BEYOND SELF-HELP

(MASTERING PERSONAL POWER)

by Gary J. Clyman

DESERVINGNESS

Copyright © 1989 by Gary J. Clyman

All rights reserved.

Printed in the United States of America.
No part of this publication may be reproduced, stored in a retrieval system, or transmitted, in any form or by any means, electronic, mechanical, photocopying, recording, or otherwise, without the prior written permission of the author.

Written and published by Gary J. Clyman
Illustrations by Alan McLuckie
MCO Illustrations by Elaina Kassouf
Original printing date: June 1, 1989

BEYOND SELF-HELP: MASTERING PERSONAL POWER™

TABLE OF CONTENTS

Acknowledgments	Page 1
Dedication #1	Page 2
Dr. Clyde Clyman's 8 Rules for Living	Page 2
Dedication #2	Page 2
Contribution To Clyman's Book by Frank Ranz	Page 3

Chapter #1 - Perspectives — Page 4

An Introductory Lecture	Page 5
Releasing the Tiger within You	Page 11
A Perspective by Doug Carter - NLP Instructor	Page 14
A Perspective by Robert Dubiel - Trance Channeler	Page 15
A Perspective by Bernie Mizock M.D. - Surgeon	Page 15
A Perspective by Gary Whitley D.C. - Chiropractor	Page 17
A Perspective by Joseph Laronge - Attorney	Page 19
A Perspective by Robert Fabino Ph.D. - Psychologist	Page 21
A Perspective by George Krueger - Cancer Victor	Page 21
A Perspective by Gilbert C. Carroll M.D. - Scientist	Page 23
A Perspective by Lou Buscemi - Chi Kung Veteran	Page 24
A Perspective by Larry Michalski - Tai Chi Student	Page 25
Choosing A System	Page 26
Finding A Qualified Instructor	Page 27
Learn What To Look For In A Chi Kung Teacher	Page 27
What Kind Of People Are Attracted To This System	Page 28
Many Martial Artists Come To Work With Me	Page 28
An Interview With A New Student	Page 29
What You Need To Work With Me	Page 35
Clyman's "4 Unbreakable Rules" For Success And Results	Page 35
Setbacks And Side Effects	Page 35
What Are "Chi Kung Veterans?"	Page 36
About Other Chi Kung Books	Page 36
Patience Is Virtue...	Page 37
How Does Chi Kung Relate To Zen Meditation?	Page 37
Pressure From Your "Loved Ones"	Page 38
Pleasing Others: The Big Trap	Page 38
How We Give Our Power Away	Page 38
Undeserving Issues	Page 39
Masturbating And Undeservingness	Page 39
Warning Signs?	Page 39
How I Fix Energy Problems	Page 39
The Chiropractic / Chi Kung Connection	Page 40
Chi Sensations Could Be Structurally Explained	Page 40
Energy: The Commodity	Page 41
What Is The Function of Tan Tien?	Page 41
Condensing Breathing	Page 41
Inside Air	Page 41
Sitting Forms With The Mind Training	Page 42

Sitting Forms With The Mind Training	Page 42
The Nature of the Moves	Page 43
Your Energy Is Directed By Your Intention (WILL)	Page 43
The Daily Practice Routine	Page 43
Defining The Issues: Focus And Applications	Page 43
About The Format	Page 44
The Whole Is Greater Than The Sum of Its Parts	Page 45
The 4 Basic Principles	Page 47
Personalization Is The Key	Page 47
"Meditation" Is Not What You Think	Page 48
You Are The Center Of Your Universe	Page 48
Changing Your World	Page 48
Misery And Trouble: A Way Of Life	Page 49
Restructuring And Rebuilding	Page 49
Reorganizing Your Life	Page 49
Choosing Your New Traits Carefully	Page 50
Life As An Experiment	Page 50
Your Soul And You	Page 50
We Are Like Tuning Forks	Page 50
Reincarnation... Who Knows?	Page 52
The Worst Signs Of Low Self-Esteem	Page 53
Hidden Eating Disorders	Page 53
Do Other Kinds Of Exercise Get These Results?	Page 54
The Chi Kung Technique In A Nutshell	Page 55
The Chi Kung / Acupuncture Relationship	Page 55
Learn From Chinese Anatomical Charts	Page 56
The Conception And Governing Vessel Involvement	Page 58
This Bears Repeating...	Page 58
Burning Through With Your Energy	Page 59
I Worked Hard So You Don't Have To	Page 59
What, When, Where & How	Page 59
The Best Time To Practice Is Early Morning	Page 60
A Little Chi Kung Is Better Than NO Chi Kung	Page 61
Too Busy To Save Time?	Page 61
Spread Out Your Condensing	Page 62
Suck Everywhere But When You're Driving	Page 62
Drinking Cold Liquids Harms Your Internal Energy	Page 62
I Suggest Skipping Breakfast	Page 62
Drink My Tea In The Morning	Page 62
Avoid Sweet Foods In The Morning	Page 63
You Should Not Practice Chi Kung After Eating	Page 63
Avoid Late Night Eating	Page 63
You Are <u>Not</u> Your Environment	Page 63
Chi Kung & Religion	Page 64
Concerning Prosperity And Happiness	Page 64
Good Urgency? Re-Capturing The Eye Of The Tiger	Page 64
The Comfort Of Confusion	Page 64
How We Punish Ourselves	Page 65
Hands On, Transfer of Power And Self-Punishment	Page 65
Understanding Income Limitations	Page 65
Creating Urgency	Page 66
Work With Your Left Foot	Page 66
"Listening to Radio Programs Can Be Harmful"	Page 66
GOD Does Not Want You To Be Poor	Page 67

Prosperity And Self-Worth	Page 67
GOD Wants You To Be Prosperous	Page 67
Chi Kung, The New Religion?	Page 67
The Three Treasures - Chi, Jing, and Shen	Page 68
A Second Explanation Of Chi, Jing, and Shen	Page 68
Converting Chi To Jing	Page 69
Shrink Before You Explode	Page 70
The Three Ingredients For Change	Page 70
Creating Results: Impregnating The Universe	Page 71
Taking The Bull By The Horns	Page 71
Practice With Urgency	Page 72
I Practiced With Passion	Page 72
The Importance Of Taking Notes	Page 72
Tai Chi vs. Chi Kung: What's The Difference?	Page 72
Chi Kung Moving Energy "With Your Mind"	Page 73
More About The Tai Chi / Chi Kung Comparison	Page 73
Is Chi Kung A Martial Art?	Page 74
What is "Gold Bell Training"?	Page 74
"Gold Bell Training" In The Martial Arts Only	Page 75
"Esoteric Explanations"? No Way!	Page 75
Health, Happiness & Longevity	Page 75
Chiropractic: Normalizing Faulty Body Mechanics	Page 76
How To Speed Up The Healing Process	Page 76
To Be Old and Healthy Is Not Just A Dream	Page 77
What is The Difference Between Life and Death?	Page 77
The Nuclear Threat Has Damaged A Few Generations	Page 77
Conscious Death - The Best Way To Go	Page 78
Death Causes Emotional Problems In The Living	Page 78
Death Issues: An Emotional Epidemic	Page 79
Peeling Off The Layers of An Onion	Page 80
Different Responses To "Hands On, Transfer Of Power"	Page 80
More Emotional Onion Skins	Page 81
Hands On, Transfer Of Power™ by Joseph Kalal D.C.	Page 81
"Hands On, Transfer Of Power" Specific Results	Page 81
"Hands On" Works Best When You Practice	Page 81
The Procedure: Hands On, Transfer Of Power™	Page 81
Five Days Of Emptiness Afterwards	Page 82
Domineering Mothers Have Left Their Marks	Page 83
If You Can't Live Here, Where Can You Live?	Page 83
Cigarette Smoking Equals Slow Death	Page 83
X-Rays Tell No Lies	Page 83

Chapter #2 - The Physical Nature — Page 84

General Principles Of "The Technique"	Page 84
Chi Kung Technical Outline	Page 85
The Basic Training Material	Page 85
The Technical Ingredients Of Chi Kung	Page 86
Definitions & Reasons Why	Page 86
Chi Kung Definitions: Basic Training	Page 89
Energy Cultivation Exercises	Page 89

Chapter #3 - The Technique — Page 91

Chi Kung Lesson Schedule: Workshop I.	Page 91
The Chi Kung Technique	Page 92
Lesson #1	Page 92
Rules And Suggestions	Page 92
A Brief Outline In Review	Page 116
Lesson #2	Page 118
Lesson #3	Page 124
Lesson #4	Page 152
Lesson #5	Page 182
The Chi Kung Daily Practice Routine	Page 182
Technical Notes - Afterthoughts	Page 195
Advanced Training: Workshop II.	Page 200

Chapter #4 - Concerning People — Page 201

The Subjects Highlighted	Page 201
PPT™ Subject Definitions	Page 202
Miscellaneous Case Histories	Page 204
A Case History by Gaye Linch	Page 204
A Case History by Doug Carter	Page 205
A Case History by Margaret Doersch	Page 206
Personality Profile I	Page 207
Personality Profile II	Page 209
Transfer of Power™ Exchange Of Traits	Page 210
Notes	Page 211
Life-Change Sheet	Page 212
Personality Profile III	Page 213
More Concerning Your Emotions	Page 215
Emotional Visualizations While Sitting	Page 215
Family Applications	Page 215
Fresh Blood In Old Relationships	Page 216
Emotionally Dysfunctional Families Are Very Common	Page 217
Keep Drinking & Keep Missing The Boat	Page 217
Why Did We Do Drugs	Page 217
Identifying With Pleasure Instead Of Pain	Page 218
Just Say "NO" To Drugs...	Page 218
Chi Kung Is The Perfect Positive Addiction	Page 218
Choosing Basic Personal Rules	Page 218
More About Belief Systems	Page 220
Recognizing Your Cage	Page 220
Expanding Your Cage	Page 220
What Gets In Your Way?	Page 221
Personal Applications For Stabilization	Page 221
Spontaneity Within Reason	Page 221
The Energy Crisis Of The Next Century	Page 222
Energy Stability IS Possible	Page 222
Chi Kung Healing: The Whole Pie	Page 222
The 6 Levels Of Healing	Page 223
The Invisible Gap - The Body / Mind Separation	Page 223
The Problems With "Astral Projecting"	Page 223
Stranger Things Have Happened	Page 223
Dumping Your Karma... How?	Page 224
More About Karma	Page 224

Your Results Equal Your WILL	Page 224
You Can Get What You Want	Page 225
Found Barefoot In The Snow, Again	Page 225
More About The Invisible Gap	Page 225
An Intellectual's View Of The Body	Page 226
Arrogance vs. Self-Confidence	Page 226
The Ego vs. Self-Confidence	Page 227
"Self-Respect" Begins With Self	Page 227
More Concerning Self-Esteem	Page 228
Take Off That "Happy Face"	Page 228
Visualizations Relating To Self-Esteem	Page 229
Your "Filter" vs. Your "Rule"	Page 229
How Do You See The World?	Page 230
Abandonment Is Wide Spread	Page 230
Women And Self-Confidence	Page 231
Decisions And Self-Confidence	Page 231
Women And Follow-Through	Page 231
Problems Women Have More Than Men	Page 232
Personal Presentation & Self-Image	Page 232
Teach 100 Doctors, Help 10,000 People	Page 232
About Concentration	Page 233
Religious Conditioning And De-Programming	Page 233
Protestant Influences	Page 233
Catholic Influences	Page 234
Jewish Influences	Page 234
Jewish Guilt And Catholic Denial	Page 234
Gary's Evaluation Of Evelyn's Story	Page 235
Evelyn's Story	Page 236
Contributions By Doug Carter	Page 237
More About Abandonment	Page 237
Regarding Co-Dependency	Page 241
Notes	Page 246
Inside Kung Fu Magazine Article, April 1987	Page 247
An Interview With Gary J. Clyman	Page 247

Chapter #5 - Concerning Emotions — Page 257

My Vision And Purpose	Page 257
Freedom vs. Bondage	Page 257
Hands On, Transfer Of Power™	Page 257
Reactions During "Hands On, Transfer Of Power"	Page 258
Hands On, Transfer Of Power™ In A Nutshell	Page 258
The Diaphragm	Page 258
"Hands On" Is Not Fun, But Is Very Helpful	Page 259
Various Tissues Effected	Page 260
Using The Hands	Page 260
Touch Without Touching	Page 261
Tai Chi Transfer Of Power	Page 262
String Of Pearls?	Page 262
How I Developed My Energy Projection Ability	Page 262
Rules and Suggestions	Page 263
Gary's Healing Story	Page 263
Medicine Man Meets Medicine Man	Page 265
Intro Questions	Page 267

The 4 Categories Of A Students' Seriousness	Page 267
Learning How To Learn	Page 267
You Can Master Anything	Page 268
Something About Wimpy Men	Page 268
Wimpy Men & Aggressive Women	Page 269
Successful People From All Walks Of Life	Page 269

Chapter #6 - Human Possibilities — Page 270

Testimonials And Case Histories	Page 270
"Real People" Testimonials	Page 270
Results Of Personal Power Training™	Page 277
Reasons Why PPT™ Helps Many People	Page 278
Motivational Sayings and Quotes	Page 279
Working With Your Affirmations	Page 280
Personalize Your Affirmations	Page 280
Affirmations Are Limitless	Page 280
The Affirmation List	Page 280

Chapter #7 - Living Healthy — Page 283

The 7 Basic Principles Of Wholistic Health	Page 283
Sugar: A Horribly Addictive Drug	Page 286
What To Expect When Converting To Vegetarianism	Page 289
Symptoms Reflect Improving Your Health	Page 290
The Four Avenues Of Detoxification	Page 290
What is Colonic Irrigation?	Page 290
Junk Food Vegetarianism	Page 291
Fiber, The Thread Of Life	Page 291
Different Kinds of Vegetarians	Page 292
Comparing Poisons	Page 293
More About Hypoglycemia	Page 294
The Chi Kung Internal Sensitivity Diet	Page 294
Proper Nutritional Supplementation	Page 295
Perspiration & Showers	Page 296
Two Kinds Of Sweat	Page 296
Sinus Flushing - Blowing Your Nose At Drugs	Page 296
Antibiotics Are Not "Harmless" Or "Wonderful"	Page 297

Chapter #8 - Sexual Kung Fu — Page 298

Radio Show: Sexual Kung Fu With Paul O'Brien & GJC	Page 298
How Much Do Orgasms Cost You?	Page 311
Sex Without Orgasms: Chi Kung While Having Sex	Page 311
Masturbation Is A Total Waste	Page 312
How Masturbation Destroys Self-Esteem	Page 312
Women And Masturbation	Page 312
Save Your Sperm	Page 312
Celibacy vs. Semen Retention	Page 313
"Blue Balls" No More	Page 313
About Dual Cultivation	Page 313
Increased Sexual Performance	Page 314
Teaching Your Women The Taoist Sexual Technique	Page 314
Understanding Her Menstrual Cycle	Page 315
The Use Of Rubbers	Page 315
Ejaculation: The Door To Depression	Page 316

Keep Your Sexual Energy To Yourself	Page 316
Sleep Less & Weigh Less	Page 316
More About Sleeping	Page 317
When Sleep Seems Like A Waste Of Time	Page 317
Positioning Your Body While Sleeping	Page 317
Dynamic Physical Presence and Awareness	Page 318
Think Of One Thing At A Time	Page 318
Importance Or Impotence: The Choice Is Yours	Page 319
The Benefits Of Celibacy	Page 319
Why Re-Invent The Wheel	Page 319
Self-Containment: The Key To Consistency	Page 320
Bigger Orgasms, Wow!	Page 320
Running Away Or Running Toward	Page 320
Experience Stability Through Celibacy	Page 320
Giving Up Sex Is Not Enough	Page 320
Internal Discipline vs. Self-Discipline	Page 321
Plugging The Leaks	Page 321
Making Room For More	Page 321
The Ultimate Challenge	Page 321
Porno Helps Your Chi Circulations	Page 322
More Concerning The Taoist Sexual Technique	Page 322
Sexual Recuperation?	Page 322
Wash Off Her Juices	Page 322
Living In Trouble and Misery Daily	Page 323
How Many Orgasms Can You Have?	Page 323
How To Choose the Best Sex Partners	Page 323
You Get Who You Are: No More, No Less	Page 323
Choosing "The Right Mate"	Page 324
Old Men With Younger Women	Page 324
Women Don't Need Young Boys	Page 325
Women Can Still Have Orgasms	Page 325
For Women Only: About Your Period	Page 325
Chi Kung Before Sex	Page 325
Chi Kung During Sex	Page 325
Sex Won't Kill You, But?	Page 325
Chi Kung After Sex	Page 326
Duel Cultivation Equals Better Sex	Page 326
The Best Kept Secret: The Grand Finale	Page 327

Chapter #9 - Specialty Applications — Page 328

For Commodity Traders	Page 328
Why Your Trading Will Improve	Page 328
Trader Sayings And Affirmations	Page 329
The Effects On Commodity Traders	Page 331
Do Mornings "Dragggg On" Forever	Page 332
When Snails Move "Too Fast"	Page 332
"Bad Choices" When Trading May Be Sugar Related	Page 332
For Health Care Professionals	Page 333
Chi Kung Will Make You A Better Doctor	Page 333
Chi Kung Will Improve Your Technique	Page 333
"Good Doctor" Or "Great Doctor" - Make The Right Choice	Page 333
Improved Communication Skills Equals More Referrals	Page 334
Your Patients Will Notice The Difference	Page 334

Chapter #10 - Q & A Section — Page 335

1)	Technical	Page 335
2)	Sex	Page 349
3)	Psychological	Page 354
4)	Health	Page 355
5)	Emotional	Page 356
6)	General	Page 356

Other Suggested Books — Page 359
Regional PPT™ Associates — Page 359

BEYOND SELF-HELP: MASTERING PERSONAL POWER™ by Gary J. Clyman

ACKNOWLEDGMENTS: I would like to express my appreciation to all my clients, students, and friends who have shared themselves with me and stimulated me to create this book. I would also like to thank Elizabeth Wirth for all her typing contributions and energy, without which this book would have taken forever to complete. I would like to acknowledge all my teachers for their "teachings and guidance" and for helping me become who I am. Above all, I would like to thank LIFE for giving me the situations and the ENERGY needed to help the thousands of people that have and will receive inspiration from my work and the words between the covers of this book.

Thanks to my special friends; Gary Whitley D.C., Joseph Kalal D.C., Daniel Garvey, Emerson Walls M.D., and to Joseph A. Laronge for his constant support, advice and encouragement, without which this book would never have been completed.

BEYOND SELF-HELP: MASTERING PERSONAL POWER™ by Gary J. Clyman

DEDICATION #1

This book is dedicated to the memory of my first teacher, my father, Dr. Clyde S. Clyman, who taught me about life and how to live your life to its fullest. May his spirit and positive influence inspire many people to be the best they can be, and more... Thanks Dad for teaching me for the first 3 years of my manhood, ages 13-16. The last lesson I received from my father was, "Gar, if you're not doing what you're suppose to do, you're not doing anything." May my readers adopt the spirit behind his message.

DR. CLYDE CLYMAN'S 8 RULES FOR LIFE

1) Use your mind, not your back.
2) A pencil is lighter than a shovel.
3) The best boss you can have is yourself.
4) As long as you sell your time, you'll never get ahead.
5) Only lend out as much as you can afford to give away.
6) People are wrong... money does grow on trees.
7) You're only as good as your word.
8) 1st time, shame on you, 2nd time, shame on me.

DEDICATION #2

The purpose of this book is to pass on to any extent possible miracles, results, and positive inspiration to my readers. I hope the vibrations attached to my work can be received by my readers, absorbed from my writing and applied to your life. I am the first to combine a physical energy cultivation technique with a modern self-improvement approach.

One of the goals of this work is to make you the best that you can be for now and to keep you inspired and excited about being alive. I hope you will continually be referring to this book for many different purposes and it will help you get more ENERGY FOR LIFE.

A CONTRIBUTION TO CLYMAN'S BOOK

by Frank Ranz   January 1989

The fact that you're here doesn't mean you are breathing, and the fact that you are living doesn't mean you're alive. This may sound strange. Learn to live again.

Some people don't have dreams. Other people dream and think how fine their lives could be. They don't change anything. This sounds strange.

It is not true when adults think that they don't grow any more. Some of them even shrink. Growing is an exciting experience. Step by step there is nothing to be afraid of. The Universe is endless.

The bare thought of the undiscovered things and adventures in my life make me so excited that my eyes shine and something restless fulfils my body that I can't wait to see tomorrow.

Frank Ranz, Leibnitz, Austria

CHAPTER #1
PERSPECTIVES

A BRIEF EXPLANATION

PERSONAL POWER TRAINING™ is a fast-paced training program designed to quickly release and eliminate the negative belief systems that limit your personal growth. I teach you to cultivate the energy you need to reach your new goals. I help you stay sharply in focus while working towards achieving the personal and professional horizons you set.

These techniques are a concentrated yet concise form of methods found at the core of many of the world's most potent mental disciplines. I will present them in a new form to meet the needs of professionals who want to change NOW.

PERSONAL POWER TRAINING™ will, in an incredibly short time, teach you how to release and eliminate negative habits, attitudes, and beliefs that place lifelong limitations on your personal, professional, and financial growth.

Once your limitations have been examined and clarified, a two stage process begins. The achievement of any goal demands an abundance of energy: Mental energy for concise, clear though; physical energy for stamina. Therefore the second stage of **PERSONAL POWER TRAINING**™ is Energy Cultivation. You will learn to generate internal physical energy on command.

The final thrust of **PERSONAL POWER TRAINING**™ is "Focus." You will learn how to focus energy on any goal in a forceful new way. Survival habits: eating, sleeping, sexual drive, etc., are the strongest instincts we possess. This Personal Power Focusing technique brings to "non-survival" characteristics (self-esteem, self-confidence, concentration and discipline) the same level of intensity as your strongest survival instinct.

PERSONAL POWER TRAINING™ not only inspects your illusions and belief systems, but replaces them with more applicable concepts that work, and brings immediate and long lasting results.

BEYOND SELF-HELP: MASTERING PERSONAL POWER™ by Gary J. Clyman

AN INTRODUCTORY LECTURE

This lecture was given in February, 1988 and is entitled, "**Releasing the Tiger Within You.**" It demonstrates an art called "Chi Kung" as I teach it in **PERSONAL POWER TRAINING™**. There are 2 parts to **PERSONAL POWER TRAINING™**.

Part one is the technique called "Chi Kung" -- translated from Chinese, it means "Energy Work" and the second part is called "Harnessing Your Vehicle."

The system I teach is my own creation. When I was taught, I had to go through the whole system to get the material I now teach first, in the beginning. I have put together a technical system in a simple way, so people with no previous experience or background can easily learn the practice.

Until this approach, learning and practicing were both difficult. Now learning is easy and practicing is simple. I have put the system together in a format. I teach you to suck in energy and then you start moving this energy around inside your body. Then you connect it with your wants and needs, affirmations & visualizations. You then learn to propel or project this personal mixture out and into the Universe. This action I have named "Impregnating the Universe." The results each of my clients receive are very personal and specific. No two clients gain exactly the same things.

In advance, you will learn the physical part because it is all rooted in the physical body. In other seminars, it is mostly or entirely in the mind, but not in my work. **PERSONAL POWER TRAINING™** gives you enough immediate internal fuel to complete what you want.

The type of clients I accept are independent business people, commodity traders, psychotherapists, Chiropractors, attorneys, medical doctors; I pick my clients very carefully. That's why I get such amazing results with nearly all my clients, because I pick them right. The kind of people that are referred to me are almost hand picked. They are successful already and need some additional inspiration. If I had to give a one sentence definition of what I do, I would say: "**I INSPIRE PEOPLE WHO ARE NOT INSPIRED.**"

I take the good things and magnify them and give my clients/students new tools for realizing, minimizing, controlling, and eliminating bad traits and habits. The first step is to recognize a bad trait or habit that doesn't work for you. When I work with a new client, I spend a lot of time talking back and forth. In the beginning, many problems are very abstract or may even seem totally invisible.

People that are dissatisfied with the way things are and want to change things for the better, come to me. Many of my clients don't know what they are coming to me for. Sometimes they have done everything they can think of; some have been in therapy, using "a passive relationship" with their therapist. Nobody has said: "Wham -- look at this!" I am about 95% correct and do just that. This work is not for wimpy people. This is not therapy or instead of therapy. It's more like "Success Counseling."

The reason I like working with commodity traders is that I can give them a tool and within a day they can use it many times. It takes people other than traders a much longer time to use their new tools. Traders use time differently. How much time does it take you to make a decision? Commodity traders think in terms of minutes or even seconds to make a decision. I asked one, "what is the longest amount of time you have to make a decision?" He said, "45 seconds." When was the last time you had to make a decision in 10 seconds? The reason I choose traders that is I can give them a tool, and they can make it work. Because of my work with traders, I am able to harness the same relationship with time for "normal people."

My clients work with me on issues of self confidence, self-esteem and internal discipline. Self-discipline is different. Internal discipline is thinking on your feet or being the same all the time, developing consistency. It is different and much more specific as to emotional balance and control. Without self-control where would we be? Or better yet, where are we?

So how do you link meditation to self-control? I usually don't use the word "meditation." "Meditation" has many preconceived ideas attached to it i.e., giving up, dispersing, leaving your body, or even praying. I use an unconventional meaning for this word.

Just look at my logo; does it look as if it represents giving up anything or dispersing anything? The energy center we use is Tan Tien (three inches below the navel and two inches in), because that is where our power comes from and it is also our physical "center of gravity."

Some people have negative ideas and associations with the word "power." When you practice "Chi Kung" the way I teach it, you suck energy in and accumulate it. All your life you have put energy out, and now, by using my technique, you can suck energy back in. There is energy all around you and you can learn how to become an energy magnet. My technique teaches you how to attract, cultivate, accumulate, circulate and project your energy.

How long does it take you to practice this? I have created what I call "The Daily Practice Routine." It ordinarily takes 30-45 minutes to run through. Many of my clients don't do the practice the way I teach it -- they do 10-15 minutes, take a break and do more. They practice everywhere they go. I have a Chiropractor friend/student, who practices all day and uses "Chi Kung" combined with his Chiropractic technique. It has made him a better, more proficient doctor. You can do it any way you want, any way that works for you. I am the survivor of my generation and have practiced at least 25,000 hours. You won't find anyone the same as me.

In 1983 I decided to re-organize the material, so "normal people" could practice the technique, understand it and use it in their lives. So when you practice "Chi Kung," about 70% is done in a sitting position -- on a chair, couch, cushion, etc., and the other 30% is done standing. Much of the sitting is done "sitting still." When you practice, it is "physical practice" but the work is taking place "inside the body," physically.

This is not exclusively Martial Art -- anyone can practice "Chi Kung" regardless of age and physical condition. You can use this as a curative or a preventative measure. Working with the energy is an exciting and direct way of improving your physical, mental, psychological, and spiritual state of being.

My weekend workshops take place once a month. Many people travel long distances to study with me privately utilizing my "Special 2 Day Private Format." On day one, we go through lessons l, 2, 3, and 4. The first 3 or 4 hours of the work are spent talking. I ask 3 things: 1) Who are you? 2) What do you do and 3) what do you want from today? When I hear people responding to those 3 questions, that is where I do what I do best. What happens is my clients find out why they are doing something they do and in **PERSONAL POWER TRAINING**™ they stop doing something that has been bothering them for years. You learn the technical practice, first you go through lesson 1, 2, 3, and 4 -- these lessons are very technical and specific. Cassette tapes review each lesson to make learning easier and less stressful. Remember, learning should be easy and practicing should be simple.

On lesson 5 there exists a self-correcting lesson, planned into the format. You put it all together into what is called "The Daily Practice Routine." You will have a self-contained unit after completing **PERSONAL POWER TRAINING**™. "The Gift" you will receive from me, is a unique relationship with the technique and I help you let all kinds of things out when I do my "hands on" stuff -- an actual energy transfer takes place. It's called "Hands on, Transfer of Power." Many things change inside you, your emotions, your belief systems, your relationship with emotional and physical pain, and even your spirit. How do you relieve "Spiritual Pain?" It has been described as being "Born Again," but not in a religious way.

I am sure you have done other workshops, but with **PERSONAL POWER TRAINING**™, you will get a lot more. What happens, because of the changes each person goes through, you will see similarities in everybody and the whole group is realizing many important things; i.e., parental deprogramming, changes in your relationship to money, and many other things. The same kind of things always come up.

Back to the "Hands on, Transfer of Power." What happens there happens because we spent 3-4 hours to change and define what we want to happen, when the "Hands on, Transfer of Power" takes place, there are emotional and/or spiritual releases, and all kinds of things are transformed. In one workshop, death issues came up and in a more recent workshop, a lot of abandonment issues came to the surface. One child was put up for adoption 28 years ago and was still carrying around the pain of this experience.

BEYOND SELF-HELP: MASTERING PERSONAL POWER™ by Gary J. Clyman

Our energy communicates many things to us. Because these things happen in the subconscious and unconscious and mind, and you are learning a physical energy cultivation practice, every time you practice, you reinforce the newly chosen traits or characteristics. This is very exciting. I gave up wanting to be a Chiropractor to do this!

Are you saying you will dispel all? No, but a very large percentage of it. There are 3 kinds of religious deprogramming -- you have Catholic, Protestant and Jewish. Catholic is dealing with "Denial," Protestant stuff deals more with money and deserving issues, like "The Protestant Work Ethic." We are still holding something our parents dumped upon us. Protestant stuff holds you back. The Jewish stuff however, doesn't hold you back, but makes you feel bad. Jewish stuff uses "Guilt." Everybody usually fits into one of those 3 categories.

The real benefit of participating in **PERSONAL POWER TRAINING™** is, you get a quick fix and then get to support it when you practice "Chi Kung" for the rest of your life.

My father raised me in a way that "this seems the only thing for me to do." Most men come to me because they don't have a real male role model. My father died when I was 16, but for the first 3 years of my manhood, he spent much time with me and we spent time talking. He set me up in a positive way.

Most people don't have a support system that feeds them. Using **PERSONAL POWER TRAINING™**, you create your own support system without needing any backup from other people.

Question: You mentioned you have several years training --- 14 years training.

A: I was one of the few people in my school who learned this material. The way I teach it, you can learn this system much quicker. This is the streamlined, 1990's version of a Taoist monastery......

This is a sucking, manifesting, attracting, becoming an energy magnet, kind of technique. My clients are not concerned with stress. If you are doing what you are supposed to do, you should not be concerned with stress because it is automatically reduced. Stress becomes a problem when what you're doing is not right for you.

What has it done for you?
I have taken this material miles ahead and you can take advantage of my 25,000 hours of practice, when you start. If I were a Chiropractor, I would have post-doctorate degrees in orthopedics, radiology, etc. So I decided to take this material, "Chi Kung," and incorporate affirmation and visualization techniques into it. When you learn it, it is as if you have spent years doing it already. Have you ever been around someone that was able to pass this kind of excitement or **"Energy for Life"** along to you?

In a recent workshop in Portland, Oregon -- to give you two specifics examples: There was a woman who had just had a miscarriage; she wasn't in touch with this trauma, so when we did the "Hands on, Transfer of Power," she completed the birthing cycle in **PERSONAL POWER TRAINING™**, and we let her sleep for many hours. I called her in the morning of the second day and she was doing great. Prior to completing Day One, she was depressed and drained; she got re-inspired prior to Day Two.

The second example is about an American Army captain in Vietnam who lost some fellow soldiers in 1967, and for the first time in 20 years, he told his story. So I did the "Hands on, Transfer of Power" with him and he let out energy that had been "blocked up" in his body for 20 years and now he is very happy and his life works much better.

One common thing I've found has been that most people are unhappy, and when we investigate why, they don't have any real reasons to feel that way. They are unhappy because it is convenient -- so understand that **you have a choice**. For this I have created "The Task/Reward Ratio." Here's how it works. You pick something you are already doing, you want to keep it simple. I use a lot of "The KISS Principle" (Keep It Simple Stupid) in **PERSONAL POWER TRAINING™**. You associate your task with whatever the reward is for yourself.

One of my traders made a lot of money last year, but when we first started working together, he was unhappy. Why was he unhappy? He had no "real" reason.... so I told him to pick a task -- He did, "drinking a cup of decaf coffee the next morning" and then he became happy; his happiness lasted a long time.

It is easier for you to get rid of your unuseful traits when you are conscious of them, then when you are unconscious.

I had another private client. His thing was, he felt confused. When someone is confused, I call that "The Comfort of Confusion." Many of us act confused because it is easier then doing what we know we are supposed to. What I do in "the work" is work; I let each client know what their act is, what they are presenting to the world, and when they do, that they are unable to get anything done. When you realize that is what you are doing, it is appealing to create action and next time the confusion comes in, you can do something about it.

I have another client who is a trader - "the Reward" was to be revitalized - "the Task" was to wash his hands and face. When he had completed his task, he was revitalized.

What happened with him is he had been a trader 5 or 6 years. When he would execute a trade, he suddenly became terrified and would act as if he didn't know what he was doing. Recently, he now trades in the pit - every time he walked into "The Merc," he would experience TERROR. So when I did the "Hands on, Transfer of Power" with him, I went in and took that terror out. Remember, this is "Energy Work" and I can encapsulate an energy problem and extract it intact. His was the hardest on me. His wasn't maintained in anger, mental or emotional, - it was in his energy. I sucked it out and his eyes became alive again.

BEYOND SELF-HELP: MASTERING PERSONAL POWER™ by Gary J. Clyman

So a lot of things happen in **PERSONAL POWER TRAINING™ WEEKEND WORKSHOPS** and/or private lessons. Depending on your personality and personal needs, the weekend format might be good to do, depending on what you want to get out of it, or private instruction.

A form called "The Personality Profile II™ saves us about 45 minutes and will give you a clearer idea of how precise our work together is. I ask the same questions to each person, because I have found these tools work consistently.

What happens when you work with The Personality Profile II™ is, you find out that the things you "LOVE" and "HATE" are related to each other. You can hate anything and some people have strong reactions to the word "HATE." Me? The "loves" come out in anything - food, sex, feeling whole, completing tasks, having self-esteem, doing a great job, feeling fulfilled, feeling self-contained, etc.

Some people put down that they "hate" riding on the El or starvation in Ethiopia. There is a right side and a left side. Right side: world issues; left side - feeling complete, etc. My work is concerned with left side -- your personal stuff. I believe that if you can't help yourself, you can't do anything for somebody else, anyway.

Look at my logo... The technique teaches you how to suck in energy. I am concerned with teaching you how to become "An Energy Magnet" and giving your body the ability to attract, maintain and store its own energy. What you will learn from me is how to cultivate the energy you have already and how to get more.

Charisma: could be natural or trained. When you practice this system, it will make a big difference. In other seminars, you usually forget what you got or who the trainer was. In **PERSONAL POWER TRAINING™**, you will never forget what you got. Here, if you practice the technique, you will have more energy than you know what to do with. What you will have are tools that help you save a lot of time and wasted energy and feel as if you are doing "the right thing."

RELEASING THE TIGER

WITHIN YOU!

Each part of **PERSONAL POWER TRAINING**™ is geared toward developing and upgrading a person's self-esteem, self-confidence, personal power, and concentration abilities. The segment of **PERSONAL POWER TRAINING**™ that makes it unique and different from every other training in the market place is that in **PERSONAL POWER TRAINING**™ a person learns internal physical energy cultivation exercises that stimulate and increase a person's sexual energy. When referring to the term "SEXUAL ENERGY," I am not referring to what you are already aware of, I am talking about a new type of energy. This energy is termed "JING" in Chinese, which means cultivated sexual energy. The purpose of **PERSONAL POWER TRAINING**™ is not to have a better, stronger sex life, although that does happen, it's about being more vital and alive.

The "sex drive" has been shown to be one of the strongest motivating forces available to us as human beings. The sex drive ranks with such forces as the survival instinct, the fear of loss, and the fear of death. Rather than concentrate on the negative aspects of motivation, let us create a mechanism to use for our own empowerment. **PERSONAL POWER TRAINING**™ contains techniques that will enable a person to create a response of the survival instinct in non-survival issues. Then a person can and does become much more in control of his or her own internal and external environments.

The social implications of **PERSONAL POWER TRAINING**™ are far reaching. When a person utilizes these concepts on a daily basis, every daily decision becomes much less threatening. Making small decisions in a new and refreshing way is how to practice and get in shape for when it is necessary to make big decisions. The application of this basic principle leads to what is uniquely referred to in **PERSONAL POWER TRAINING**™ as "Releasing the Tiger Within You."

As a rule, daily stress and strain has been responsible for many of the negative traits we as humans exhibit on a daily basis. And due to the prominence of many suppressive situations in our modern lifestyle, we rarely operate from a position of strength. We usually find ourselves reacting to some external stimulation or some recurring incident from our past, which might be a recent incident, but is usually an experience from our distant past.

In **PERSONAL POWER TRAINING**™, many of these past incidents are discovered, and reactivated. Then we are capable of a complete release. This process is known as "retracing" and has been proved to be a valuable tool in erasing the harmful effects of many of these stored experiences. After a person has retraced, we see a type of cleansing that affects a person on all levels: mentally, physically, emotionally, and spiritually. This is where "Hands on, Transfer of Power" fits in.

From that point on, a person who has completed **PERSONAL POWER TRAINING**™ can view life from a new perspective, one of confidence with a higher sense of self-esteem. When you view yourself as a powerful and secure individual, the universe will show you the respect you so rightly deserve. This concept is known as "Commanding Respect vs. Demanding Respect."

The internal energy cultivation exercises taught in **PERSONAL POWER TRAINING**™ have their roots in "Taoist Meditation" which is still practiced in a few monasteries in China. In ancient times, these techniques were of great value in daily living conditions related to a threatened existence. However, in these modern times, we are not faced with the same forms of dangers as in the past. Our new dangers are disguised. In this modern lifestyle we all live in, our dangers expose themselves as daily stress and strain, such as suppressive working conditions, miscommunicated love relationships, financial risks, risks of public life such as street violence, environmental pollutants such as poor quality air and water, as well as terrible food. Expectations from parents, lovers, and peers also add to many of our lethargic personality traits and habits. When we realize more fully that many of these traits and trigger responses can be eliminated by simply exposing and willing them away in conjunction with the support techniques available in **PERSONAL POWER TRAINING**™, can we take charge of our own fate and destiny. We can make "giant steps" towards mental, physical, emotional, and spiritual independence and self-containment by utilizing the techniques available in **PERSONAL POWER TRAINING**™.

What you will get from **PERSONAL POWER TRAINING**™ is the ability to tap into your "Personal Power" in a way that was unavailable to you previously.

PERSONAL POWER TRAINING™ will prove to be one of the most positive and empowering experiences of your life.

Copyright 1983 by Gary J. Clyman. All Rights Reserved.

NOTES

A PERSPECTIVE BY DOUG CARTER

When I first realized that I had an opportunity to write a forward for Gary Clyman's new book, I found myself thinking back on when I first heard about him. I was conducting an instructor training conference for a well- known international training company. One of the instructor candidates was an assistant Attorney General for the State of Oregon. One day he and I began discussing how people become energized, that is "full of energy, excitement and personal power." After a few minutes, the candidate looked at me and said, "Doug, you've just got to meet Gary!," and so I asked him, "Gary who?" He said, "Gary Clyman," and I replied, "So, who's Gary Clyman?" Little did I recognize at the time how difficult it would be for anyone to describe who Gary Clyman is, or what he does. Because as he so succinctly put it on numerous occasions, "I'm not who you think I am. This isn't what you think it is, and it's different than anything you've ever seen, so don't try to put it in a box." Based on the trust and respect I had for my instructor candidate, I agreed to attend a weekend seminar.

Many of the things that occurred that weekend are in this book. You'll read about Gaye and her miscarriage, and about the ex-Green Beret and his pent up guilt about leaving a young soldier along a dike in Viet Nam. You'll have an opportunity to discover a lot about yourself and how you react in the world around you. And if you're open enough, you'll discover techniques, and ways for you to begin the process of "breaking out" of some of the bonds that are holding you back from really being who you want to be. All I can suggest is, that you realize that what is in this book and what Gary does is unlike anything you've probably ever seen or heard, although similar to many things, but it's definitely different than anything you've ever experienced. In order to really understand all the implications... **You've just got to meet Gary!**
Doug Carter, San Diego, CA

A PERSPECTIVE BY ROBERT K. DUBIEL

Gary's system represents a departure from conventional self-improvement modalities, in that he focuses on body changes as well as on reforming habits of mind. Through the discipline of Chi Kung, I, for example, have been able to consistently center my energy in the here and now, as never before. In addition, I am developing the capacity to collect this focused energy so that I have a pronounced effect on my environment, just by being. This occurs whether I find myself in formal positions of leadership or not.

An important principle: Energy which is focused has a stronger reverberation than diffused energy.

I am a professional trance channel and a teacher of metaphysical principles. Use of the principles of Chi Kung has brought my spirit more firmly into my flesh. I am no longer hovering around the fringes waiting to take off for a better plane. In my experience, Gary's practices are a good antidote for excessive "crown chakra-itis" (too much concentration in other realms of consciousness at the expense of the physical). I do not feel that Chi Kung replaces spiritually oriented systems for enhancing sensitivity or strengthening channeling ability. However, I do find emphasis on Tan Tien (3 inches below the navel and 2 inches in) very helpful in the quest of "knowing thyself."

Focussing on Tan Tien and on energy meridians throughout the body, is a good way to become attuned to one's own "body wisdom." The body is very much connected to the Soul's larger purpose, even when the intellect is blocked. Through the practice of Chi Kung, one learns to listen to the body sensations going on inside, and to use them in making decisions. This is a form of listening to the inner self, the most valuable meditation tool there is. Robert K. Dubiel, Chicago, IL

A PERSPECTIVE BY BERNIE MIZOCK M.D.

The purpose of this "Perspective" is to instill inspiration in the future reader. Prior to this attempt, oral teaching has been the only way to transmit these gifts of knowledge. There have been a few moments in my life, during which I have become fully awake and alive. Those few moments were connected with some external catastrophe of some sort or another. It was out of those few moments of aliveness, that I came to the realization that my normal state of being is a "walking sleep."

It has been possible to awaken to a sense of heightened aliveness and energy by putting myself into a group conference, where intensive processes of interaction gradually generated an elevated level of group energy and sensitivity. I have worked with alchemical agents that have produced profound shifts in my level of consciousness.

Participating in the heightened attention of an operating room has also provided a source of increased attention levels. Yet, in all of my searches, experiencing these heightened states of energy, have always seemed to me to be contingent upon my proximity to a group process, ingestion of an alchemical agent, fasting, or alteration of sleep patterns.

It is now clear to me, that a technology for transformation of consciousness exists and has always existed. It's existence has been secret, because there are specific requirements that must be met for such vehicles of transformation to be potent, rather than vapid, abstract ideas and philosophies.

The 2 basic requirements are 1) the contents of the discipline and 2) a capacity for energetic transmission. That is to say, Gary, has the ability to teach the specific technique and has the energetic capabilities to induce the student. Therefore, a clear understanding of the mechanical steps in and of itself are not sufficient. However, in actuality to relationship with Gary, it is indeed possible to achieve a "higher energetic state of awareness and physical presence."

It has been my experience that upon completion of PERSONAL POWER TRAINING™, the ability to condense energy does not diminish over time; and this, even if the daily practice in a formal fashion is not done.

I feel extremely fortunate and appreciative to have experienced the transmission of "The Clyman System" which has been so empowering for me. He is readily accessible and for those of you who are ready to take this "Quantum Leap" in your energy levels, you will enjoy this book and the subsequent life challenges that await you. Bernie Mizock M.D.

BEYOND SELF-HELP: MASTERING PERSONAL POWER™ by Gary J. Clyman

A PERSPECTIVE BY GARY WHITLEY D.C.

I first became acquainted with Gary Clyman in 1980, when he became a distributor of the nutritional formulas that I and Dr. Lamar Rosquist formulated. Gary became interested and then got very excited about determining his "own" nutritional needs. He became fascinated with the uniqueness of our formulations and the results that he was getting for himself. He began testing his friends and clients and got them on the formulas and they too were getting great results.

Over the next few years, Gary developed quite a following of people who were looking for "better health." But this is not where Gary Clyman's greatest talent lies, for Gary Clyman is a very gifted Master in the arts of Tai Chi and Chi Kung. This is where the "true genius" of Gary Clyman really lies.

Through his discipline of the past 15 years that he has been studying and practicing the ancient arts of Tai Chi Chuan and Chi Kung, he has developed an incredible insight into the positive and negative energy flows that people express through their behavior patterns. Gary can talk to you for a few minutes and through "listening and observing" how you communicate with him, he can determine your negative behavior patterns that you are totally unaware of. By helping you to recognize these negative patterns that you have adopted, he can help you in all aspects of your life.

He then teaches you the art of Chi Kung or "Energy Cultivation" which provides The Power through increased personal energy to make a clear break from the negative behavior patterns that may be holding you back from living a total and successful life.

I went through this experience with Gary when I attended his PERSONAL POWER TRAINING™ which he taught in Portland, Oregon about 2 years ago. The reason I went to his seminar was to learn to become a better public speaker. I found out that my problem related to public speaking was locked up in "self-defeating patterns" of behavior that had become so ingrained that I wasn't even aware I had them. I hope this makes sense to you, it certainly did to me.

During the seminar, I was asked to tell the group why I came and what I wanted to get out of it. While I was expressing myself, Gary was able to pinpoint behavior patterns that I was using that were negative and self-defeating and pointed them out to me and the group. It was a very uneasy feeling to be put on the spot at the time, but it was extremely rewarding for me. Since then, I have dropped those "negative patterns" and have become a much better communicator with the people I speak to and more importantly, with myself.

Thank you Gary Clyman for your talent in this very important area of "The Human Experience," which so many of us don't know how to access by ourselves, but so deeply need.

Gary Clyman sent me a copy of his book entitled BEYOND SELF-HELP: MASTERING

BEYOND SELF-HELP: MASTERING PERSONAL POWER™ by Gary J. Clyman

PERSONAL POWER™ a few weeks ago. I have been very excited about the possibilities that it will open up for thousands of people just like me, who can benefit from the "truths" that Gary teaches. This book contains some of "The Secrets of the Universe" and I would exhort you to read this material with an open heart and mind and to practice the principles taught within its covers. In so doing, you can become a "Master of Personal Power" in your own personal life.

I love you Gary, for the person you are and for the great contribution that you are making to mankind by providing a book such as this for our use. GOD has and will continue to bless you abundantly for your years of dedicated service to humanity and your sincere desire to help others to have a more meaningful life experience. Gary Whitley D.C., S.L.C., UT

BEYOND SELF-HELP: MASTERING PERSONAL POWER™ by Gary J. Clyman

A PERSPECTIVE BY JOSEPH LARONGE

If I could talk about Chi Kung I would like to relate to you an incident in which I found, in a way that I think was representative of the way Chi Kung has helped me in my law practice.

It was the fall of 1987 and I found myself sitting at a trial table. I was in the 4th week of a month long trial. In fact, it was the longest trial of my career. It had been brutal. I was up against 3 other lawyers just by myself. They really had a strategy for trying to wear me down, before we got to the trial. About 3 weeks before, they just hit me with tons of papers that required responses, answers, and a lot of attention so that I would lose some footing and some momentum in approaching the trial. As the things moved along, it was really a battle of wits and endurance.

On the last day of the 4th week of trial, I had a particularly troublesome "expert" witness. He was a Doctor of Finance from the East coast and was really sharp. It was a cross examination of their witness. It was funny. I stood up. I was about to start this tense cross examination. I picked up this water pitcher from the table I was using. You could just cut the air with a knife. I mean, it had been that way the whole trial because there were 10 million dollars in question. You could imagine people were pretty tense. So I picked up the water pitcher and I went to pour the water. The table was just filled with all these detailed notes and all that. The cap fell right off of the pitcher and all the water just poured all over the table... you know right in front of me and on my lap. Well the other side started laughing and it was kind of humorous.

What I found very interesting was, it didn't throw me at all. You know, I had spent the whole trial practicing the things I had been training in in Chi Kung. Every night I would be "Condensing," channeling my energy and in fact, one of the best things I was doing was taking the assaults that the other attorneys were throwing at me and using them. You know, I could absorb what they were doing and channel it for my own purposes. So when this happened and the water fell all over the papers in this tense incident, I just laughed like everyone else and was really relaxed. I just took the "add humor" of it that I was getting from the other side and just churned it into being even more effective in the cross examination.

BEYOND SELF-HELP: MASTERING PERSONAL POWER™ by Gary J. Clyman

I could almost just feel it condensing into my bones and saying "I'm going to sink this down into my Tan Tien, put it into the Earth, and send it send it back out, the way I want it to be." Well, it worked just that way. I was very effective against their "expert" witness. I mean, they were shaking their heads. They could not believe the way things were going.

When the trial was over, I knew that I had done what I needed to do. I had kept my endurance. I had been sharp and quick and never really lost a step. I would attribute a lot of that to the mental, physical, and emotional stamina that I got from practicing Chi Kung and of course, also to my many years of Tai Chi which act as a foundation that gives my Chi Kung a place to blossom. So, it was a really enjoyable experience to see it in action.

GJC: Please explain a little bit about what does Chi Kung means to you? It's not just meditation.

JAL: I think that's an interesting question. You know, many years ago, in my 20's, I had come across some of the Eastern philosophies, and although I had trained in the martial arts for many years, meditation was very new to me then. It was not Chi Kung or the other things that I had practiced then. I had found that while it was restful, it was more "up in my head." It wasn't something concrete, that I could actually use or do something with. With Chi Kung, when you really feel yourself getting control of parts of yourself, first of all, you didn't even know exists and secondly, didn't believe you could ever have a handle on, you begin to feel a sense of "POWER," and also a sense of connection to things outside of yourself. Instead of alienating and separating you from other people and things, I think it connects you to "The Source" in a way that you can feel your own individuality, at the same time feeling part of the system as a whole. And that's very empowering.

Chi Kung opens you up a lot of options you didn't even know were available before you begin to realize that your capacities as a person were really limited by your own belief systems. As those belief systems change because you see the growth from your practice, what you can do sometimes feels limitless. I mean your rational mind knows perhaps this is not so, but usually when you're practicing and trying to accelerate your energy beyond the speed of light, and sense some of the things that are happening, and the results that you can produce, you, at least I, get kind of an inner smile inside and say here's something that's really worth while. It allows me to make things happen. I would say, "that's what Chi Kung is." Joseph A. Laronge, Portland, OR

BEYOND SELF-HELP: MASTERING PERSONAL POWER™ by Gary J. Clyman

A PERSPECTIVE BY ROBERT FABINO Ph.D.

Learning to generate internal energy that can be available to a person as is needed involves the highly complex coordination and relationship of mind, breathing, and physical movement. An individual's ability to accumulate, cultivate, circulate, and distribute his or her personal internal energy is positive, exciting, and powerful.

Chi Kung is an ancient art that can be found recorded in history over 2,000 years ago. It is an art that has many purposes and provides many different benefits. Although it is still considered an art - its techniques and applications have drawn the attention of the scientific community on an international level.

Training in Chi Kung has been simplified and made easier to understand by Gary Clyman in PERSONAL POWER TRAINING™. This ancient art is effectively and positively presented in a basic program that can be taught in 8 private weekly sessions, a weekend intensive format, or 2 days of private, one on one instruction.

Benefits of "The Training" for an individual are highly personal and developmental. Success in the training of mental conditions will be determined and reflected in an individuals quality of practice, commitment, and perseverance. Outcome of the practice and benefits can be seen immediately and or developing over a period of time, with the utilization of the "Chi" as is needed by the individual for their individual program. Change is an integral part of the practice.

PERSONAL POWER TRAINING™ is a fun way to participate in an action- oriented program. Learning can be quick, the benefits are numerous and on-going. Dr. Robert Fabino, Psychologist

A PERSPECTIVE BY GEORGE KRUEGER

I came to Gary Clyman in September of 1987. I had been taking some acupuncture treatments from Dr. Joseph Kalal and he and I had a pretty good relationship. He told me exactly what I should do. He said "go talk to Gary Clyman and have a conference about the prostate surgery you are going to have." Prior to that, I received some very radical radiation treatments done to me out at Fermilab. I was one of their "guinea pigs." This was not traditional radiation. This burned my insides out. It did a real good job of it, but it stopped the cancer that I had growing there.

I had a very "late stage" cancer, "first stage" being the easiest. I was a "third or forth stage" and I was "terminal." They did a nice job on me on that, but it didn't completely take and I had the surgery scheduled in March of 1988. Now I knew that I was going to have a lot of pain because I had an extreme amount of pain before. You don't get away with that with cancer, it's a bad thing. As I said, I was going to Dr. Kalal for another thing that wasn't related to my cancer, but he knew what I had coming up. He said, "Why don't you go talk to Gary." He said he had a weekend workshop set up where I could learn a little bit more about controlling my pain.

BEYOND SELF-HELP: MASTERING PERSONAL POWER™ by Gary J. Clyman

It was the best move I ever made in my life. It was unbelievable. With what I learned, I had complete control going into the operation. I wasn't worried about the operation at all. The anxiety definitely was decreased, but you still have that, but going into the operation, I just knew that I had absolute control. I wasn't worried about it. God, you have to know that mine was a bad thing, 6 hours and 15 minutes on the operating table.

An interesting thing, I don't know if it had anything to do with it or not. They anticipated a "considerable blood loss." I had no blood loss. 6 hours and 15 minutes, they were operating. They had me absolutely laid open. I had no blood loss, transfusions, nothing along those lines. I would think that this particular element of Tai Chi (Chi Kung) had me prepared for this. I was just "ready."

They were taking me into the prep room before the operation and I guess they might have thought I was a little bit nuts. I was doing my thing while they were doing theirs. I used my Chi Kung practice to be aware at the "going out" part of my surgery. I did my little thing and it worked. Gary had taught me a technique to use after the operation, for gathering my pain into my toe. I probably had the sorest toe that anybody ever had, after the operation. I put all the pain right in that damn toe, and I really didn't have a bad time getting out of that.

If you can imagine, "late stage" prostate cancer; which had been burned. My insides, my guts are burned, you know there's no question about that. Then I had this operation and that was a little bad. You know all I have inside of me is scar tissue. It hurt and there's no question about the aggravation connected with it. I don't have a normal set of guts. All I've got is scar tissue and it's extremely slow in repairing itself. I'm not a "usual" case, I'm a "bad" case. My guts just don't exist, they're scar tissue. So I had a pretty bad time recuperating. But again, if they would have left me alone after surgery, I wouldn't have really had too many problems.

After the surgery, they gave me very, very heavy doses of morphine, which I really didn't need. They were just processing me through like a normal patient. The morphine interfered with my own process of eliminating the pain. They didn't understand. Finally, after a couple of days, I made them understand, I didn't need those narcotics. It wasn't helping me any. It effected me and I didn't like it. Finally, I didn't know they were going to do this to me. After a couple of days of the narcotics, I asked the nurse "What the hell are they jamming into my sides?" Then she told me and I said "I don't want any more of that, I'll handle this myself." I did very well after that, no problem. I had a lot of other problems, but that wasn't one of them.

I'm a strong man, but Chi Kung made me much stronger. Really Gary, your technique made me much, much stronger. My wife laughs at me. She thinks I'm a little bit of a kook, but she understands, I'm able to handle things real well.

My advice for other people is "take PERSONAL POWER TRAINING™ by all means." You know, I'm really scared for other people. I just feel so sorry for people that are not as strong as I am that have to go into something like this. I don't know what they can do. I feel so sorry for them. You helped me and I'm strong to start with. I don't know what other people would do. Take it and practice. Tai Chi (Chi Kung) has just been "super" for me.

You know, the operation put me out of commission for a year's time. Mine was very, very bad., But I tell you, I can hardly wait 'till this summer when I can practice Chi Kung for my golf game. I can hardly wait! You know that Azinger practices this for his golf, and I can hardly wait to do it for my own. My game can be great again, or at least passable. You know, I'm not a young man. When I went to Gary, I was 63. I'm 64 now and I'm looking forward to a lot of great golf. George Krueger, Chicago, IL

A PERSPECTIVE BY GILBERT C. CARROLL M.D.

I am a physician and a scientist. Consequently, I concern myself primarily with what works and then try to discover how it works. My wife and I first became acquainted with Gary through his Tai Chi class.

After 9 months of Tai Chi, my wife (also a physician) underwent Gary's PERSONAL POWER TRAINING™/Chi Kung. Her increase in vigor, effectiveness, and equanimity were remarkable. Likewise her mood was uplifted generally. The changes were so profound, we refer to it as her "transformation."

Next I began PERSONAL POWER TRAINING™. Within 2 weeks, my work seemed less stressful. I found new freshness and beauty in food, art, and music. People became more amusing to me. My sexual interest increased. As my practice continued everyone - even my opponents - seemed to treat me with more respect. Conflicts were resolved more quickly and amicably.

These changes have persisted for months now. I believe they will be maintained indefinitely.

The above is a partial account of what happened. My own ideas regarding the mechanism of how it happened are not important. Suffice it to say, I think the explanation for all of my experiences can be translated from Chinese mysticism into Western formulations based upon biophysics and neurobiology.

Gary has begun to develop an American version of an effective technique for self-improvement based on Tai Chi/Chi Kung. His method has many elements based not only on experience, but also on guess work and intuition. With time, I think he will discard what is ineffective, extraneous, or incorrect, and focus and refine what is effective.

Hopefully more systematic investigation by him and others will continue to develop what he has begun: a new science of coping. Gilbert Carroll M.D.

BEYOND SELF-HELP: MASTERING PERSONAL POWER™ by Gary J. Clyman

A PERSPECTIVE BY LOU BUSCEMI

I had been studying Tai Chi for over 9 years and Chi Kung for about 5 years before I met Gary Clyman. The 5 years before I met Gary was a living hell. I was having severe, adverse reactions since beginning Chi Kung work. As I inquired more about Chi Kung, I found many discrepancies in each system and between systems. I never got a straight answer from anyone.

In theory, all the books and experts had the ultimate system, but in practice all were unreliable. It was not fun being in a state of psychic shock. I had heard of Gary several years before I actually met him, and when I saw his ad, I remembered he had come highly recommended several years earlier. Gary Clyman was the first person in all the years I have been in living hell to understand what I told him. This is in itself an accomplishment.

His reworking my knowledge of Chi Kung has changed my life dramatically. My questions were completely understood and answered clearly and fully. He is the first one to demystify, simplify, and put it into a practical, usable, safe, and effective form, Chi Kung.

During the "living hell era," I had been having severe adverse reactions since I began practicing Chi Kung. I was having headaches, severe itching, and I could hardly eat any foods without having these side effects. Since learning Chi Kung with Gary Clyman, I can now eat whatever I want, whenever I want to, without any trouble as before. According to all the doctors, acupuncturists, Chiropractors, herbalist, psychic healers, you name it, none of whom helped me in the slightest, the symptoms of my previous Chi Kung side effects masked themselves in 2 major ways. The first was as having hypoglycemic reactions to nearly everything I ate and the second was appearing as if I had a severe case of Candita Albicans (Systemic Yeast Infection). Now I can eat anything I want to; everything I was told was bad for me, without worrying about or having any problems. I've got no fear of food any more.

I now have a safe and understandable Chi Kung system to work with and my life has dramatically changed for the better by it. This practice makes me feel stronger than I have ever felt. I would say The Clyman System™ is The Coca Cola of Chi Kung, An American Original, The Real Thing. Lou Buscemi, Natick, MA.

BEYOND SELF-HELP: MASTERING PERSONAL POWER™ by Gary J. Clyman

A PERSPECTIVE BY LARRY MICHALSKI

I've been involved with various martial arts styles and systems over the last 12 years. I came to Gary 20 months ago in search of a quality Tai Chi Instructor, which, by the way, is extremely difficult to find.

At the initial interview, I was immediately impressed by Gary's excellent communication skills, honesty, and patience in understanding the student's needs and perspectives. He's an impeccable Tai Chi Master who sweats the details and loves the Art.

Shortly after I began to build a solid Tai Chi foundation under his guidance, I became aware of Gary's other activities and interests, along with his workshop, PERSONAL POWER TRAINING™. He takes ancient Taoist, Tai Chi, and Chi Kung practices, then strips them of their mystical shrouds through clear explanations and practical exercises.

After 8 months of Tai Chi, I took PERSONAL POWER TRAINING™ which created (and is creating) a new me! It not only has eliminated past negative belief systems and energy blockages, but sensitizes me to present ones before they can manifest themselves. More importantly, I replace them with "seed ideas" of a positive and creative nature. Only the "best dressed" thoughts are admitted.

"The Clyman System" isn't some mystical-etheric bull-jive, but rather is rooted in a condensed and unified mind, body, and spirit. It's taught me to focus my energy, increase my self-esteem, seed future realities, recognize and develop latent creative abilities, and improve my health and virility. It's a tool that becomes geometrically more effective the more one develops it.

It's been 11 months since PERSONAL POWER TRAINING™ and I feel it's the perfect intermeshing compliment to my Tai Chi practice.

Gary still proves to be the most perceptive teacher to ones "real" needs that I've ever met. He's a fluid, but structured Master of Practical Life that unselfishly shares his knowledge and experience; whose enthusiastic attitude is contagious. Larry Michalski, Des Plaines, IL

CHOOSING A SYSTEM

People are constantly striving to raise the quality of existence at every level, whether it be in relationships, occupations, or favorite hobbies. People utilize different approaches to realize improvement at these different levels. Choosing the correct approach for you can be a difficult task.

This section is directed at helping you choose the system and teacher that best suits your personal needs. Much confusion is associated with this work. Listed are some warnings and guidelines to help make this part of the work easier.

You must engage in a relatively progressive system, whether it be meditation, Yoga, Tai Chi, cooking, music, or any other discipline. You should find a person capable of teaching by example and who is willing to work with the student's interest at heart, and not just trying to confuse or manipulate the students by taking advantage of their inexperience. Nobody will hold your hand through the work, but if you can find an advisor who could help reduce stress and give you some encouragement, you will stand a better chance of making it through your training.

Beware of the mystical approach. If you fall for it, you will fall into it. You could become sidetracked and waste a lot of time wandering in the wrong direction. Looking back at the period could be painfully awakening. The system you choose must be well rounded, mentally, physically, and spiritually. Beware of one-sidedness. Since humans are multi-leveled beings, what ever you get involved in or dedicate your time, thought, practice, and lifestyle to, it must deal with as many sides of you as possible. If any one side is left out or dealt with more than the others, you run the risk of becoming out of balance. Only by devoting yourself to a well-balanced system can you hope to exceed the system itself. If the fundamentals or basic principles of that system are small and limited, what do you think the extensions and outgrowth will be? This is why you must look to the basic philosophy that is at the heart of each system.

Physically speaking, it must be accessible and approachable to a multitude of individuals regardless of age, physical condition, or adverse attitudes. Fanatics, and one hour a day practitioners must stand a good chance of developing. Don't look too far ahead, it could seem a lot more difficult or easier than it really is. Many people tend to become discouraged early because they do not have a good understanding and therefore quit before they give themselves a chance. You must not only look at where your teacher is, but how and by what means he got there. It is reasonable for one to wish to be farther along, but don't be disillusioned by the amount of work that it takes.

Enjoy "being," being where you are, moment by moment, only then can your training take a positive effect on your total being. Please remember, masters are made at the beginning, not at the end. Courage, sincerity, and stubbornness are important always.

Mentally, you must be alert and ready to receive change at all times. Look ahead at your seniors (people who have been involved longer than you). Does it appear more palatable to be in their shoes, than in your own?

You must take into consideration many things such as, their personalities, approach, background, motivation, stage in their process, and amount of work which they put in. You can learn something from everybody. Is your teacher willing to spend the amount of time it takes for you to absorb the material?

Most seekers only see a small portion of what they could. Ego, frustration, refusal to give up the old, negative habits, and hearing but not paying attention, are just a few obstacles to be overcome. Beware of an exclusive approach to an end result. Your practice must be devoted to the improvement of the human condition of life without creating any selfish attitudes.

Now the hard part, spirituality and physically. This is a very touchy subject because many people are locked up even though they believe they are free. One must be very careful not to create any friction with one's self. You didn't become the way you are overnight, so don't expect to change it overnight. The process starts out by making small additions. As you get used to the process of change, or acceptance, the other side of you will learn to release the unproductive aspects of your spiritual being. This work is very closely related to your mental side but has some subtle differences. These changes are usually harder to distinguish, such as having more tolerance, having and keeping a quieter mind and taking control and responsibility for your own destiny.

Your spiritual practice must follow a step by step process. One thing must lead to the next. Don't get excited. Take it one day at a time and try to avoid straying away from your true path. This requires constant monitorization of your actions, attitudes, and efforts. Please avoid excesses. Remember, too much is just as bad as not enough. You must be responsive to change.

FINDING A QUALIFIED CHI KUNG TEACHER

Some Chi Kung students have problems associated with learning from unqualified teachers. I use the word "unqualified" not to imply that there is some regulatory body that determines who's good and who isn't. I look at a Chi Kung teacher's qualifications by the results he produces in his students and the people he has taught. There are a few well-known teachers circulating, and every once in a while, one of their students comes to me for help, because they are not getting what they had hoped for or expected. Sometimes they have problems directly related to learning from these other teachers.

LEARN WHAT TO LOOK FOR IN A CHI KUNG TEACHER

To choose the correct system for you may appear to be a complicated task. Unlike Tai Chi, which can be judged or gaged by somebody's martial art ability, appearance, physical endurance, rootedness, fighting application creativity, and/or other factors, Chi Kung is not so obvious to the beginner's eye.

Chi Kung is easier to fake; lately, in the last few years, a lot of bad Chi Kung teachers have surfaced. I don't mean their characters are bad. I'm referring to the material they teach that is so watered down. They should call what they do something else, completely. I'm sure some simply "translate" without actually personally contributing anything. Speaking 2 languages is not enough reason to be called "Master." Look out for them.

What I teach is clearly different. After many thousands of hours of personal practice, I have formulated my own Chi Kung system. I teach a system which has been extracted and developed from my extensive Tai Chi training. My system in not some modified or bastardized version of some larger system to teach to us "Dumb Americans," but has been designed and simplified to give you all the technique you need in the most precise and shortest time frame. I believe that learning should be easy and practice should be simple, not easy. This is not simply a self-improvement book. Learning my system from my book will actually give you a specific procedure to perform on a daily basis.

Most people that show an interest in learning Tai Chi have certain ideas, personal goals, and criteria that can be addressed, answered or fulfilled in the initial 2-3 months of their Chi Kung practice. These are quickly satisfied so each new student can go on with his or her work without continuing the desperate and long search for the truth.

WHAT KIND OF PEOPLE ARE ATTRACTED TO THIS SYSTEM?

"Self-starters" who are already somewhat successful but who realize there's always room for improvement come to learn from me. You can excel even more at what you do by applying these valuable principles. "Losers" are rarely attracted to my system, they usually justify why they are not operating at their full capacity. Winners attract winners.

MANY MARTIAL ARTISTS COME TO WORK WITH ME

I attract a lot of martial arts students and also "experts" as my students. One of the reasons these people come to me is, because of my level of expertise and willingness to give them what they both want and need. To develop internal energy (Chi) there are a few methods. The word "Ki" or "Chi" has become quite generic over the last 15 years. Every art uses these same words to some extent, however, in The 4 Major Chinese Internal Systems (Tai Chi Chuan, Pa Kua Chang, Hsing I, and Lu Ho Ba Fa), each of these arts teaches its own interpretation and utilization of Chi and Jing.

I do something that is different from everybody else. I take my students where they are and give them a well rounded, self-contained, working knowledge of how they can convert their internal energy (Chi) into internal power (Jing). As I've mentioned in another section the book, my approach to developing internal energy through "The Clyman System" has been extracted from my extensive Tai Chi and Chi Kung background and improved. The important thing to understand here is "I take you from where you are and help you get to where you want to go."

An analogy is helpful here to understand the conversion process. An internal combustion engine must have an energy source, gasoline, and a method of igniting the energy, the ignition system, into the more usable form of energy, horsepower. For us, "Chi" is the energy source, "Jing" is the power, and Chi Kung is the method of transformation.

AN INTERVIEW WITH A NEW STUDENT

(This is an interview with Darryl Lyzun who has been practicing Tai Chi for 12 years as of 1988, prior to his learning Chi Kung

DL: How do people find you?

GJC: They find me by looking. I mean, I advertise, I'm around. In the Tai Chi Community, not just Chicago, but nationally, I am somewhat well known now. I've been doing Tai Chi for a long time. Plus, because of my personality traits, people don't forget me easily. They try... but they can't.

DL: Do you get a lot of referrals from other Tai Chi people or martial artists in the community?

GJC: No, no I don't. Because everybody thinks that they know everything. So, my primary target of the population is not the martial art community. I've even met Karate people who think they already know what I'm teaching. They have no idea what I'm doing. Most Tai Chi teachers have no idea of what I'm even talking about. So they really have no idea what I'm teaching. But when I run across a guy doing Tae Kwon Do or some other external art, who thinks he knows what I'm doing, that's truly ridiculous! You've got to be a Tai Chi Master to even get the concept of how I've done this, not just somebody who knows how to kick and punch. What I do has nothing to do with martial arts any more.

DL: So, how can people learn Chi Kung from you in a weekend?

GJC: Well they can learn it in one weekend because I worked so hard to make it simple enough for people to understand. It's important to understand that when you learn Chi Kung from me, as you learn the different phases and parts of the system, you change as you learn it. It's not like something you have to practice for years to see a result. People see results with me in a very, very short time. For instance with Lou Buscemi, he flew in from Boston and spent 2 days with me. He did the 2 Day Private Format. He had 5 years of bad Chi Kung in the past and all kinds of problems. His other teacher was very confused.

The first thing I did with him was to make him agree to forget everything he learned so I could start with a fresh slate in the training and that's exactly what I did. He only spent 2 days with me, privately. I have a lot of people fly in to do that on a regular basis. They never come back, but they find me, fly in, learn it and that's it. A large part of my business is these traveling students.

DL: What other applications does Chi Kung have? I mean can it be used with Tai Chi, from what you've learned from Tai Chi?

GJC: Yes, although when I teach my Chi Kung system, it's a separate entity. You can also practice Tai Chi but you don't really mix them. I've combined a few things in a minor way in The Daily Practice Routine but that has nothing to do with Tai Chi. Yes, it's Tai Chi, but you don't need a Tai Chi background to be successful in my Chi Kung system.

DL: If you have Chi Kung, could you make applications to the Tai Chi movements to give your movements more power or to transfer internal energy?

GJC: That's automatic. The first thing I teach in my Chi Kung system is "Condensing Breathing." "Condensing Breathing," which I've explained in many other sections of the book, "gives you the ability to condense 18 inches of movement into 1 inch of space." So expanding on this principal, if you're doing a "ward off form" or you're doing some other Tai Chi move, you would be doing "Condensing Breathing" and then you practice your Tai Chi differently. I'm not saying you do "Condensing Breathing" when you're practicing Tai Chi, but because you already have been practicing "Condensing Breathing" prior to this, it affects your Tai Chi in a very positive way. It makes your Tai Chi more dense.

DL: How good would your Tai Chi have to be in order to transfer from one to the other?

GJC: Just fundamental. You don't have to be advanced in either. Chi Kung can actually help practitioners of other martial arts improve their skills.

DL: Is there any relationship between Chi Kung and Kundalini Yoga?

GJC: No. Chi Kung and Kundalini Yoga are not really related except that Kundalini was taken from Chi Kung a long time ago, but they, the Indians, did not reproduce the whole system. There are similarities in that we're saying about energy but we're really not talking about directing energy in Kundalini. Kundalini Yoga many years ago was taken from Chi Kung. Most people don't know this.

In Chi Kung you direct the energy with your mind. That's different. The difference between the circulation is, in Kundalini Yoga they only concentrate on "bringing it up" or "letting it flow up," whereas with Chi Kung you direct the energy with your mind or intention, "up," and you in turn also direct it "down." So it's clearly different.

DL: What do you mean by "circulating the energy up and down." I know how it works "up" but what is the "down" part.

GJC: Right, you know something about Kundalini Yoga.

DL: Right.

GJC: Well, the "down" part in Chi Kung is that you turn the corner at the top of the head and direct the energy down again until it's made one complete cycle.

DL: O.K., what are the benefits of directing it down.

GJC: It maintains your stability. You develop a "constitution" and you are in charge or in control of your energy instead of being a victim to it, which is a common problem with Kundalini Yoga.

DL: Because Kundalini Yoga is not a circular movement, it's just raised up only.

GJC: Right. They never pay attention to "down" that I know of.

DL: Maybe this is why people have trouble with convulsions and a lot of shaking.

GJC: Right. Convulsions, shaking, and all that stuff that I've already explained in the book as "side effects" are not supposed to be looked at, in my opinion, as a negative, if they're related to people that get their technique from me. Now if people learn Chi Kung from somebody else, well then there are problems, but if they ever happen with me, which they hardly ever do, it's O.K. You've been working really hard to get your energy to do something, so if you ever have shaking, so what, it's no big deal.

DL: I remember you talking about your own experience.

GJC: Yeah, right. I shook my brains out all the time.

GJC: So the question is how much practice a day is required, or do I advise, and the answer is, because The Daily Practice Routine only takes approximately 45 minutes to run through, that's all you really have to do.

Q: Do you have to do it every day?

A: No, 3 to 5 times a week would be sufficient.

DL: Using compressing breathing or "Condensing Breathing" in doing "the short punch," is that the same as Chi Kung?

GJC: No. I do teach "Condensing Breathing" in lesson #1 of the training, but the difference between being able to "zap" somebody while barely moving using Tai Chi or just learning Chi Kung is, when you learn just Chi Kung, you don't have the physical/structural relationship that you'll get from developing in Tai Chi. You don't have it. It's not supposed to be there. It's not important.

DL: So what response do you have for the people that say "you really can't learn anything in two days."

GJC: Well if somebody has really got their mind set that they can't learn anything in two days, they're right. I'm not going to argue with them. If they're positive and absolutely sure that they are incapable of learning something that is going to change their life from a very serious single long two day experience, then they're right. They don't belong studying with me. I'm not trying to change. You know, I need people with certain tools. What I'm talking about is, I need somebody who is ready to do something. If somebody is so hesitant that they just can't believe they can be helped or they can't believe they are capable of learning, or that it's possible to teach them, they're absolutely right. They don't belong with me. They should stay with somebody else for the rest of their lives. But that's not who comes to me. People that come to me are people that are ready, willing, and able, and know that there are possibilities when I present my system to them. They grab it and they run with it. And they do it and they change their lives. Self-starters are who come to me. There are enough of them out there that I can be selective with whom I choose.

DL: That's interesting because I was reading something the other day from the book I was talking about, how change happens and how a big barrier to change is people's concept of time.

GJC: I agree.

DL: And how they get tied to the idea that something important has to take a long time. They are going to change, but it's going to take a long time. And what is that? That is just a faulty perception.

GJC: That's a belief system.

DL: What you're saying is "change can and should take place immediately."

GJC: Now in the book, I've already explained something called "The 3 Ingredients to Change." These are Jing, Chi, and Shen. That is original Chinese, "The 3 Precious Things" (see Chapter #1). However, I've related them to how to get a result, make a difference, or change. Read that part. Basically, if you have an end result in mind, and spirit, then creating it and following through is easy. The problem that most people have is, they don't know what they're going to get, what it's going to look like, or what it's going to do, so of course, they get nothing but trouble. I call that "banging your head against the wall." But if someone works with me, they're able to program what they want and quickly get it.

BEYOND SELF-HELP: MASTERING PERSONAL POWER™ by Gary J. Clyman

DL: O.K., but from my understanding the Chinese or the Taoists, weren't they great believers in change, gradual change?

GJC: Right, but we'll soon be in the 1990's. We're not talking about the 1400's where if you wanted to go 200 miles, it was going to take you 3 days on a horse or 7 days walking. We're talking about, if I want to go to Portland, Oregon, in 4 hours... I'm there. I've adapted this for the 90's, the 21st century. This is different. Yeah, it's the same technique, but who says the applications have to remain the same?

DL: I've been running every day for about 6 or 7 years now and what I notice is the days that I don't run, I feel bad. Kind of achy, depressed, just don't have any energy. How could you compare that to the Chi Kung system?

GJC: O.K., running stimulates the production of endorphins. Doing Chi Kung, even though it's not as physically grueling as long running, also produces endorphins. So you can use Chi Kung as a mood elevator, to stabilize your personality, or to get out of certain environmental or emotional spaces the same way, except you don't ever have to go anywhere. You don't have to dress up and run in 40 below zero weather.

DL: But as far as physical benefits?

GJC: It improves your posture, strengthens your legs.

DL: You're not saying that it can take the place of some exercise.

GJC: Yeah, it can, but you'd have to modify it somewhat. You see it's not really set up as a physical exercise program. If that's what you want, then go into Tai Chi after you learn Chi Kung. You finish the training which is a two day format, eight sessions a week, and then you go into Tai Chi.

DL: With Tai Chi, can you achieve an aerobic effect?

GJC: When you're good at it, later. Like after 2 or 3 years.

DL: What do you recommend in the meantime?

GJC: From a Chiropractic perspective running is not good because it stresses the major joints too much and sometimes causes injury. Swimming seems to be me to be the most compatible exercise instead of Tai Chi or with Tai Chi. Now for me, swimming is boring. I can't do boring things. Now for me Tai Chi is not boring. It is so challenging that it's not boring. Some people think its boring but that is because they don't have the spirit of it.

Why was Chi Kung protected so long? That's the question. Well, I believe that the generation before me, my teachers, used the output, the dispersing and controlling of information as power. As for myself, I use the dispersing of information as power.

BEYOND SELF-HELP: MASTERING PERSONAL POWER™ by Gary J. Clyman

They used the controlling of information as power. So, my teachers wouldn't teach things until they had a very specific time and use and other criteria so, in the fact, their "holding back" of information made them more powerful. Whereas the fact that I give out so much information makes me more powerful in the world. Now why did I hold onto Chi Kung all that time until I finally started teaching it in 1983? Because I already knew that it made no sense to teach it in the format that I learned it, because no one could learn it that way. It would take too long. I had to have someone who had gone through the whole Tai Chi system before I could even teach them Chi Kung. That was 1978 or 79. I learned Chi Kung in 77, so in 78-82, I practiced Chi Kung on my own, many hours a day. In 82 I had the experiment where I tried to teach it for $25 a month and I got shit on, totally taken advantage of, totally unrespected. It was like throwing pearls before swine. So then in 83, I had another idea, let's change the format and teach it so people needed NO previous experience and that's what I now do and it worked and I haven't changed it since. I use an old rule... "If it's not broke, don't fix it." Make sense?

DL: So are you the only one who has this system?

GJC: Yes, I made it up. It's my system. No one taught me how to teach this. Somebody taught me the ingredients of what I teach, but nobody formatted it and said O.K., first do this, then do that, then do...

First teach some sort of "Condensing," then teach "Standing Meditation" because you need some sort of "physical connection" in relationship to your energy and your body. Then I teach "Inside Air" because "Inside Air" actually will be a precursor for The Micro Cosmic Orbit, then insert "The Sitting Forms with The Mind Training" which are moving forms combining Chi circulations while physically moving. Nobody ever teaches these. Other teachers teach movements, but they don't teach "The Mind Training." Then after "The Sitting Forms with The Mind Training," then I will teach you "The Micro Cosmic Orbit." Then on top of all that, you put it together into what is called "The Daily Practice Routine." This format is my creation. Last but not least, I included affirmations, visualizations, and what I call "Impregnating the Universe" to close with what is called "Layered Condensing." I made up the whole concept of "Layered Condensing." This is mine, I am the originator of this system, and it works.

The unique thing about my system is, that simply by learning it, you get the transformations without having to practice. Now if you practice, it makes it easier and more powerful, but even if you don't practice, you still change. Because as you learn and go through your transformations, you go through different phases with yourself, and by the time you finally do The Hands On, Transfer of Power™, it is the culmination of all the different things that we've worked on and with all this time. You will be different because you are in the driver's seat. It works that easy and that simple.

GJC: Any other questions?

DL: Not right now.

WHAT YOU NEED TO WORK WITH ME

I accept new students and clients who already possess certain positive qualities. As I've mentioned elsewhere, you must be a self-starter and have the "hunger for more" regardless of your profession or station in life. I bring out the best from the people I accept to work with. I share the responsibility of their results when they use the valuable principles I teach. Usually, when I interview new prospective clients, they think they are interviewing me, when in reality, I am screening and interviewing them. This again, is how I get such amazing and consistent results with almost everybody I choose to work with, by choosing exactly the right people to work with. The saying "Results Talks, B. S. Walks" has never been more true.

CLYMAN'S "4 UNBREAKABLE RULES" FOR SUCCESS AND RESULTS

There are "4 Unbreakable Rules" that must be followed in order to obtain your desired results from this system:

Rule #1 - No Drinking alcohol
Rule #2 - No Using Drugs
Rule #3 - No Smoking Marijuana
Rule #4 - No Masturbating (this one counts the most)

These rules must be followed. Not following them leads to dispersement and scattering of your spirit and all your energies.

SETBACKS AND SIDE EFFECTS

Setbacks and side effects are minimal to nonexistent in my clients. When you begin to make changes in your life for the better, the people that are suppose to love you the most, have tendencies to react many times in negative ways. This is because their balance is being upset or shaken up. They don't know where they will stand with you when you're different. This is a situation that comes up with some of my clients. This is understandable because they feel threatened. They must be assured that "things will be alright."

Many times after working with one of my clients, the spouse decides to work with me because they realize how they can benefit greatly from the training also. Working with me has actually "energized" or saved many troubled marriages and relationships that might not have survived without utilizing me. This happens more often than you might think.

WHAT ARE "CHI KUNG VETERANS?"

I have met many people who have had "bad side effects" from practicing Chi Kung the way other teachers teach it. I call these people "Chi Kung Veterans." Many have come to me for help after many years, living or trying to live, with their Chi Kung problems. Sometimes the symptoms associated with these Chi Kung problems resemble Hypoglycemia or Candita Albicans (System Yeast Fungus Infection) or Epstein-Barr Virus. In any case, the way I help these people is by teaching them my Chi Kung system. It is as simple as that. When they learn "The Real Thing," their symptoms usually go away immediately. The problem nowadays is that if they went to an alternative health care professional, they would probably be diagnosed as having one of the before-mentioned conditions. Usually the wrong diagnosis. Most western doctors would probably tell you "it's all in your head." This is even worse than making the "The Missing Diagnosis."

In these special cases, the first thing I do, is have them "discard all their previous experience and training." When I repair "Chi Kung Veterans," first I retrain them. In almost 100% of these cases, all these "Chi Kung Veterans" needed was to learn from "a genuine expert." People fly in to work with me from all over the country for my specialty. It can usually be completed in about 2 days.

My best friend and Tai Chi brother had these same symptoms in 1977 and we could not find anyone who could help him. He lived in "hell" for a long time. I did the best I could for him, but I was not an expert yet. Today everything is different.

The results these "Chi Kung Veterans" get from this re-training are permanent and far-reaching. Read what Lou Buscemi wrote in his perspective in this book. He had learned from one of these so called "masters" and I fixed him in just 2 days. These problems are simple to eliminate permanently when you understand "the true nature" of the problem.

ABOUT OTHER CHI KUNG BOOKS

Many of my readers have read many other Chi Kung books that have already been published. Almost everybody tells me "they really didn't know what to do with those books." A common response is "I looked at it, put it away and never touched it again," or "I tried some of the techniques in the other books, but found they didn't lead anywhere." This will not be true with my book. My intention is to give you a self-contained, workable, complete system that you can use immediately to help improve your life.

Some Chi Kung books on the market today, I am sure are mere translations of some other Chinese books. The important point to understand here, is that if somebody is translating, they don't have to have a working knowledge or have to have mastered Chi Kung. All they really have to be able to do is be able to translate. This is the condition of the Chi Kung books in the United States.

These "Chi Kung Veterans," the people with previous experience, will find great joy and appreciation in working with my system.

PATIENCE IS VIRTUE...

Everyone has heard this famous saying at one time or another. What most people do not understand is that patience is a virtue only when it is appropriate. This means you must be doing the right thing, first, then patience is an asset. If you are doing the wrong thing, then all your patience is a liability. For instance, I recently went to a Chi Kung lecture by a very well known author and teacher. The people in his crowd were very lost and confused. They were all attracted to him, because he is also very lost and confused.

By reading his books, I always had a hunch that he was only a collector or translator, but after seeing and hearing him in person, now I am sure he does not know what he is doing. If "patience" is applied to this teachers system, absolutely nothing will come from it and "patience" will be a liability. Remember, Chi Kung is to help improve your life, not take the place of it. This means "YOU" are more important than any system. This "Holier than Tao" attitude is so far in left field, you could not be any more wrong. This is the same teacher that Lou Buscemi spent 5 years studying with. What worse crime is there than wasting people's time?

HOW DOES CHI KUNG RELATE TO ZEN MEDITATION?

The major difference between Chi Kung and Zen Mediation is that when you practice Zen, you do not "direct your energy" with your mind. You simply "let the energy flow" on its own. In 1979-80, my Tai Chi brother and I spent a great deal of time with 2 Korean Zen Buddhist monks. We exchanged techniques and information extensively and at the end of our relationship, we realized that we had technical skills and practices that were not related to Zen. We were actually at a higher level than our 2 monk friends. These monks respected us as "masters of our art," and this gave us a new perspective of our own abilities and knowledge.

These monks were shocked when they began to understand what we were practicing. They had seen similar things done when they were in Korea, in the temple, performed only by their "high level" masters. They said nobody was ever taught how to do these techniques. These monks were in Zen for over 20 years each. We had been practicing Tai Chi and Chi Kung for only 6 or 7 years at the time. In Chi Kung, you move and direct your energy with your mind, consciously.

Many people have some experience with Zen meditation. While practicing Zen, if a thought passes your mind, the idea is to let that thought go. But if you're spending 8-12 hours a day looking for "the thought" and while you're practicing your Zen meditation, your thought finally appears, it makes no sense to "let it go." I guarantee you, when you finish meditating and go back to try and recapture your thought, you will have great difficulty recovering it. I have rarely seen anybody with the ability to forget what they saw and remember it again. This is not like dreaming. Here you are purposely wiping it out. How can you expect to read what you purposely erased?

Meditation has a funny problem. My advice is, when you're practicing Chi Kung and a thought, realization, project, or some other creative idea comes up, write it down. Capture it on paper, then let it go. This way, when you're done practicing, you can take your clipboard and you've retained what came up instead of just "letting it go." Millions of dollars worth of great ideas can be captured by simply writing down these "semi-objective thoughts" as they pass through your mind. In the long run, many great ideas come up in the funniest places. What funnier a place for a great idea to come up then while meditating, and while you're not looking for it? That's why Chi Kung the way I teach it, is the meditation system for this modern, fast-paced lifestyle we all have.

PRESSURE FROM YOUR "LOVED ONES"

The reaction of my client's spouses to the client's improved lives and changed personality traits is quite remarkable. The first and initial reaction is that they encourage them to improve, until about 2-3 weeks after they've started, then all of a sudden, they feel threatened and want them to assume their old status and position, again, so they can maintain controlling them as before. At this phase, the spouses sometimes try creating many problems in my client's lives. This phase of the cycle only lasts about 2 weeks.

Finally, their relationships land on a more even keel, with balanced communication between the two. This cycle is very common when you start to go for what you want. You might "catch some flack" from the people that are suppose to love and support you. Be prepared, but don't be antagonistic. "When you stop taking shit is when it always hits the fan." The wives of many of my clients begin working with me a few months after their husbands do. This has a great stabilizing effect on their relationships.

PLEASING OTHERS: THE BIG TRAP

It's a big trap to try to please people, but when you have self-confidence you don't care if you please them. When you don't care if you please them, many times you will. If you try to please them, you can't do it anyway, so trying to please everyone is "a double edged sword." If you're not happy, you can't possibly ever make anybody else happy, so you have to first do "what's right" for you and not worry about the others.

HOW WE GIVE OUR POWER AWAY

Most people associate "giving your power away" with women, but actually, women do it in a more traditional way, while men do it in a much more sneaky and sophisticated way. In men, these are related to "masculinity issues." Traditionally speaking, women have been trained to give their power away. Depending on their era and background, this problem may be more or less serious. Now a days, with all these emotional dysfunctional issues, this is becoming more common. Being raised in an alcoholic environment is the most obvious family situation. Child abuse in my opinion is a close and intermingling second.

BEYOND SELF-HELP: MASTERING PERSONAL POWER™ by Gary J. Clyman

UNDESERVING ISSUES

In rare cases, "an undeserving issue" or self-esteem problem prevents people from actually accepting what they know is good for them even while working with me. Under normal circumstances and since I choose "stable people" as clients, many problems can be eleviated or won't last as long as they could. Many people have "an undeserving issue" that gets in their way their whole lives. When it comes to accepting what is rightfully theirs, it is usually difficult to get around this, especially since most people are unconsciously holding on to these "undeserving issues."

MASTURBATING AND DESERVINGNESS

Masturbating reduces your ability to accept more. It reduces your self-esteem levels, your ability to deserve. That shows up as not getting something you truly deserve because you believe you don't deserve it, or being easy to please. For instance, instead of making a lot of money, you will settle for less money, less than what you're worth. The only time I really have trouble with interviewing a client, is if he masturbates more than 3 or 4 times a week. I pretty much know that I'm not going to be able to accept him as a client. He will probably say that he doesn't want to work with me and will have plenty of excuses such as, he can't afford it, it will be better for him to do it in a couple of months (a favorite among procrastinators), or his life really isn't as bad as he made it out to be when we spoke last.

Because they have this problem with their ability to deserve already, they just don't work with me. And they don't know that the reason that they came to me is to eliminate this exact limitation.

It's as if they're surrendering to the problem instead of overcoming it. What do you do if I tell someone "your days for masturbating are over?" They listen to me and say "Ooops, what am I going to do instead?" They would rather continue masturbating than work with me. But men that masturbate don't understand this. It's as if they fall asleep before the sun rises each day, and never get to see what a sunrise looks like.

WARNING SIGNS?

Other teachers stress the dangers of Chi Kung, usually more than the benefits. I stress the benefits, not the dangers. My students rarely ask or are concerned about the dangers. You see, I've found that if you keep warning or scaring people, a certain percentage will complete a self-fulfilling prophecy. I don't spew warnings and my students don't worry about them. "Be a warrior or a worrier, the choice is yours."

HOW I FIX THESE ENERGY PROBLEMS

I help these other teachers' students when I help them balance their energy by examining what is going on inside of them. Sometimes I sit back to back with them which enables me to feel and detect what is wrong. Most of these people know how to bring on their undesirable symptoms because the symptoms are directly related to their previous practice. I have them practice and describe what they are doing. I am amazed at the "vagueness" of most of the other teachers' details.

Careful examination and consultation is the first step. Then, I go inside their energy system and reproduce it in myself. I then experience what they are experiencing. Next, I fix the circuitry in myself and finally, I fix theirs in them and teach them a new, more powerful and specific technique. These problems are usually very simple, regardless of how long they have endured or how serious the symptoms. "Retraining" usually replaces any apparent problems immediately. If you have this problem, you know exactly what I am explaining. Contact my office immediately for help.

THE CHIROPRACTIC / CHI KUNG CONNECTION

Quite often many of the sensations or feelings that are interpreted by some Chi Kung practitioners are misconceived as energy related problems and sensations. Many of these problems and sensations have been proven to have actually been Chiropractic problems. A simple visit to a Chiropractor's office could have alleviated many of these so called energy problems. Many of these problems are not energy problems at all but are simple joint or bone-out-of-place problems. Due to their naivety or ignorance in some cases, some people that have these feelings have interpreted them to be these huge energy-related problems. I can recall having back pain, literally thousands of times as a Tai Chi student.

The difficulty I had was I did not understand what and how Chiropractic worked. I put up with all kinds of pain that I probably never had to if I would have only gone to see a Chiropractor. These aches and pains were probably simple mechanical dysfunctions and irregularities, but in those days, who knew?

CHI SENSATIONS COULD BE STRUCTURALLY EXPLAINED

The sensations could be tingling in the face, shoulder pain, spinal pain, hip discomfort. Sometimes people that have upper thoracic problems actually think it their Chi. It could be and yet, if they were to practice Chi Kung and had the availability of Chiropractic treatment, it would make their practice of Chi Kung that much easier. Even when I asked my teachers, do you think they had enough insight to refer me to a Chiropractor? No way. This ignorance feeds the mystique associated with Chi Kung and Tai Chi. I am telling you, "if you hurt, don't just put up with it, put a Chinese liniment on it and if if it doesn't get better in 1 week, go to a Chiropractor."

BEYOND SELF-HELP: MASTERING PERSONAL POWER™ by Gary J. Clyman

ENERGY: THE COMMODITY

The long term goal in Chi Kung is to accumulate, cultivate, circulate and direct energy with our mind, in that specific order. Energy cultivation starts scattered, with no particular pattern or apparent origin. The first step in achieving our goal and developing a relationship with our own energy is to first distinguish the boundaries of our physical bodies. This is the easiest part.

Regarding energy and Chi Kung as taught in **PERSONAL POWER TRAINING™**, the first step is to organize the energy that is scattered within the confines of the physical body. The next step in this system after organizing is collecting and preventing unnecessary energy leakages still remaining inside the physical body. A further step in this system is called adding to our energy accumulation.

WHAT IS THE FUNCTION OF TAN TIEN?

The process of what you do to Tan Tien, when you are developing an excess amount of sexual energy is to suck it into 3 inches below your navel and 2 inches inside. The purpose of Tan Tien is to perform as a boiler. So imagine you are heating or boiling water, and instead of the boiler exploding under the pressure build up, what you do is you leak a little out, intentionally, and feed it into your Micro Cosmic Orbit.

So you do Condensing and you boil. This is why when you practice Condensing Breathing, you begin to feel very hot. Then you use the release valve to channel accumulated energy from your condensed energy from Tan Tien to your Micro Cosmic Orbit. So you are developing a system. Suck, overload almost to the point of explosion, and drain off to your Micro Cosmic Orbit. You want to develop a self-generating system. Tan Tien is your physical center of gravity, approximately even with your 5th Lumbar Vertebrae. Tan Tien is also related to your animal instincts such as sex, survival, and physical urgency.

Technique #1 - Condensing Breathing

To accomplish our initial goal of organizing the energy in the confines of the physical body, "Condensing Breathing" is the major technique and principle used. After some energy has been accumulated, the energy inside the confines of the physical body must be directed with the mind, first crudely & grossly in upward and downward directions separately and systematically, next we learn a more refined procedure for working with our energy.

Technique #2 - Inside Air

To accomplish our goal and the next step, "Inside Air" is utilized.

The next step is connecting our newly accumulated energy to the body through repetition of very specific movements. The importance of this step is to connect or link our energy with the identification of our own physical body.

Technique #3 - Sitting Forms with the Mind Training

So far what we have done is 1), organized and accumulated the energy inside the confines of the physical body; 2), projected that energy in gross movement directions; 3), we have connected our stored energy to the identification of our physical body through various pathways and movements and 4), we come to a very important part of the system called Torso Circulation. This particular part of the system can be performed only after steps one through three have been performed successfully. Torso Circulation has several names -- The Micro Cosmic Orbit, The 10 Step Cycle™, The Lesser Circulation and a few others.

The names are not important. What is important however, is the part of our practice where the energy we have already accumulated and identified is circulated throughout our central nervous system. As you probably have noticed from reading so far, is we have mentioned The 4 Basic Principles which are 1) Condensing, 2) Torso Circulation, 3) The Macro Cosmic Circulation and 4) Projecting.

We have dealt so far with our own individual energy, exclusively. We will now expand our practice to include energy outside and beyond our own.

SITTING FORMS WITH THE MIND TRAINING

This section of your practice has been neglected by everybody I have ever seen writing or lecturing. Most other teachers emphasize the physical movements. My contention is, the physical movements are secondary and not important. Yes, we do exist in our physical bodies; that is not being disputed here; however, when practicing "Sitting Forms with the Mind Training," the primary concentration and importance should be on the "Chi Circulations." In my system, this is a piece known as "6 Forms and 7 Circulations." This name is not to be construed to have some mystical or esoteric meaning. "6 Forms and 7 Circulations" is a primary part of the Chi Kung practice and the effects from this will help you to embody and link your internal energy to your physical body. Prior to this, there has probably been no true relationship between the two.

The other segments of your practice have different functions. Those will be dealt with later, individually. "The Sitting Forms with The Mind Training" are done in the sitting position with the body repeating simple movements and the emphasis is on "drawing energy in through the open doors and expelling energy out through other open doors." These openings will be explained in the technical chapter in more detail with each movement.

There is no time frame for performing this section of your practice. They can be done for 10 seconds each or 30 minutes each. When practicing "Sitting Forms with the Mind Training," you can use the image of gathering on the inhale and expelling on the exhale like a volcano. On the inhale the movement expands, the energy contracts and is sucked into your body, while on the exhale, the movement contracts and the energy expands and is projected out.

This part of the training appears to be quite complicated to the novice but it is not. The details are visible and physical. New students should not assume the attitude that they are doing them wrong. Don't forget **the movements don't matter--The Mind Training is more important.**

THE NATURE OF THE MOVES

The end of one move is the beginning of the next. There should be no visible gaps or "jerky" changes. The movements should flow in and out of each other. Don't forget, in every technique you practice, your mind should remain in Tan Tien unless you are told otherwise.

YOUR ENERGY IS DIRECTED BY YOUR INTENTION (WILL)

It is important to remember your energy automatically follows the position that your body takes. That's why you have your toes turned in at all times, because that draws your energy in, towards the center of your body.

THE DAILY PRACTICE ROUTINE

I have designed "The Daily Practice Routine" to fulfill certain requirements to all students and practitioners. "The Daily Practice Routine" contains Condensing Breathing, Tai Chi Connective Meditations, The Macro Cosmic Circulations, Inside Air (prenatal breathing), and The Micro Cosmic Orbit. All of these should be important technical concepts in any real, traditional Chi Kung system.

DEFINING THE ISSUES: FOCUS AND APPLICATIONS

This section is called "Drawing the Line" or on which side of the line are we working?

This question comes up in my initial interviews and consultations with many of my perspective clients. When they first come in the door, and they sit down and start talking, and I ask them what do they want, they don't exactly know what to say or how to respond to this question. Their answer reflects their level of self-deservingness, self-esteem, and confidence.

What happens is, I'll ask the question, What do you want to get from working with me?

BEYOND SELF-HELP: MASTERING PERSONAL POWER™ by Gary J. Clyman

Many people, not most, are totally confused in knowing how to respond because of the undeserving issue that they have, they don't know that they can have things and personal improvements. A lot of my prospective clients respond by saying they want to end world hunger, they want to get rid of the threat of nuclear destruction, they want to eliminate poverty, and many other global problems.

As far as I'm concerned, my work does not deal with any of these issues. For explanation purposes, we will categorize these previously mentioned issues "the left side of the line." So if world issues are labeled "the left side" than I do all my work on "the right side."

Some of "the right side issues" are developing self-confidence in the individual person, self-discipline, and self-esteem. If you have these specific problems or if your levels of these important aspects are low, you can't help anybody anyway, including yourself. So to try and talk in global issues or in response to problems on a large scale in reaction to the question "what do you want?," makes no sense whatsoever. The feeling is of pure impotence. So what we do in the initial consultation is we outline, it shows up that most people feel that they really don't deserve anything. So when I ask them "what do you want?," they don't have anything to say. This is more common than you might think.

I have to go through a "mind shift" with my prospective clients before we can even have this conversation to start with.

Remember, your levels of self-deservingness and self-esteem will reflect your comfort in asking for what you might truly deserve. It is not uncommon to be extremely uncomfortable when confronted with this question. The amount of your discomfort is reflective and indicative of your self-esteem deficiency levels. Right now, ask yourself the question and make a list, "what do I want to get from reading this book?" Don't forget to gauge your discomfort levels.

ABOUT THE FORMAT

In 1983 I decided there had to be a more efficient way of teaching Chi Kung because only the most determined of my Tai Chi students ever got to even hear about it. The success rate of ratio of my Tai Chi students that made it to Chi Kung was near to 1%.

The major hurdle was making it through "the system" before you could even qualify to learn Chi Kung. That is exactly how I learned Chi Kung, by completing the system of Tai Chi Temple Style. This, needless to say, is not a very efficient way to teach the masses. "The Mother System" was set up to not teach the masses, but rather to produce a few extremely proficient Tai Chi career professionals.

In order to help more people and not make the requirements for acceptance so tremendous, I had to create my own way of teaching what I had considered "the most important material in the system." I decided it was more practical to teach these important techniques in the beginning, and not at the end, as an afterthought.

By learning Chi Kung the way I teach it in PERSONAL POWER TRAINING™, you can learn to utilize these valuable techniques and apply them to your daily life.

I decided to reformat what I was taught in 1983, and create a new system that would be the way I would have wanted to retrain myself, if I had had the opportunity. I had spent so much time practicing, that when I finally decided to restructure the system and create my new way of teaching, I did it right the first time. I have not changed my original system or method of teaching Chi Kung since 1983.

What I teach is technically what I was taught, but the way I teach it and the applications are totally different. The applications are much larger in relationship to living. That's where the name of the book comes from, **BEYOND SELF-HELP: MASTERING PERSONAL POWER™**.

Remember, I was taught Chi Kung almost as a second thought and an extension of my Tai Chi practice. My Tai Chi teacher tried to "get rid of me" numerous times to avoid teaching Chi Kung to me. I was persistent. I didn't even know Chi Kung existed but knew I wasn't "finished" with him.

The way I teach Chi Kung, I haven't watered it down. In fact, I actually have refined it. If you are going to spend a few months learning Chi Kung from me, you are going to learn much more in a shorter time then I learned. This is the most "streamlined" version of Chi Kung I know about.

The most important feature here is I have formatted this material, so you, my students or readers, can actually learn it, absorb it, and apply it to your lives, easily.

Chi Kung the way I teach it in PERSONAL POWER TRAINING™ is actually much larger than the actual technique I was taught. This material has saved my life and I am sure that many thousands of people will help save themselves through this practice also.

Repetition is a very important part of learning. So taking that fact into consideration, I have repeated my self frequently in explaining some of the more important things and details relating to Chi Kung.

THE WHOLE IS EQUAL TO MORE THAN THE SUM OF ITS PARTS

It only takes 3 or 4 sessions of working with me before you can actually begin seeing this practice as a system or a "interrelated web," where each technique is related to the total system. Don't forget the way to learn the system is to go through lessons 1-4 and then learn "The Daily Practice Routine" which has a self-correcting function for reviewing and reformatting everything you have learned up to that point.

Learning the system can be compared to learning about a car. You have tires, a steering wheel, and an exhaust system. When most people teach Chi Kung they teach it fragmented with no continuity.

What I do that no other Chi Kung teachers do is, I give you a whole car. First I give you all the parts, then I put the parts together for you in what's called "The Daily Practice Routine." All you do is drive the car. You don't have to be a mechanic, I'm the mechanic. You don't have to be a designer, I'm the designer. You don't have to be the maintenance man, I'm even the maintenance man. I put the whole thing together so the end result of learning my system, is you just drive the car. In 1983 I decided I really wanted to teach people a way of improving their lives without requiring them to first complete the Tai Chi system. Since 1983 I have not deviated from my original outline. I got it "right" the first time. And a practical common sense rule is "If it's not broke, don't fix it."

BEYOND SELF-HELP: MASTERING PERSONAL POWER™ by Gary J. Clyman

THE 4 BASIC PRINCIPLES

Many of the details you learn in the beginning of PERSONAL POWER TRAINING™, you will later be advised to discontinue and discard. Remember, the way I teach Chi Kung utilizes a principle called "stacking details." While learning this system, you will learn 30 or 40 different tools and techniques. You will end up grouping all these diverse techniques into 4 basic categories.

These are the 4 basic categories:

1. The Condensing principle
2. The Micro Cosmic Circulation
3. The Macro Cosmic Circulation
4. Projecting

Everything I teach in the system boils down into 4 basic principles. You can't learn "The 4 Basic Principles" first. You must learn the 30 or 40 individual techniques so you can have a prospective for seeing the interrelationships among these various techniques. I have revolutionized Chi Kung because of this presentation.

All the techniques fall into one primary category. It might be a member of secondary categories. But primarily one. This basic principle sheet will categorize most of the techniques.

WARNING: Do not try to make sense out of this until you have a greater overview of the system.

PERSONALIZATION IS THE KEY

Practicing Chi Kung is in and of itself a system separate from the benefits that come from doing it. For instance, each person's list is important usually to that person only and is not important to anyone else. The technical system I teach in PERSONAL POWER TRAINING™ is exactly the same for everyone I teach it to. I never alter it. I got it right the first time when I organized it and I just keep teaching the same way.

By learning the system this way, you get to apply each part of the technique to yourself in your own unique way. It's a very personalized system.

You must distinguish where your physical body is in relationship to your external environment. That's why many people invade another person's "personal space" without recognizing the other person's boundaries. Many people have trouble setting limits for themselves and respecting others. I call this invasion by another person. The antidote for this problem is what I call "Developing Personal Space."

BEYOND SELF-HELP: MASTERING PERSONAL POWER™ by Gary J. Clyman

"MEDITATION" IS NOT WHAT YOU THINK

I have stated this previously, when I explain Chi Kung, I don't like using the word "meditation" because many people have preconceived ideas about what "meditation" is. What you, the reader, and I think of "meditation" are probably not the same. Most people think of "meditation" as some sort of scattering, dispersing, or perhaps even leaving your body, practice. That is not what Chi Kung Meditation is about at all.

YOU ARE THE CENTER OF YOUR UNIVERSE

Chi Kung helps you become present in your body by raising your level of physical presence and awareness to the point that you're not concerned about when you're going to meditate. Because you have a heightened awareness and physical presence, it's as if you are meditating 24 hours a day. This practice is not "scattering" whatsoever. Just look at my logo. All the arrows are pointing and focusing inward, toward the center and the center is YOU.

A common complaint that I hear from other people that have read other Chi Kung books already on the market, is that they don't know what to do with the material. My book will instruct you in what and how to practice exactly. I always tell my clients that no experience is better than bad experience.

If you only have 15 minutes to practice and you want to use your time most efficiently, this is what you should do. Understand that you are going to have to steal some time during your day, 5 minutes here, 5 minutes there, that's fine, it all adds up and that's what everybody else does. Start with Condensing Breathing (the Stickman), Upward & Downward Meditation, Inward & Outward Meditation, and Tai Chi Stance Meditation, then you go to work and start with Inside Air, The Micro Cosmic Orbit, you can save The Sitting Forms with The Mind Training for when you get home. Do another 10 minutes of these. You can break it up. That's why I tell people "you can practice my system all day long." It's especially easy to do this if you can close your office door and create some personal privacy.

CHANGING YOUR WORLD

When you practice Chi Kung, it takes you from being "ordinary" to becoming "other than ordinary." You just won't be the same. "Won't be the same" could show up in almost any combination... being more motivated, more solid, etc. Whatever and however you decide you want to be.

Most people don't make decisions concerning what they want, so what do they get? Whatever falls in their path. This is not the most predictable way to live your life. This is equivalent to eating out of garbage cans, or having the waitress in the restaurant bring you what she decided to bring you. You wouldn't let the waitress make your decisions for what to eat, then why let fate make even more important decisions for you.

Sorry Charlie. When you start to practice Chi Kung, you begin to make decisions. That's why relationships and marriages change. That's why many of my clients change their professions. That's why if you decide you want to move to a different city, you just make the decision and do it.

These kinds of changes are what practicing Chi Kung with me is all about.

MISERY AND TROUBLE: A WAY OF LIFE

As I have said before, many people come to me who look like their lives are working, but they know deep down inside that they are miserable and in trouble. The level of misery and trouble they exist in depends on how carelessly they have structured their lives. Many successful people appear to have it together when in reality, they've just been "lucky" or they really have no reason how they got to where they are. When these successful people come to work with me, they can understand the "true nature of success" and can literally multiply their successes, not effortlessly, but much easier than without my help.

RESTRUCTURING AND REBUILDING

A process I call "Restructuring and Rebuilding" is when I work with clients to help them figure out what they're supposed to do with their lives, whether it's "the right thing" or whether it's just something. Whether it's "big perfect," whether it's "little perfect." What they're supposed to do in their marriage, their business, how they're supposed to treat themselves, or how the different levels of self-esteem, self-confidence and self-discipline fit into the pattern that they've been living and how they want to change it. This is called "Restructuring and Rebuilding."

REORGANIZING YOUR LIFE

You start by making lists of various things. The first list should be things that you "do not want to do." Now, "do not want to do" can be applied to relationship, profession, or any other aspect of your daily life. After you've created the lists and decided "what you don't want to do," "things you do want to do" will be more in the light. You will have many ideas. By the time you finish "your disqualification list," you will have some ideas of what you do want. I also suggest that you make a list of aspects that you want if you're concerned about having "the right relationship."

Outline exactly the traits that you want in your mate, spouse, boy friend, girl friend, and as a couple, etc. When this is being done, an important part to understand is that you probably won't get everything on your list, but if you get 70% you'll be happily satisfied. Many people think, they in fact will get "the perfect mate." I disagree with this. The reason I disagree with this is, if you are not the best you can be, how can you expect to get anything better than yourself? The limitations that you'll get in your partner can be based in your own personal limitations.

CHOOSING YOUR NEW TRAITS CAREFULLY

I discovered in myself and while working with my clients, that most people never made any decisions about who and how they wanted to be. I call this "who do you want to be when you grow up?" I think it takes place around 18-21 years of age. But I find a lot of people that skipped this step in their maturation cycle. They never did this. This is referring back to what my athlete friend told me. The true questions are, "what traits do you want to represent you, what's important to you, or pick 3 things that are important to you." Most people never have. Many people have an idea of how to act, but rarely does anybody follow through on those ideas. Using Chi Kung helps you "follow through" with what you know you're supposed to do.

LIFE AS AN EXPERIMENT

What happens when people learn this system is that they use their current environment as an experiment so that when they go to a new environment, they already carry their new traits with them, as opposed to trying to work them out everywhere they go, all the time. Now, you work them out now, and they're yours next time around.

YOUR SOUL AND YOU

There are certain phases that the soul goes through. This is contrary to what some organized religions teach and might be similar to some non-traditional ones. I am not concerned with finding agreement. I feel that if you have "strong WILL," you can control your own fate and destiny. Most people can't control their own minds, let alone their own fate and destiny.

I made a decision many years ago that I was going to do so much in this life time, that I would not have to come back again. So can you. If I can help 1,000 people in "a big way," then those people will effect possibly 10,000 other people that I will probably never get a chance to meet.

WE ARE LIKE TUNING FORKS

When you are learning from me, whether privately or in a group, my vibration is what changes you, not Chi Kung, not your personal practice, because some of my clients don't practice faithfully. If I vibrate at 1,000 per second and you vibrate at 200 vibrations per second, my velocity increases yours automatically. So if you just sit in the presence of this vibration and argue with me for an hour a week, that's what helps to create your desired changes. It is my spirit helping your spirit. It's like a spiritual transfusion.

The way I work with people is by causing them irritation on purpose and out of that irritation comes a reaction and a response mechanism that actually gives you the ability to respond in a live situation. Responding in your sessions with me is not really a live situation, because if I want you to be quiet, I'll tell you to be quiet and you'll be quiet. But if you're responding out in the world, at work, in a relationship, or anywhere else, they're not going to say "be quiet" and you'll do it. So, in working with me, you get to exercise and learn to use the tools that are necessary to "create your world the way you want it."

I have met a few people in the last 20 years that have experienced things like this and they had been thought to be crazy, to be out of control, to be having psychic experiences. However, because of my constitution derived and developed from my Tai Chi and Chi Kung practice, when these experiences happen to and around me, I understand them and I can assimilate these experiences and put them to work, using them for the betterment of humanity. When I say "humanity," I mean my clients, one person at a time. That is another reason why I can help people in such a short period of time. So, where do I go from here with this? Well that's pretty much up to you, not up to me.

Many people that read this and understand what I'm talking about will see the importance and how they can use these abilities in their own lives, to help them be healthy, happy, prosperous and make a difference in their lives. In the old days (pre-1985), when this healing ability that came through me, I was using it to help people with very serious, I won't say diseases, but we'll say health problems, or conditions. I was able to help people walk that hadn't been able to walk for many years. I was able to help joints work that have been turned off through stroke or turned off through "willed disabilities." This relates to the old Apache medicine man I treated in 1979. I worked with him for 2-1/2 weeks. He had been paralyzed for over a month due to a stroke and in 2-1/2 weeks, I had him walking on his own, using a cane, but free.

The traditional western doctors in Arizona had given up on this man and I was hired over the telephone and I went to "fix him." They hired a Jew doing Chinese medicine on an Apache medicine man, if you can understand the strangeness of this whole situation, and it worked nevertheless. This experience is labeled in the book, "medicine man meets medicine man" and is true. But now in the 1990's, what and how can you benefit from this "intuitive truth" that works through me? Remember, I'm not saying I channel like other people with lesser constitutions, I'm not saying a spirit entered me and talks through me which is so common nowadays. I am saying "the spirit is me," lives in me, works through me, to help people around me that are attracted to this.

Most people don't even know what they're coming to me for in the beginning of our relationship. They just have a feeling and experience a bonding that I can help them. They don't really know how or why. It takes a few weeks of working with me before this intention is discovered and refined. I am here for you, to give you service. That's the important underlying factor.

BEYOND SELF-HELP: MASTERING PERSONAL POWER™ by Gary J. Clyman

REINCARNATION... WHO KNOWS?

There exists in some ancient writings a very strange process. In modern times, in the New Age Movement, a lot of talk about this process has been dramatized. The original dramatization of this principle I saw many years ago in "The Reincarnation of Peter Proud," which seemed to be a movie that a lot of people went to see, just as a movie. However, I have experienced what I call "multiple deaths." I will explain what I mean.

The spirit goes through individual transformations and changes. This is my opinion. It actually happens two different ways. The body dies and the spirit takes on a new body, or what happens more frequently is, the body remains alive and the spirit changes. This has happened to me numerous times in the last 20 years. It has recently happened to me again. That is why some of my work has changed so drastically in such a short period of time. The old spirit that lived in me, Gary Clyman, has reached its expiration date and a new spirit moves in or takes over.

Now a days a lot of people do "channelling" and do some sort of... it's not really esoteric, it's more like New Age... do some New Age "spirit" work, where another spirit "comes in and talks through them." Because of my physical and spiritual constitution, when the channelling takes place inside of me, my body remains the same, my expressions remain the same, my personality remains the same, all because of the stability I've developed over the last 15 years in practicing Tai Chi. A lot of these transformations appear to be dreams. However because of my consciousness, sensitivity, and awareness, I have been able to recognize these changes in a very specific sequence. This is actually one of the reasons that I'm able to help people in such a quick and permanent way.

I understand things about being a human that most people never pay attention to. Some of these basic principles are written in very ancient Taoist texts that aren't even available in English. Much of the advise that I give people does not come from Gary Clyman, does not come from God like many West Coast people would like to believe, but it actually comes from an innate knowledge that I have developed from understanding myself. People from all over the country and soon from all over the world are attracted to this reservoir of spiritual understanding.

Creating change in the world must start with individuals, one at a time. This is an important step in my work. Changing the World begins with changing individuals. Remember a lot of this work has been kept secret inside various groups. I have, through my Tai Chi and Chi Kung practice, tapped into this "secret knowledge" that has never been brought out to mainstream America.

Advice through different mediums is available to people who realize the importance of having the right information and doing "the right thing." The underlying principle here is, I help people do exactly what is right for them, regardless of what the rest of your environment including your parents, your friends, your peers, your spouses, or your children think. You do what's real for you and don't worry about the rest of the people.

It's their responsibility to accommodate it. That's a very self-centered way of being, but this is the only way that you can actually be yourself and make a difference in the world.

THE WORST SIGNS OF LOW SELF-ESTEEM LEVELS

To extend a self-esteem problem in men that produces a man willing to accept being beaten by a women is pathetic. This is also related to the problem with setting personal boundaries. You are willing to let other people invade your personal space and abuse you to an excessive and unreasonable degree. This problem is more common than one might think on the surface. <u>Physical violence should not be accepted under any circumstances from another person</u>, regardless of who they are. This type of "invasion of privacy" is totally out of the question and is very wide spread. Only through an extreme lack of self-respect can this even be allowed to happen.

An example: you are "here" (defined), and everything is around you. A very common problem many people have is that they are "not here" (undefined) and everything is around them. They believe their bodies are equal to everything else in their environment, and no more important. Many people put the same importance on their possessions as they do their own physical bodies, which is totally ridiculous and way off base.

HIDDEN EATING DISORDERS

Bulemia without the symptoms of "The Binge/Purge Mechanism" is more widespread than most people would believe. Many people, due to their own internal discipline or level of control, have Bulemia or a very similar eating disorder, but do not express the obvious external symptoms that are most commonly found with this condition.

I have recently worked with a client who has had an eating disorder his whole life. He would have never recognized and identified himself as a Bulemic.

The origin of this particular eating disorder and psychological profile is that "Bulemics" as a rule choose their eating disorder very carefully as their own self-contained set of control devices. For instance, they are the only people that can have any input. They use their eating disorder as their own prized possession that no other person can influence, effect, or intrude upon.

I will list the Bulemic causes I have noticed:

Being ignored as a child, always wanting attention and never getting it, being told or instructed how to act, appear, and feel, always having your personal space invaded by other people which includes many variations of emotional, physical, and sexual abuses, as a child and as an adult. Also playing the game of life and having the rules changed frequently by an external source.

I do not require my students or clients to practice every day. 4 or 5 times a week is more than enough and if a person is anger-motivated or compulsive, and misses one day of practice, they usually have tendencies to make a string of missed days out of it. It's sort of like an alcoholic on a binge.

DO OTHER KINDS OF EXERCISE GET THESE RESULTS?

A question many people ask me is, "Do other kinds of exercise do what Chi Kung does?" No, they don't. You could be a marathon runner and never ever get any of the benefits of just 2 or 3 weeks of practicing Chi Kung. This has been proven to me many times over. I have actually interviewed some very proficient athletes who have had the same kinds of problems that other people have had. Their athletics put their bodies in shape, but did nothing for their WILL, their souls, or their minds.

You see, strengthening one's soul or one's WILL requires different tools than any other kind of therapeutic work. This is as far as I know, the only way to strengthen one's WILL in a short period of time for long term benefits.

Strengthening one's WILL is tied into the various damages that daily life puts on us.

BEYOND SELF-HELP: MASTERING PERSONAL POWER™ by Gary J. Clyman

THE CHI KUNG TECHNIQUE IN A NUTSHELL

Phase #1 - is distinguishing where your body is in relationship to your environment.

Phase #2 - is determining where the energy is in your body. For instance, inside your extremities and torso.

Phase #3 - is taking the energy that you've already discovered and cultivating it into the core of your extremities and your torso.

Phase #4 - is taking the energy and driving all of it from the extremities into the inside of the torso to the center line, inside the torso.

Phase #5 - is drawing all your the collected energy from all the other areas of the body and storing it in a spot called Tan Tien which is located 3 inches below your navel and 2 inches inside.

Phase #6 - is circulating and moving your essence throughout your body, to be more specific inside the Central Channel of your nervous system (spinal cord). This is a very specific and important part of your Chi Kung practice.

The question often comes up, "how do you circulate your energy inside your spinal cord if you don't have the slightest idea where your body is in relationship to your environment?" You should begin to understand why you have to learn the grosser techniques first, then you will become more refined and specific as you learn more.

Learning this system is like having someone give you the wheel as opposed to re-inventing the wheel every time.

THE CHI KUNG / ACUPUNCTURE RELATIONSHIP

A question that comes up frequently is, "What is the relationship between Chi Kung and acupuncture?" In most books and according to some other teachers, they rely heavily on acupuncture as a way of explaining how the energy flows in the body. In my opinion, using acupuncture as a way to explain Chi Kung has certain problems associated with it. First of all, it implies that in order to practice Chi Kung, a student must have an extensive understanding of acupuncture. This is not true. I am a retired acupuncturist since 1985. I started learning acupuncture in 1975.

Acupuncture was quite difficult to learn in the old days, because of "a shroud of secrecy" that surrounded it. It took my friend and I a long time to locate our acupuncture teacher and convince him we were "safe and serious" enough for him to teach us. Acupuncture is only remotely related to Chi Kung and is not necessary to learn and practice in order to make your Chi Kung more proficient.

The principles of acupuncture may help in describing and explaining how the energy flows in the body, but should be discarded after your Chi Kung practice is under way.

LEARN FROM CHINESE ANATOMICAL CHARTS

The important principles to grasp are: the body should be viewed as in Chinese anatomical charts, with the arms extended over your head, palms facing forward, unlike the western charts. The front side of the body or the yin side, is the softer and lighter surface of the body including the face, chest, abdominals, front of legs, and most importantly the palm sides of the arms and forearms are exposed and focused on. To determine the yang side or the harder side of the body, imagine your body with your arms extended over your head. The yang surfaces are on the back of the head, the back of the neck, the shoulders, back, buttocks, back of thighs and calves. These surfaces are considered tougher or more protected than the front side of the body. Now, in relationship to yin and yang, the inside of the thighs. are considered yin and the outside are considered yang in comparison. This is the only relationship to acupuncture that you really have to understand or recognize. (See Illustration #1)

THE HUMAN BODY
(ILLUSTRATION #1)

When you practice the Chi Kung standing meditation, which I named "Basic Path Training," you are going to be sucking energy in the yin surfaces of the body, on the inhale, which again includes the inside of palms and the forearms, and the inner surface of the thighs. You will be expelling energy out through the finger tips, on the exhale. It is not important at this time that you have a direct or specific path for the energy to flow through.

Remember, you are going to be sucking in through the palms and the forearms and blowing out the fingertips. This is a very common practice in Chi Kung. How the energy gets to the finger tips through other areas in your body is not important, because the energy knows how to get there on its own. The destination of what I call opening and closing the doors, is a very important part of your daily Chi Kung practice.

THE CONCEPTION AND GOVERNING VESSEL INVOLVEMENT

In regards to the Chi Kung relationship with The Conception and Governing Vessels, it is important in my opinion. In describing The Micro Cosmic Orbit, it makes sense to use the concepts of the Conception and Governing vessels. But in my opinion, this is really not important, even in a the most basic beginning stages.

The energy is not really circulated inside the conception and governing vessels. It is much more applicable if understood that the energy is actually circulated inside "the central channel" of the spinal cord, which is in the center of each spinal vertebrae. I **use The Conception and Governing Vessels only for teaching purposes in the beginning.**

At the top of the spinal cord, near the brain stem, the energy then circulates directly up through the top of the skull, and on the exhale, it will then decline, dropping through the back to the spinal cord, down through the spinal cord to the tip of the tail bone (coccyx). It will then pierce the core of the body to the floor of the perineum (point at the base of the torso) and change direction. When circulating your energy in The Micro Cosmic Orbit, it is important not to drop your energy from Tan Tien (3 inches below the navel and 2 inches in) down to your genitals. What you should do is cut a corner from Tan Tien, across by passing your sex organs, to the tip of the tail bone and then rise up on the inhale. **Do not pass through the genitals.** This will cause you trouble and extra work to remedy in advance of developing a minor problem.

THIS BEARS REPEATING...

It seems to me that many other authors combine acupuncture text into their Chi Kung books. In my opinion, a basic understanding of acupuncture is not necessary in order to excel in the practice of Chi Kung. It is easy to write a thicker book if you include a substantial amount of acupuncture theory. In my book, you won't find it. I have had great success teaching people from all walks of life without even the slightest mention of acupuncture. Remember, the reason for writing this book is to bring Chi Kung to the masses. Requiring any understanding of acupuncture, needing a Tai Chi background, reading the Tao Te Ching will begin to limit my readership as well as this books ultimate usefulness. When I accept students for my Tai Chi class, I recommend and require them to take PERSONAL POWER TRAINING™, where I teach Chi Kung, prior to joining my Tai Chi class.

BURNING THROUGH WITH YOUR ENERGY

Many of these pathways have yet to be "burned through" by you directing your energy through various kinds of body tissue. This is an important concept, "burning through." Acupuncture offers us a convenient concept, but to be more exact the "burning through" concept is much more accurate.

The way I was taught Chi Kung early in 1978, was as an extension of my own Tai Chi practice and instruction. My teacher had decided that he had taught Tai Chi long enough and went into the business world. He taught me Chi Kung almost as an afterthought in his living room a year or so after he had closed his Tai Chi school.

When I speak of acupuncture, I do have some experience with it. You see, at around the same time I was learning Chi Kung, I was also learning acupuncture. The concepts are similar but not the same.

When you practice Chi Kung the way I teach it, You need no previous experience what so ever.

I WORKED HARD SO YOU DON'T HAVE TO

After many years of practicing these techniques, I teach the updated version of how I personally practice. I was practicing this way for years before I ever considered teaching anybody else. When you the reader learn Chi Kung from my book, it is very important for not to skip around. I have put the technical part of this book so your only responsibility is to learn these simple techniques in the prescribed order and fashion. I repeat, learn the system in the order presented. Do not skip around.

Each technique the way I teach it, leads to each other techinique. I have had excellent results in teaching this way and Insist this is the best way to learn.

WHAT, WHEN, WHERE & HOW

When practicing Palms On Knees Meditation, you do not have to be concerned with the question, "Where does the air go after it enters through the knees?" Caring any more about this is like trying to guide your breath into your lungs consciously. It is just not necessary and makes no difference. When you pour water on a table top, do you have to know how the water will reach the floor? No, the water knows how to all by itself.

THE BEST TIME TO PRACTICE IS EARLY MORNING

Concerning the time of your daily practice, early morning is best for a few reasons. Before practicing I advise my students to take regular hot or warm showers and finish with 30 seconds to a minute of ice cold water with no hot. This is very good because the ice cold shower has the same effect as practicing Condensing Breathing in that, it makes your energy and your body heat thrust toward the inside of your body, inside the limbs and inside the torso. This is also achieved when practicing Condensing Breathing. Never take a shower immediately after practicing Chi Kung. This will rob your body of valuable body heat, energy, and can create energy imbalances.

The best time to practice Chi Kung is in early morning, after your cold shower and before eating. Before practicing, you might want to drink some hot herbal tea to get your insides warmed up. I even sit and practice Condensing Breathing directly in front of a very hot space heater. I let the heat blow directly on the small of my back. This is used as an aid in "heating up" your body and to help absorb and circulate that external heat into your Micro Cosmic Orbit. You will be surprised at how fast this will improve your winter health, the way you feel, and keep your day better and easier, all day long.

When practicing Chi Kung, you tend to get hot. I do not advise taking your clothes off, but actually remaining hot and trying to absorb the heat into the center of your torso. For health maintenance purposes, you should wear a turtleneck as soon as the temperature drops to around 60 degrees and you might include a very thin cotton or wool sleeveless and collarless sweater vest. This will help you retain your body heat and maintain a warm torso.

Body heat is one of the most important things that we are dealing with here. If you don't conserve and maintain your internal body heat, it becomes very difficult to circulate internal energy. Body heat is very necessary for cultivating and developing your internal energy. As I have explained elsewhere in the book, the first benefit derived from your Chi Kung practice is improving your health.

The best time to practice differs from person to person, depending on your daily schedule. If you practice Chi Kung the way I teach it, you will be able to fit it into your busy schedule. You can do the complete Daily Practice Routine in less than an hour, closer to 40-45 minutes without skimping any of the important parts.

I have students all over the country that practice many different ways. They don't all practice the way I teach. Some students practice for 15 or 20 minutes in the morning and take little breaks of practice, when they can get more in.

I have some students that are Chiropractors. One of them works on his patients all day long, using Chi Kung combined with his Chiropractic technique. His Chiropractic technique is extremely proficient and since he learned Chi Kung from me a few years ago, he is able to work all day on over 100 patients and not become tired by the end of the day. So this doctor is actually practicing Chi Kung all day long.

A LITTLE CHI KUNG IS BETTER THAN NO CHI KUNG

A common question many of my clients ask is, "how do I practice all this when it seems like I have no time to do it?" The answer to this question is elsewhere in my book and bears repeating. Answer: Try to get in one substantial practice in the beginning of your day. "Substantial" means approximately 15-20 minutes. After this first practice is out of the way, this frees you up to practice in small increments throughout the rest of your day.

TOO BUSY TO SAVE TIME?

Many people ask me since they have no time to do the whole Daily Practice Routine because they're busy, "how does one break up the Daily Practice Routine so it's workable on a daily basis?" Busy people can't be spending a lot of time practicing."

O.K., this is the "busy person's" Chi Kung practice. Start with condensing breathing - The Stickman, then do your Upward and Downward Meditation, Inward and Outward Meditation, Tai Chi Stance Meditation, then sit down. This takes 15 minutes or so. Everybody has 15 minutes, I don't care how busy they are.

MEF: After Tai Chi stance, what did you say?

GJC: Tai Chi stance, I didn't say anything after Tai Chi Stance. Then, whether you're in your car or on the train, you can practice Inside Air. You can do it on the train because you're really not supposed to be making any noise anyway after you learn it Inside Air. Then you can do The Micro Cosmic Orbit. I don't advise doing that while you're driving, but if you're on the train or someone else is driving, it'll be fine. No problem. Then you can do The Heaven and Earth Meditation any time, any place, anywhere, even in business meetings, and that's where you're throwing in your Affirmations, your Visualizations, and your Impregnating.

But you really do want to have control of your environment when you're doing the Impregnating practice. You don't want to have to have to answer the phone or to be interrupted. You want to finish that and then you want to finish your Layered Condensing. Then you're done. You also want to take your cold shower in the morning, <u>before</u> you practice.

MEF: Even if you don't do Preparation?

GJC: Sure. Now most people say then, they need a second shower after they practice. I say you really don't because if you do the first shower, you're not going to smell that much unless you're extremely "toxic." You're not going to stink like a pig after a 20 minute practice. I mean, you'll be sweaty sure, so you wash you face and you're done. It's not like you're going to the gym for 3 hours, or you're in my Tai Chi class.

SPREAD OUT YOUR CONDENSING

"Condensing Breathing" can be practiced all day long, in your car, at work, when talking to other people, at meetings, or anywhere else that you can fit it in. After just a short amount of time of condensing breathing you will begin to notice that you will begin to experience higher energy levels on a frequent basis, almost immediately. When I say "higher energy levels," I don't mean that you'll run farther, play sports with more endurance, which you will, but these external benefits are side effects of these higher energy levels.

SUCK EVERYWHERE BUT WHEN YOU'RE DRIVING

"Condensing Breathing" as I have said previously, can be practiced anywhere but should not be practiced while driving your car because as it raises your physical presence and awareness and it could distract you from your driving responsibilities.

I have seen myself many years ago, actually having concentration problems while driving because I was meditating everywhere I went. I didn't have any accidents, luckily, but I found myself "spacing out," which is not the best defensive way to drive.

DRINKING COLD LIQUIDS HARMS YOUR INTERNAL ENERGY

I do not suggest drinking cold fluids in the morning because your body's energies are not flowing strongly and are organized yet.

I SUGGEST SKIPPING BREAKFAST

I personally have skipped breakfast for many years. I advise this because it is easier to practice without having any food in your system. When I used to practice 6-10 hours a day, eating breakfast interrupted and conflicted with my training schedule.

Skipping breakfast also gives you a chance to burn off food from the day before. Most people eat on schedule, regardless of whether they are actually hungry or not. This makes no sense and is probably a carry over from childhood when we had no control over our "feeding schedule" just like animals in the zoo.

DRINK MY TEA IN THE MORNING

With all the "coffee substitutes" on the market these days, why would anybody want to drink coffee. I have been told that these "substitutes" are no substitute to coffee. I personally don't and never have liked coffee, but I have been drinking the same tea mixture for nearly 15 years now. I will give you the recipe my favorite tea mixture.

1 teaspoon of 1 tea bag of Kuki Cha Tea (Japanese Twig tea)
1 teaspoon of 1 tea bag chamomile flower tea

1 tea bag of Red Zinger (Celestial Seasonings Brand)
1/2 teaspoon of Chinese Gun Powder (Green)*

Chinese Gun Powder Tea is a green tea in which the leaves that are rolled into very hard little balls that look like they blow up when you put them in boiling water. Never boil the water with the tea already in it. Boil the water first, then add the tea. Add this tea mixture to a full pot of tea. This will be enough for many large cups. Try it, you'll like. If desired, you can add 1/2 a tea spoon of buckwheat honey in a large cup of tea.

AVOID EXCESSIVELY SWEET FOODS FIRST THING IN THE MORNING

You should eat only when you are hungry unless you have the symptoms of hypoglycemia (low blood sugar). Do not start your day off with sweets, you will have nowhere to go from there. This will lead to "The Roller Coaster Effect" that will feel like hell.

YOU SHOULD NOT PRACTICE CHI KUNG AFTER EATING

If you practice immediately after eating, most of your energy is going to digesting your food. This means that you are not going to have any energy available to circulate through your body. If you have a 1 hour lunch break, and you don't know whether to eat first or practice first, <u>always practice first</u>. For best results, avoid eating food 20 minutes before and an hour after you practice, if at all possible.

AVOID LATE NIGHT EATING

Avoid eating after 10PM because this leads to many digestive problems and can you fat. Your digestive organs do not get a chance to rest. Late night eating leads to "next day sluggishness."

What you eat the night before effects your next day's energy levels. If you practice Chi Kung, you can still whip your energy levels back to where they should be, but that's a lot of extra work.

YOU ARE <u>NOT</u> YOUR ENVIRONMENT

Understanding this principle is one of the first necessary steps in developing your internal energy.

The purpose for keeping your eyes "half opened and half closed" is, if you close your eyes totally, you will day dream and fall asleep. If you keep your eyes wide open and glaring, you will only be aware of your external environment. You want a good balance between the two, aware of your internal and external environments, that is, your body and your environment at the same time. When some people begin to experience a change in the way they "see," it as if their eyes don't focus as usual. Don't worry, this is a normal phenomona. It will go away soon.

BEYOND SELF-HELP: MASTERING PERSONAL POWER™ by Gary J. Clyman

CHI KUNG & RELIGION

CONCERNING PROSPERITY AND HAPPINESS

People that don't have a lot of money and are operating in "survival" have a certain sense of urgency. Of course, people that have this "lack of" consciousness also believe that their unhappiness will be solved or their happiness is based on the amount of possessions or income they have.

Many of my readers will agree that their happiness appears to be based on their financial security. When practicing Chi Kung, you develop an ability that is very hard to get otherwise. Your happiness becomes less related to your finances and you realize that your happiness is based on doing what's best for you, doing what <u>you</u> want as opposed to what others want.

GOOD URGENCY? RE-CAPTURING THE EYE OF THE TIGER

Because many people have very low levels of self-esteem, practicing Chi Kung will elevate your self-esteem and so, up goes your happiness with it. I have worked with a few clients that are millionaires and they have been no more happy than the average person. As a matter of fact, sometimes because they have so much money, financial abundance and stability, this actually causes them problems. Severe boredom, lack of challenge and lack of urgency. For the extremely well-to-do, this is a serious yet common problem.

In the early stages of millionairship, it appears that some of my clients have had a carry over attitude, and feel that they don't have enough, when in fact they really do. It's as if their wealth has not registered with them yet.

Something that many people don't have is "The Eye Of The Tiger" which is bringing your spirit up to its full potential. What is needed here is what I call "Rules for Living." If you don't have them, you can't expect any more than what you already have. The key to being successful is not what you're going to do, the key to being successful is what you're prepared and committed to do.

To be confident in fighting and self-defense, you don't have to kill somebody, but you have to be prepared to kill somebody. If the decision comes up, you have to know in your heart and soul, that if it's between him and me, it will definitely be him that takes the fall. If you have a bad marriage, you don't have to get divorced, but you have to be prepared to get divorced in order to make your marriage work. Whatever you're prepared to do is the gauge of how much you're going to get back from it.

THE COMFORT OF CONFUSION

"The Comfort of Confusion" relates to people who for one or many reasons chooses unconsciously to act confused because this act prevents them from doing what is best or right for themselves. A poverty attitude can be carried long after you have more than you ever thought you would have. In some cases, sudden prosperity carries with it the fear that someone is going to take it away from you.

This common worry is a carry-over from the old days. I have found this in people who have "sudden success." I help my clients get over this problem almost immediately. This belief also appears as the feeling that life is too good, and something is going to happen that will change all this. These beliefs are related to self-esteem and self-confidence problems. "Do I deserve as much as I have?" is a common question.

HOW WE PUNISH OURSELVES

This Part is concerning self-punishment and how it relates to the practice of Chi Kung. I have found many people, if told to practice every day, will convert missing one day into a week long ordeal. This means they extend their "lack of discipline" into a much longer cycle. With some of my clients, I tell them they don't have to practice. This tends to alleviate the guilt related to not practicing and they then end up actually practicing more. This self-punishment cycle shows up in many people, in many different ways.

In commodity traders, the self-punishment cycle shows up as deliberately making two bad trades in reaction to the first bad trade.

"HANDS ON, TRANSFER OF POWER" AND SELF-PUNISHMENT

Many times, after a person has received "Hands on, Transfer of Power," it eliminates his or her "self-punishment cycle." The reaction after having the "Hands on, Transfer of Power" gives you the ability to recognize your self-punishment from a new perspective, because you are different than you were previously.

UNDERSTANDING INCOME LIMITATIONS

I have discovered that some people have money-making capability problems relating to the amount of money they were told was a sufficient amount when they were young. Realize that in 1968, $10,000 was about an average income and people that were making $30,000 a year were thought of to be "exceptional." If you use that as a basis for comparison, the same $30,000 is $150,000 nowadays.

What you haven't taken into consideration is inflation and how much the dollar really is worth these days and all those other comparisons. So $60,000 is not a lot of money any more in the 80's. In 1968, $60,000 was an enormous amount of money. This problem is directly related to a person's "comfort zone," "Sense of Urgency," "The Protestant Work Ethic" and other "undeserving issues."

Practicing Chi Kung is an excellent way to adjust your "sense of urgency," your perspective on income and what you're worth. This concerns the issue of prosperity and creating urgency related to your income.

There are so many people making more money than they ever thought they were going to make before, but in relationship to how much they are actually capable of making, are barely scratching the surface.

CREATING URGENCY

This is directly related to what I call "Creating Urgency" or "Using Survival Instinct in Non-survival Situations." If people waste 50% of their energy on trying to assimilate and digest the way they're treated by other people, that is 50% of their energy that they are not directing on furthering themselves toward personal or professional goals. What I am saying here is, if you are wasting a lot of energy trying to accommodate for the way you treated, you can't do what you're suppose to do. You are operating with only half your cylinders working.

So to create a "sense of urgency" is a very important part of becoming happy and living a fulfilled life. In order to develop this sense of urgency, a handful of things are important. First of all, you must realize what characteristics are yours personally, and what characteristic are from your background or from the way you were taught. After you have isolated these specific characteristics and traits, you must then make decisions about whether you want to continue to own them or whether you would rather just let them go and replace them with something that does not necessarily have to be its opposite.

This is part of what I do with each of my clients prior to do "Hands on, Transfer of Power."

WORK WITH YOUR LEFT FOOT?

A part of what has to happen to create change is that you get so disgusted with the way things are that you're willing to do anything to prevent remaining the same. "You should be able to work with your left foot." This was told to me by one of my Tai Chi seniors in 1975. This means that Tai Chi people should be able to earn a living with their left foot. This means you can spend 95% of your energy and intention on cultivating yourself and 5% of your energy and intention on making a living.

"LISTENING TO RADIO PROGRAMS CAN BE HARMFUL"

The idea that this is true relates to the Catholic or Protestant Work Ethic, "If you don't work hard, it's not worth it, it's dishonest or you didn't earn it."

When driving my car on Sunday nights, I sometimes hear Christian radio programs. Nothing infuriates me more than hearing the preachers talk about how horrible it is to have wealth. They don't call it prosperity, they call it "wealth" as if it's dirty. When I meet new people, I can see the effect of being raised around these types of guilt-ridden belief systems.

GOD DOES NOT WANT YOU TO BE POOR

It certainly seems that these radio preachers spend more time and energy trying to justify to their listeners why they should live in poverty and be poor, as opposed to stimulating or inspiring them to obtain the most out of life, such as prosperity, happiness, and love.

According to these belief systems, "if you have a lot of money or wealth, you are missing something else," or "you really can't be happy if you're wealthy" or "you're really better off having nothing because then you will be closer to GOD." What kind of garbage is this? These kinds of beliefs have caused enormous amounts of indirect suffering. I can't say "direct" because I hope these preachers don't wish their listeners to feel miserable. They may, I don't know. But, they are trying to get money from their listening audience, so they use guilt.

I don't think they are trying to make their listening audience depressed. As I ride in my car myself, I find myself feeling what they're saying and then the other part of me clicks in and I say "no, don't do that." Many times I feel like writing letters to these preachers, but then I realize it won't help, so I don't bother. If this stuff effects me, I hate to imagine how badly "normal people" might be effected.

PROSPERITY AND SELF-WORTH

I have found in working with people, when asking the question, "How much money are you worth?" or "How much money do you want?" is that people usually say about 2 and a half times what they have had in the past. Example: if a person says they want to make $50,000 a year, they are probably currently making about $20,000, or if they say they want to make a million dollars, they are probably making about $400,000. It is funny but the spoken amount is usually slightly less than half. How much do you want?

GOD WANTS YOU TO BE PROSPEROUS

The concept of prosperity is a new one in this country. There are a few good books on this subject. A few books that I've read, that I advise my clients to read are <u>The Dynamic Laws of Prosperity</u> by Katherine Ponder and <u>How to Have MORE in a Have-Not World</u> by Terri Cole-Whittaker. Katherine Ponder has a handful of other books concerning prosperity. Find them and read them yourself.

CHI KUNG, THE NEW RELIGION?

When I say this is "not religious" I mean this is not giving up to Jesus, GOD, Buddah, or Mohammed, or any other representation. It has nothing to do with that. Chi Kung is not to be used instead of religion. Whatever religion you are, that's up to you. Chi Kung is an application and a self-contained system that does not require you to give up any religious beliefs, rituals, or anything else.

Anybody that thinks that Chi Kung is the new religion is extremely confused. Just like Macrobiotics is not a new religion. Macrobiotics is a way to eat. Now the problem that many people in Macrobiotics have, and I'm not exactly sure of the origin of this particular belief is that they feel that the spirit is in the food. The spirit is not in the food. The nutrients are in the food, but the spirit comes from somewhere else. Just like in Chi Kung, the spirit is not in Chi Kung, the spirit comes from you. It's already there.

Chi Kung gives you the ability to develop and bring out the qualities that you make a conscious decision to bring out. If you practice Chi Kung for 2 years, and you have been giving up regularly, obviously you will be much different. When you first learn this stuff, you will be looking at a lot of things that will come to the surface. You will learn to make very specific decisions about giving things up, one at a time. That's just the way it is. You will get amazing results using this system.

THE THREE TREASURES OR PRECIOUS THINGS: CHI, JING, AND SHEN

Your first goal is to accumulate and cultivate Chi, and convert our Chi to Jing (cultivated sexual energy). If you ejaculate, it is like making a huge cash withdrawal on a very small savings account. What is the sense in that? So first we develop Jing. After you have cultivated Jing, you go through a similar process of converting Jing into Chi. Chi is more of a mental energy, with a much faster vibration. Remember, Jing has a more physical and noticeable vibration because it is vibrating more slowly. That is why it is heavier and more physical. On the other hand, Chi is much faster so the body does not have a chance to respond to its movement by physically vibrating.

What comes next after transforming Jing to Chi, is a very commonly asked question. This question was on my own mind for many years. I never got a satisfactory answer, and I'm sure you haven't either. I will give you my answer. In the Chi Kung article in Inside Kung Fu Magazine 1987, we defined Shen as "Your level of assertiveness in the World." This definition comes about as close as you will probably ever get to making sense of this word. What good does all your energy do you, without a vehicle to utilize it? That's where Shen comes in.

A SECOND EXPLANATION OF CHI, JING, AND SHEN

First is Jing, which is level one, Chi which is level two, and finally Shen which is level three and the highest of the three.

Jing is cultivated sexual energy which is the physical vibration, the way the energy moves inside the body. Chi is more like "the speed of the mind" as opposed to the vibration. Chi moves too fast to create a physical vibration. Shen is your spirit, or your level of assertiveness in the world.

So you cultivate Chi or Jing first depending on how you practice, then you transmute or convert Chi into Jing, and then you transmute your Chi and Jing into Shen, Spirit. Shen is last.

Different kinds of practice develop different aspects of Jing, Chi, and Shen. But Shen is always last. It is the end result of your Jing and Chi cultivation and transmutation.

If people aren't doing what they are supposed to do, they has no Shen. But if people have a picture of how they're supposed to be, what they're suppose to do, what their life's mission is and all that, they are actually performing it or "living it out," then they have a large amount of Shen.

If you want to be the best at what you are, and you're not, what's the point?

CONVERTING CHI TO JING

So when some people say they "feel their Chi" or they "feel their Jing," they don't feel their Chi, they feel their Jing. The word "Chi" has become too generic a term. Too many meanings and associations have been tied to the word "Chi." Even when people feel tingling in their fingers or shaking in their legs, this is not "Jing." I am talking about "Cultivated Sexual Energy," not just some muscular contractions and shaking.

I feel my Chi and Jing, you feel my Jing only. My Jing can be measured by my ability to make you feel it, Chi is my own, you can't feel my Chi at all. Jing can be expressed out of my body, Chi can not.

When Chi is converted to Jing, this is the same as converting your internal energy (Chi) into your internal power (Jing). Internal power can also be thought of as "explosive energy." Your internal energy you feel, your internal power has the quality of being able to be transmitted and expressed outside of your own body. When a Tai Chi Master touches someone and makes them fly into a wall with what looks like "no effort," this is a demonstration of using his JING, or his cultivated sexual energy. _Internal power must be stored in the body and cannot be converted when needed._ It must already be present.

In my own experience, I feel the same all the time, and cannot detect any change in my internal energy or power reserves. This has been this way in me since I can remember having "my energy awakening" in 1977. Since then, I have never been the same as before. This can also happen to you, if you practice the right material, the right way.

Jing is cultivated sexual energy, Chi is the energy of the mind that cannot be felt or expressed to another person, and Shen is spirit, not "spiritual" like some "New Age" people associate with the word "Spirit." Shen is "The Size of Your Balls in The World."

SHRINK BEFORE YOU EXPLODE: AN IMPORTANT SECRET

This is a very important saying: "Your ability to explode is directly related to your ability to contract," or "your ability to project is directly related to your ability to condense." <u>Without practicing "Condensing Breathing," there can be no explosion.</u> Just as in Tai Chi, the form named "rollback" helps you create power in and for all the other forms. All the other moves are expansive in nature, whereas "rollback" is the only form contractive in nature.

THE THREE INGREDIENTS FOR CHANGE

The first is -- The Physical -- JING.
The second is -- The Mind -- CHI.
The third is -- Spiritual -- SHEN.

To create anything, most people attempt the physical aspect first, then the mental. That is the hard way. A more effective and efficient way of going about creating change is to first have "The Spirit." Knowing it will happen and seeing the end result as it has already been accomplished or already exists in the world, even though it hasn't showed up yet is how you get what you want.

You have the ability to have what you want, and knowing that is already half the battle. That's Shen or Spirit. Now how do you get to the end result? That is the million dollar question. It is a lot easier to get to the end result when you have a clear picture of what the end result looks like. If you are vague or have no idea, then you are trying to "bang" your way through it.

So, then the mind comes in. For all practical purposes we will call this aspect of change Chi. With the mind, you structure the steps to achieve the end result, regardless of what it is. Then after you first have "the Spirit" and "the steps to achievement" or the Chi of the mind, then you incorporate the physical aspects to your change.

This is contrary to the way most people work. They just physically do and they're lucky if they ever get what they're looking for or want.

If you set up in advance what you already want, you stand a much better change of getting it. You must know and have faith that the picture you have created is going to happen, otherwise, you are only shooting in the dark. Even if you have no physical evidence to prove you are right, faith in yourself is more than enough to see it through.

If you know where you want to go, you'll probably get there. If you have no idea where you want to go, you will probably never get there, wherever "there" is.

If you don't have vision about what you want, you're not going to have what you want. It's as simple as that. Most people go through their entire lives physically trying to create changes, which is the stupid way of doing things. Some think that they're going to be a little smarter and they're going to know the steps before they move. That's how most people do it who are smart. But what I'm talking about is seeing the end result in advance and then figuring out how to get there. What we're talking about here is "Visualization of the Change."

CREATING RESULTS: IMPREGNATING THE UNIVERSE

If you are having trouble with getting a result, you must realize there are 3 steps in getting something to happen. I have explained this in another section of my book under "The 3 Ingredients of Change." This is an important principle so I will repeat it again. The first level is physical, the second is the mind, and the third is spiritual. Impregnating the Universe uses what I call "Shen" or spiritual change. That means you already know what the end result is going to be. Then when you use the mind, you're going through the steps that create the change, the second level. Then when the change is finally completed.

The 3 levels are: the physical, the mind, and the spirit. These are the 3 things that go into creating any change. You begin with spirit and it becomes physical. You go with spirit, then you figure out the steps, which is mind, then you end up with the result which is physical. The problem that most people have is they don't do any preplanning anywhere, in the spirit or mind. They don't even have an idea of what they are trying to do. They are just physical, they just "bang" their way through it, which is stupid. That's how most people live. It's like smashing your head against the wall. Imagine how much easier your life would be if you knew what the end result of your work looked like before you even started.

So the difference and what you learn from me is how to set it up in advance and then get it. This principle is not only true but important in every endeavor whether it be starting a new business, writing a book, starting a relationship or marriage, losing weight, learning something new, or starting a new exercise program.

TAKING THE BULL BY THE HORNS

What is this stuff we call ENERGY FOR LIFE? Nothing more than the ability to take life by the horns and break them off, one or both at a time. To create the reasons why you should do something to be greater than the restrictions and reasons why you should not attempt to have life the way you want it, to live life to the fullest extent and raise and continue to raise your natural abilities to accept more than before.

This material is dedicated to the expansion of your horizons and the stretching of your own personal boundaries and limitations and beating your own personal best.

A common question my client/students ask me is "Do we do all the details on all the techniques?" The answer is NO. The only details that I want you to practice, I will tell you to practice. Because of the different levels of the practice itself, you don't try to pile everything on top of the previous details. Yes, you do use "the stacking method" for collecting and organizing your information, but you don't do everything all at the same time. For instance, you would not do Inside Air while you're doing The Micro Cosmic Orbit, but squeezing the urinary and anal sphincter muscles is a very common detail that is in most of the techniques.

Remember, the method of learning is different than the method of practicing. I repeat, the method of learning is different than the method of practicing.

PRACTICE WITH URGENCY

"Practicing as if your clothes are on fire" in relationship to being deliberate, on the point, and full of aliveness is a concept I use to illustrate how to be alive and raise your level of physical presence and awareness. You can imagine how wide awake you would be if your clothes were burning. This is the attitude you should use when practicing Chi Kung.

I PRACTICED WITH PASSION

I used to practice Tai Chi as if I were running a marathon. In this I mean, I would practice frequently to insure the flame would not go out, usually 6-10 hours per day. This would consist of about 3 practice sessions lasting about 2-3 hours each. This was the only way I could maintain the fire inside me and the pure excitement for learning Tai Chi. "Practicing" is thoroughly performing your material while "running through," is simply going through the motions. Recognize and understand the difference.

THE IMPORTANCE OF TAKING NOTES

I have only one regret from my personal training. I wish I would have taken notes for the purpose of being able to teach Chi Kung and use my own experiences as a student in the training. However, the end result of learning Chi Kung as taught in PERSONAL POWER TRAINING™ is that you don't remember how you used to be before you changed. So I actually represent the end result of this process. My advice to you as a beginner is to take notes but don't dwell on re-reading them. Just take them so that months or years from now, you can use them to help yourself understand from where you came.

TAI CHI VS. CHI KUNG: WHAT'S THE DIFFERENCE?

The practice of Chi Kung is physical in that it involves and takes place in the physical body. It is not a mind thought or a thought process, but neither is Chi Kung physical like Tai Chi. Tai Chi concentrates primarily on changing your physical structure, improving your posture, taking off your weight, strengthening your lower body, improving your breathing and many other physical benefits. Chi Kung focuses more on what the mind is doing and not so much on "physical details," at least in my system.

Chi Kung concentrates more on cultivating your WILL. These two arts are clearly different. Chi Kung is not physical in nature but it's not mental either. Training your mind is quite different than "being mental" or learning new ways to think. It is not learning new belief systems, it is breaking old belief systems and becoming free, that's more important.

If practicing Chi Kung can help you realize and break you personal limits, so that your limits have less control over you, that's more important than giving you some new way of thinking. Keeping the old limits and using a new way of thinking means you're still stuck.

Learning and practicing Chi Kung is totally different than going to "therapy" where the therapist is usually passive and just a professional listener. My Chi Kung approach is very, very aggressive, but not physically aggressive.

CHI KUNG MOVES ENERGY "WITH YOUR MIND"

What is it if it isn't physical and it isn't mental? It is directing energy with your mind. An example is trying to move a golf ball with your mind, under your skin or to use a vacuum cleaner to pick up something that travels through the hose. That is easier to understand. The idea of moving the golf ball under your skin is like a mouse running under your skin, energetically speaking, of course.

At advanced stages, you can feel a person putting his mind at any point in his body by expanding any specific part of their body, at WILL. Some people can feel expanding and contracting with their mind. Many people can develop this ability but this is an impressive yet insignificant show of a mind training application compared to the big one, which is actually developing your WILL.

MORE ABOUT THE TAI CHI / CHI KUNG COMPARISON

A common question that always comes up is "What is the difference between Tai Chi and Chi Kung?" The primary difference is that when practicing and learning Tai Chi you concentrate primarily on developing internal energy in relationship to your physical structure. That is, when you develop your internal power in Tai Chi, you are able to develop what is called "Transfer of Power" (Fah Jing), which allows you to release the energy that is stored in Tan Tien. "Condensing Breathing" is very important in this process.

What you are able to do is vibrate your skeletal system, direct the energy with your mind, and as you do this, you are able to move other people with your vibration. This takes a great deal of time to develop. Remember, Tai Chi concentrates primarily on restructuring the physical body.

Yes, in Tai Chi you will learn different ways of breathing, but they are not as specific as in Chi Kung. Tai Chi breathing techniques are much more general, such as learning how to "abdominal breathe" as opposed to the way most people breathe, with the upper third or half of their lungs.

When you learn Chi Kung, you will learn much more specific breathing techniques that are combined with very specific mind training, whether it's driving energy up through the sky and down through the earth, circulating energy throughout your arms and legs in relationship to your torso, or in The Sitting Forms with The Mind Training, doing a very simple movement repetitiously while the most important part is not the physical movement of the body, but what the mind is doing? It's much more important to direct your energy with your mind while doing The Sitting Forms with The Mind Training than to be concerned primarily with physical details.

IS CHI KUNG A MARTIAL ART?

Tai Chi concentrates primarily on structure and is practiced as a martial art. Chi Kung is not really considered a martial art. Since I've updated my system so that people don't need any previous experience or background, most people that come to me are not even slightly concerned or aware that Chi Kung is related to martial art.

The way Chi Kung is taught in my system is, you learn these mind training exercises which are very specific and in the long run Chi Kung can help your martial art. In the long run you will learn things about yourself through the feedback and the realizations that you'll have while you're practicing Chi Kung. Developing internal energy will have dramatic effects on your current martial art ability.

Generally speaking, Tai Chi is 80% physical and 20% mind training, compared to, Chi Kung being 80% mind training and only 20% physical. When I say mind training, I am not referring to philosophy or any specific way of thinking, I mean directing and moving energy to and from, in and out, and/or through very specific pathways with your mind. When I say "pathways," it is important for you to understand that these pathways are not already in existence, like the acupuncture meridians. You must create and burn through them.

WHAT IS "GOLD BELL TRAINING?"

I teach "Gold Bell Training" or what some people call "Iron Shirt Chi Kung" but I restrict this to the martial art aspect because until my basic system has been practiced and understood, and you have become proficient, for you to learn "Gold Bell Training" makes no sense at all.

Remember, more material is not more important than the quality of what you already know. Quality is more important than quantity. Repetition increases consistency and reduces variations. A thing must be done many times the wrong way before it can be done right.

The traditional and the same reason that I teach "Gold Bell Training" now is to develop the ability to absorb punches from an opponent or a practice partner. <u>This is very important in martial art training.</u> I don't consider this important in daily life unless you are a martial artist. I would like to try out these other teachers' "Iron Shirt" to see if they can actually do what they profess. "Try out" means to exchange punches with them. If your Gold Bell doesn't work, what's the point in talking about it. Mine works and I've demonstrated it thousands of times. "Put up or shut up," is what I always say. The system I teach is real and will stand true to all the tests. Will the others? "Gold Bell Training" will be handled in detail in my Tai Chi book.

"GOLD BELL TRAINING" IN THE MARTIAL ARTS ONLY

To practice what is called "Gold Bell Training" or "Iron Shirt Chi Kung" without having an extensive internal martial art or Tai Chi background and a good Tai Chi ability is pointless. The purpose of using "Gold Bell Training" is to bounce or repulse punches and kicks off the body. To practice "Gold Bell Training" as an addition to Chi Kung is not necessary.

If you have the right basic technique, everything you're doing in your basic practice should be covered anyway. It is if you study Tai Chi with me. If you think you're going to be able to take punches simply because you're practicing Chi Kung and "Gold Bell Training" without an extensive Tai Chi background, you have a terrible surprise to look forward to. You need a physical, structural relationship with your "Gold Bell Training" explosion ability. I repeat, "learning Gold Bell Training without an extensive Tai Chi background is pointless."

"ESOTERIC EXPLANATIONS?" NO WAY!

In regard to the explanation of "The Taoist Sexual Technique" and Chi Kung, I have purposely avoided using any "esoteric explanations." I do not believe that "esoteric explanations" actually help you to understand anything anyway. I believe they are an easy way of not having to explain what is really meant.

HEALTH, HAPPINESS & LONGEVITY

In regard to the benefits of practicing Chi Kung, health, happiness, and longevity are automatic. When I ask people "What do you want from life?," I expect more specific answers than generic health, happiness, and longevity.

Ultimately, the end result of all this work is to have more ENERGY FOR LIFE, be alive, help improve your environment, and care for yourself and the people around you. I am of the strict belief that you can not help anybody until you first help yourself. You have to be stable before you can contribute and help anyone else. Changing the world starts with helping one person at a time. This is a very important part of my approach.

I have a reputation as being very aggressive. That reputation is correct and accurate. When you practice Chi Kung, it's a very masculine art. Women do practice it, but the primary benefits of the practice are developing internal energy, becoming a warrior, and developing your WILL.

Your WILL in my system is what is worked on first. People come to me with all sorts of problems. Don't misunderstand me, their problems are not usually their main concern, but they are to be dealt with. People come to me with weight problems, WILL problems, and spirit problems. I recently interviewed a man that had had a health problem with one of his sons a few years ago. Within the first 10 minutes of meeting this man, I guessed he had a wounded spirit related to his son's illness from a few years ago. What I said to him was exactly right. He never did work with me because he had given in to his problem. He had lost his inspiration to be happy again and live life to it's fullest. I feel sorry for people that don't give life their best shot, but it's <u>their</u> choice, not mine.

By practicing Chi Kung in the method I teach, many people are actually able to recuperate and rejuvenate their wounded souls and wounded spirits. It is important to understand that this is not just a technique that applies to cultivating your sexual energy. The extension of this technique, or the extension of the application of Chi Kung actually leads to improving your life in all aspects. This system can not only save your live, but give it meaning.

CHIROPRACTIC: NORMALIZING FAULTY BODY MECHANICS

Why does Chiropractic benefit most people? That is because we do exist in the physical world. We are exposed to many different kinds of stressors on a regular and ongoing basis. We have physical bodies and to help our physical bodies operate more efficiently, we require some "fine tuning" in our physical structure. This is where Chiropractic fits into the picture.

Western medicine has its strengths and weaknesses. For instance, in emergency situations Western medicine is extremely valuable. I would not want to go to an acupuncturist or herbalist immediately following a car accident. Many alternative modes of therapy offer great assistance in restoring your health, but after emergency medicine has been administered and the patient is safe and out of a dangerous situation. But what about all those situations where there are not "life threatening" circumstances. Chronic and acute pain, poor posture, misplaced and disfunctional joints which are not truly malformed, and many other conditions are regularly helped by Chiropractic treatments.

HOW TO SPEED UP THE HEALING PROCESS

Many people are afraid of Chiropractors primarily because of their own lack of knowledge. If you have a pain in your body somewhere, it is quite possible it is a minor problem that can be eleviated quickly by a Chiropractor. Most people, however, reach for a pain killer in response to their discomfort instead of finding out the true cause of their pain. Suppressing a symptom (pain) does nothing but to buy you time so your body can heal itself. Sometimes the drug you take can actually hamper the healing process and does you no real good.

Chiropractic, on the other hand, does not poison your body with chemicals. And if the problem is structural in origin, chances are it can be normalized immediately. Give it a try, you might be surprised at how quickly you feel better. Many of these improvements are permanent.

TO BE OLD AND HEALTHY IS NOT JUST A DREAM

A commonly asked question is, "If I practice Tai Chi/Chi Kung, how will it effect me when I get old?" I have seen only a handful of perfect examples of good health throughout my Tai Chi career. It only makes sense that if you have to get old, you might as well keep your faculties and be as strong as you were when you were 30 or 40, be happy, keep your "marbles" and your vitality. Wearing your body out by 50 years of age and taking 20 or 30 years for it to kill you is not my idea of a good way to go.

Look at most of the senior citizens in this country for example. If you don't take the steps to prevent these conditions, you have nothing else to look forward to when you get old.

Many years ago, I decided I wanted to be that "freaky old man" that still has more vitality than everybody 20, 30, 40 years younger than him.

WHAT IS THE DIFFERENCE BETWEEN LIFE AND DEATH?

What is the difference between LIFE and DEATH? When the energy leaves the body and the body loses the ability to respond to the external world or the outside environment, that is DEATH.

What is the Taoist way of dying? This is a very interesting subject. The ideal way to leave this world is consciously. I mean to make a conscious decision to leave this world and go into the next. Not many people want to admit thinking about this subject, but it is on some peoples minds.

THE NUCLEAR THREAT HAS DAMAGED A FEW GENERATIONS

If you are a product of the 1960's, you were raised with the constant threat of nuclear destruction and The Cuban Missal Crisis. Some people have been effected by this threat more than others. This threat has caused many people to adapt an "I don't care" attitude. This is tragic and very wide spread in our younger generations. I see this in my own generation and even worse in younger people. This fear over our heads has robbed many people of their inspiration to live life to it's fullest, in fact, some people don't even try. Their attitude is that it's all going to be destroyed anyway, so why bother.

I have interviewed many people, and in some interviews, I have traced a procrastination issue back to its origins; that is, when my client first noticed it showing up. Many times in people that were children during the early 60's, those bombing drills while in grade school effected us in ways most people are still not aware of. Look into your own personality for any remnants that you might have.

CONSCIOUS DEATH - THE BEST WAY TO GO

When a Taoist prepares for death, the dying process may take many years.

Resolving with the person who is about to die is one of the most important and valuable steps you can take toward being complete with your loved ones. This resolution can save you much work, emotional stress and trauma in the long run. A tremendous amount of worrying and feeling incomplete appears as a result feeling as if you didn't respond or do the right thing at the right time. This resolution process can waste many years of your life to reach completion. The pain and suffering associated with this situation is a great loss of human energy.

If you know that a friend or relative is dying, and take the extra energy to show the love to have the resolution, prior to his or her death, the death experience can actually be one with more joy in it, rather than suffering and misery, as most people experience.

So with this in mind, understand that the only difference between being alive and being dead is your ability to respond to your environment. Being dead is simply losing the faculty or the tools to communicate with your external environment including your own physical body.

For instance, my own father's death; he died suddenly of a heart attack at the age of 49. I was only 16 years old. He had no previous poor health but all his older brothers had died at 52 or younger. I believe that he had hung around to help take care of me and help me grow up, for probably about 10 years until I finally had the intuition and courage to resolve with him, even though I had a wonderful relationship with him. He had been taken away from me and I was determined to hang on to him.

DEATH CAUSES EMOTIONAL PROBLEMS IN THE LIVING

The way my father was taken away from me had created certain emotional imbalances in myself. The first level of emotional imbalance, at least on the surface, was jealousy. The jealousy had converted from my being very aggressive and jealous in relation to my girl friends and lovers to when in 1982 I finally started doing some work on this problem, the jealousy converted to anger and soon after, the anger converted to a feeling of abandonment. This feeling was directly caused by my father dying and leaving me suddenly, with no advance warning in 1968.

This realization, although it took me many, many years to understand, has actually given me the ability, the intuition and the personality skills to be able to help many people resolve their "death and dying issues" with friends and relatives.

Also, 9 days prior to my father's death, my uncle, his older brother, died of a heart attack also. These 2 deaths directly led to my adoption of a more serious and healthy lifestyle. This has caused me to become a vegetarian, and to lose a lot of weight. I went from 205 pounds to 145 pounds in less than 3 years. My martial art practice also contributed immensely. The life changes all happened at the same time.

When a person dies, we must do our share to let them go. By holding on to them we delay their passing on to the next world. That's not fair and is quite selfish, but most of us don't know we do this.

DEATH ISSUES: AN EMOTIONAL EPIDEMIC

As I do my weekend workshops and deal with the various topics and subjects that come up with people in relationship to their emotional well being, Death Issues related to the people around us are very common problems that have shown up in a very high percentage of my weekend participants. If you have these issues giving you trouble in your life you should contact me after completing reading my book. There is a way out for you. This has even been a major concern in my relationship with my wife. This was her "first level" of material that we resolved.

Our emotional states in this work should be viewed as the layers of an onion, or the many layers of paint on a wall. As we uncover, discover, and resolve each level, we are exposing new issues that can be realized and dealt with. In my experience, the hardest layers seem to be those that surface first. As my students expose and resolve these issues, this leads directly to more happiness and joy in each of their lives. These results speak for themselves.

The rationalization of these Death Issues and their relationship to anger and abandonment is extremely wide spread and you would be surprised to discover that most people have the same kind of problems. Abandonment, anger, jealousy, guilt, rage, fear, bitterness and any combination of these emotions and their derivatives can possibly be the end result of having someone close to you die. The age factor is not as important in these circumstances.

I have worked with a lot of clients who have had their parents die when they were very young, ages 4-6 years old. This has surfaced as a very serious and deep overshadowing problem for most of their lives, until they worked with me.

When I perform the "Hands on, Transfer of Power" many of these issues are resolved forever.

PEELING OFF THE LAYERS OF AN ONION

Human beings are like onions, not that we stink, but we have many emotional crusts and things that exist inside of us, around us, and motivate us.

What I have found in my work with clients is that many people are anger-motivated. The various emotions that people carry are anger, abandonment, guilt, fear, rage, terror, grief, and a few others. While as a person is participating in a "Hands on, Transfer of Power," these specific "emotional onion skins" come up to the surface, are reexperienced, realized and released. Everybody has these. Some people come knowing what their problems are or at least having some notion of what's going on, while others realize these human conditions only after 2 or 3 sessions with me. Realizing the condition or the nature of your being, the ingredients of your personality is the first step in actually giving up these unwanted traits and personality qualities. After these traits have been identified, which happens in a very short time, then it is my job to assist you in making specific decisions concerning retaining these specific traits and personality qualities. This all still takes place within the confines of the application of the "Hands on, Transfer of Power."

It is a natural human tendency to believe or feel that your problems are more serious than other peoples'. This tends to make you, in your own eyes, appear more individual and special. However, the depth of the problems that all people have is basically the same. You are no different than anybody else. The flavor of your "onion skins" is what make you appear to yourself to be quite different. The process of eliminating these unwanted traits, belief systems, and natures is the same process. It is my job to bring these to the surface so you can make "yes" or "no" decisions, then I can remove them. It is that simple.

Please realize that many of these "onion skins" appear to be quite irrational. That always makes them look as if they're more serious, or incurable, than they really are. Everything can be changed if you can make a "yes" or "no" decision concerning it.

DIFFERENT RESPONSES TO "HANDS ON, TRANSFER OF POWER"

While receiving the "Hands on, Transfer of Power" technique, some people respond quite differently than others. Some people have visions of their original incident, some hear voices, some actually yell and scream because they are actually there dealing with the people that they have had incomplete communications with over all these years. This could be related to an ex-wife or husband, abusive parents, or, there has even been cases where women have come up with visions of their fathers raping or molesting them that they have piled way back in their subconscious minds to the point that they can't remember anything about the incident at all.

These images have come up to be crystal clear and even in color sometimes.

MORE EMOTIONAL ONION SKINS

What we're talking about here... it's almost like the level of being (and I'm not saying one is higher than the next or any of that), it's almost like if I do a "Hands on, Transfer of Power" on you once, that's one time. If we're working on different issues, for example, if originally you start out with abandonment and that switches to guilt, anger or GOD knows what else, that's like your second level. Some people I've worked with, they're up to level 4 with me by now. That means they've started out one way and they have changed topics, material, and issues a few times.

HANDS ON, TRANSFER OF POWER™ by Joseph Kalal D.C.

The other day I was telling a friend of mine about Gary's Hands On, Transfer of Power™. As a Chiropractor and acupuncturist, I know that there are acupuncture points associated with these areas. However, what my training doesn't tell me is, when Gary stimulates these points, why are such phenomenal responses illicited? I compare these experiences to being in a sweat lodge, fasting for days, sweating for days, preparing your mind and your body for the vision quest.

After receiving Hands On, Transfer of Power™, I was emptied and was able to fill my body with all the positive things I wanted to. I recommend this to people whose spirit needs a jolt forward. Joseph Kalal D.C.

"HANDS ON, TRANSFER OF POWER" SPECIFIC RESULTS

"HANDS ON" WORKS BEST WHEN YOU PRACTICE

I have tried "Hands on, Transfer of Power" on people that do not practice Chi Kung or have no experience and the results are not as good as on those who do practice. You see, the practice not only keeps your old issues from returning but also helps to nourish "the new you." So the way for the "Hands on, Transfer of Power" to really work best is when the person actually has a relationship with their own energy and energy cultivation system.

When I'm doing the "Hands on, Transfer of Power," my function is like a spiritual surgeon and you get a spiritual transfusion. I go in and remove the obstacle in a very specific way and take it out so you can function more normally. It doesn't sound like acupuncture or some "new age" interpretation of energy flow. That's not what I am talking about here. I am saying I can help you like nobody else can.

THE PROCEDURE: HANDS ON, TRANSFER OF POWER™

When I am performing the "Hands on, Transfer of Power," first I stimulate various areas. I do the same procedure on every person I work with. It's not as if everybody's the same, but when I do the procedure, each person's issues are different.

I start with the "diaphragm palpation" first, while they are breathing deeply, then I start working on the various spots. The is remotely related to "5 Element Acupuncture Theory," but only remotely. I start with the kidneys and fear. I have worked with a few hundred people and I have only had 3-4 people have kidney / fear related issues. These people are very rare, for fear to be their major emotional motivators. Next I do the spot in the center of their chest slightly above the thymus gland near the heart. That area is always related to abandonment and death-related issues. I continue to work these spots and stimulate them the client is actually living the actual original incident. Please note: When I am doing the "Hands on, Transfer of Power," my clients are not "remembering" these incidents, they are actually "living" them.

Next I go to the Liver and Anger area. Many people have this anger / liver involvement; most I would say. When I stimulate the anger area, I drain their destructive liver energy off, then they are not angry any more.

Each individual's relationship with anger and their response mechanism or what I call their "Anger Cycle" is much different. So, for instance, if someone would have been getting angry over something previously, no matter how major or minor, now they get mad for only 2 seconds and then they let it go, and they're not angry any more, instead of walking around being angry for days or weeks over one incident.

The next area to be worked is half way down between the xyphoid process and the navel, about 2-3 inches to the left of the midline. This is where I have located "Bitterness." "Bitterness" is tied in with stomach involvement in 5 Element Theory. In my recent work, I have discovered some people that have reactions at this spot related to being controlled or manipulated by other people, regardless of who does the controlling. That's where "Stubbornness" fits into the picture.

The next area I do is over the ovaries in women and next to the testicles, on the torso not the legs, on men. In this area I have discovered "Guilt." After I stimulate these various areas, I then suck the damaging energy out, while coaching the person I'm working with to "encapsulate it and pass it to me." I then ask the question, "What percentage of it is gone?" When they get close to 100% gone, (and some people can't get it down to 100% gone), I go inside the body with my energy and "comb" for any residual energy remnants related to their issue.

I have the ability to enter other people and keep my energy intact upon my exit and return. I function like a drug-sniffing customs dog, but sniffing for any hidden charges still left behind relating to these specific issues. I act as a human vacuum cleaner to remove what I find left.

FIVE DAYS OF EMPTINESS AFTERWARDS

The next phase is going through five days of emptiness after I perform "Hands on,

Transfer of Power." "Hands on, Transfer of Power" can many times be the most torturous experience of your whole life, not because of the physical pain, but because you are actually re-living the "Original Incident." These "original incidents" can range from being ignored as a child to being raped by family members. Some other examples can be witnessing your little brother getting hit by a car, seeing our father beat your mother, having your spouse or boy friend/girl friend leave you, or anything else, you name it.

DOMINEERING MOTHERS HAVE LEFT THEIR MARKS

Many men are suppressed constantly by their dominant mothers. This is a very common problem that many men are expected to live with. This affects many relationships with their future girl friends. "Hands on, Transfer of Power" changes peoples lives and is always effective. This is the most remarkable thing I have ever done to help people.

IF YOU CAN'T LIVE HERE, WHERE CAN YOU LIVE?

Do remember that any aspect of this PERSONAL POWER TRAINING™ and the principles that are being explained in the book are still basically on a physical plane with a physical relationship, not mental. This is not mental stuff we are talking about.

CIGARETTE SMOKING EQUALS SLOW DEATH

Smoking cigarettes is one of the most self-destructive acts known to man, and you can't complain when the end result of your cigarette smoking is your destruction. Approximately 350,000 people die per year due to cigarette-related illnesses.

X-RAYS TELL NO LIES

As a matter of fact, I quit smoking in 1969 after smoking for 9 years, and in 1987 I went to a Chiropractor for some treatments. We took a full set of X-rays and my bronchial tubes showed up as "black" in the X-ray all these years latter. This "black" represents damage done by smoking cigarettes 20 years ago. Take care of your body, 'cause if you can't live in this body, where can you live?

CHAPTER #2
THE PHYSICAL NATURE

GENERAL PRINCIPLES OF "THE TECHNIQUE"

There are 4 basic categories that each individual Chi Kung technique falls into. Many techniques do indeed fall into multiple categories, but all are clearly members of one primary type. I have included this section so you can understand and get an overview of Chi Kung more fully. It will assist in understanding "The System" the way I teach it.

The following is a list and explanation of the 4 basic categories in my "Chi Kung" system.

#1 THE CONDENSING PRINCIPLE - This is the single most important ingredient and the first principle to understand. Condensing Breathing is the source of all the energy cultivation exercises. Without practicing this, there will be no "alchemical agent" or "essence" to be circulated. Practicing Condensing Breathing is a meditation that will cause consolidation on all levels. This practice can and will aid in the transformation of one's constitutional properties.

#2 TORSO CIRCULATION - The Micro Cosmic Orbit or The 10 Step Cycle™. This principle is used in regard to Chi circulations limited to the torso only.

#3 MACRO COSMIC CIRCULATION - Combining the whole body as a single unit. Each body part is in communication with each other body part. This term is used when relating the extremities and the torso as a single unit with intimate communication.
    A)   Mother Meditation
    B)   The Macro Cosmic Orbit
    C)   The Tai Chi Connective Meditations

#4 PROJECTING - IMPREGNATING THE UNIVERSE - Sending your SPIRIT out, into the world. Practicing the following exercises in the prescribed order will produce profound results, immediately. These practices are distinctly different from other affirmations and visualizations in that they are performed after practicing Condensing Breathing. They are linked to your body and will manifest in a real, physical, and obvious way when applied.
    A)   Affirmations B)   Visualizations
    C)   Projecting into the Universe

BEYOND SELF-HELP: MASTERING PERSONAL POWER™ by Gary J. Clyman

CHI KUNG TECHNICAL OUTLINE WORKSHOP I.

THE BASIC TRAINING MATERIAL

1) PREPARATION FROM TAI CHI INCLUDING DETAILS

2) CONDENSING BREATHING

3) BASIC PATH TRAINING

4) BREATHING TRAINING

   A. OUTSIDE AIR

   B. INSIDE AIR

5) SITTING FORMS WITH THE MIND TRAINING

6) PALMS ON KNEES MEDITATION

7) STILLNESS SITTING WITH CONDENSING BREATHING

8) THE MICRO COSMIC ORBIT / AKA - THE 10 STEP CYCLE™

9) CLOSING THE CIRCUIT

10) HEAVEN AND EARTH MEDITATION

11) CREATING YOUR DAILY AFFIRMATIONS

12) CREATING YOUR VISIONS COMBINED WITH YOUR AFFIRMATIONS

13) PROJECTING YOUR WILL / IMPREGNATING THE UNIVERSE

14) LAYERED CONDENSING

BEYOND SELF-HELP: MASTERING PERSONAL POWER™ by Gary J. Clyman

THE TECHNICAL INGREDIENTS OF CHI KUNG

DEFINITIONS & REASONS WHY

1)   PREPARATION FROM TAI CHI INCLUDING DETAILS
What it is... The warm up exercises from Temple Style Tai Chi.
What it's for... To loosen each joint and body part, individually, prior to practicing Chi Kung.
Long term implications... To consistently help your body relax and release tension as well as gauge your relaxation progress.

2)   CONDENSING BREATHING
What it is... The most important part of Chi Kung. The precursor for all the circulation practices.
What it's for... To compress your being into a more dense space, increasing your intention, WILL, concentration, and vibration capacity and velocity.
Long term implications... Continual increase of your energy levels, awareness, decision making abilities, and general performance.

3)   BASIC PATH TRAINING
What it is... Tai Chi conversion meditations used to orientate your mind in and with your body.
What it's for... To develop basic "Energy Pathway Circulations."
Long term implications... Constant increase of your BODY/MIND relationship and connection.

4)   BREATHING TRAINING

    A.   OUTSIDE AIR
What it is... Basic abdominal breathing found in many other disciplines.
What it's for... Used for comparison purposes only. This never has to be practiced.
Long term implications... Calming effect only.

    B.   INSIDE AIR
What it is... Basic mind training in how to direct your energy circulation in a gross, single direction. Up and down ONLY. This method of breathing is also known as "pre-natal breathing" or "fetal breathing" because it is the same way you were breathing while in your mother's womb.
What it's for... Important preparation for "The Micro Cosmic Orbit." THIS MUST ALWAYS BE PRACTICED PRIOR TO DOING "THE MICRO COSMIC ORBIT."
Long term implications... Puts a snap in many of your circulations. Develops internal coordination and improves your posture when not practicing.

BEYOND SELF-HELP: MASTERING PERSONAL POWER™ by Gary J. Clyman

5) SITTING FORMS WITH THE MIND TRAINING AKA / 6 FORMS AND 7 CIRCULATIONS™

What it is... Movements performed in a sitting position, using the arms in connection with the torso. These are used to create the pathways the energy flows through. Remember, the energy circulations are more important than the actual physical movements. Don't be concerned with the correctness of the movements. Be more concerned with your intention in circulating your energy through these specific pathways. Don't forget any internal details.

What it's for... Connecting the body as a single unit. To create communication with all your cells.

Long term implications... Helps to "bore out" and increase the energy pathways. These circulations are unique to "Chi Kung" and should be practiced for many years.

6) PALMS ON KNEES MEDITATION

What it is... Connecting meditations through your knees and your palms.

What it's for... Connecting your condensing breathing through your arms and legs. This opens your major energy channels.

Long term implications... Helps to create "a vacuum" in your body for storing and attracting more energy.

7) STILLNESS SITTING WITH CONDENSING BREATHING

What it is... Condensing breathing without the effort placed on the physical body. Done in a sitting position, the is also to reduce the harmful effects of gravity.

What it's for... Another version of condensing breathing.

Long term implications... Great for increasing internal sensitivity and rooting for "The Micro Cosmic Orbit" and your affirmations and your visualizations.

8) THE MICRO COSMIC ORBIT / AKA - THE 10 STEP CYCLE™

What it is... Major torso circulation at the heart of "Chi Kung."

What it's for... Increasing vital force and transmuting cultivated sexual energy (Jing) to spiritual energy (Shen). Leads to long term constant accumulation and circulation of cultivated sexual energy. The width and velocity of your pathway will increase with consistent practice.

9) CLOSING THE CIRCUIT

What it is... The final step or conclusion of "The Micro Cosmic Orbit." The downward drop of your energy and return to "Tan Tien" (3 inches below your navel).

What it's for... The return home of your essential energy where it is stored in "Tan Tien."

Long term implications... Absolutely necessary to preserve your Jing.

10) HEAVEN AND EARTH MEDITATION

What it is... Condensing in from the top and in from the bottom. It is also called "Twin Tornadoes Meditation" signifying the purpose.

What it's for... Embodiment. To add an added dimension to your Condensing Breathing.

Long term implications... Adds density to your Condensing Breathing and roots your affirmations and visualizations to your body.

11) CREATING YOUR DAILY AFFIRMATIONS
What it is... An important ingredient in acquiring your dreams. Extracting the exact words, lead to accepting your vision.
What it's for... Clarification of your dreams and visions.
Long term implications... Updating and integrating your dreams into your LIFE.

12) UNITING YOUR VISION WITH YOUR AFFIRMATIONS
What it is... Just what it's name denotes.
What it's for... Actualizing your vision and your affirmations to each other and cultivating your own reality.
Long term implications... Trimming the fat off your picture. Keeping negative influences to a minimum distraction.

13) PROJECTING / IMPREGNATING THE UNIVERSE
What it is... Formatting your own future. Connecting your visualizations, affirmations, and your Condensing Breathing, physically.
What it's for... Implanting or setting up your environment the way you want it. Releasing your dreams into the universe.
Long term implications... Strengthening all your Chi Kung practices. The final connection to your own reality. External actualizations.

14) LAYERED CONDENSING
What it is... Calling you own energy back to you. It is like the opposite of an onion skin. The more you can "fit in," the better and more valuable this technique will prove to be.
What it's for... Regrouping after "Impregnating the Universe."
Long term implications... Your Personal Power can be multiplied by ending your Chi Kung practice with "Layered Condensing."

THIS IS THE END OF THE DAILY PRACTICE ROUTINE

BEYOND SELF-HELP: MASTERING PERSONAL POWER™ by Gary J. Clyman

CHI KUNG DEFINITIONS: BASIC TRAINING
ENERGY CULTIVATION EXERCISES

1) PREPARATION: These are exercises used to help your bodies learn to relax and release tension. These exercises are done in a circular fashion and a specific order. These exercises can be performed at any time and any place, with or without other techniques.

2) CONDENSING BREATHING: This is, in my opinion, the single most important part of Tai Chi, Chi Kung, and other related internal meditation, and energy cultivation exercises. Incorporating "condensing breathing" into your daily practice will increase your energy levels, Chi awareness, personal power intensity, and spiritual stamina.

3) BASIC PATH TRAINING: In order to prepare you for the upcoming training and work, I have incorporated into the training basic Tai Chi forms. These exercises are to help beginners with no previous experience to express themselves and become more present. These exercises have been incorporated to help keep you grounded as well as give you a physical vehicle to build your Chi Kung practice upon.

These exercises are designed to teach each practitioner the location of the basic channels, their doors, which are the specific location in which the Chi enters and leaves the body, and the directions and pathways the energy flows through in the body.

4) BREATHING TRAINING
There are only two basic breathing techniques.

    A. OUTSIDE AIR: This type of breathing has also been referred to as stomach or abdominal breathing. This is very similar to the breathing done in Zen meditation. This will be used for comparison purposes only.

    B. INSIDE AIR: This type of breathing is very special and import-ant. This particular technique has also been referred to as "pre-natal breathing" or "fetal breathing." This is a type of breathing that does not rely upon the lungs and general circulation for air, but refers rather to the breath as used in your mothers womb, before you were born. "Inside air "is an internal system of breathing which should be at the heart of "Chi Kung."

5) SITTING FORMS WITH THE MIND TRAINING / AKA - 6 FORMS AND 7 CIRCULATIONS™: These exercises are what I consider the heart of "CHI KUNG." These are the exercises that make "CHI KUNG" an internal exercise system. It is important to understand that these are not just physical movements, and that there are very specific Chi circulations involved in each exercise.

6) THE MICRO COSMIC ORBIT / AKA - THE 10 STEP CYCLE™: This is the most important part of the "CHI KUNG" system. This is directly related to how you cultivate

and circulate your Chi, and is one of the most sought after techniques, by both meditation and TAI CHI students alike.

7) STILLNESS SITTING WITH CONDENSING (TAOIST MEDITATION): This is a general term used to describe many of "The Chi Circulations" practiced in this Chi Kung system. There are many techniques that can be as specific as possible.

BEYOND SELF-HELP: MASTERING PERSONAL POWER™ by Gary J. Clyman

CHAPTER #3
THE TECHNIQUE

CHI KUNG LESSON SCHEDULE: WORKSHOP I.

HOW TO PRACTICE INSTRUCTIONS: This is basically a 6 Week Training Course. Each individual lesson should be practiced for one week without adding the next lesson. When you do add the next lesson, you should then practice them in their entirety, without deleting any details. All the material will be restructured in Lesson #5 (The Daily Practice Routine).

LESSON #1

1) PREPARATION WITH TAI CHI WITH DETAILS
2) CONDENSING BREATHING
3) BASIC PATH TRAINING
    A. UPWARD AND DOWNWARD MEDITATION
    B. INWARD AND OUTWARD MEDITATION
    C. TAI CHI STANCE MEDITATION

LESSON #2

4) BREATHING TRAINING
    A. OUTSIDE AIR
    B. INSIDE AIR

LESSON #3

5) SITTING FORMS WITH THE MIND TRAINING
   AKA - 6 FORMS AND 7 CIRCULATIONS™
6) PALMS ON KNEES MEDITATION

LESSON #4

7) THE MICRO COSMIC ORBIT / AKA - THE 10 STEP CYCLE™
8) CLOSING THE CIRCUIT

LESSON #5-#6-#7-#8 / CREATING "THE DAILY PRACTICE ROUTINE"

9) HEAVEN AND EARTH MEDITATION
10) CREATING YOUR DAILY AFFIRMATIONS
11) UNITING YOUR VISION WITH YOUR DAILY AFFIRMATIONS
12) PROJECTING YOUR WILL / IMPREGNATING THE UNIVERSE
13) LAYERED CONDENSING / CALLING YOUR ENERGY BACK

BEYOND SELF-HELP: MASTERING PERSONAL POWER™ by Gary J. Clyman

THE CHI KUNG TECHNIQUE

LESSON #1

The purpose of this text is to teach my readers the Chinese internal art of Chi Kung (Energy Work). This text has been written to teach you Chi Kung as taught in Gary J. Clyman's PERSONAL POWER TRAINING™. Your Daily Chi Kung practice can enrich all aspects of your life. Regular practice will lead to regular results. Remember "Masters are made in the beginning, not in the end." This means, if you pay attention to all your details, from the very beginning, you will become GREAT almost automatically. This text may not be duplicated under any conditions and is protected under copyright by the creator of Gary J. Clyman's PERSONAL POWER TRAINING™.

The format of PERSONAL POWER TRAINING™ is structured in a sequence of individual lessons. Each portion of "the technique" is formatted in a priority fashion that makes it necessary to learn each individual part of the technique in the proper order. The first 4 lessons should be learned one at a time.

After completion of the first 4 lessons, all the lessons are then restructured in what is called "The Daily Practice Routine," which is the end result and finished product of learning Chi Kung in PERSONAL POWER TRAINING™.

When learning Chi Kung from this book, the details should be learned and applied as if each detail is an addition to each last detail. This process of piling or layering information is called "stacking details." This form of detail organization will be practiced throughout your entire Chi Kung education.

RULES AND SUGGESTIONS YOU SHOULD REMEMBER, PRIOR TO LEARNING "THE TECHNIQUE"

All breathing is done through the nose regardless of the technique.
As the breathing is performed, <u>INHALE</u> to the right, <u>EXHALE</u> to the left, for purpose of simplicity.
Your mind should remain in "Tan Tien" at all times regardless of what other technique you are practicing.
You should never lock your elbows, except in "Preparation."
Your elbows should always be dropped down, never raised up.
Your spine should always be extended up as if trying to reach for the sky or as if you are pushing a hook up toward the ceiling, but can barely reach.
Your sacrum (base of spine) should always be tucked under your torso, regardless of the posture or technique.
Keep your chin gently tucked with your neck straight.
Don't close your eyes unless specifically instructed, keep them half opened and half closed.
Don't eat before practicing.

BEYOND SELF-HELP: MASTERING PERSONAL POWER™ by Gary J. Clyman

It will be helpful to use a mirror to check your postures regularly.

REPEATED NOTE: When you change from one technique to the next, your changes should be abrupt and clean, not gradual and sloppy. This stands true throughout your entire Chi Kung practice.

WARNING - DO NOT GET BOGGED DOWN IN PHYSICAL DETAILS. The internal details relating to the circulations are much more important. You can do all the physical details wrong and if you are doing the circulations correctly, you will be O.K. "Preparation" is not important compared to everything else in Lesson #1. "Preparation" is important for the purpose of relaxation and to help develop an awareness of the body, and can be discontinued after learning "The Daily Practice Routine."

LESSON #1 - **Preparation from Tai Chi with Details**
(See Illustration #2)

Preparation - The Warm-Up Exercises

Hang by a string from the top of your head. Keep your tongue up, teeth together, lips together, eyes half open, half closed.
Keep your feet 2-1/2 to 3 feet apart with your toes turned in slightly. Gently, let your shoulders drop, relax your chest, and breathe through your nose.
Keep your mind in Tan Tien, which is 3 inches below your naval and 2 inches in.
Let your thumb and first finger touch near the seam of your pants.
Turn the back of your hands forward. Keep your feet flat, your knees pulled apart, and concentrate on Tan Tien. Gaze into infinity. Don't stare or day dream. Try to remain as relaxed as possible.

Keep your tongue up, this will enable you to breathe through your nose more easily.

We will now do each individual part of the body in Preparation.

Turn your neck to the right, 90 degrees to the front as you INHALE
Turn your neck from the right, EXHALE all the way past the center to the left side, 90 degrees from the front.
Every time you move, coordinate your movement with your breath.
Do not close your eyes or tense up your shoulders. Remain as relaxed as possible. Continue to push up as if you are hanging by a string at the top of your head, also keeping your chin gently tucked so it doesn't stick out. Each part of preparation should be done until you feel very comfortable. Stop in the center, facing the front.

Right shoulder
INHALE as you rotate your right shoulder up and toward the back.
EXHALE down making large oval.
Make sure each movement is performed evenly coordinated with the breathing.

Keep your mind on Tan Tien which is 3 inches below your navel and 2 inches inside.
Right shoulder INHALE up, EXHALE down.
Now you are about to change shoulders.
Left shoulder
INHALE as you rotate your left shoulder up and toward the back.
EXHALE down making large oval.
Be sure you are relaxed.
Do not close your eyes.
INHALE
Relax your hands
EXHALE
Keep your spine as straight as you can without becoming rigid.
INHALE Tuck your pelvis under your torso.
EXHALE
INHALE
Each time you inhale you should be moving up.
EXHALE
Each time you exhale you should be sinking down.

You are about to change direction on the **Left Shoulder**
INHALE change direction.
Now, rotate your left shoulder up and toward the back
EXHALE roll your left shoulder down.
INHALE
EXHALE
Don't forget to remain as relaxed as possible.
INHALE
All the movements are circular
EXHALE
Take your time on each movement.
INHALE
EXHALE
We are about to change back to the **right shoulder**.
INHALE bring your **right shoulder** up and toward the back.
EXHALE rotate it down.
INHALE
EXHALE
You want your body to feel very heavy but not tense.
INHALE
The heavier it feels, the more you are using your mind and not just performing a physical movement
EXHALE
INHALE
Remember to stay as relaxed as possible, still keeping your feet flat, still holding your pelvis tucked and under your body.
EXHALE

INHALE
Keep your head erect. Do not look down. Do not close your eyes.
EXHALE
Still hang by the string at the top of your head. We are about to change to **Both Shoulders**.
INHALE
Rotate both shoulders up towards the front
EXHALE
Rotate both shoulders down.
Stay as relaxed as you can.
INHALE up.
Make the your movements circular.
EXHALE down.
INHALE up. At the top you are going to change directions for the last time.
EXHALE down. Now go down toward the back.
INHALE up
EXHALE Do not close your eyes.
INHALE
EXHALE
Stop in the center.

We are going to do **The Waist**.

INHALE as you turn the waist to the right at a 90 degree angle to the front
EXHALE as you turn to the left.
Each movement must be connected with the breath.
INHALE
The amount of time it takes you to breathe should be the amount of time it takes you to do the movement.
EXHALE to the left
INHALE
In Tai Chi, the hips are very, very important. If you have tight hips, your Tai Chi will be very tight so that is why we are doing preparation for each individual part of the body.

The Waste, Hips, Spine, and Neck. Turn as far as you can.

This time on the inhale, INHALE all the way around. Turn as far as you can to your right.
EXHALE all the way around to the opposite side. That includes the neck, all the way, but still stay erect and reach for the sky with the top of your head. Remember to keep your chin dropped.
INHALE Don't lean. Do not close your eyes. Keep your mind in Tan Tien.
EXHALE Keep your feet flat on the floor, relax your arms
INHALE
EXHALE We will now switch to the **Knees Only**
INHALE Push up keeping the feet flat, and your pelvis under, and your knees pulled

apart.
<u>EXHALE</u>
Knees Only
Keep your feet flat on the floor
<u>INHALE</u> Rise slightly.
<u>EXHALE</u> Sink slightly. (Repeat)
<u>INHALE</u>
<u>EXHALE</u>

Stretch Your Forearm Muscles

The last part is **Stretching Your Forearm Muscles**. You may do that on your own. Keep your **Palms Facing Out**. Push against your fingers, with your elbow parallel with the ground.
<u>INHALE</u>
<u>EXHALE</u>

End of Preparation.

Preparation in Review.

Hang by a string from at the top of your head, tongue up, teeth together
lips together, eyes half opened, half closed. Keep your feet 2-1/2 to 3 foot widths apart (slightly less than shoulder width).

Keep your toes turned in slightly and pelvis tucked under. Turn the back of your hands facing forward, gently touching your leg where the seam of your pants is with your thumb and first finger of both hands. Keep your mind on Tan Tien.

BEYOND SELF-HELP: MASTERING PERSONAL POWER™ by Gary J. Clyman

PREPARATION FORM
(ILLUSTRATION #2)

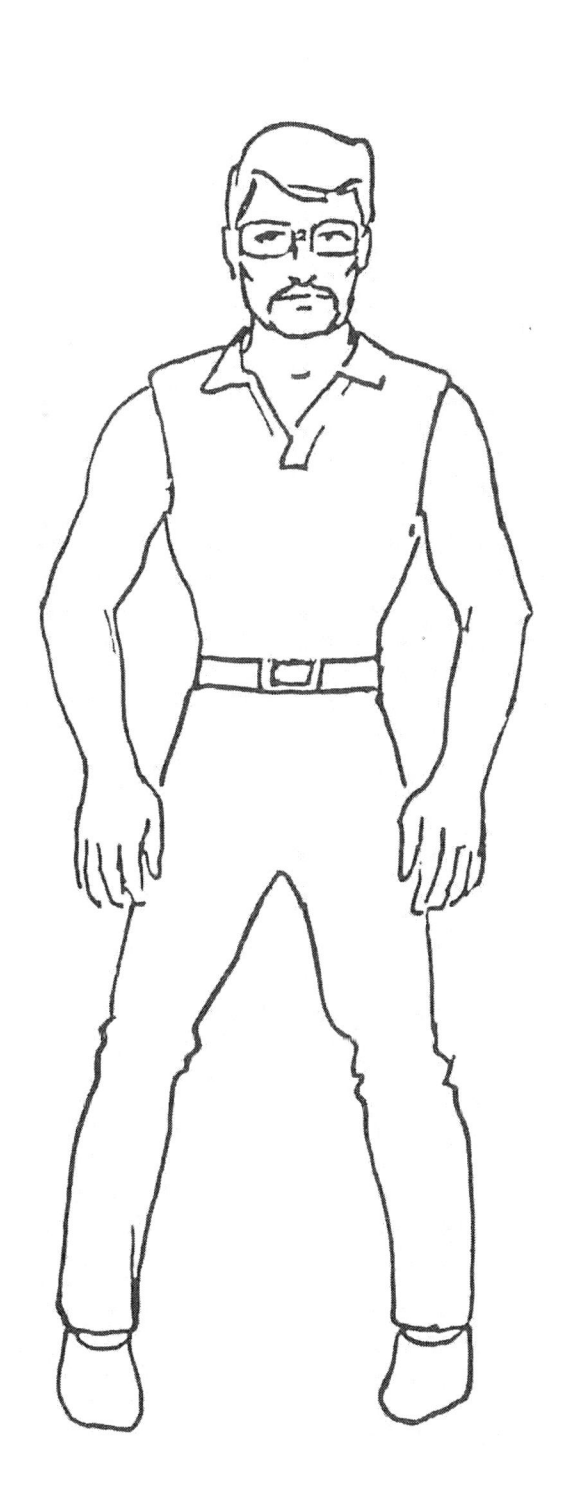

BEYOND SELF-HELP: MASTERING PERSONAL POWER™ by Gary J. Clyman

LESSON #1, TECHNIQUE #1 (See Illustrations #3A & 3B)

We will now learn **CONDENSING BREATHING**.

Condensing Breathing in Tai Chi is the single most important factor. Condensing Breathing squeezes 18 inches of movement into 1 inch of space.

In Chi Kung the way I teach it, **Condensing Breathing** is the beginning, the basis for all the energy cultivation work. When you practice Condensing Breathing, it has effects on all things in your environment.

First of all, it makes you "the most important single factor in your environment." People don't understand that they are more important than everything around them.

Second of all, when you practice **Condensing Breathing**, first you are drawing energy into your body in a gross fashion. After you have been practicing Condensing Breathing for a relatively short time, the technique becomes more and more specific. (See Chi Kung In A Nutshell)

We will now start **Condensing Breathing**. (See Illustration #3A)

Take a posture with your feet about three feet apart, about a shoulder width and a half. This is wider than in the distance used in Preparation. Tuck your pelvis under.
Hold your arms slightly in front of you and totally relaxed.
Gently sink your chest.
Drop your shoulders.
Hold your head erect and keep your tongue up on the roof of your mouth.
Keep your mind at what is called Tan Tien 3" below your naval and 2" inside your body.
Make sure your pelvis stays tucked under and you are relaxed.

Step 1 of **Condensing Breathing** (See Illustrations 3A & 3B)

Hold your arms slightly forward but not tense. We will now start **Condensing Breathing - Perform Each Series At Least 4 Times.**
With your **right hand** on the inhale **touch your left arm.**

INHALE Touch the surface of the skin on your left arm.
EXHALE Take your hand away.
INHALE Touch the surface of the skin on your left arm.
EXHALE Take your hand away, etc.

We are now going to switch sides. On the inhale take your **left hand** and **touch your right arm.**
INHALE Touch the surface of the skin on your right arm.
EXHALE Take your hand away.

INHALE Touch the surface of the skin on your right arm.
EXHALE Take your hand away. Etc.

Always touch very gently

We will now do the legs.

Stop doing the arms.

INHALE Touch both legs at the same time. While keeping your torso erect, bend your knees.
INHALE Touch both your legs at the same time.
EXHALE Take your hands away.
Your pelvis must remain tucked under at all times. Don't tense up.
INHALE Touch both your legs at the same time.
EXHALE Take your hands away.

Stop doing the legs.

We will now **touch the torso.**
INHALE Gently touch the torso with your fingertips.
EXHALE Take your hands away.
INHALE Gently touch the torso with your fingertips.
EXHALE Take your hands away.

Now **add the face and head with the torso.**
INHALE Gently touch the torso, head and face, on the inhale.
EXHALE Take your hands away.
INHALE Gently touch the torso, head and face, on the inhale.
EXHALE Take your hands away. Stop

Step #2 of **Condensing Breathing** (See Illustration #3A)

Do the arms again, except this time, on the INHALE draw into your arms with your mind, in from all 4 directions at the same time.
INHALE Draw in with your mind.
EXHALE Relax
INHALE Draw in with your mind.
EXHALE Relax

BEYOND SELF-HELP: MASTERING PERSONAL POWER™ by Gary J. Clyman

CONDENSING BREATHING
(ILLUSTRATION #3A)

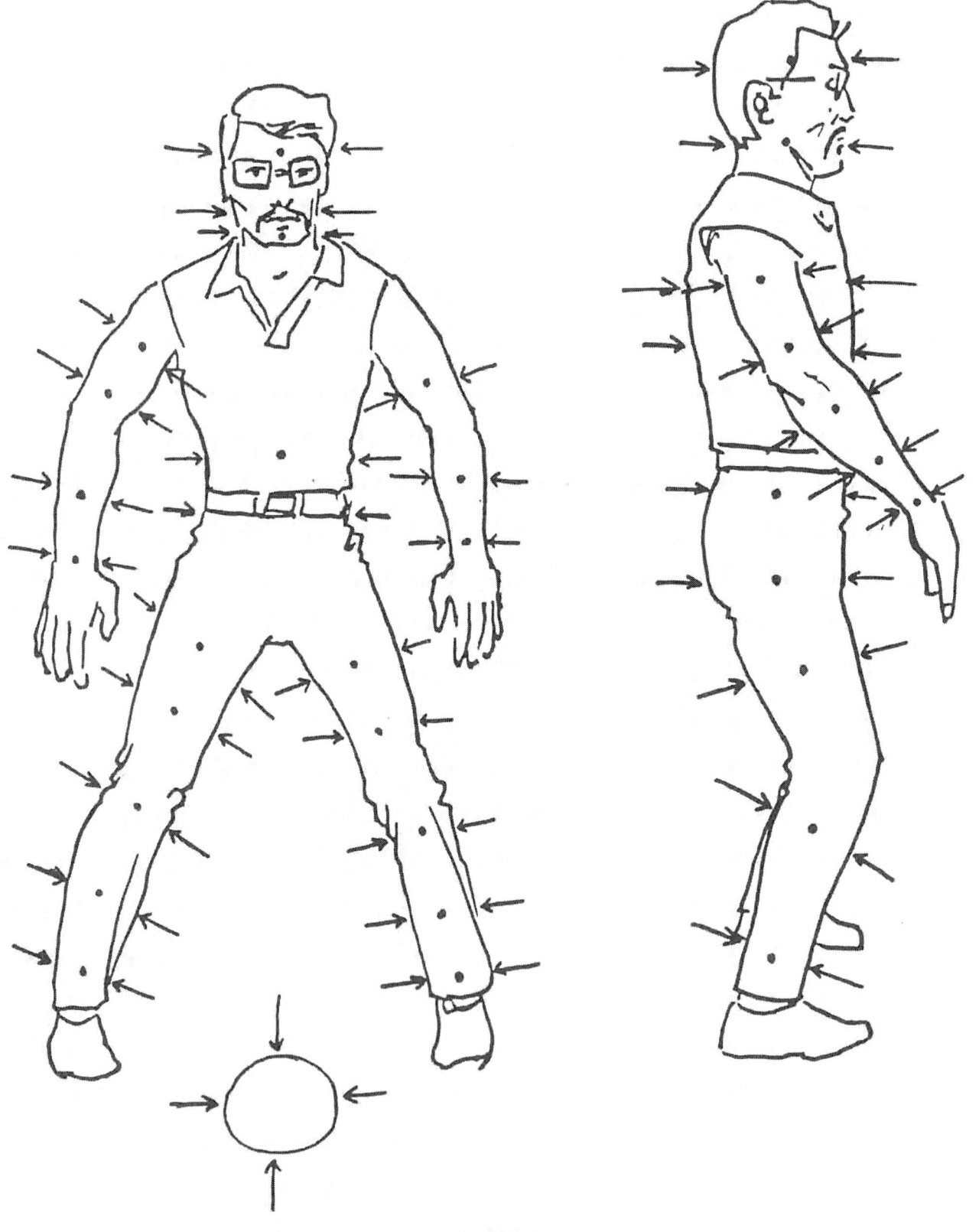

Step #3 of **Condensing Breathing** (See Illustration #3B) This time do both arms at the same time. As you draw into your arms, **imagine a line running down the center of both arms**, draw into that center line on the inhale. On the exhale just relax and do not be concerned about what to do on the exhale.
INHALE Draw into the center line on both arms at the same time from all 4 directions.
EXHALE Relax.
INHALE Draw into the center line on both arms at the same time from all 4 directions.
EXHALE Relax.

Stop doing the arms.

We will now do **the legs.** (See Illustration #3B)

INHALE Draw into both legs at the same time, in from all 4 directions at the same time. Imagine a center line running down the center of the legs.
INHALE Draw in.
EXHALE Relax.

You're not touching your arms now. You are not touching your legs only. Just draw into your legs.
INHALE Draw in.
EXHALE Relax.

Stop doing the legs.

We will now do **the torso only.** (See Illustration #3B)

INHALE Draw into the center of the torso as if you have a single line running down the center.
EXHALE Relax.
INHALE Draw into the center line of the torso, in from all 4 directions at the same time.
EXHALE Relax.
INHALE Draw into the center line of the torso, in from all 4 directions at the same time.
EXHALE Relax.
You are not touching with your hands on this part.

Now add the head and face to the torso centerline.
(See Illustration #3B)
INHALE Draw into the head, the face, and the torso center line running through them all.
INHALE Draw in.
EXHALE Relax. REPEAT

Don't close your eyes or daydream.

EXHALE Remember to keep your mind 3" below your naval and 2 " in. Keep your

tongue up at the roof of your mouth at all times.
INHALE Draw into the center line in the torso, head and face.
EXHALE Relax.

Stop doing the torso, head and face centerline.

Step #4 of **Condensing Breathing - THE STICKMAN**

On the inhale, you are going to imagine **The Stickman** inside your arms, legs, torso, head and face. (See Illustration #3B)

INHALE Suck into the centerline of each and all body parts, in from all 4 directions at the same time.
EXHALE Don't do anything, just relax.
INHALE Suck in, contract your urinary and anal sphincter muscles. Condense in from all 4 directions at the same time.
EXHALE Relax. You should never condense on the exhales, ever.

We are doing the whole body at the same time in **The Stickman**.
INHALE Draw into **The Stickman** inside your body, arms, legs torso, head and face.
EXHALE Relax. Do not close your eyes or daydream.
INHALE Draw into **The Stickman** inside your body, arms, legs torso, head and face.
EXHALE Relax. You may spend as much time as you would like practicing The Stickman. You will practice Step #4 forever, as a single practice.

BEYOND SELF-HELP: MASTERING PERSONAL POWER™ by Gary J. Clyman

CONDENSING BREATHING
(ILLUSTRATION #3B)

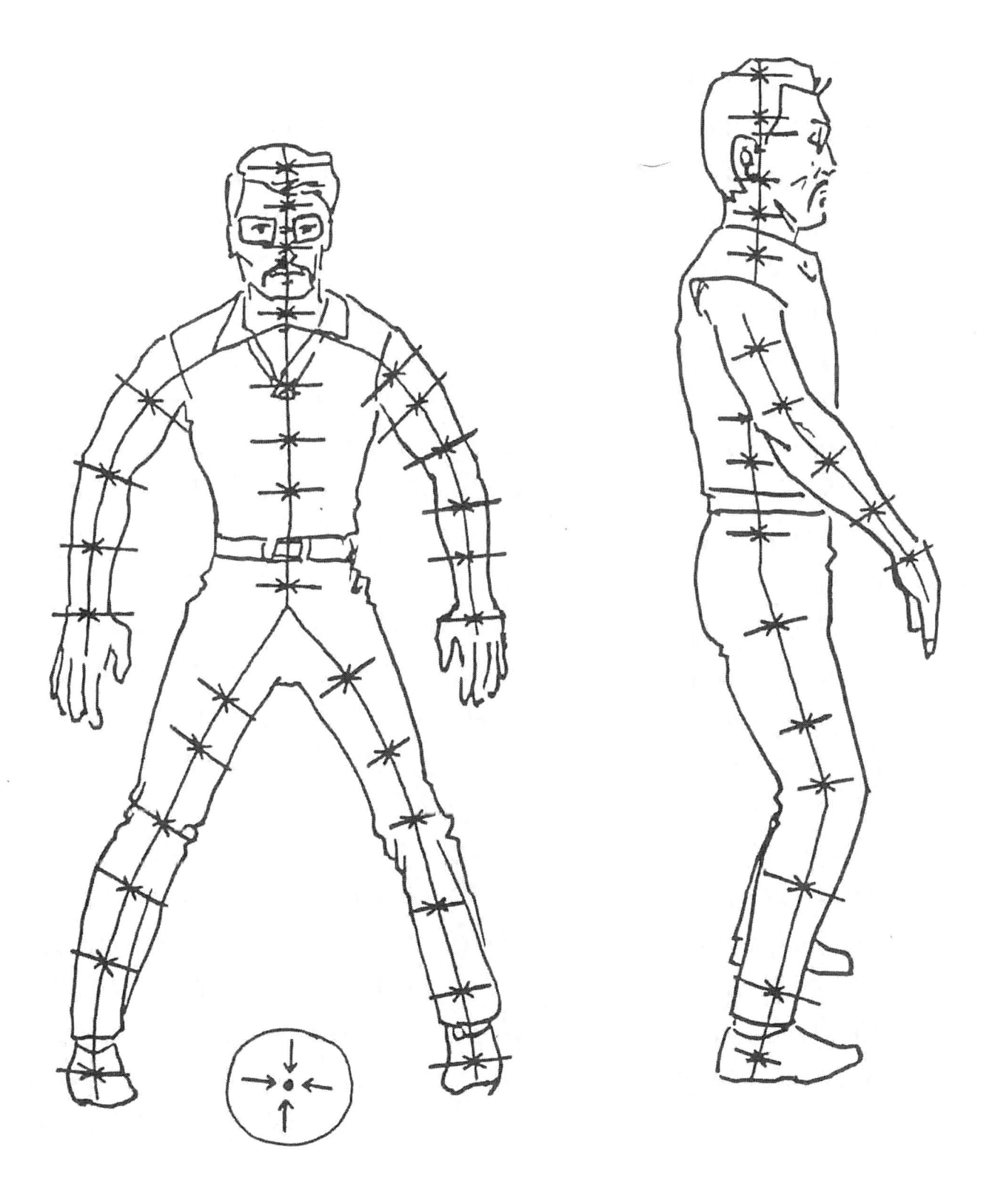

Step #5 of **Condensing Breathing - Sensitizing Your Spine**
(No Illustration Needed)

With the thumb from either hand, and gently touch your spine, behind you, on the inhale. Move your hand away on the exhale. Only touch your spine on the inhales.
<u>EXHALE</u> Take your hand away.
<u>INHALE</u> Gently touch your spine.
<u>EXHALE</u> Take your hand away.
Don't close your eyes or daydream.
Don't lose your posture and always keep your mind 3" below your naval.

We have now completed the first level of details in Condensing Breathing.

Commentary: A question that many students ask is, "What do you do on the exhale? Do you imagine energy going out? What do you do?" The answer is: It is very important to understand that in the beginning stages of doing Chi Kung or Tai Chi for that matter, you **are not concerned about what do you do on the exhale**. Do this or that. It makes no difference as long as you don't condense or squeeze your sphincter muscles on the exhale. What's important in the beginning, is that you spend most of your time drawing energy into the body, condensing energy into the body. On the exhale, it makes no difference. The exhale is not important while practicing Condensing Breathing. <u>NEVER CONDENSE ON THE EXHALE.</u>

IMPORTANT MUSCLES YOU'VE NEVER EXERCISED

How to squeeze your urinary and anal sphincter muscles is very important. A small percentage of the people I work with do not know how to contract these muscles. In order to contract your urinary sphincter muscle, imagine you are urinating and it's time to stop and you don't want to "wet in your pants." To contract your anal sphincter muscle is as if you ate Mexican food for lunch and your going back to work in a <u>very crowded elevator</u> and you don't want to embarrass yourself or the people with you. Physically squeeze both sphincter muscles, don't just do it with your mind.

Another question commonly asked by beginners in Chi Kung and Tai Chi is "how do you keep your mind on Tan Tien while you are practicing everything else?" The answers to this question is quite simple. First of all, no one promised you it was going to be easy. Second, keeping your mind on Tan Tien is of utmost importance. It is difficult in the beginning. So what. It would help if you were to touch gently 3" below your naval periodically to remind yourself to keep your mind down there.

We will now run through **Basic Path Training**. It is very important to understand that **Basic Path Training** is something you learn in about three years of Tai Chi into the system. Basic Path Training is combining basic Tai Chi postures and adding in **The Mind Training**. The percentage of physical to mind training in Basic Path Training is 80% mind training and 20% physical.

BEYOND SELF-HELP: MASTERING PERSONAL POWER™ by Gary J. Clyman

The physical postures, whether they are correct or incorrect, are unimportant and insignificant. **The Mind Training** in these postures is really important.

Don't get distracted about whether you are doing it right or not. It makes no difference.

LESSON #1, TECHNIQUE #2

We are now going to learn **Upward and Downward Meditation**.
(See Illustrations #4A & 4B)

Take a posture with your feet about three feet apart, about a shoulder width and a half. Tuck your pelvis under, pull your knees out, hang by a string from the top of your head. Keep your tongue up, always breathe through your nose.

Reach forward, directly in front of you. Create two, 45 degree angles with your arms. Hold your arms gently in front of you as if you are reaching for something. (See Illustrations #4A & 4B)

<u>INHALE</u> Suck in through your palms and forearms, like a vacuum hose.
(See Illustration #4A)
<u>EXHALE</u> Expel out through your fingertips on both hands.
(See Illustration #4B)
<u>INHALE</u> Suck in through your palms and forearms, like a vacuum hose.
(See Illustration #4A)
<u>EXHALE</u> Expel out through your fingertips on both hands.
(See Illustration #4B)
Keep your posture, keep your tongue up.
<u>INHALE</u> Suck in through your palms and forearms, remember to keep your elbows dropped gently at 45 degree angles, gently reaching in front of you.

Keep your pelvis tucked under your torso. Keep your mind 3" below your naval.

<u>EXHALE</u> Out your fingertips
We have now completed **Upward and Downward Meditation**.

BEYOND SELF-HELP: MASTERING PERSONAL POWER™ by Gary J. Clyman

UPWARD AND DOWNWARD MEDITATION
(ILLUSTRATION #4A = INHALE)

IN PALMS, NOT FINGERS

UPWARD AND DOWNWARD MEDITATION
(ILLUSTRATION #4B = EXHALE)

BEYOND SELF-HELP: MASTERING PERSONAL POWER™ by Gary J. Clyman

LESSON #1, TECHNIQUE #3 (See Illustrations #5A & 5B)

We are now going to learn **Inward and Outward Meditation**.

Again, gently hold your arms out about 45 degrees from the center, down and out, with your elbows slightly bent. With your palms slightly facing the ground. This is called **Inward and Outward Meditation**.

INHALE Suck in through your palms and forearms. (See Illustration #5A) This is very similar to Upward and Downward Meditation but slightly different.
EXHALE Expel out through your fingertips. (See Illustration #5B)
INHALE Suck in through your palms and forearms, like the vacuum cleaner. (See Illustration #5A)
EXHALE Expel out your fingertips. (See Illustration #5B)
INHALE Suck in through your palms and forearms, like the vacuum cleaner. (See Illustration #5A)
EXHALE Expel out your fingertips. (See Illustration #5B)

Relax, drop your shoulders, keep your body erect and continue to keep your mind 3" below your naval.

Remember your arms are about 45 degrees out from the center line

We have now completed **Inward and Outward Meditation**.

BEYOND SELF-HELP: MASTERING PERSONAL POWER™ by Gary J. Clyman

INWARD AND OUTWARD MEDITATION
(ILLUSTRATION #5A = INHALE)

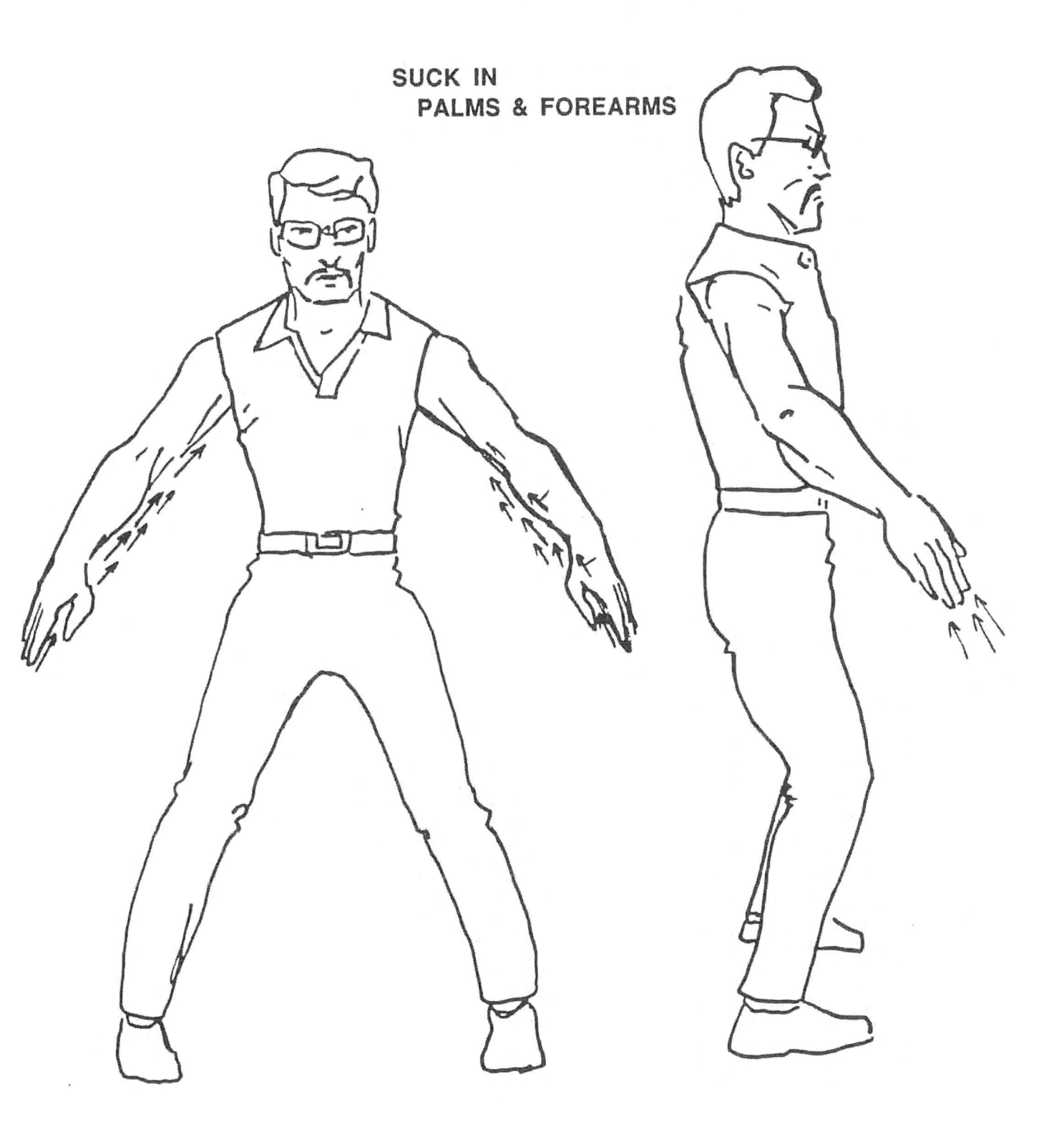

SUCK IN
PALMS & FOREARMS

INWARD AND OUTWARD MEDITATION
(ILLUSTRATION #5B = EXHALE)

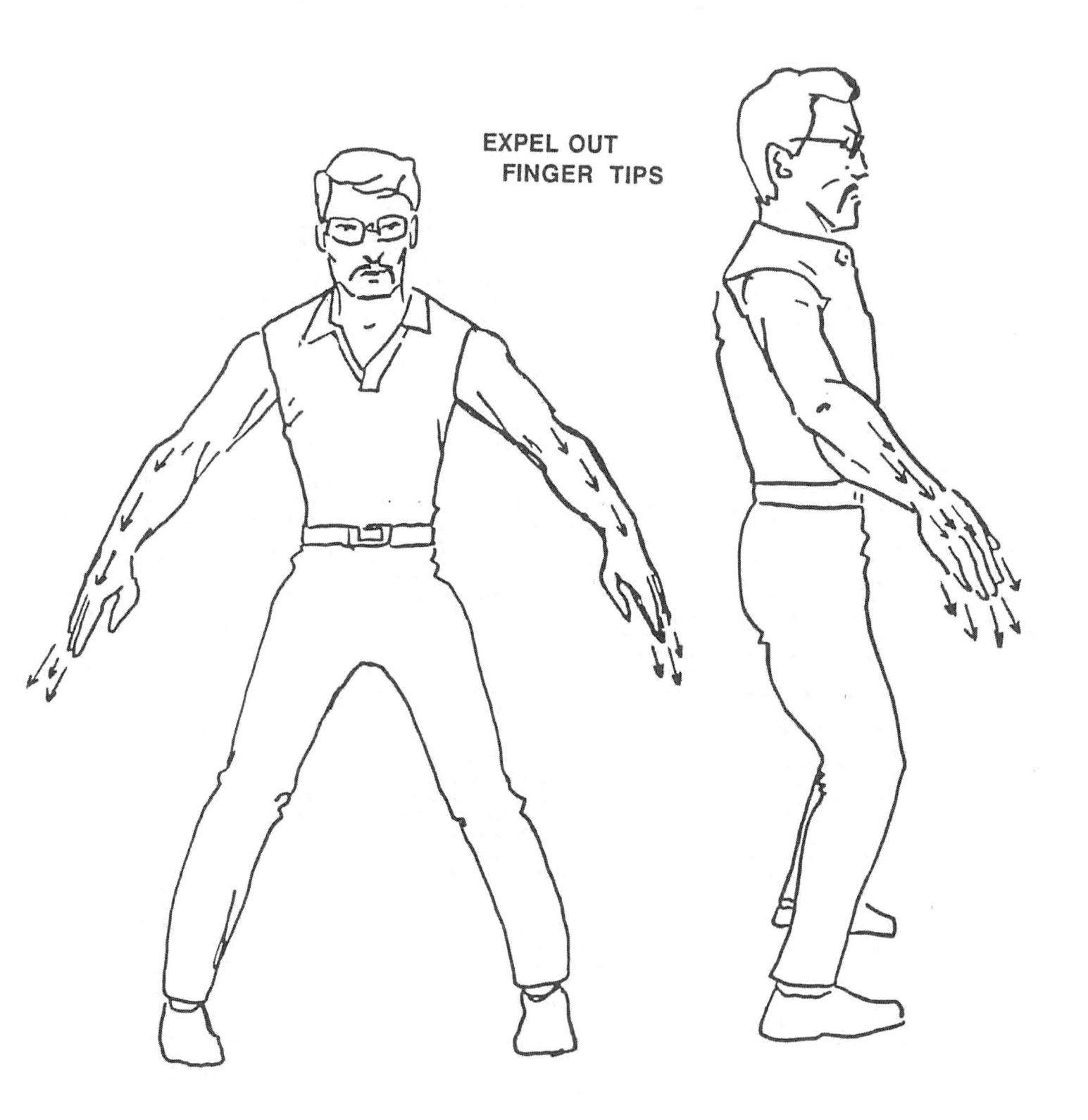

EXPEL OUT
FINGER TIPS

BEYOND SELF-HELP: MASTERING PERSONAL POWER™ by Gary J. Clyman

LESSON #1, TECHNIQUE #4 (See Illustrations #6A & 6B)

We will now learn **Tai Chi Stance Meditation**.
(See Illustrations #6A & 6B)

This is the final meditation in what I have named **Basic Path Training**.

Take a posture with your feet about three feet apart, about a shoulder width and a half. Tuck your pelvis under, pull your knees out, hang by a string from the top of your head. Keep your tongue up, always breathe through your nose.

Hold your torso upright. Hold your arms gently in front of you at about shoulder height. Imagine your arms around a barrel or a "hula-hoop" with your fingers are pointing toward each other. Your thumbs are gently relaxed. Your arms are about shoulder height. Drop your shoulders, make sure you are relaxed.

INHALE With your mind, start from your right palm. Draw the energy in and circulate, from your right palm to your right elbow, to your right shoulder, across your chest, to your left shoulder, to your left elbow, and to your left palm. (Inhale as in Illustration #6A)

EXHALE Reverse, go back around. Back to the right palm, to the right shoulder, across your chest, to your right shoulder, and back to your right palm. (Exhale as in Illustration #6B)

INHALE Circulate from the right palm, all the way around the arms across the chest to the other arm, to the left palm, again. (Inhale as in Illustration #6A)
EXHALE Reverse. Do not cross the center line between your finger tips.
(Exhale as in Illustration #6B)
INHALE Repeat.
EXHALE Repeat.

This is called **Tai Chi Stance Meditation**. (See Illustrations #6A & 6B)

Tai Chi Stance Meditation was the final meditation in what is called **Basic Path Training**.

TAI CHI STANCE MEDITATION
(ILLUSTRATION #6A = INHALE)

ACROSS THE BACK

112

TAI CHI STANCE MEDITATION
(ILLUSTRATION #6B = EXHALE)

ACROSS THE BACK

We will now do a **Calming Down Exercise** so when you go back out into the world, you are not hyper or wild, and you are under control.

This posture is what I have named **The Lock Off Position**.
(See Illustration #7) I have chosen the name **The Lock Off Position** to signify the conscious action of forgetting you have arms and forgetting you have legs.

Have a seat on a chair or mediation cushion. Sit down and gently cross your ankles. Place your left palm facing up on your lap. Put your right hand inside your left palm facing up also. Gently, hold your left thumb in your right palm. Forget your got arms and legs. This is called Locking Off.

The body is not important, but what you are going to do with your mind, that is.

INHALE Silently say to yourself, "where am I coming from?"
EXHALE Silently say to yourself "where am I going to?" Repeat

INHALE Silently say to yourself, "where am I coming from?"
EXHALE Silently say to yourself "where am I going to?" Repeat
Relax as much as you can. Practicing this will help reduce your accumulated anger and help you keep control of yourself.

It is very important to understand that this is only the first time running through Lesson #1. Later on in the tape series, I will add more details to what you just learned.

Remember not to get "hung up" on "having to do it right" because you have to do it wrong many times before you can do it right.

END OF LESSON #1

BEYOND SELF-HELP: MASTERING PERSONAL POWER™ by Gary J. Clyman

THE LOCK OFF POSITION
(ILLUSTRATION #7)

A BRIEF OUTLINE IN REVIEW

1) PREPARATION WITH TAI CHI DETAILS (See Illustration #2)

2) CONDENSING BREATHING IN A HORSE STANCE (See Illustration #3A)
   A. FEEL THE SURFACE OF YOUR SKIN. Touch in the following order: Arms, Legs, Torso, Head, and Face. TOUCH ON THE INHALE ONLY! (See Illustration #3A)
   B. DRAW INTO EACH BODY PART. Condense in from all 4 directions with your mind and any other visualizations you can use. (See Illustration #3B)
   C. DRAW INTO EACH BODY PART again but this time create a single line running down the center of each body part: Arms, Legs, Torso, Head, and Face. (See Illustration #3B)
   D. DRAW INTO EACH BODY PARTS AT THE SAME TIME: Arms, Legs, Torso, Head, and Face. This will be called "The Stickman." Don't forget to always keep your mind at Tan Tien. (See Illustration #3B)
   E. DRAW INTO YOUR SPINE FROM ALL 4 DIRECTIONS while tapping your spine with you thumb on the inhale only. (See Illustration #3C)

3) BASIC PATH TRAINING USING TAI CHI STANDING MEDITATIONS

   A. UPWARD AND DOWNWARD MEDITATION
   (See Illustrations #4A & 4B)
   Suck in the palms and forearms on the inhale (Inhale as in Illustration #4A); expel out the finger tips on the exhale. (Exhale as in Illustration #4B) Squeeze your sphincter muscles on the inhale only.

   B. INWARD AND OUTWARD MEDITATION
   (See Illustrations #5A & 5B)
   Such in the palms and forearms on the inhale (Inhale as in Illustration #5A). Expel out the finger tips on the exhale (Exhale as in Illustration #5B). Squeeze your sphincter muscles on the inhale only.

   C. TAI CHI STANCE MEDITATION
   (See Illustrations #6A & 6B)
   Circulate around in each direction, inhale one way and exhale the other. (Inhale as in Illustration #6A). (Exhale as in Illustration #6B). Do not cross the center space between your hands. You may switch directions when you choose. **Squeeze your sphincter muscles on the inhale only.**

4) CALMING DOWN EXERCISE - This is to be used only if necessary. This should be practiced in "The Lock Off Position." (See Illustration #7)

    A. "Where am I coming from? (Inhale)
    B. "Where am I going to? (Exhale)

LESSON #2

This is practiced in a sitting position called **The Lock Off Position**. All 4 sets of details should be learned separately and practiced together. Add each level of details to each existing level. (See Illustration #7)

What we are going to do first in Lesson #2 is what is called **Outside Air**.

Leave your hands right where they were at the end of Lesson #1. Lesson #2 is practiced in **The Lock Off Position**. With your legs or your ankles crossed gently, depending on what you are sitting on, your left palm should be facing up with your right hand inside holding onto your right thumb.

Forget you have arms and legs. They do not matter and are unimportant during the duration of Lesson #2.

INHALE Let your lower abdominal area expand as you breathe. When practicing Inside Air, we are only concerned with the air that goes in your nose. Relax as much as you can. Don't fall asleep. Keep your eyes opened.
Sit up straight, reach for the ceiling with the top of your head.

EXHALE Stay relaxed.

INHALE Breathe all the way down to your lower abdominal area. Fill up your abdominal area like a sack of rice, filling at the bottom first, gently filling up to the top.

EXHALE Stay relaxed.

REPEAT

EXHALE Let the air out - deflate your abdominal area.

Remember, **Outside Air** is not important. The only reason I am teaching you **Outside Air** is to use for comparison purposes. You don't have to practice this technique.

BEYOND SELF-HELP: MASTERING PERSONAL POWER™ by Gary J. Clyman

OUTSIDE AIR - IN THE LOCK OFF POSITION
NOT IMPORTANT
(ILLUSTRATION #7)

We are going to learn **Inside Air**. **Inside Air** is very important. **Inside Air** is equivalent to pulling the cord on a lawn mower to get the motor started. Begin in **The Lock Off Position**. (See Illustration #7)

Inside Air is equivalent to priming the pump to get the pump started. It is very important to practice **Inside Air** specifically because later on in Lesson 4, when you have learned The Micro Cosmic Orbit, which is an internal circulation, inside the torso. **Inside Air** is a pre-requisite and is very important to practice before The Micro Cosmic Orbit. So, now we are going to learn **Inside Air**.

On the inhale, you are going to take a short inhale, followed by a long inhale. Remember you are still in the posture that you were at **the end of Lesson #1.**

<u>INHALE</u> Snort in, short inhale followed by a long inhale.
<u>EXHALE</u> Snort out, short exhale, followed by a long exhale.
<u>INHALE</u> Short inhale followed by a long inhale.
<u>EXHALE</u> Short exhale followed by a long exhale. This is very important.

REPEAT

<u>INHALE</u> Short inhale, followed by a long inhale.
<u>EXHALE</u> Short exhale, followed by a long exhale.
<u>INHALE</u> Short inhale, followed by a long inhale.
<u>EXHALE</u> Short exhale, followed by a long exhale. Remember the body does not matter while practicing **Inside Air**.

We have now completed Detail #1 of **Inside Air**.

We will now learn Detail #2 of **Inside Air**.
On the <u>INHALE</u> your mind goes up through the ceiling.
On the <u>EXHALE</u> your mind goes down through the floor.
Remember, your are still practicing Detail #1 which is short inhale followed by a long inhale, short exhale, followed by a long exhale.

So <u>INHALE</u> as your mind goes up through the ceiling.
<u>EXHALE</u> your mind goes down through the floor.

REPEAT

Review Detail #1 and Detail #2 one more time together.

<u>INHALE</u> Short inhale followed by a long inhale, your mind goes up through the ceiling.
<u>EXHALE</u> Short exhale followed by a long exhale, your mind goes down through the floor.

We have now completed Detail #1 and Detail #2 we will now add Detail #3 to what we have just learned.

I will now explain Detail #3.

On the INHALE, pull your diaphragm up, like a guitar string and you let go on the short inhale only. INHALE Perform Detail #1, which is on the inhale, short inhale followed by a long inhale, short exhale followed by a long exhale.

Detail #2 is on the inhale, direct your mind goes up through the ceiling, on the exhale your mind goes down through the floor. Detail #3 is, on the inhale, pull your diaphragm like a guitar string. EXHALE and relax.

Perform Details #1, #2 and #3, all at the same time.

We have now completed Details #1, #2 and #3 of **Inside Air**. We will now add Detail #4.

Detail #4 is on the inhale contract or squeeze your urinary and anal sphincter muscles on the inhale only. Remember, whenever squeezing your urinary and anal sphincter muscles, always squeeze on the inhales only.

We will now do **Inside Air** combining all 4 sets of details.

INHALE Short inhale followed by a long inhale, your mind goes up through the ceiling, you pull your diaphragm like a guitar string, and you squeeze your urinary and anal sphincter muscles, on the inhale.

EXHALE Short exhale followed by a long exhale, your mind goes down through the floor, there is no diaphragm attention and you release your urinary and anal sphincter muscles.

We have now completed **Inside Air**.

A commonly asked question at this point is: how do you pull the diaphragm like a guitar string? It is very important to understand that you only pull the diaphragm in the beginning of the inhale and immediately let go. Do not hold it in until you exhale. So on the inhale, you pull the diaphragm and you let go immediately independent of what you are doing with the breath. This is very important.

Detail #1 - On the INHALE, short inhale followed by a long inhale.
On the EXHALE, short exhale followed by a long exhale.
Detail #2 - On the INHALE, your mind goes up through the ceiling, on the EXHALE your mind goes down through the floor.
Detail #3 - On the INHALE, pull your diaphragm like a guitar string and let go immediately. There is some abdominal tension or contraction of the muscles but only momentarily.
Detail #4 - On the INHALE, condense your urinary and anal sphincter muscles and hold them the whole time of the inhale, on the exhale release them. Not forcefully, gently, remain relaxed.

These are all 4 Sets of Details for Inside Air.

Lesson Commentary: **Inside Air** is of utmost importance when practicing Chi Kung because it is a direct priority that you practice this prior to learning The Micro Cosmic Orbit.

That is the only purpose for it. We have now completed Lesson #2. Do not go further in the system unless you have already fully absorbed Lessons #1 & #2.

NOTE: SQUEEZE YOUR SPHINCTER MUSCLES ON THE INHALES ONLY. NEVER SQUEEZE YOUR SPHINCTER MUSCLES ON THE EXHALE. IMPROPER MUSCLES CONTRACTIONS MAY CAUSE WET DREAMS.

Lesson Commentary: When projecting your mind up through the ceiling, it starts on the short inhale and continues the whole time you are doing the ling inhale. When projecting your mind down through the floor, it starts on the short exhale and continues the whole time of the long exhale.

BEYOND SELF-HELP: MASTERING PERSONAL POWER™ by Gary J. Clyman

INSIDE AIR - IN THE LOCK OFF POSITION
VERY IMPORTANT
(ILLUSTRATION #7)

BEYOND SELF-HELP: MASTERING PERSONAL POWER™ by Gary J. Clyman

LESSON #3

SITTING FORMS WITH THE MIND TRAINING
(AKA - 6 FORMS AND 7 CIRCULATIONS)

This is called **The Sitting Forms with the Mind Training** or **"The Sitting Forms"** for short. I have given these moves practical names for your convenience. There are no hidden meanings, just names. It is very important to understand that the way you move your body when you are practicing **The Chi Circulations** or **"The Sitting Forms"** is not important. Don't waste a lot of energy worrying about whether you're doing them correctly or not. Don't get frustrated or upset. Don't act like you can't remember how to do the moves. It makes no difference. The important part here is the mind training. This section of your Chi Kung practice begins in **The Lock Off Position** (See Illustration #7).

Bow Fists: Begin in **The Lock Off Position**. Draw in through the knees on the inhale and expel out through the right fist on the exhale. (See Illustration #8)

Sit on a chair, a couch, or on a meditation cushion, in **The Lock Off Position**, with your legs gently crossed. Expand your arms to form **Bow Fists Position** (See Illustration #8). Your right fist will be gently closed with your left hand very close to touching but not touching, over your right fist. Make sure the outer part of your right fist is facing out. That means your thumb of your right hand is facing towards your sternum, which is the center of your chest. Keep your elbows dropped at all times. Don't close your eyes, keep your posture upright.

INHALE Let your arms open while opening your right fist.
EXHALE Gently bring your arms and hands close together, gently closing your right fist and almost covering your right fist with your left open hand, but not touching.
INHALE Let your arms gently go around again.
EXHALE Gently close your right fist while your left hand nearly covers your right hand.

Remember, the physical movement is not important. What is more important is **The Chi Circulation.**

INHALE Let your arms go around on the inhale,
EXHALE Gently let your hands come closer together with your right hand gently forming a loose fist, covering your right fist, with your left hand.

The Chi Circulation in Bow Fists Form.

INHALE Expand your arms, draw in, suck in through both knees, and squeeze your urinary and anal sphincter muscles.
EXHALE Expel out through the heel of your right fist as its facing out with your thumb facing toward your sternum.

<u>INHALE</u> Suck in through your knees, let your arms go around and expand.
<u>EXHALE</u> Expel out through the heel of your right fist.
<u>INHALE</u> Suck in through your knees, both knees at the same time.
<u>EXHALE</u> Expel out through the right heel of your hand.

Remember, the physical movement is not important. **The Chi Circulation** is much more important. **Now ends Bow Fists - Form #1, Circulation #1.**

BOW FISTS
Form #1, Circulation #1
(ILLUSTRATION #8)

Tai Chi Ball Meditation. (See Illustration #9)
Hold your arms slightly down at an angle with your right arm slightly inside your left arm.
INHALE let the ball expand, but don't use your shoulders.
EXHALE Contract the ball. Keep your right arm always inside, your fingers are pointed slightly downward.
INHALE Expand the ball.
EXHALE Contract the ball. Keep it simple.
INHALE Expand the ball, remember the physical movement is not important.
EXHALE Contract. I don't care what it looks like when you are doing it.

The Chi Circulation in Tai Chi Ball Meditation.

INHALE Draw in through your knees as the ball expands.
EXHALE Contract and project your energy into your spine.
INHALE Draw in through your knees as you let the ball expand.
EXHALE Project into the spine, in from all 4 directions, into your spine on the exhale.
INHALE Expand the ball suck in through your knees
EXHALE Project into your spine as the ball contracts.
That is the first circulation of **Tai Chi Ball** sitting form.

The second Circulation of **Tai Chi Ball Meditation** is physically exactly the same but **The Chi Circulation** is different.
(See Illustration #9)

INHALE Suck in through your knees as the ball expands.
EXHALE Expel out through "your third eye" (spot between your eyebrows).
INHALE Let the ball expand, suck in through your knees.
EXHALE Let the ball contract, expel out through "your third eye."
INHALE Let the ball expand, at the same time, suck in through your knees and squeeze your urinary and anal sphincter muscles.
EXHALE Let the ball contract. Expel out through your third eye.

Now ends Tai Chi Ball Meditation - Form #2, Circulations #2-3. At this point many of you are wondering, how does the energy get from the knees, to other parts of the body? How does the energy get from the knees into the spine? How does the energy get from the knees and out "your third eye?" Don't worry it doesn't make any difference. The important thing to do is just practice and not worry about other details.

BEYOND SELF-HELP: MASTERING PERSONAL POWER™ by Gary J. Clyman

TAI CHI BALL MEDITATION
Form #2, Circulations #2-3
(ILLUSTRATION #9)

EXHALE

OUT

IN

IN

Sideways Fan Through Back: Begin with your fingers facing up and both palms facing toward each other, in front of your sternum with thumbs facing toward your chest. Start in **Prayer Hands Position** (See Illustration #10A). Don't worry, this is not religious. From **Prayer Hands Position,** take your right palm, gently face it 90 degrees to the front, straight out towards your side. Turning your head to the right side, let your right hand "push out" to the right side.

Pull your hand back to the center **Prayer Hands Position,** with both palms facing toward each other fingertips facing up and your thumbs facing toward the chest.

Now we are going to do the left side. Push your Left palm out 90 degrees to the front, straight out to your left side as you turn your head to the left. Now pull your hand back gently to **Prayer Hands Position** with both hands facing toward each other, fingertips facing up with your thumbs facing toward your chest.

Always turn your head in the direction of your move.

INHALE Pull your hands toward each other to **Prayer Hands Position.** EXHALE Push your right palm out to the right side, your head turns toward the right side and you extend your right palm. Keep your elbow slightly bent.
INHALE Pull your right hand back in to **Prayer Hands Position.**
EXHALE Push your left hand out to the left side, turn your head towards to the left side.
INHALE Pull your left hand back to the center to **Prayer Hands Position.**

The physical posture in all of these movements are not important. What is important is what you are doing with your mind.

Start with both hands in front of your chest, fingers facing up, thumbs facing your chest, palms facing each other, **Prayer Hands Position.**
(See Illustration #10A)

The Chi Circulation in Sideways Fan Through Back.

INHALE Suck in through both knees at the same time.
EXHALE Expel out through your right palm.
INHALE Pull your right hand back to **Prayer Hands Position.**
EXHALE Push your left hand out to the left side as you turn your head to the left.
INHALE Pull your left hand back to **Prayer Hands Position.**

>Note: **The Palm Exit** is where you exhale out through.
>Exhale Only. (See Illustration #10B)

A brief review of **Sideways Fan Through Back.**

EXHALE The right arm goes out, the right hand goes out, 90 degrees to the front, to the right side, as you exhale out the heel of your right palm. (See Illustration #11R)

INHALE Your right hand comes back to form **Prayer Hands Position**, suck in through your knees.
EXHALE Your left hand goes out, 90 degrees to the front, to the left side, you exhale out the heel of your hand on the left palm. (See Illustration #11L)
INHALE Bring your left hand back to **Prayer Hands Position,** as you suck in through both knees.
EXHALE Push your right hand out, 90 degrees to the front, to the right side. Make sure you don't straighten your elbow.
EXHALE Your energy goes out the heel of your right hand.
INHALE Bring your right hand back to **Prayer Hands Position**. Suck in through your knees.
EXHALE out the left palm to the left side turning your head, the energy goes out the heel of your left palm, facing out to the side.
INHALE as your left hand is coming back toward **Prayer Hands Position**, Suck in through your knees.

Lesson Commentary: The physical movements are _not_ important. **The Chi Circulations** are _extremely_ important. **The Chi Circulations** have been ignored or purposely left out, in every other Chi Kung book I've ever seen.

REVIEWING THE CHI CIRCULATION - Such in through your knees, expel out through the heel of your right and left **Palm Exit** (See Illustration #10B). **The Palm Exit** is the location on your hands where you expel your energy out from. This same principle is used in all **The Moving Forms**.

Now ends Sideways Fan Through Back - Form #3, Circulation #4.

BEYOND SELF-HELP: MASTERING PERSONAL POWER™ by Gary J. Clyman

PRAYER HANDS POSTURE
(ILLUSTRATION #10A)

BEYOND SELF-HELP: MASTERING PERSONAL POWER™ by Gary J. Clyman

THE PALM EXIT
(ILLUSTRATION #10B)

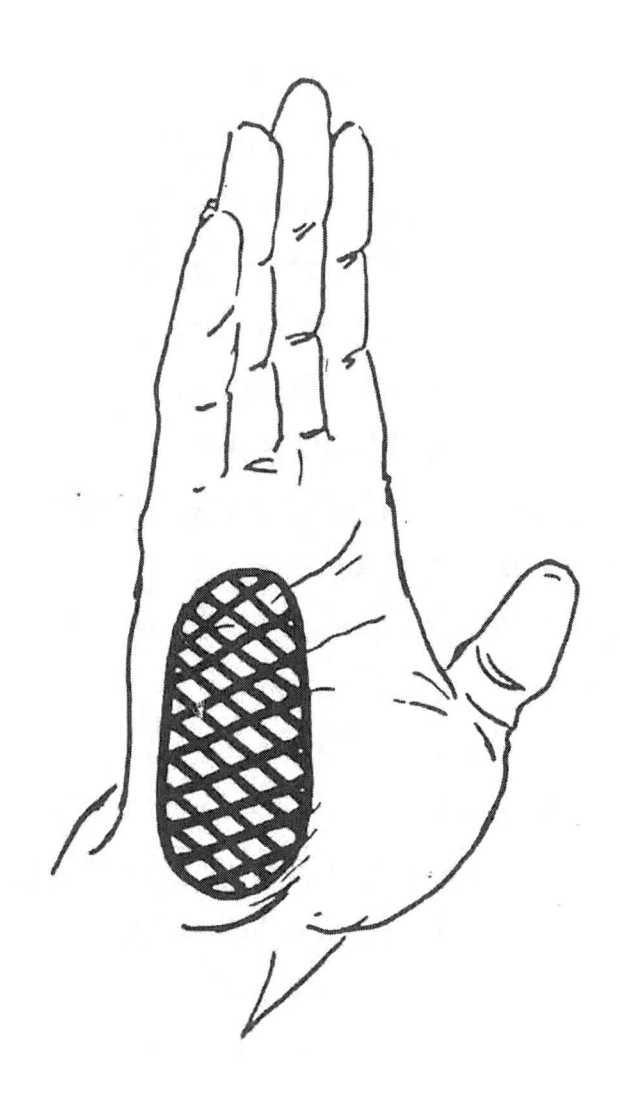

BEYOND SELF-HELP: MASTERING PERSONAL POWER™ by Gary J. Clyman

SIDEWAYS FAN THROUGH BACK
Form #3, Circulation #4
(ILLUSTRATION #11R)

OUT

PRAYER HANDS POSTURE
(ILLUSTRATION #10A)

BEYOND SELF-HELP: MASTERING PERSONAL POWER™ by Gary J. Clyman

SIDEWAYS FAN THROUGH BACK
Form #3, Circulation #4
(ILLUSTRATIONS #11L)

PRAYER HANDS POSTURE
(ILLUSTRATION #10A)

BEYOND SELF-HELP: MASTERING PERSONAL POWER™ by Gary J. Clyman

Forward Fan Through Back: Begin with one hand in front of your chest while the other hand extend out toward the front, with the heel of your palm facing forward. Inhale in as you draw your hand in toward your center, exhale out as you go away from the body. Inhale in through the knees, and exhale out through the heel of your outgoing hand. (See Illustrations #12R & 12L)

> Note: **The Palm Exit** is where you exhale out through.
> (See Illustration #10B)

We will do **Forward Fan Through Back**.

INHALE Suck in through your knees.
EXHALE Expel out through your right palm as it goes straight out toward the front with your fingers facing the ceiling and your thumb pulled back toward your chest.
INHALE Let your right hand come back to the **Prayer Hands Position**.
EXHALE Let your left palm go straight out in front of you with your fingertips on your left hand facing up, with the left thumb facing back toward your chest.
INHALE Go back to the **Prayer Hands Position**, with both palms facing each other, fingertips facing up, and thumbs facing toward your chest.
We will now insert the mind training in **Forward Fan Through Back** as the right hand goes out toward the center, you exhale out through the palm of your right hand.
INHALE as your right hand comes back toward the **Prayer Hands Position**, you suck in through your knees.

Left side, Forward Fan Through Back

EXHALE with your left hand straight toward the center and forward
EXHALE the energy is going to go out the heel of your left palm, straight forward.
INHALE bring your left hand back, sucking in through your knees back to the center **prayer position**. The right hand now goes out. The energy goes out the heel of your right hand, toward the center.

Right side, Forward Fan Through Back

EXHALE with your right hand straight toward the center, forward
EXHALE the energy is going to go out the right heel of the right palm, straight forward.
INHALE bring your right hand back, sucking in through your knees back to the center prayer position. The left hand now goes out. The energy goes out the heel of your left hand, toward the center.

Remember your left or right forward hand is still directly in front of your sternum, fingertips pointing up, thumb pointing toward your chest. (See Illustration #10A)

INHALE your right palm comes back to the center prayer position, as you suck and draw in through both knees. Now we are going to let the left hand go forward.

This is called **Forward Fan Through Back**. The energy goes out through the palm of the left hand with the fingers pointing up, thumb pointing toward you, keep your elbow bent, don't straighten it.

INHALE let your left hand come back to the center prayer position as you suck in through your knees.
EXHALE out the right palm going out, keep your elbow dropped, the energy travels out through the right palm.
INHALE pull your right hand back to the center prayer position, sucking in through both knees.
EXHALE the left hand goes straight toward the front. Remember the right hand is still in the prayer position, fingertips facing straight up, thumb facing straight toward your chest and upright.
INHALE your left hand comes back to the center prayer position, sucking in through your knees.

Now ends Forward Fan Through Back - Form #4, Circulation #5.

FORWARD FAN THROUGH BACK
Form #4, Circulation #5
(ILLUSTRATION #12R)

BEYOND SELF-HELP: MASTERING PERSONAL POWER™ by Gary J. Clyman

PRAYER HANDS POSTURE w/ PALM EXIT
(ILLUSTRATIONS #10A & 10B)

BEYOND SELF-HELP: MASTERING PERSONAL POWER™ by Gary J. Clyman

FORWARD FAN THROUGH BACK
Form #4, Circulation #5
(ILLUSTRATION #12L)

Double Hands, Down and Out: Begin by drawing in through your palms and knee-caps simultaneously on the inhale. Expel out through your palms as your hands go "down and out" at your sides, as you exhale. (See Illustrations #13A, 13B, 13C & 13D)

We will now do **Form #5, Circulation #6** which is called **Double Hands, Down and Out.**

This is done in the sitting posture with your legs gently crossed. Remember it doesn't matter what the physical body is doing, however, it matters a little. You got to do it relatively O.K. but don't worry about specific details. First we are going to build the physical part of **Double Hands, Down and Out** which is the 5th of **The Sitting Forms with The Mind Training.**

Begin in **prayer hands** with both hands facing each other in front of your, fingertips pointing up, thumbs facing toward your sternum. This will be easier than some of the previous moves.

<u>INHALE</u> don't worry.
<u>EXHALE</u> gently turn your wrists around toward the outside and your are going to do Down and Out 45 degrees to the center with your palms facing down and fingertips pulled up.
<u>INHALE</u> let your hands gently rise up, keep your elbows dropped. Do not worry about the specifics with the physical details.
<u>EXHALE</u> down and out 45 degrees to the front. Not straight sideways, not straight forward, down 45 degrees.
<u>INHALE</u> as you draw in.
<u>EXHALE</u> down and out 45 degrees down toward the floor. Make sure you are pulling your fingertips back and your palms are forward, forward toward the floor.

We will now add **The Mind Training** to **Double Hands, Down and Out.**

<u>INHALE</u> suck in through your knees and through both palms at the same time.
<u>EXHALE</u> expel out through the palms of your hands with your fingertips being pulled back and your palms facing down 45 degrees to the ground. <u>INHALE</u> suck in through your knees and both palms at the same time. <u>EXHALE</u> out both palms at the same time. Not out through your knees, never out through your knees.
<u>INHALE</u> suck in through your knees and both palms. Do not worry about the physical details, just get **The Chi Circulation** correct.
<u>EXHALE</u> out your palms. Remember to pull your fingertips up. I want a little bit of attention at your wrists.
<u>INHALE</u> let your arms gently float up as you suck in through your knees, suck in through your palms on both hands.
<u>EXHALE</u> down and out 45 degrees. **Now ends Double Hands, Down and Out - Form #5, Circulation #6.**

BEYOND SELF-HELP: MASTERING PERSONAL POWER™ by Gary J. Clyman

TRANSITION TO DOUBLE HANDS, DOWN AND OUT
Form #5, Circulation #6
INHALE ON TRANSITION
(ILLUSTRATION #13A & 13B)

OUT PALMS

OUT PALMS

IN

IN

BEYOND SELF-HELP: MASTERING PERSONAL POWER™ by Gary J. Clyman

DOUBLE HANDS, DOWN AND OUT
Use whole palms for exhale, not Palm Exits
(ILLUSTRATION #13C)

OUT PALMS

OUT PALMS

BEYOND SELF-HELP: MASTERING PERSONAL POWER™ by Gary J. Clyman

TRANSITION TO DOUBLE HANDS, UP AND OUT
Form #6, Circulation #7
INHALE ON TRANSITION
(ILLUSTRATIONS #13D & 14A)

Double Hands, Up and Out: Begin by drawing in through your palms and kneecaps simultaneously on the inhale. Expel out through your finger tips as your hands go up and out at your sides. (See Illustrations #14A, 14B & 14C)

We will now do **Double Hands, Up and Out, Form #6, Circulation #7.**

Start from **prayer hands** in front of you.
INHALE don't worry about anything yet.
EXHALE gently let your palms face 45 degrees to the ceiling. Not straight up, yet not straight out, 45 degrees. (See Illustration #13A)

INHALE drop your elbows and gently pull your fingertips back so you're slightly flexing your wrists. (See Illustration #13B, 13C, & 13D) Now remember it is 45 degrees out to the side, it's not forward. This is one of the most complicated to do correctly, but if all you are doing wrong are the physical details, don't worry about it.
EXHALE out the palms, gently pull your fingertips back. You want a little tension at the wrists.

We are now going to do **The Chi Circulation.**

This is called **Double Hands, Up and Out.**

INHALE bring your arms in, suck in through your palms, pull your wrists back slightly, suck in through your knees at the same time.
EXHALE still keeping your fingertips pulled back slightly, expel out through the palms of both hands.
INHALE suck in through your knees, suck in through both palms, while gently pulling your fingertips back.
EXHALE out through the palms while still pulling your fingertips back. INHALE suck in through your knees, suck in through your palms.
EXHALE out through the palms of your hands.

INHALE remember, your arms are out 45 degrees to the side and up. EXHALE out through the palms of your hands.

We will now do **The Second Version of Double Hands, Up and Out.** This time the only difference is we are going to lead on the exhale with our fingertips facing out 45 degrees to the ceiling (No Illustration Needed). This time we are not pulling our wrists back.
INHALE pull your wrists back on the inhale, suck in through your palms, suck in through your knees at the same time.
EXHALE gently out through your fingertips, <u>not out through your palms</u>.

This is **The Second Version of Double Hands, Up and Out**.
INHALE pull your wrists back, suck in through your knees and your palms at the same time.

EXHALE Expel out through your fingertips. Relax as much as you can as you exhale.
INHALE suck in through your palms and in through your knees while gently pulling your fingers back.
EXHALE Expel out through your fingertips, keeping your hands 45 degrees to the ceiling, 45 degrees to the side, fingers pointing up toward the ceiling. (No Illustration Needed)

We have now completed **Form #6, Circulation #7** of **The Sitting Forms with The Mind Training**. This is the hardest part of the training because it relies on physical form, but don't be frustrated and depressed over whether you are performing the movements correctly or not, they don't matter. **The Chi Circulations** in these forms are much more important than what you are doing with your physical body.

DOUBLE HANDS, UP AND OUT
Form #6, Circulation #7
"ON THE INHALE"
(ILLUSTRATION #14B)

BEYOND SELF-HELP: MASTERING PERSONAL POWER™ by Gary J. Clyman

DOUBLE HANDS, UP AND OUT
Form #6, Circulation #7
Use Finger Tips for exhale, not Palm Exits
(ILLUSTRATION #14C)

OUT FINGER TIPS

OUT FINGER TIPS

PALMS ON KNEES WITH CHI CIRCULATION

As you sit in **The Lock Off Position**, on a chair or cushion, gently place the palms of your hands on your kneecaps

INHALE draw in through your knees.
EXHALE expel out through the palms of your hands.

Keep your palms on your knees at all times.

Practice this as "a closed circuit." (See Illustration #15)

BEYOND SELF-HELP: MASTERING PERSONAL POWER™ by Gary J. Clyman

PALMS ON KNEES MEDITATION
(ILLUSTRATION #15)

LESSON #4

THE MICRO COSMIC ORBIT
Performed in The Lock Off Position
(See Illustrations #7 & 16A-16P)

Begin in **The Lock Off Position**. Put your left hand down by Tan Tien on your lap, palm facing up. Next, put your right hand inside your left hand, holding on to your left thumb in your right palm, and cover your left thumb with your right. Again, we are "Locking Off" your arms and your legs intentionally, forgetting we even have arms and legs. **The Micro Cosmic Orbit** is a very essential and important part of your Chi Kung practice. **The Micro Cosmic Orbit** is developing and refining the energy that circulates inside the torso. Prior to learning and practicing **The Micro Cosmic Orbit,** a student in my Chi Kung system has to perfect **Inside Air**. **Inside Air**, as I have mentioned before, is absolutely essential prerequisite and it's already set in order, in a priority fashion.

<u>**If you don't know how to do "Inside Air,"
do not attempt to practice The Micro Cosmic Orbit.**</u>

We will now learn **The Micro Cosmic Orbit**.

The term **Ten Step Cycle**™ is my own idea. The reason I chose the Ten Step Cycle™ is because there is 10 steps we are going to be doing, each individually and most in succession.

Take **The Lock Off Position**, your sitting posture. Cross your legs, and "lock off" your arms and legs. Keep your tongue up against the roof of your mouth. Do not close your eyes. Gently and slightly sink your chest. Drop your shoulders. Take your pelvis (sacrum) and gently tuck it underneath your body. What you are doing is pushing your lumbar region of your spine or the low back outward by tucking your pelvis under.

Step #1 at Point #1: With your mind, go from your nostrils to the tip of your sternum (breast bone) Xyphoid process. So with your mind, you are going to draw a line from your nose (nostrils), down to the tip of your breast bone. (See Illustration #16A) Do that now.

<u>INHALE</u>, draw from your nose, down past your lips, past your chin, down past your neck, to the tip of your sternum, on the inhale.
<u>EXHALE</u>, with your mind, come back up. Back out your nose. Do not be concerned if you are circulating your breath or you are circulating what? What is important is <u>your mind</u>, not the breathing. However the breathing should be in conjunction with the motion of your mind, but don't worry about the actual breath. Back down again.

INHALE, from your nose, breathe down to the tip of your sternum. Gently, keep your eyes open, do not daydream.
EXHALE, back up.
INHALE, down from your nose to the tip of your sternum.
EXHALE, back up past your nostrils. Practice this step on your own a few times until you can do it smoothly, with no distractions.

INHALE down, tip of the sternum. EXHALE, back up. We've just completed **Step #1 at Point #1**.

THE LOCK OFF POSITION
(ILLUSTRATION #7)

BEYOND SELF-HELP: MASTERING PERSONAL POWER™ by Gary J. Clyman

THE MICRO COSMIC ORBIT
(ILLUSTRATION #16-A)
Step #1 at Point #1

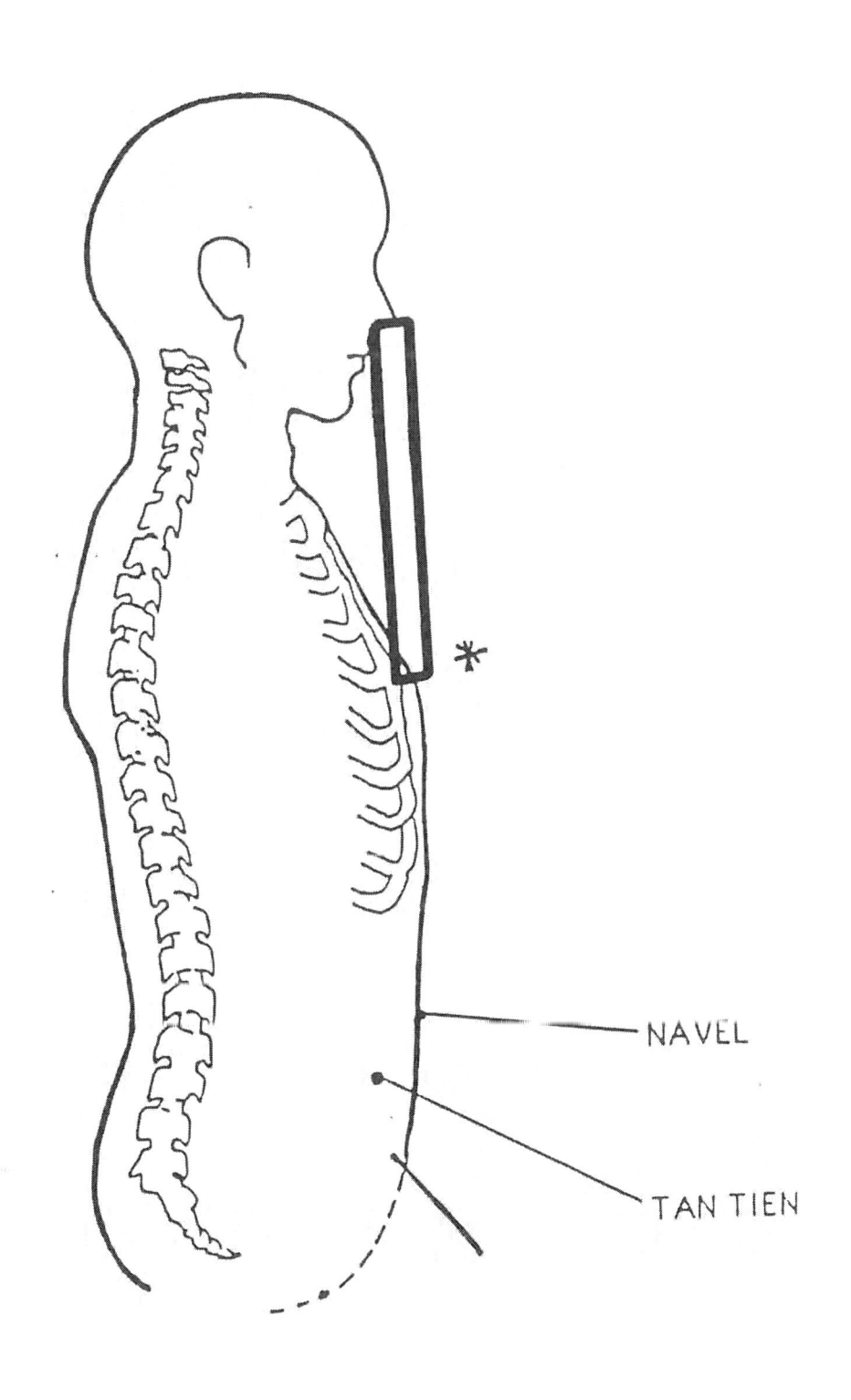

NAVEL

TAN TIEN

Now we are going to go to **Step #2 at Point #2**. With your mind on the inhale, go down to the point between your anus and your genitals (point #2). This point is in the same area in men and women. However, anatomically it is slightly and insignificantly different.

INHALE, starting at your nostrils., with your mind, go down, pass Point #1, past your abdominals, all the way down to the point between your genitals and your anus. That's on your way down.

On the way up, you're going to go back up and out your nostrils.
INHALE, bring your mind all the way down, pass everything to the floor of your torso, on the inhale.
EXHALE, bring it back up to your nostrils.
INHALE, bring it down from your nostrils, all the way down to the floor of your torso.
EXHALE, bring your mind, back up to your nostrils.

**It is very important to do each individual point in order.
Don't skip any steps while learning The Micro Cosmic Orbit.**

INHALE, go down, exhale, back up.
EXHALE, go back up to your nostrils.

Practice this step on your own a few times until you can do it smoothly, with no distractions.

For references purposes we are going to use point #2 for Step #2, Step #3, Step #4, and Step #5. The location of the Steps #3-5, is exactly in the same place. However, the distinctions between Step #2, #3, #4 and #5 are, you are going to do totally different things with your mind at this particular location.

BEYOND SELF-HELP: MASTERING PERSONAL POWER™ by Gary J. Clyman

THE MICRO COSMIC ORBIT
(ILLUSTRATION #16-B)
Step #2 at Point #2

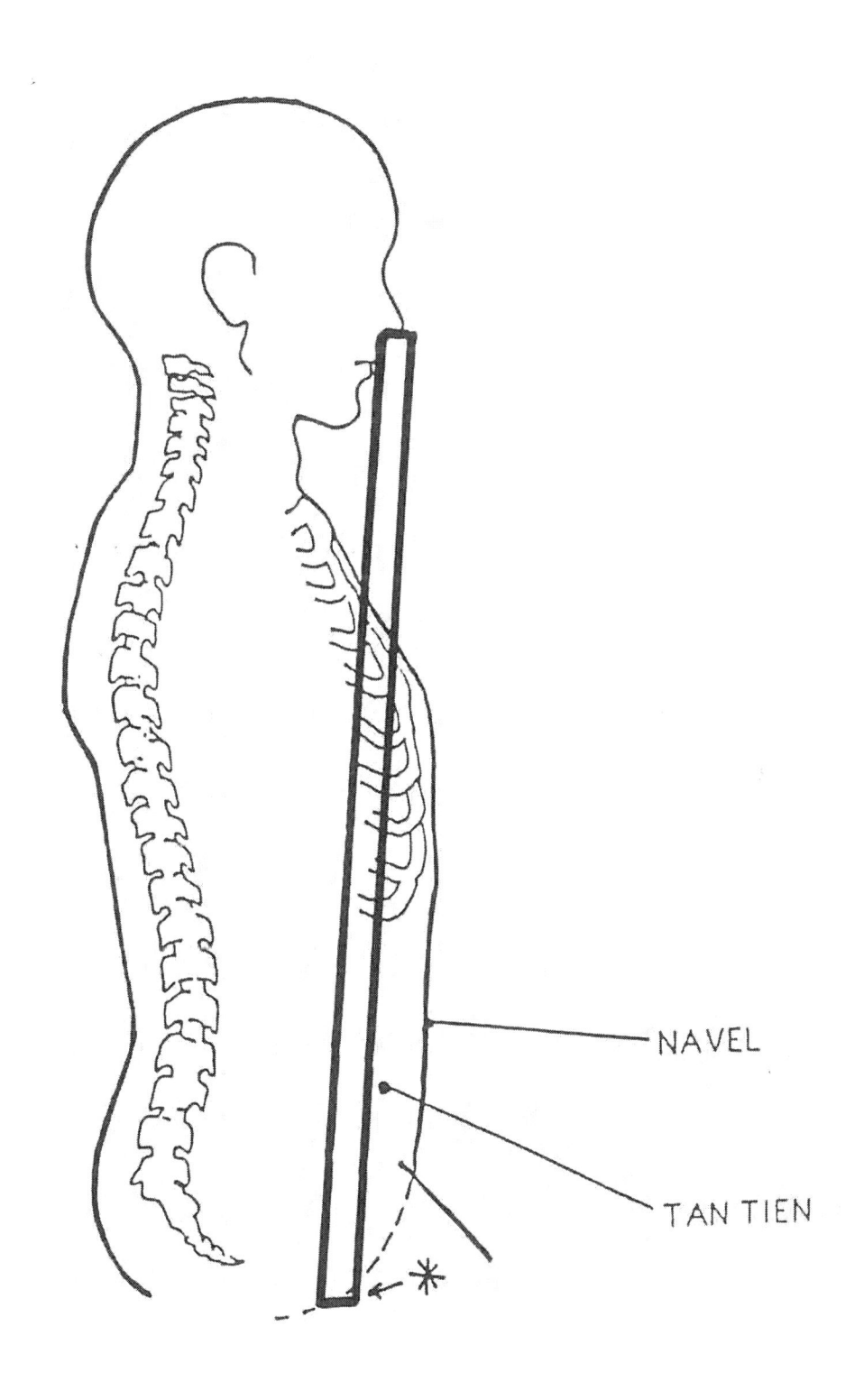

- NAVEL
- TAN TIEN

Step #3 at Point #2: With your mind, go from your nostrils, all the way down as fast as you can get there, to the bottom (point #2). When you get to the bottom of your torso, on the inhale, continue the inhale and squeeze your urinary and anal sphincter muscles. Focus your mind on the spot between your anus and genitals.

INHALE, suck and go down, squeeze, hold, contract, hold, contract as you move to Point #2.
EXHALE, relax and go back up to your nostrils.
INHALE, direct your mind down to Point #2 as fast as you can. Squeeze on the way getting there. At Point #2, squeeze your urinary and anal sphincter muscles and concentrate your mind at the point between your genitals and your anus.

INHALE squeeze.
EXHALE relax. On Step #3, do not be concerned with bring your mind back up to your nostrils. This is not important. This means there is nothing to do on the exhale with Step #3.

INHALE, direct your mind back down to Point #2, as fast as you can. Squeeze your urinary and anal sphincter muscles on the inhales. **Focus your mind between your anus and genitals.**
EXHALE, relax. That is **Step #3 at Point #2.** Practice this step on your own a few times until you can do it smoothly, with no distractions.

BEYOND SELF-HELP: MASTERING PERSONAL POWER™ by Gary J. Clyman

THE MICRO COSMIC ORBIT
(ILLUSTRATION #16-C)
Step #3 at Point #2

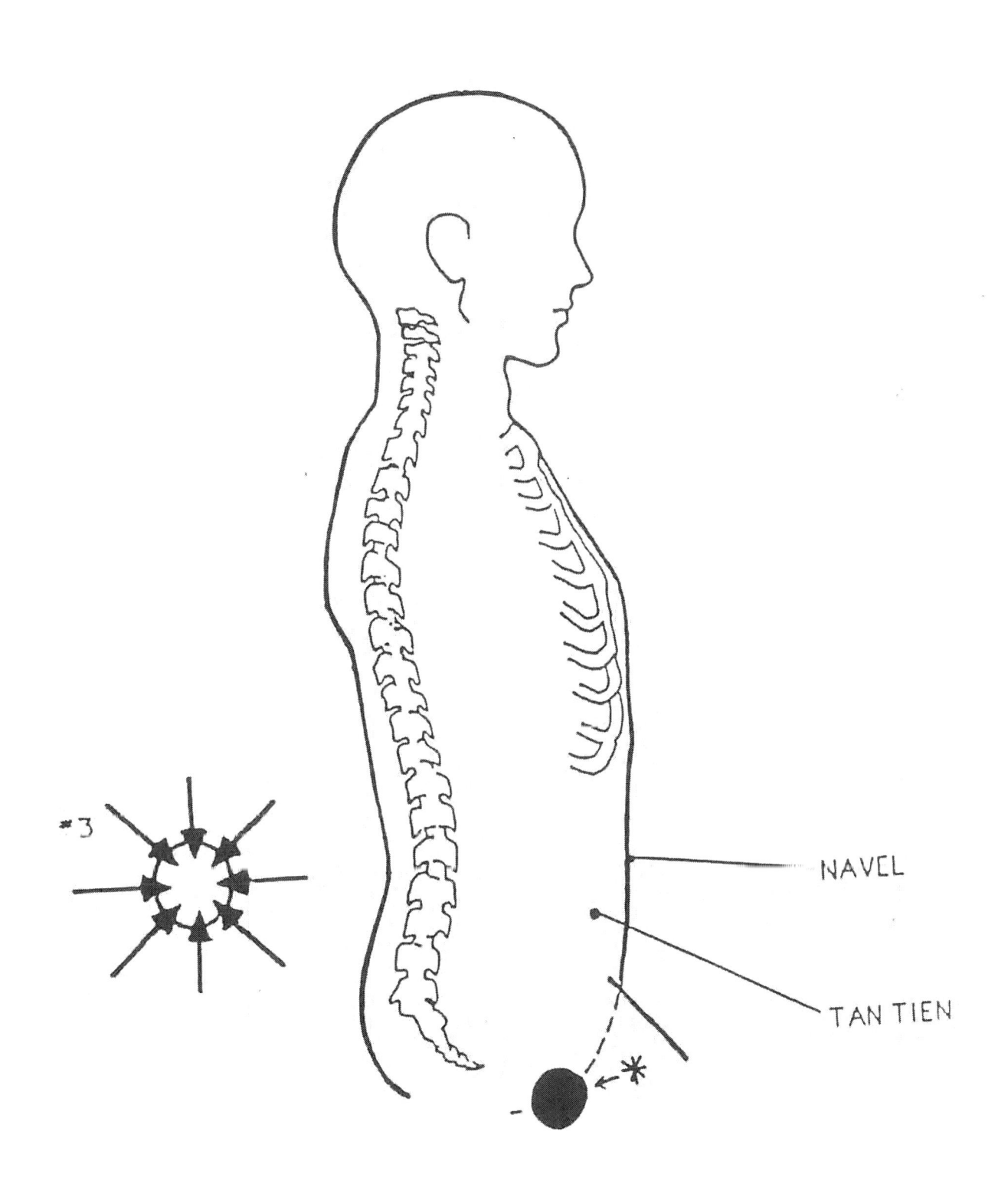

Step #4 at Point #2: With your mind, go down to Point #2, as fast as you can. Squeeze on Step #3. It's as if you're doing Step #2 and Step #3 at exactly the same time. INHALE, direct your mind, down to Point #2, squeeze on Step #3.

Everything is exactly the same as Step #3. However, in Step #4 you explode on the exhale. By the way, don't have any physiological accidents.

INHALE down to Point #2, squeeze on Step #3 while you contract your urinary and anal sphincter muscles. Focus your mind between your anus and genitals (Point #2).
EXHALE, explode at Point 2. Don't worry about how to bring your mind back up. It is not important. What's important is the explosion. Do Step #4 again.
INHALE, drop your mind down to the floor of your torso as fast as you can get to Point #2. Squeeze on Step #3. On Step #4, when you are almost fully inhaled, **EXPLODE** with your mind in all directions, but don't explode or snort the breath out. That's not important. **The Mind Explosion** is important, not the breath explosion. Do it one more time.
INHALE, go down to Point #2, squeeze on Step #3. On Step #4, **Explode!**

BEYOND SELF-HELP: MASTERING PERSONAL POWER™ by Gary J. Clyman

THE MICRO COSMIC ORBIT
(ILLUSTRATION #16-D)
Step #4 at Point #2

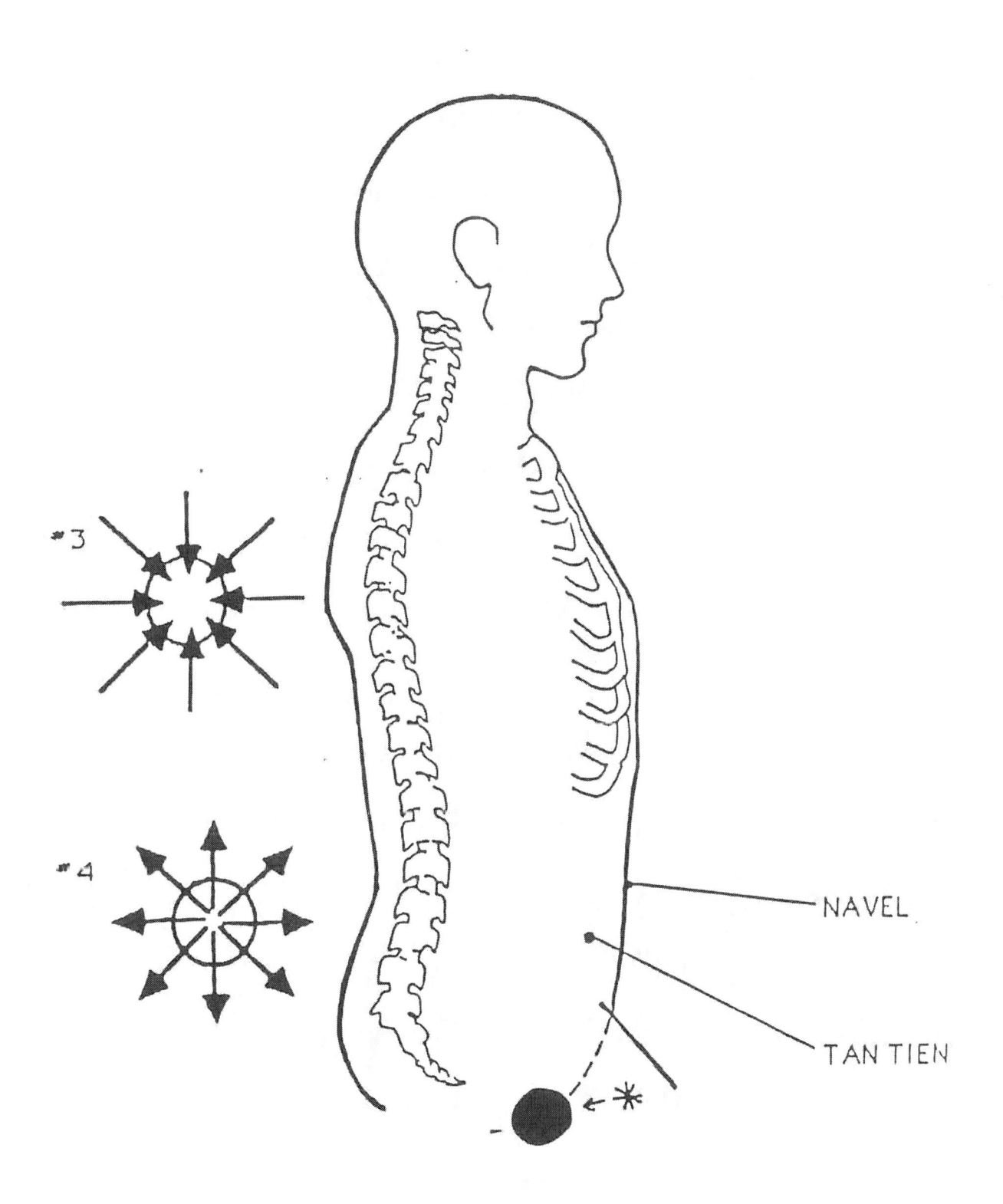

Step #5 at Point #2:
INHALE, with your mind go down to Point 2 as fast as you can. Squeeze on Step #3, skip Step #4, and on Step #5, it's as if you're holding everything in place, spin like a small roller-skate wheel or a drill bit, in place at Point #2. You're not going anywhere but you are "rotating in position" at Point #2. **THE DIRECTION THAT YOU ROTATE IS ABSOLUTELY IMPORTANT.**

When rotating you are going to rotate as if you're turning down toward the front and up the back. (See Illustration #16-P) So it's down, toward the back, up the spine and then forward again, rotating. I can't say clockwise or counterclockwise because we're not facing right or left. You are rotating over the top and down the front, over the top and down the front. If you have already learned this from me, this will be "no problem" to understand. If you don't understand it, read it over again until you do.

Step #5 at Point #2: With your mind go from your nose, down to Point #2, squeeze on Step #3, skip Step #4, and on Step #5, **EXPLODE** in a rotating fashion and hold it in place at Point #2. Don't worry about how to get back up to your nose, it is not important. Repeat.

INHALE, direct your mind to Point #2, squeeze on Step #3, skip Step #4, rotate on Step #5, in place as fast as your mind can turn.

INHALE, down to Step #2, squeeze on Step #3, skip Step #4, rotate Point #5. It is very important to realize at this time that anytime from now on that you are going to be doing any of the points, including Point 2, you're going to squeeze your urinary and anal sphincter muscles. That's an unsaid law which I just said. A further visualization or explanation of Step #5, which is done at Point #2 is: "imagine a drill bit coming in from your side and turning in the direction of, down the front, up the back. Down the front, up the back; down the front, up the back." Or another picture is a tiny, tiny gear or a roller-skate wheel standing up, turning down the front, up the back, down the front, up the back, down the front, up the back, in the location of Point #2.

ABSOLUTE RULE: Never at anytime, whether you are doing Step #5 or the complete circuit, turn in the other direction.

We have now completed **Step #5 at Point #2**.

BEYOND SELF-HELP: MASTERING PERSONAL POWER™ by Gary J. Clyman

THE MICRO COSMIC ORBIT
(ILLUSTRATION #16-E)
Step #5 at Point #2

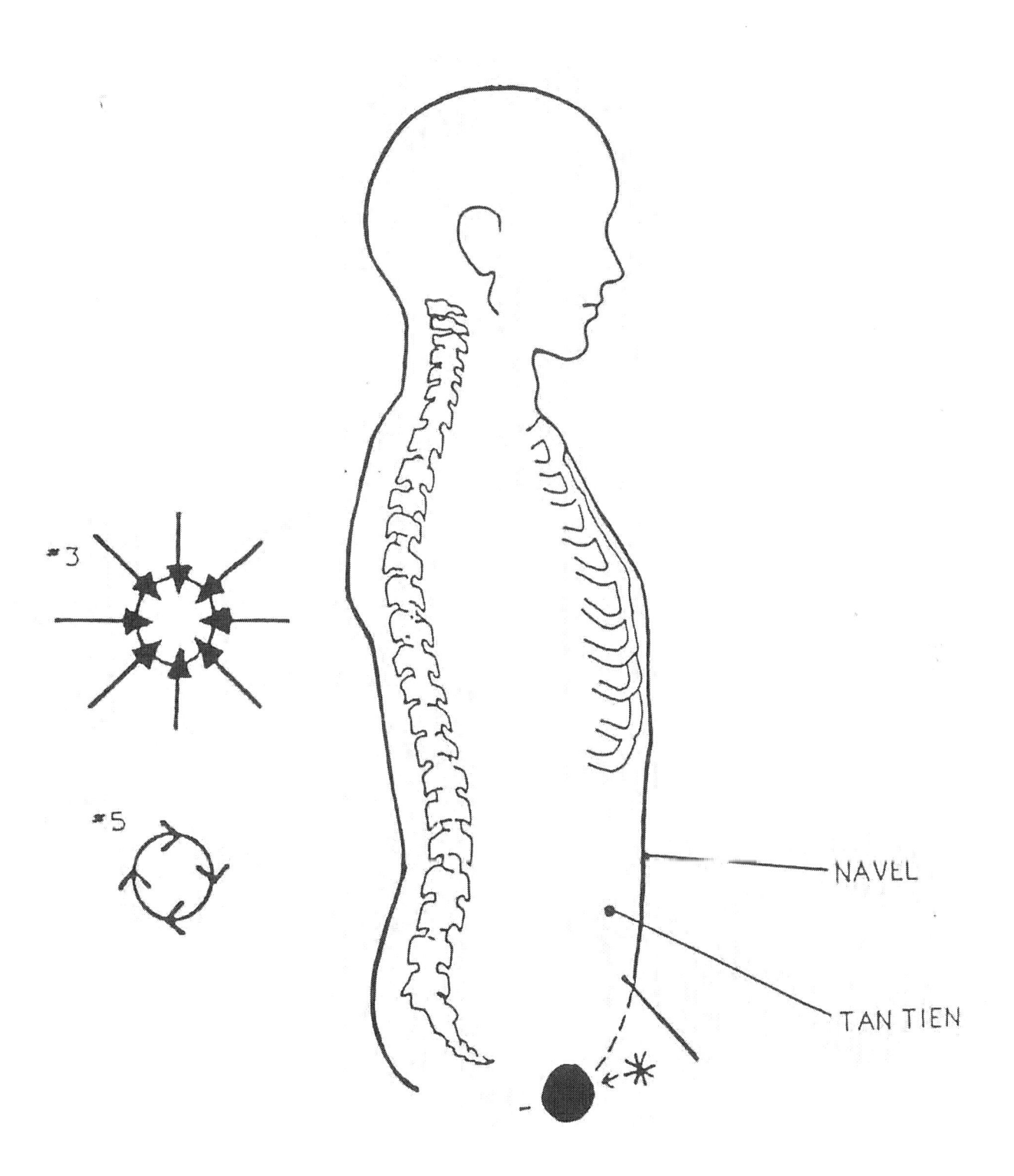

Step #6 at Point #3: This step is totally different from Steps #2, 3, 4 and 5.

INHALE, with your mind go from your nostrils, down past Point #2, turn the corner with your mind and visualize the image of an umbrella handle going up to the tip of your tail bone (coccyx). Touch the tip of your tailbone with your finger to be able to direct your mind to that spot.

EXHALE, return back down and around up the curve, to your nostrils. INHALE, go down, turn the corner, go to the tip of the tailbone on the inhale.
EXHALE, go down and around, back out to your nostrils.

I would also like to remind you on the inhale when you are going down, you are still squeezing your sphincter muscles, you're still going to be focusing your mind down at Point #2, etc.
INHALE, go down past Point #2, turn the corner up to the tip of the tailbone.
EXHALE, back down and around and out. An important way to help yourself direct your mind to your tail bone is to touch it with your hand.
INHALE, go down past Point #2, turn the corner up to the tip of the tailbone on the inhale.
EXHALE, relax your sphincter muscles, relax your mind, let your mind go down and around and back up and out to your nostrils.

Practice this step on your own a few times until you can do it smoothly, with no distractions.

THE MICRO COSMIC ORBIT
(ILLUSTRATION #16-F)
Step #6 at Point #3

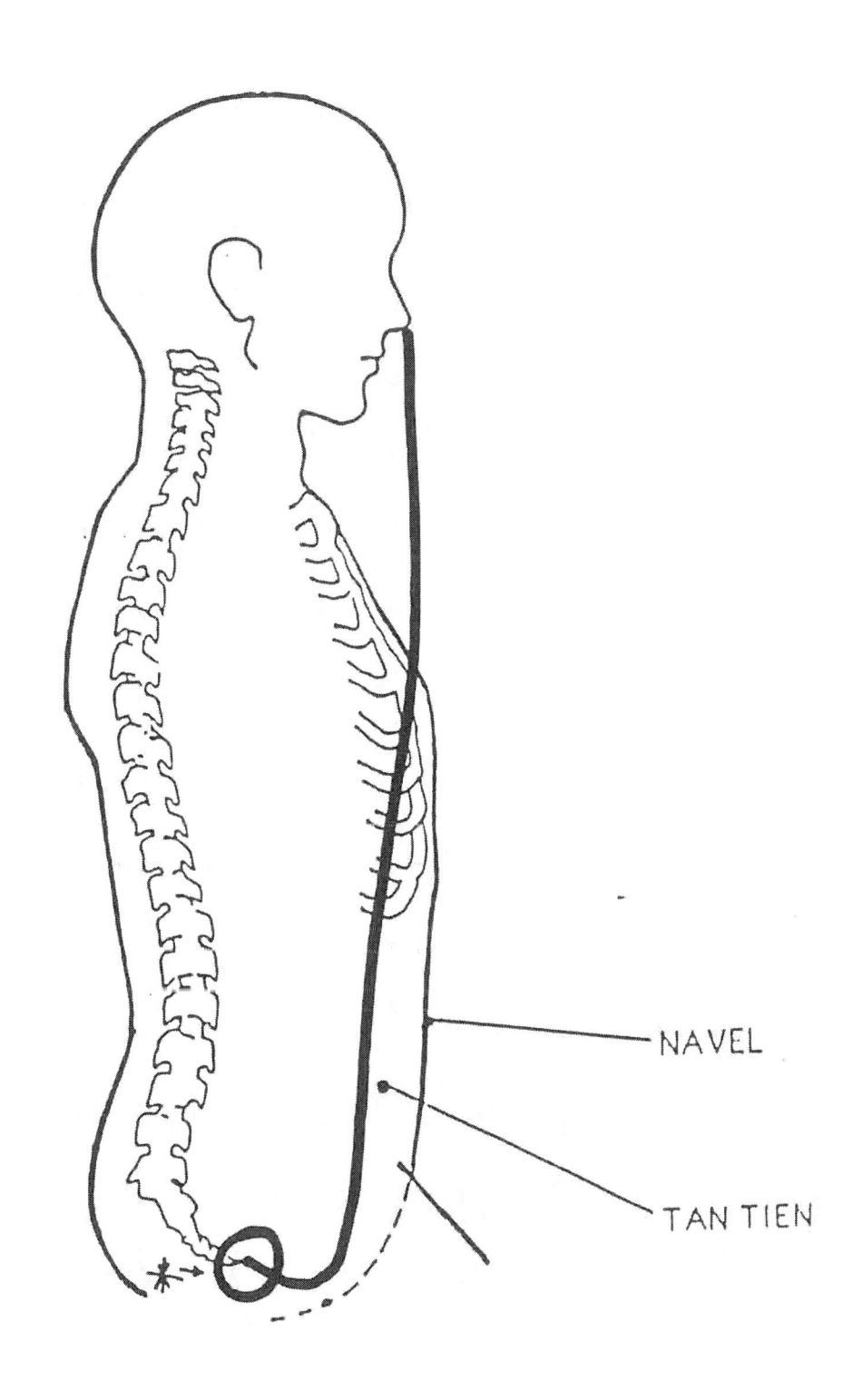

— NAVEL

— TAN TIEN

Step #7 at Point #4: With your mind go from your nose as you inhale, down and around, down to Point #2. Turn the corner and pass your tailbone. Go to an area on your lumbar spine even with your navel (Approx. L2) on the spine. That's Point #7. INHALE, Drop down past Point #2 and turn the corner and go past your tailbone all the way to around to even with your navel level on your spine. EXHALE, go back down around the umbrella handle, turn the corner, go back and up to your nostrils.

Repeat **Step #7 at Point #4** one more time.

INHALE, with your mind, start at your nostrils go down to Point #2. Turn the corner without hesitation, pass Point #6, and go up to Point #7 which is even with your navel on your lumbar spine.

EXHALE, go down and around and back out up to your nostrils, with your mind.

NOTE: What you want to do is you want to travel with your mind as fast as you humanly can. We're not trying to stop anywhere except for the destination. We are not "sightseeing" when we practice this. We are passing right through the whole circuit to the point of destination and we're going back down and around in return.

BEYOND SELF-HELP: MASTERING PERSONAL POWER™ by Gary J. Clyman

THE MICRO COSMIC ORBIT
(ILLUSTRATION #16-G)
Step #7 at Point #4

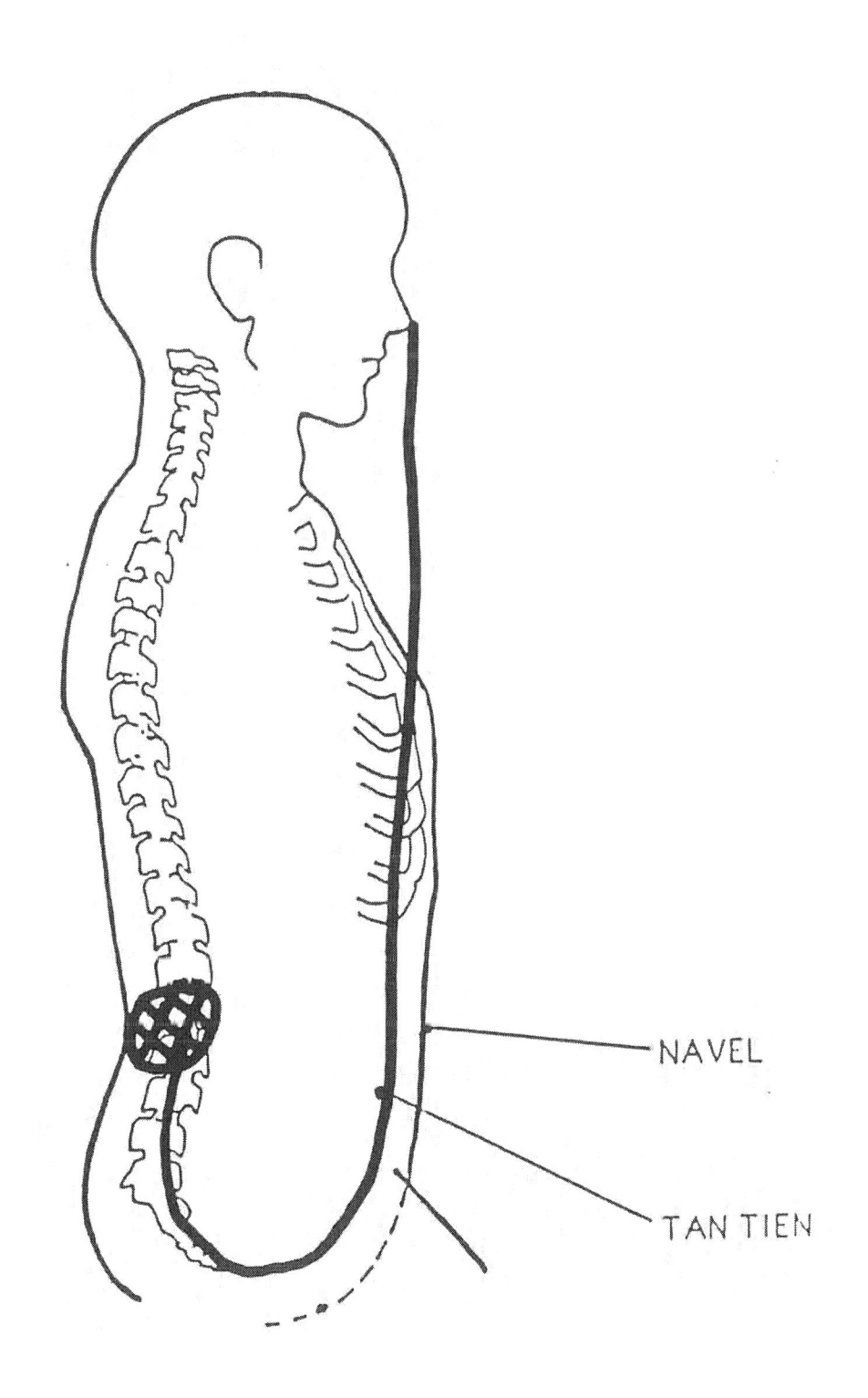

- NAVEL
- TAN TIEN

Permanent Step #8 at Point #5: The reason I am putting Temporary Step #8 in here is only for practice purposes. In my experience as a teacher over the many years, I have found that people sometimes have trouble "closing the circuit" from Point #7 up to **Permanent Point #8 at Point #5.** I'm giving you an "interim point." Take your finger and touch the Xyphoid process which is the lower tip of your breast bone. Imagine sticking your hand straight through your body all the way to your spine, at the level of your Xyphoid process. That is **Temporary Step #8 at Point #5.** Use exactly the same principles we've been using.

INHALE, direct your mind down from your nostrils, down to Point #2. Turn the corner, pass Point #6 and pass Point #7 which is even with your naval on your lumbar spine. Go up to the Xyphoid process level on your back. If you need help, you can take your thumb and gently touch your spine, even with the tip of your sternum.

EXHALE, go back down, around and out. Repeat. After you've practiced this a few times, you never have to do this again, except for "review purposes."

BEYOND SELF-HELP: MASTERING PERSONAL POWER™ by Gary J. Clyman

THE MICRO COSMIC ORBIT
(ILLUSTRATION #16-I)
Temporary Step #8 at Point #5

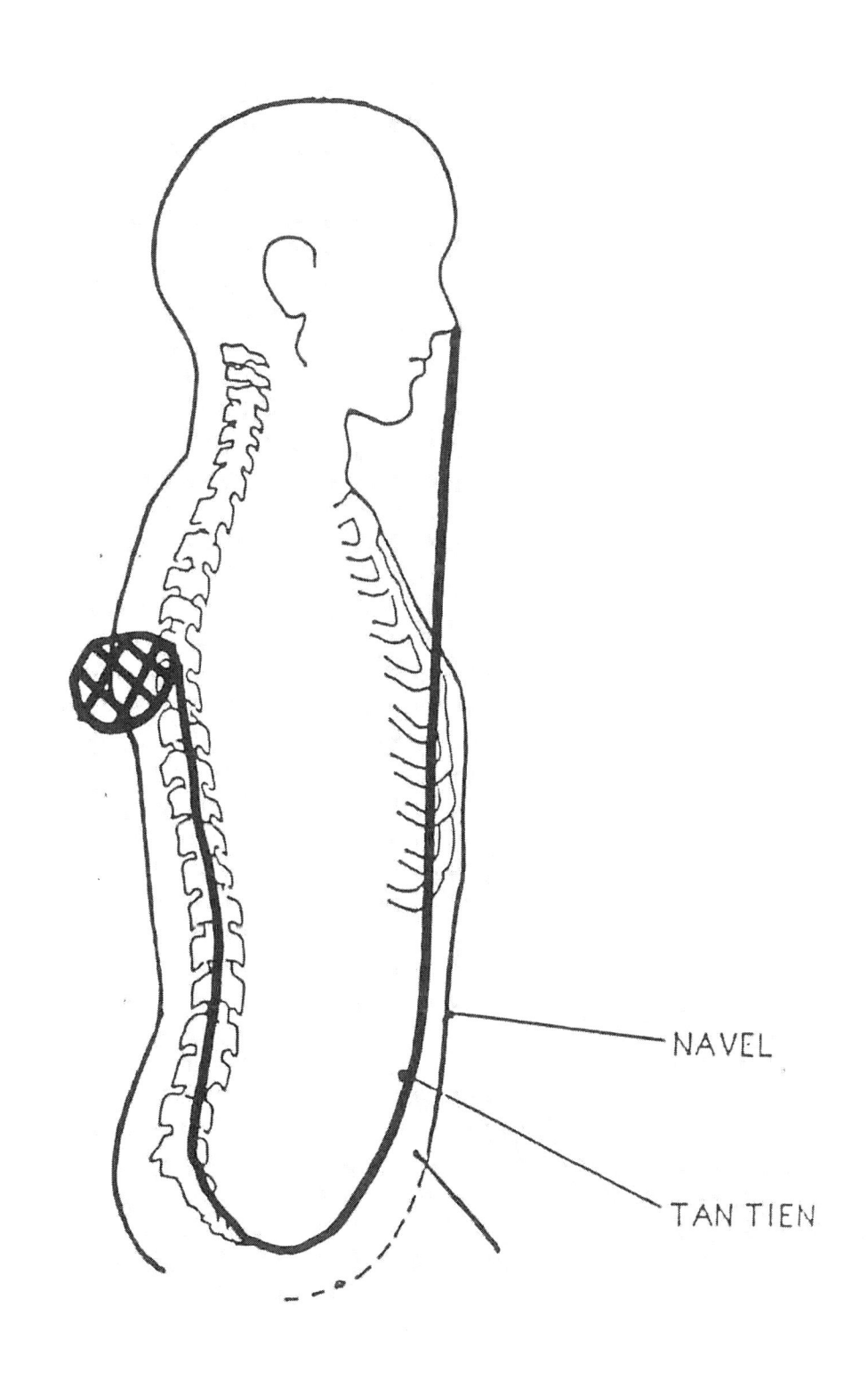

NAVEL

TAN TIEN

Permanent Step #8 at Point #6: Direct your energy with your mind starting at your nostrils. Go down to Point #2, turn the corner, pass your tailbone, pass even with your naval, and pass the center of your back. Go all the way up to 7th Cervical Vertebrae, which is the largest bump at the base of your neck. It's also the largest Cervical Vertebrae.

INHALE, with your mind go all the way to C7.

EXHALE, go down and around and back out. This is exactly the same principle, this is not complicated, if you think this is hard, start over again from the last step you understood.

INHALE, with your mind go from your nostrils, down and around, turn the corner. Go all the way up to the base of your neck, your 7th Cervical Vertebrae, on the inhale.

EXHALE, drop down with your mind, turn the corner, go back out to your nostrils. We will repeat this one more time.

INHALE, go down, squeezing the sphincter muscles as I explained to you before. Turn the corner at Point #2 and go all the way up your 7th Cervical Vertebrae, at the base of your neck.

EXHALE, go down, around, and back out.

BEYOND SELF-HELP: MASTERING PERSONAL POWER™ by Gary J. Clyman

THE MICRO COSMIC ORBIT
(ILLUSTRATION #16-J)
Permanent Step #8 at Point #6

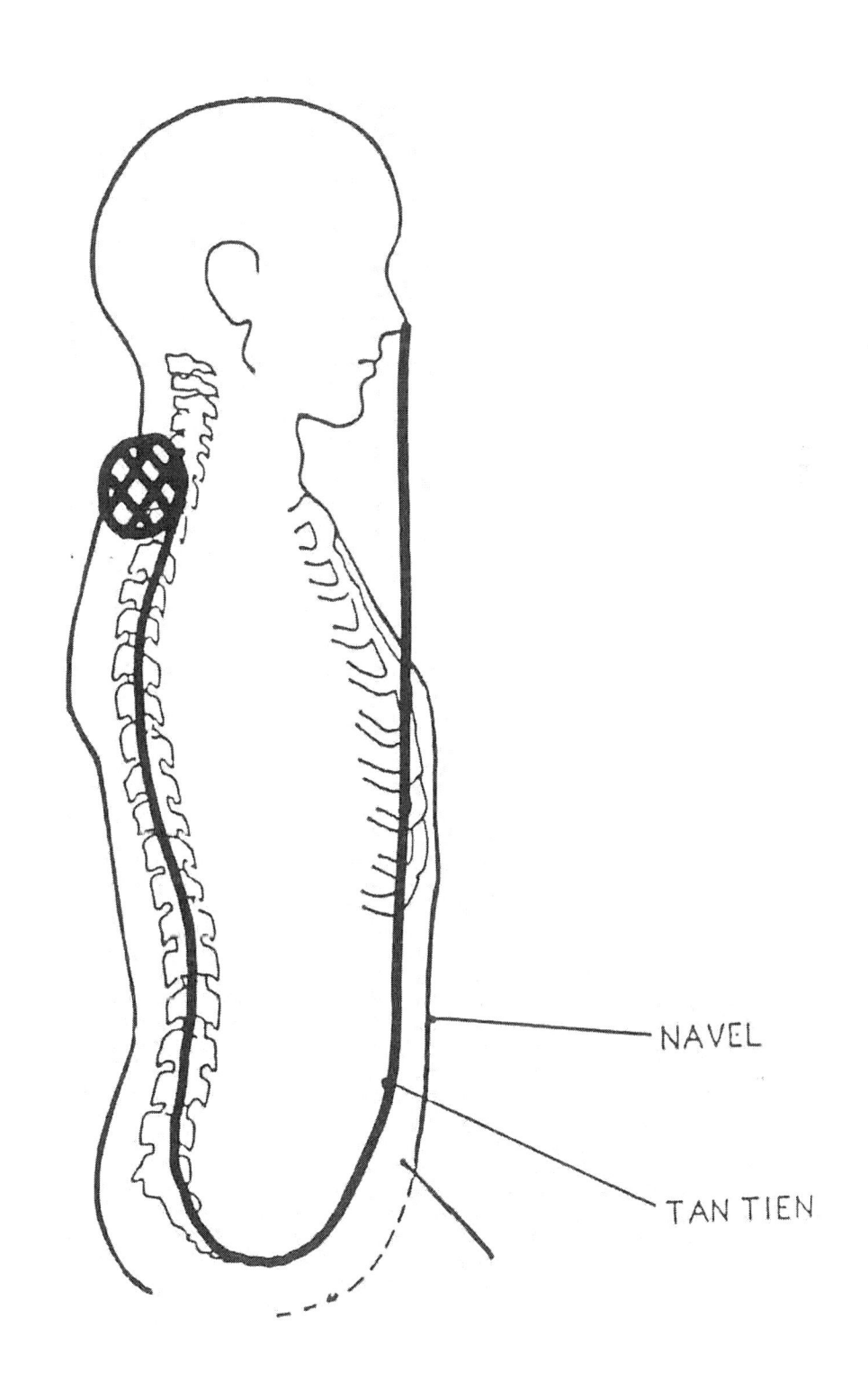

NAVEL

TAN TIEN

Step #9 at Point #7: This point is at the crown point which is exactly at the highest point on the top of your head. We will use exactly the same principles.

INHALE, with your mind go from your nostrils, down and around. Turn the corner at Point #2. Go all the way to the top of your head. If you have to, take your finger and gently touch/tap the top of your head.

EXHALE, with your mind go down and around in the direction you came and back up and out to your nostrils. This should be easy by now. Repeat. INHALE, with your mind go down and around, turn the corner, keep squeezing your sphincter muscles the whole way up to the top of your head.

EXHALE, go down, around, and back out.

BEYOND SELF-HELP: MASTERING PERSONAL POWER™ by Gary J. Clyman

THE MICRO COSMIC ORBIT
(ILLUSTRATION #16-K)
Step #9 at Point #7

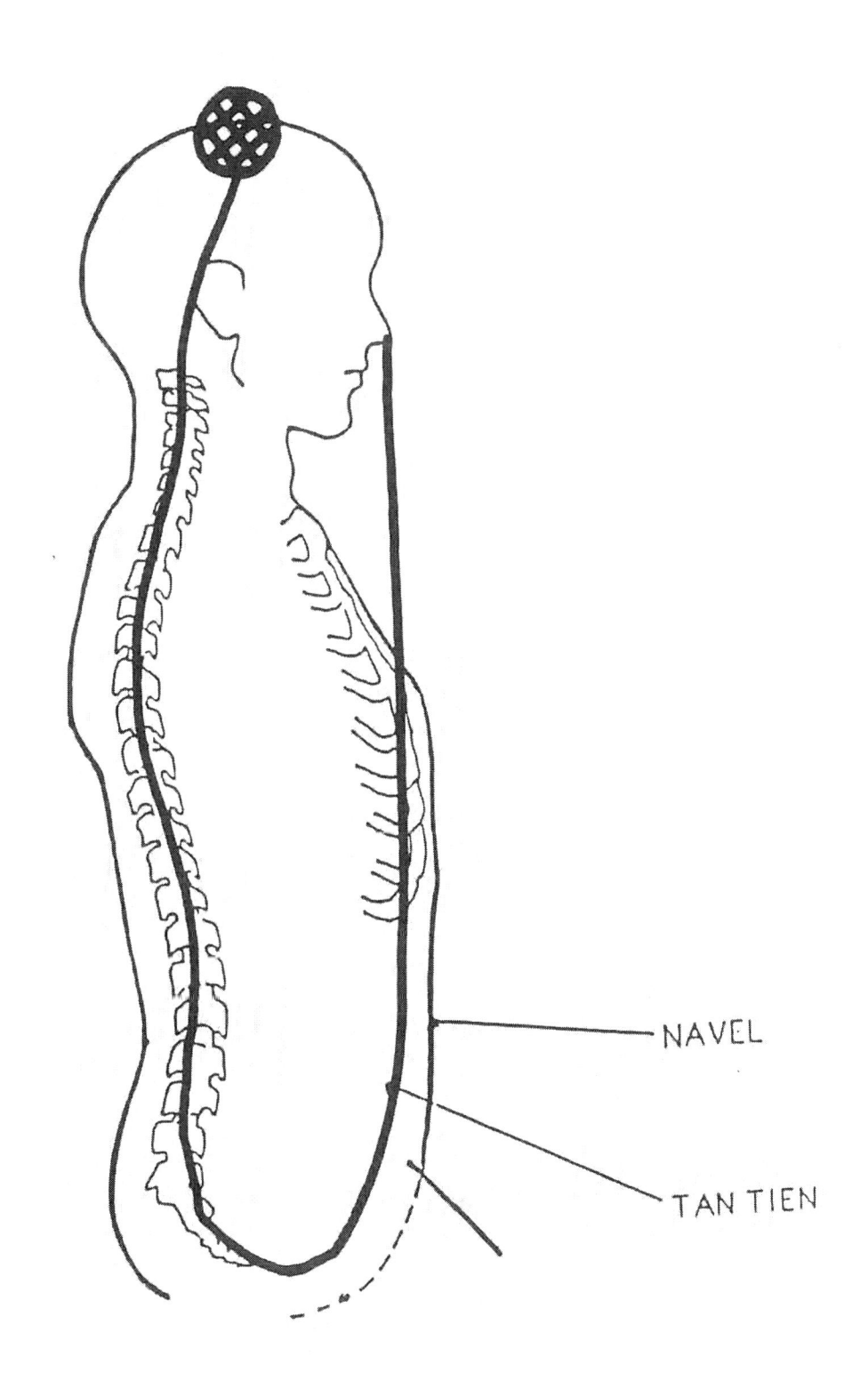

— NAVEL

— TAN TIEN

Step #10 at Point #8: This point is between your eyebrows, what is called "Your 3rd Eye."

INHALE, with your mind go from your nostrils, down and around. Turn the corner, go all the way up your spine to the top of your head, turn the corner again and go to Point #8, between your eyebrows

EXHALE, reverse the direction and go back down the way you came.

INHALE, go from your nose, down, around, turn the corner, go all the way up to the top of your head, and turn the corner to your eyebrows.

EXHALE, reverse the direction, turn the corner, go down, around, and back out.

BEYOND SELF-HELP: MASTERING PERSONAL POWER™ by Gary J. Clyman

THE MICRO COSMIC ORBIT
(ILLUSTRATION #16-L)
Step #10 at Point #7

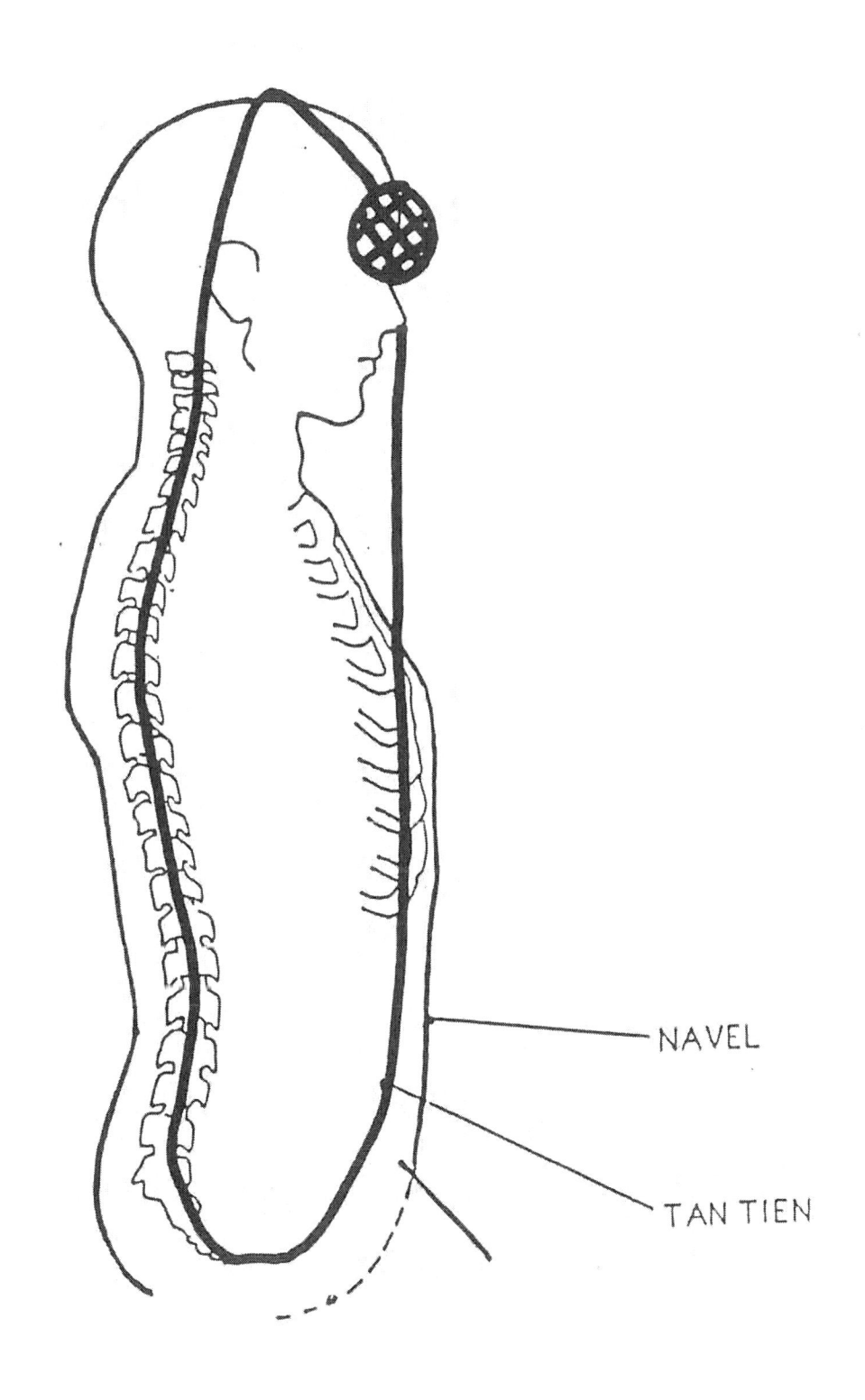

- NAVEL
- TAN TIEN

BEYOND SELF-HELP: MASTERING PERSONAL POWER™ by Gary J. Clyman

We have now finished the instructional part on **The Micro Cosmic Orbit**.

Now we are going to do "Closing The Circuit."

Closing The Circuit: With your mind, start at your nose.

<u>INHALE</u>, with your mind, go down and around squeezing your sphincter muscles all the way. Go all the way down past Point #2, past your tailbone, up your spine to the top of your head and finally turn the second corner to the point between your eyebrows.

<u>EXHALE</u>, with your mind, drop down the front this time. Down the front and back to Tan Tien (3 inches below your navel and 2 inches inside).

<u>INHALE</u>, starting at Tan Tien, drop down with your mind past Point #2 and turn the corner. Go up your spine to the top of your head to the spot between your eyebrows.

<u>EXHALE</u>, with your mind go down and around the front and back to Tan Tien (3 inches below your navel and 2 inches in).

<u>INHALE</u>, starting from Tan Tien, go to the tip of the tailbone, shoot straight up your spine to the top of your head, turn the corner to the point between your eyebrows.

<u>EXHALE</u>, with your mind, drop your energy down the front and back to Tan Tien. We have just practiced what I call **"Closing the Circuit."**

BEYOND SELF-HELP: MASTERING PERSONAL POWER™ - by Gary J. Clyman

THE MICRO COSMIC ORBIT
(ILLUSTRATION #16-M)
CLOSING THE CIRCUIT

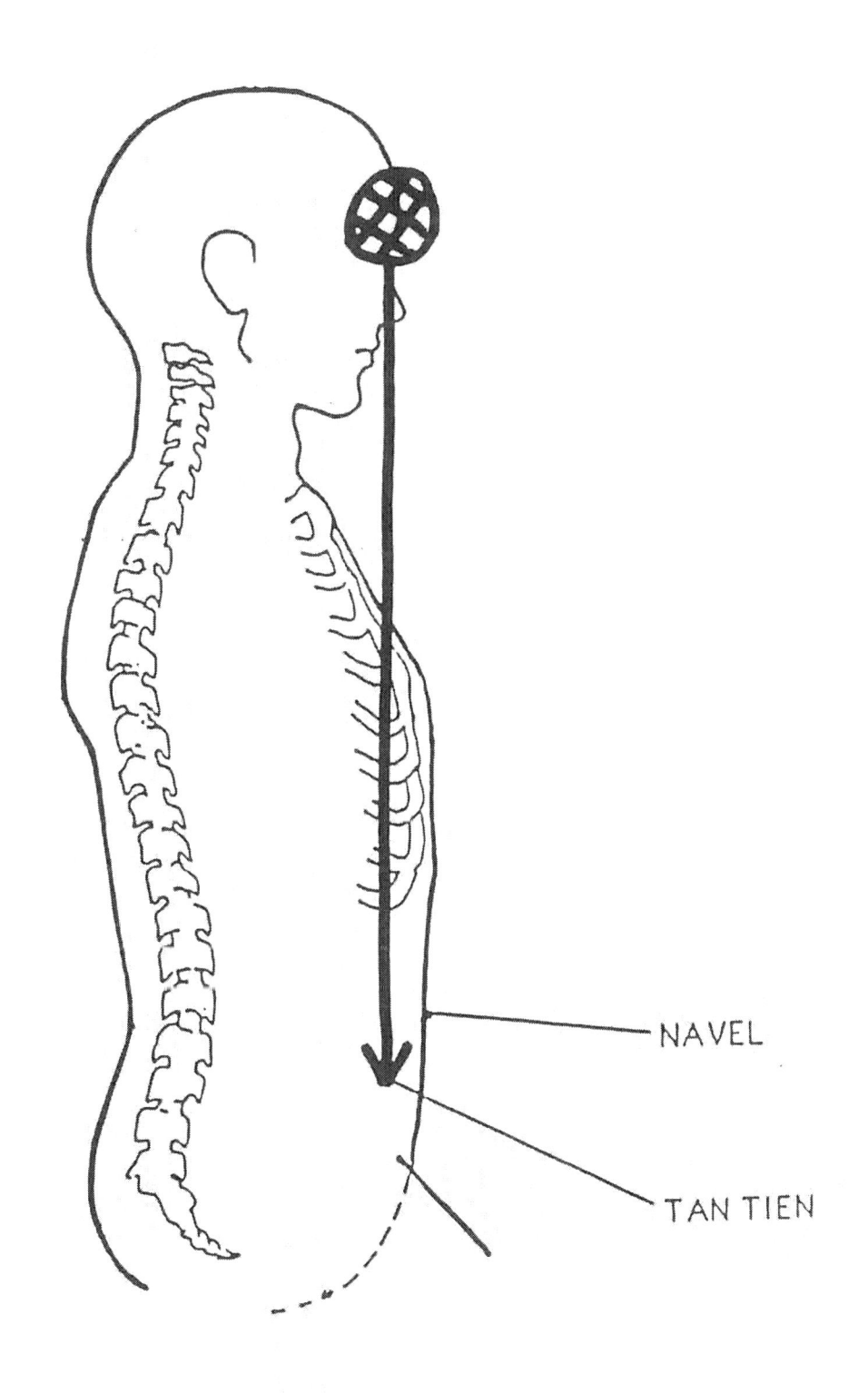

— NAVEL

— TAN TIEN

Congratulations, you've successfully made it through **The Micro Cosmic Orbit**.

You will actually have **The Daily Practice Routine** timed perfectly and specifically for everything you need. **The Daily Practice Routine** is a self-contained daily practice unit.

Congratulations! You made it through the instruction. It's very important for you as a relative beginner in this practice of Chi Kung, to make sure you understand all your essentials. If you're not sure, go back and review.

Heaven and Earth Meditation, Your Daily Affirmations, Your Visualizations, Projecting/Impregnating the Universe, and Layered Condensing are all performed at the tail end of **The Daily Practice Routine**. We have now completed Lessons #1, 2, 3, and 4. **The Daily Practice Routine** will combine the first 4 lessons into a simple, concise, and streamlined format.

Remember: Masters are made in the beginning, not in the end!

BEYOND SELF-HELP: MASTERING PERSONAL POWER™ by Gary J. Clyman

THE MICRO COSMIC ORBIT
(ILLUSTRATION #16-N)
FINAL INHALE

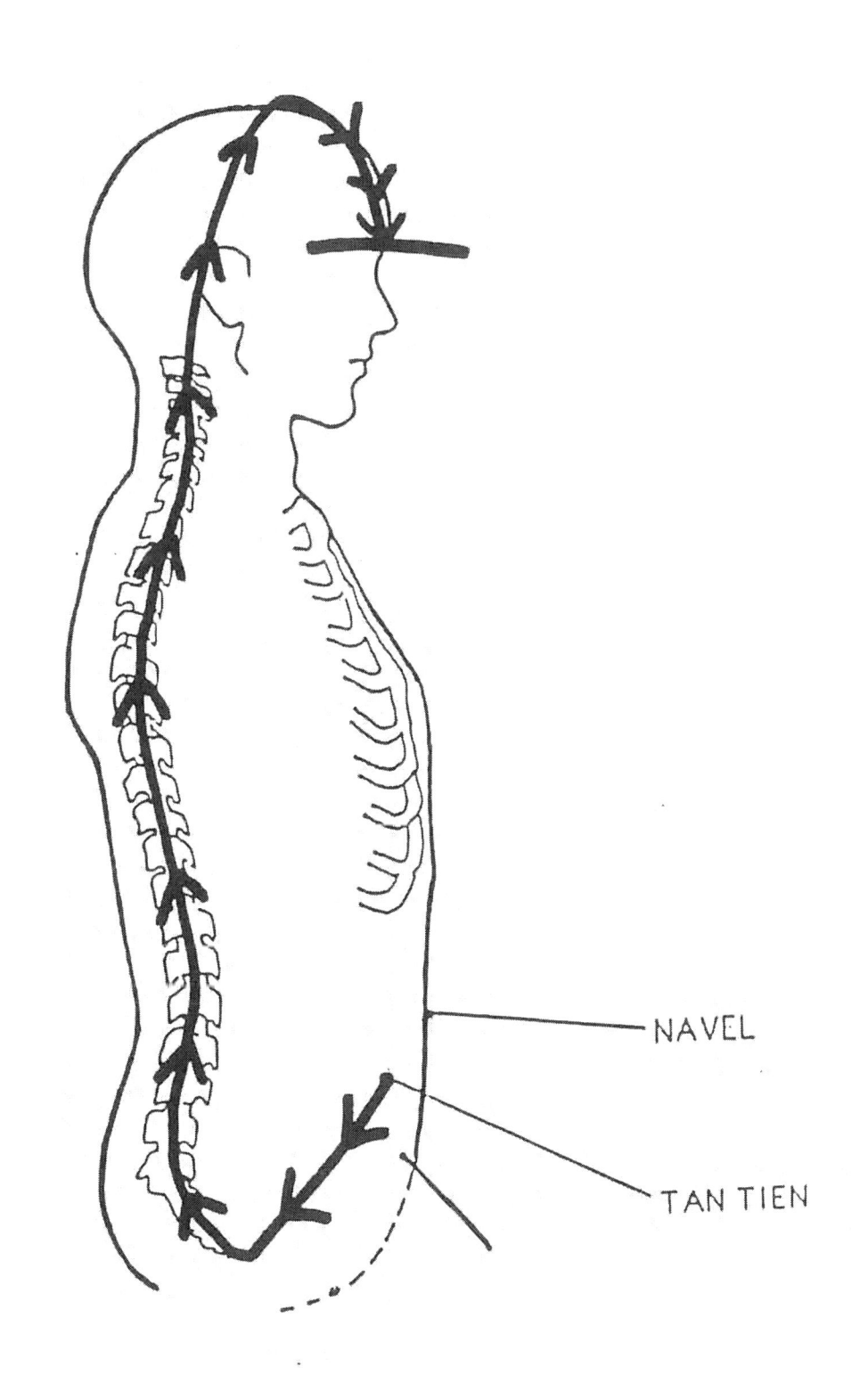

— NAVEL

— TAN TIEN

BEYOND SELF-HELP: MASTERING PERSONAL POWER™ by Gary J. Clyman

THE MICRO COSMIC ORBIT
(ILLUSTRATION #16-0)
FINAL EXHALE

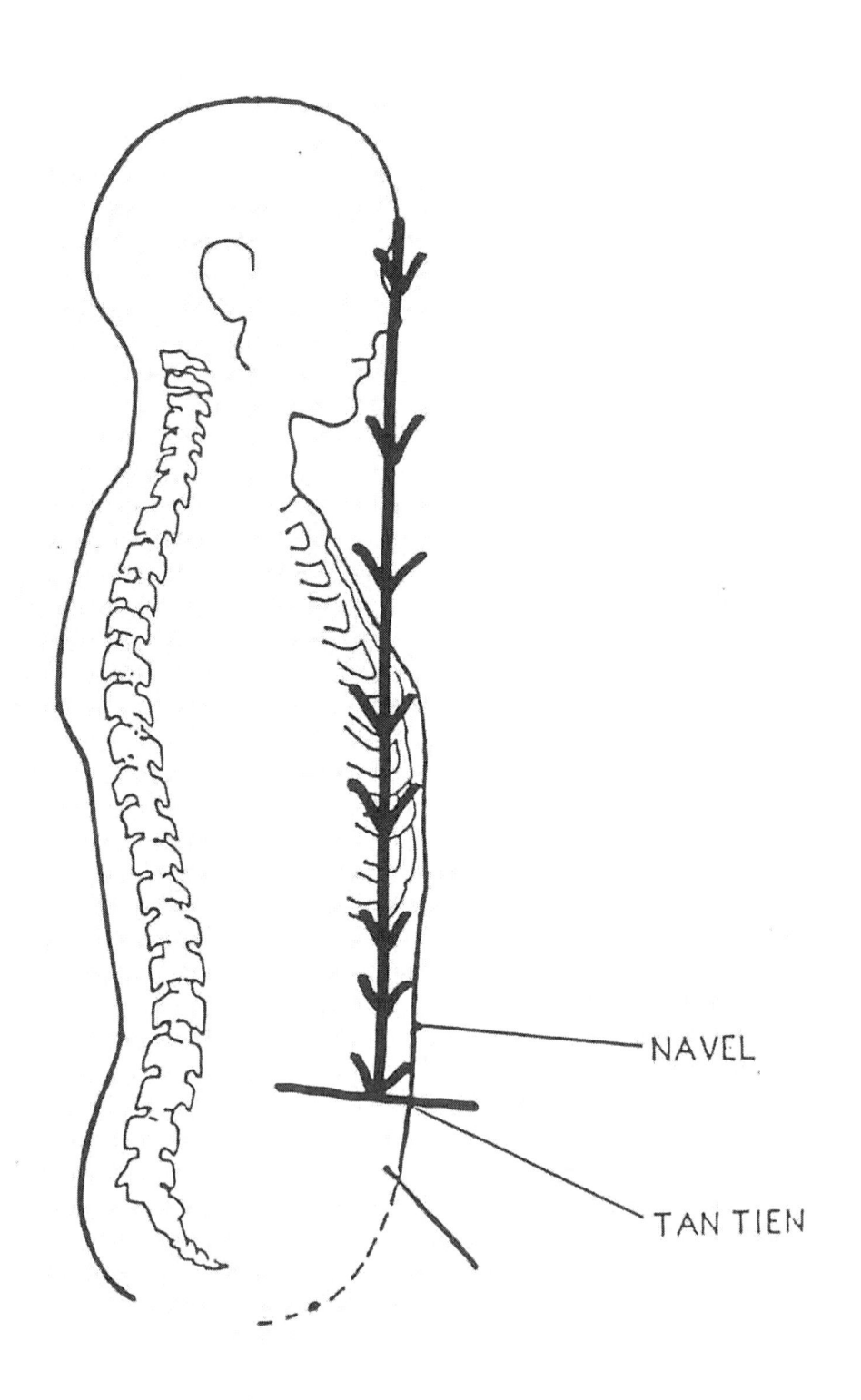

— NAVEL

— TAN TIEN

BEYOND SELF-HELP: MASTERING PERSONAL POWER™ by Gary J. Clyman

THE MICRO COSMIC ORBIT
(ILLUSTRATION #16-P)
ALL FOLLOWING TOTAL CIRCULATIONS

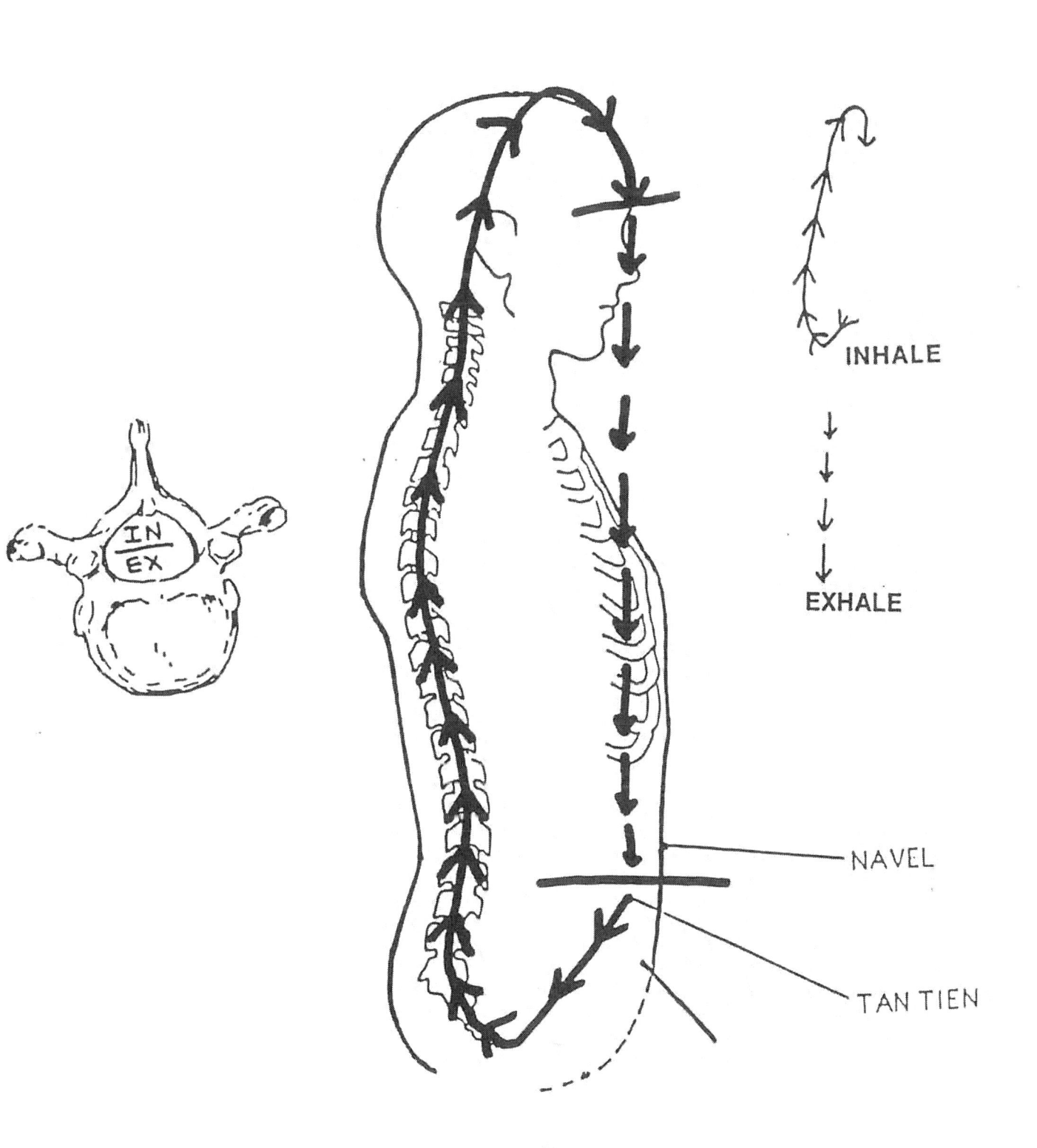

INHALE

EXHALE

NAVEL

TAN TIEN

BEYOND SELF-HELP: MASTERING PERSONAL POWER™ by Gary J. Clyman

LESSON #5

THE DAILY PRACTICE ROUTINE OUTLINE

The beginning and the first part of **THE DAILY PRACTICE ROUTINE** is done in a standing position.

> **Important note: Each new version of each technique replaces each old technique. Make sure you know each part well before you construct The Daily Practice Routine.**

1) <u>CONDENSING BREATHING</u> - STANDING

Done in a horse stance. Draw into your Stickman from all 4 directions. Keep your mind in Tan Tien, 3 inches below your naval and 2 inches inside. (See Illustrations #3A & 3B)

2) <u>BASIC PATH TRAINING</u> - STANDING

    A.   Upward and Downward Meditation (See Illustrations #4A & 4B)

Draw in your palms and forearms on the inhale, expel out your fingertips on the exhale.

    B.   Inward and Outward Meditation (See Illustrations #5A & 5B)

Draw in your palms and forearms on the inhale, expel out your fingertips on the exhale.

    C.   Tai Chi Stance Meditation (See Illustrations #6A & 6B)

Hold your arms at should height with your fingertips facing each other. Keep your palms facing your chest with your shoulders dropped and relaxed.

This is the second part of The Daily Practice Routine. It should be done in a sitting in The Lock Off Position, on a meditation cushion or a chair.

3) <u>INSIDE AIR</u> - SITTING (See Illustration #7) All 4 sets of details are listed. When practicing, add each level of details to each existing level.

Detail #1 - Short inhale followed by a long inhale. Short exhale followed by a long exhale.
Detail #2 - On the inhale, direct your mind, up through the ceiling. On the exhale, direct your mind, down through the floor.
Detail #3 - On the inhale, pull your diaphragm like a guitar string and let it go immediately. On the exhale, don't do it.
Detail #4 - On the inhale, squeeze your urinary and anal sphincter muscles. On the exhale, don't do anything. **<u>SQUEEZE ON THE INHALE ONLY.</u>**

BEYOND SELF-HELP: MASTERING PERSONAL POWER™ by Gary J. Clyman

4) <u>SITTING FORMS WITH THE MIND TRAINING (CHI CIRCULATIONS)</u>
(AKA - 6 FORMS AND 7 CIRCULATIONS™)

    1. Bow Fists: Draw in through the knees on the inhale and expel out through the right fist on the exhale. (See Illustration #8)

    2. Tai Chi Ball Meditation: 1) Draw in through the knees on the inhale, expel out, and into the spine on the exhale. 2) After you can do this well, expel out through "your third eye," the spot between your eyebrows. (See Illustration #9)

    3. Sideways Fan Through Back: Begin in **The Prayer Hands Position** (See Illustration #10A). Keep one hand in front of your chest while the other hand extends out to the side with the heel of your palm facing out (See Illustrations #11R & 11L). Inhale in as you draw your hand toward your center, exhale out as you go away from the body. Inhale in through the knees, and exhale out through the heel of your outgoing hand.

    4. Forward Fan Through Back: (See Illustrations #12R & 12L) Begin in **The Prayer Hands Position** (See Illustration #10A). Keep one hand in front of your chest while the other hand extend out toward the front, with the heel of your palm facing forward. Inhale in as you draw your hand in toward your center, exhale out as you go away from the body. Inhale in through the knees, and exhale out through the heel of your outgoing hand.

    5. Double Hands, Down and Out: (See Illustrations #13A, 13B, 13C & 13D) Draw in through your palms and kneecaps simultaneously on the inhale. Expel out through your palms as your hands go down and out at your sides, as you exhale.

    6. Double Hands, Up and Out: (See Illustrations #14A, 14B, 14C) Draw in through your palms and kneecaps simultaneously on the inhale. Expel out through your finger tips as your hands go up and out at your sides.

5) <u>PALMS ON KNEES WITH CHI CIRCULATION</u> (See Illustration #15)
As you sit in the cross legged posture, gently place the palms of your hands on your kneecaps. On the Inhale, draw in through your knees. On the exhale, expel out through the palms of your hands. Keep your palms on your knees at all times. This should be practiced like "a closed circuit."

6) <u>STILLNESS SITTING WITH CONDENSING</u>

    A. The Micro Cosmic Orbit: This is practiced in **The Lock Off Position** (See Illustration #7). Just practice **The Total Circulation**, not each step (See Illustrations #16A-P).

    B. Heaven and Earth Meditation: (See Illustrations #17A & 17B) (AKA - Twin Tornadoes, The Hour Glass, or Double Funnels Meditation). The is also practiced in The Lock Off Position.

INHALE, draw in from the top funnel from Heaven while drawing in from the bottom funnel from Earth.

EXHALE, mix the two different energies and "blow out" the top and the bottom funnels. Spend as much time as you need.

BEYOND SELF-HELP: MASTERING PERSONAL POWER™ by Gary J. Clyman

HEAVEN AND EARTH MEDITATION
(ILLUSTRATION #17A)

BEYOND SELF-HELP: MASTERING PERSONAL POWER™ by Gary J. Clyman

C. Creating _Your_ Daily Affirmations: This is also practiced in **The Lock Off Position** add while practicing Heaven and Earth Meditation. These will vary with each person. Use the affirmations that best suit your needs. Practice every day! This will become part of your Prosperity Training. Perform _Your_ Daily Affirmations, both on the inhale and on the exhale. (See Illustrations #17A & 17B)

D. Creating _Your_ Daily Visions: This is also practiced in **The Lock Off Position** add while practicing Heaven and Earth Meditation. This is extremely individualized to each persons needs. This is the place in Your Daily Practice Routine where you create and see your world exactly the way you want it. This is one of the most important steps in creating a constructive, permanent change. Your Vision Creation Practice will keep evolving as your practice grows. Perform _Your_ Daily Visions, both on the inhale and on the exhale. (See Illustrations #17A & 17B)

E. Projecting _Your_ WILL / Impregnating the Universe: This is a technique that combines Condensing Breathing, Heaven and Earth Meditation, _Your_ Daily Affirmations, _Your_ Visualizations, and a special releasing technique for helping to program your life, environment, and future. Continue doing Heaven and Earth Meditation, except now **project out the top funnel only on the exhale**. (See Illustration #18)

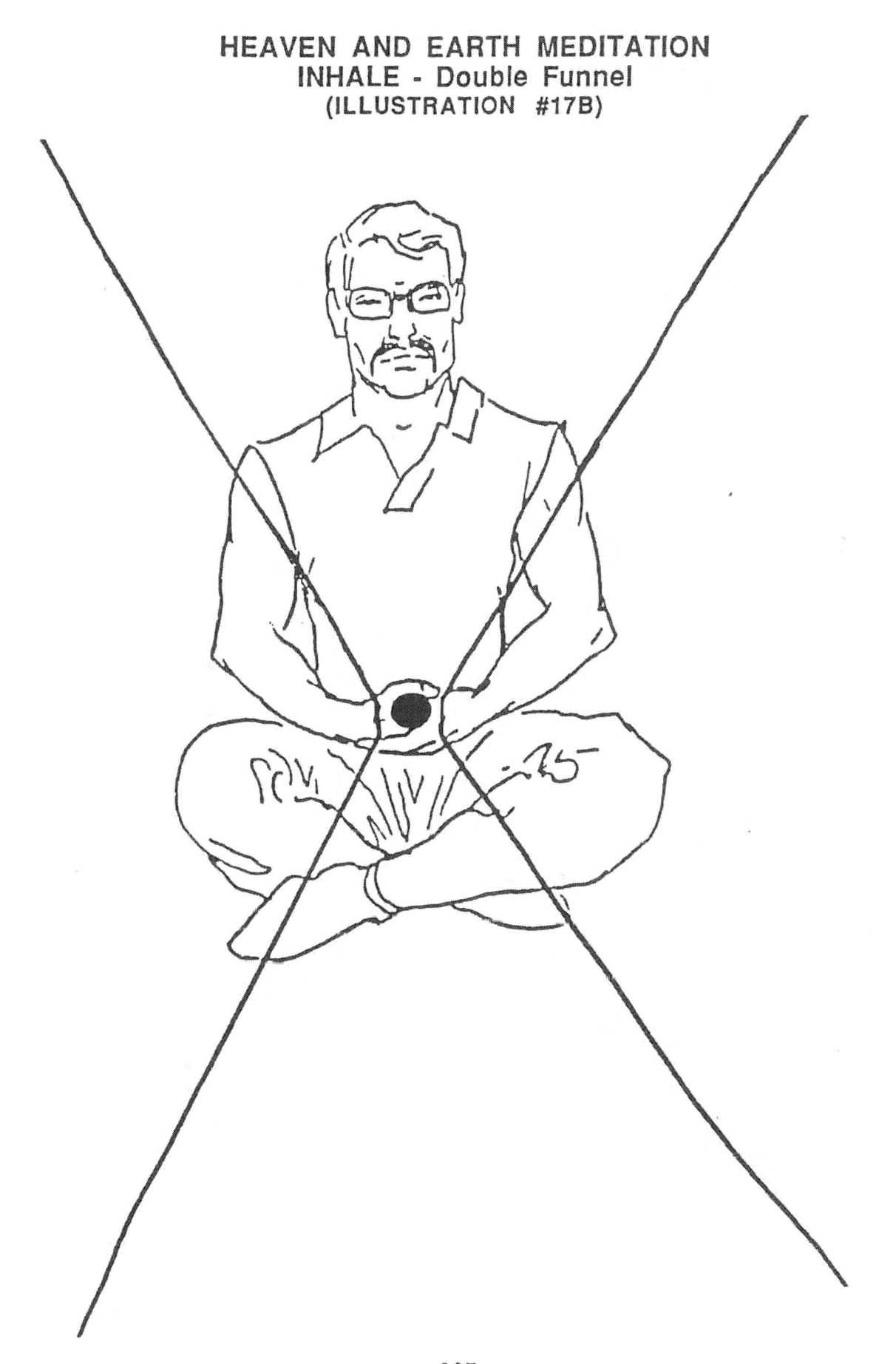

BEYOND SELF-HELP: MASTERING PERSONAL POWER™ by Gary J. Clyman

HEAVEN AND EARTH MEDITATION
INHALE - Double Funnel
(ILLUSTRATION #17B)

PROJECTING INTO YOUR UNIVERSE
EXHALE- Single Funnel
(ILLUSTRATION #18)

F. Layered Condensing: Re-calling your WILL. Regrouping your-self and your internal energy after Impregnating the Universe. Collecting your energy and yourself back into Tan Tien to complete. On the inhale, suck in form all directions at the same time. On the exhale, "blow out" in all directions at the same time, except for the last exhale. On the last exhale, only let the air out, not your energy or your WILL. (See Illustration #19)

BEYOND SELF-HELP: MASTERING PERSONAL POWER™ by Gary J. Clyman

LAYERED CONDENSING
-INHALE ONLY-
(ILLUSTRATION #19)

BEYOND SELF-HELP: MASTERING PERSONAL POWER™ by Gary J. Clyman

LAYERED CONDENSING
-EXHALE ONLY-
(NO ILLUSTRATION IS NECESSARY)

<u>Important note:</u>
On the exhales, explode out and fill the universe, except for on the last breath. On the last breath, let the air out,
but retain your energy and WILL.

THIS IS THE END OF THE DAILY PRACTICE ROUTINE

The Daily Practice Routine: The purpose now is to teach you how to put together "the format" that you will in a very short time be practicing on a daily basis.

I am now going to organize Lessons #1, 2, 3, and 4 in a daily practice format for you. This is a very important and fun part of **The Clyman System™**. If you still do not understand what I am explaining here, that means that you don't get it. You should go back and review until you understand and can do all the individual parts. This is not where I am going to explain everything from scratch. I am using the attitude that "you already know the material." This is like shuffling the cards, not creating the deck.

Instruction in The Daily Practice Routine: You can do **Preparation** first if you wish. It's totally up to you. I am not attached to whether you do it or not. The reason I taught preparation in Lesson #1 is that most people who do "The Training" are so physically tense, that doing anything while being that tense is "worthless." You can't get anything done that way, so at this point you have been doing this for awhile. You know whether you have to do it or not. Some days you might do it and some days you might not. We are starting here with **Condensing Breathing**.

<u>Remember, **Condensing Breathing** is the single most important factor in whether you are going to be good in Tai Chi or not.</u> If some of you are not in Tai Chi and I am assuming most of my readers are not, **Condensing Breathing** has very important application to your daily life.

Condensing Breathing: Start by spreading your legs, 2-1/2 to 3 feet apart. That's almost double shoulder width. Tuck your pelvis under, gently let your elbows "bow out" just a little bit, but your fingertips are still pointing down to the ground, slightly in front of you. Do not touch your body with your fingertips. Keep your tongue up, breathe through your nose, reach to the ceiling with the top of your head and make sure your chin is tucked under. You don't want your chin going forward. Then you will get a stiff neck from practicing.

Condensing Breathing is what we're starting with. You're in the posture already. I will go through some important details. Remember, I told you touch all the different body parts. At this stage of The Training, you can discontinue that. You don't have to do that any more. The purpose I gave you that originally was so you can distinguish what is you and what is your environment and start separating them. Forget that. Now you already know where your body is in relationship to your environment. Now we are going to go right into **Condensing Breathing**.

Condensing Breathing: INHALE, suck into The Stickman. Suck into the centerline of your arms, legs, torso, head and face. Immediately suck into the centerline of **The Stickman** inside of you.
INHALE, suck in from all 4 directions at the same time. INHALE - EXHALE. Don't worry about letting anything out. Just let the air out.
INHALE, suck in, don't forget to squeeze your sphincter muscles. Squeezing your sphincter muscles is very important. If you leave the sphincter muscles out of your practice, then you are almost "intellectualizing" the practice. You want this to become a physical practice.

INHALE, condense.

EXHALE, relax.

In the beginning of **Condensing Breathing** on a daily basis, the first thing you are going to do is suck into all 4 limbs and your torso in from all 4 directions. **Keep your mind in Tan Tien at all times.**

The next detail that you will do on a daily basis is after you have practiced the first line of details, suck in and take all the arms and the legs and the torso, the centerline and now center your attention 3" below your naval so that Tan Tien, which is 3" below your naval and 2 inches in. Suck into the center of all the lines that you are condensing.

INHALE, suck in all the lines and center all the lines 3" below your naval. EXHALE, relax. INHALE, suck in. EXHALE, relax. INHALE, suck in. EXHALE, relax. Do it one more time. INHALE. EXHALE. O.K., relax.

Shake your body for about 10 seconds just to relax it. Go back into the standing position that you were using for **Condensing Breathing**.

BEYOND SELF-HELP: MASTERING PERSONAL POWER™ by Gary J. Clyman

Basic Path Training:

Upward and Downward Meditation: If you are in my Tai Chi system, Temple Style, you'd be doing the Tai Chi forms and about 2-1/2 to 3 years before learning this set of **Standing Meditation.** After you have learned them you would then get **The Mind Training** that goes in on top of the physical Tai Chi forms. However, in **The Clyman System of Chi Kung,** I give you **The Mind Training** first, not last.

We are not going to spend any time practicing Tai Chi. You can do that later if you want to.

Upward and Downward Meditation: Your feet are still 2-1/2 to 3 ft. apart except this time reach forward with your fingertips almost like your elbows are straight and you are reaching forward. Form **Upward and Downward Meditation** by leaving from your elbows to your fingertips relatively straight but slightly sloped at the wrist. But sloped so that the wrist is actually higher than the elbow, not dropping your wrist, but raising your wrist so you're gently curved (See Illustrations #3A & 3B).

From this position, drop your elbows down to about a 45 degree angle to the ground. You should also have about a 45 degree angle from your elbow to your fingertips. Do not make it almost straight. I want it much more curved than you might think. Check the illustrations.

If you are viewing your body from the front view in a mirror, what you are going to be looking for is to make sure that your elbows are "no wider" than your wrists. That means you don't want your elbows lifted. You want to keep your elbows "dropped" at all times regardless of what form you are meditating in. So lower your posture more, sink more down, but do not fall forward. Keep your arms exactly where they are.

Remember this is not Tai Chi, this is Chi Kung so we are not concentrating on the physical movement. I don't care what it looks like as long as it is relatively O.K.

<u>INHALE</u>, suck in through your palms and your forearms. Suck in.
<u>EXHALE</u>, expel out through your fingertips. Remember this is **Upward and Downward Meditation.**

<u>INHALE</u>, suck in through your palms and forearms.
<u>EXHALE</u>, shoot it out through your fingertips.
<u>INHALE</u>, suck in.
<u>EXHALE</u>, shoot it out through your fingertips. Stay right in the position you are in.
<u>INHALE</u>, suck in and squeeze your sphincter muscles on all these meditations.
<u>EXHALE</u> shoot it out through your fingertips. If you feel a little tension when you first start this it's not a big deal. It's O.K. because as you practice more and more, it will get more and more relaxed. But you don't want to be standing up "sleeping." Do not close your eyes. Don't lose your posture. Don't rise up. Every time you notice you are rising up, push yourself down a little more.

INHALE, suck in.
EXHALE, shoot it out through your fingertips.
INHALE, suck in. Remember your arms are directly in front of you, with your elbows down at a 45 degree angle to the ground with your fingers up at a 45 degree angle to your elbows. Squeeze your sphincters on every inhale.
EXHALE shoot it out through your fingertips. You have just completed **Upward and Downward Meditation**.

Now we are going directly into **Inward and Outward Meditation**. Keep your body in exactly the same position as before. The only thing that is going to change is the position of the arms (See Illustrations #4A & 4B). So hold your arms out at a 45 degree to the front and a 45 degree to the side with your fingertips still pointing down toward the ground at a 45 degree angle. We are not pointing straight down and we are not pointing forward or to the side, we are down 45 degrees.

Gently sink your chest, keep your pelvis pulled under, keep your neck straight, reach for the sky with the top of your head, keep your tongue up, breathe only through your nose and do not close your eyes. Sink down a little.

INHALE, suck in through your palms and your forearms and both arms at the same time.
EXHALE, shoot it out through your fingertips, exactly the same as in Upward and Downward Meditation.
INHALE, suck in. Squeeze your sphincters on every inhale.
EXHALE, shoot it out through your fingertips.
INHALE, suck, squeeze, condense.
EXHALE. Repeat.
INHALE, suck, squeeze, condense in the palms and the forearms.
EXHALE shoot it out through your fingertips. We have just completed **Inward and Outward Meditation**.

BEYOND SELF-HELP: MASTERING PERSONAL POWER™ by Gary J. Clyman

TECHNICAL NOTES - AFTERTHOUGHTS

It always helps to hear it important details one more time.

Condensing Breathing / The Stickman

When sucking into the torso part of **The Stickman**, do not go down from the top and up from the bottom. Go in only from the 4 directions (in, out, back, & front).

The Stickman Extras: You can include an auxiliary exercise of standing in front of a wall from 2 inches away, with your mind in Tan Tien, with your eyes half opened, half closed, while **Condensing**. <u>INHALE</u>, expand your body and shrink your energy. <u>EXHALE</u>, shrink your body, and expand your energy. This is tricky but very important if you can do it.

Condensing Breathing: Your ability to explode is directly reliant and proportionately related to our ability to contract.

Basic Path Training - Tai Chi Stance Meditation: It doesn't really matter when you're doing **The Daily Practice Routine** on **Tai Chi Stance Meditation** where you begin, where you stop, or change direction of the circulation from one direction to the other. You can do it anywhere. It's easier to do when you can see it with your eyes, but it doesn't really make that much difference.

Basic Path Training - The Tai Chi Standing Meditation: After you know what you are doing with **The Standing Meditation**, you should practice for 3 sets to "leg tolerance." That means there is not real amount. Your ideal amount of repetitions per set will vary according to your levels of endurance on each particular standing meditation. These standing meditations are the hardest part of your Daily Practice Routine. Make them that way, the harder, the better.

The Sitting Forms with The Mind Training: You want to duplicate the standing postures, you don't want to break the consistency. This means you want to duplicate the Tai Chi forms while you are sitting, if you are a Tai Chi student.

Bow Fists: Start in **The Lock Off Position** with your ankles crossed, with your hands in place already.

<u>INHALE</u> open. <u>EXHALE</u> close. Gently form a fist with your right hand with the little finger side of your fist pointing out from the center of your chest. On the inhale open, your arms go apart. On the exhale, immediately, you start to close in.

The Chi Circulation is: <u>INHALE</u>, suck in through your knees, <u>EXHALE</u>, expel out through the heal of your right fist pointing out. INHALE in through your knees, squeeze your sphincter muscle. EXHALE project out the heal of your right fist and let go of your sphincter muscles. <u>Only squeeze on the inhale.</u> It is also important to remember that the physical details of the move are not important; the mind training part of it is the important thing.

Tai Chi Ball Mediation: Now, drop your hands, open your hands almost touching your lap. <u>INHALE</u> open; <u>EXHALE</u> close. Make the movement gradual and smooth. Keep the right hand slightly inside at all times.

The Chi Circulation is: <u>INHALE</u>, suck in the knees, squeeze sphincters. <u>EXHALE</u>, suck into the spine from all directions. (Completely different from Condensing Breathing. In Condensing Breathing you are sucking into the spine or into The Stickman, on the inhale.) This is called "Projecting," not "Condensing." On the exhale, project into the spine. Keep your eyes open, sit forward on the edge of your chair in an anti-gravity position (leaning slightly forward). Reach for the sky with the top of your head, drop your chin, tip forward slightly with your whole torso.

When doing these moves you want to feel like your wrapped with strong duct tape, so on the inhale, your lower abdominals do not expand and on the exhale your lower abdominals do not contract. You're breathing internally, but your lungs, chest and stomach are not expanding and contracting, so it stays tight. I call this being "Wrapped." Continue doing same move...

<u>INHALE</u> in the knees, <u>EXHALE</u> project out through the third eye, between your eyebrows.

The Sitting Forms with The Mind Training - The Tai Chi Meditation, Circulation #2: Remember to project into the spine on the <u>exhale</u>. <u>This is not considered Condensing Breathing.</u> This is the only time you are actually "projecting into" anything, on the exhale. You always Condense on the inhale, this is the only time it's different.

Sideways Fan Through Back: <u>INHALE</u> suck in through your knees. This time on the exhale, your palms are pointing towards each other, finger tips pointing straight up, do not touch. Turn your head to the left or right, either side. Back to center to form **Prayer Hands Position.** <u>INHALE</u> move to the center. <u>EXHALE</u> push out to the opposite side. Alternate arms. Point fingers up toward the sky, elbows dropped, pull your thumb back toward your face, project out through the area between the second to the last finger and the little finger on your palm (See Illustration 10B).
Sideways Fan Through Back is a converted Tai Chi single form.

The Chi Circulation is: <u>INHALE</u>, squeeze your sphincter muscles. <u>EXHALE</u>, project out through the heal of the right or the left palm. Expand more and reach more.

Forward Fan Through Back: This is exactly the same are Sideways Fan Through Back except for the directions the arms move, that's all.

Forward Fan Through Back: <u>INHALE</u> in toward center to form **Prayer Hands Position,** while you suck in the knees. <u>EXHALE</u> switch to the other hand. Thumb pulled towards you, fingers up towards the sky and pulled back. Project out though "The Exit Door" part of hand, by the wrist (See Illustration #10A).

<u>INHALE</u>, pull in, <u>EXHALE</u>, push out. The movements are not important, but the circulations are. The movements can be improved later. It is important to keep your elbows dropped because you don't want to create an energy blockage in your structure.

Double Hands, Down and Out: <u>INHALE</u>, start in **Prayer Hands Position.** Now drop your palms to facing 45 degrees out and 45 degrees down, keep your elbows dropped. <u>EXHALE</u>, move your hands, down and out. <u>INHALE</u> when pulling your arms up, you don't want your arms to come past the center line. <u>INHALE</u>, pull up at that plane, palms facing down and out. <u>EXHALE</u>, make sure you have your wrists bent, with your fingers being pulled back toward your head. Keep shoulders dropped, relax as much as you can.
<u>INHALE</u>, suck in the knees, squeeze the sphincters, pull hands back. <u>EXHALE</u> push your palms, down and out. <u>INHALE</u> in the knees and in the palms. <u>EXHALE</u>, project out your palms.

The Chi Circulation is: Suck in the knees and your palms at the same time, but <u>never project out the knees.</u>

Double Hands, Up and Out: <u>INHALE</u> and let your wrists float up toward the ceiling, drop your elbows, point your fingers up and out, 45 degrees to the sky. <u>EXHALE</u> out your finger tips. Lead with your fingers.

The Chi Circulation is: Suck in the palms and in the knees while squeezing your sphincter muscles. Project out your fingertips.

This is very simple yet very important. This set of exercises connects your whole body on a cellular level to each other cell.

Palms On Knees Meditation: With this meditation, end up with your palms on your knee caps. <u>INHALE</u>, suck in your knees, squeeze your sphincters. <u>EXHALE</u> out your palms. Go back to starting position which is the lock off position. When you do **Palms On Knees Meditation**, it is almost like you've got 2 circulations going on at the same time. You have a circulation that comes up the legs, up the side of body and down the arms. You don't have to be able to visualize or complete the circuit, if you just <u>suck in your knees</u> and <u>blow out your palms</u>, your energy knows how to get from one place to the other. You don't have to direct it with your mind.

Palms On Knees Meditation: When you pour water on a table top, you are not concerned about how the water will get to the floor, you just know it will. This should be the same attitude used while practicing this sitting meditation.

BEYOND SELF-HELP: MASTERING PERSONAL POWER™ by Gary J. Clyman

The Micro Cosmic Orbit: Remember, when you're doing step #1, Point #1 of **The Micro Cosmic Orbit**, how you get from your nostrils to the tip of Xyphoid process is not important. You can visualize the outline of the body or it doesn't even have to follow your body at all. Keep it as simple as possible.

When doing Step #2, Point #3 of **The Micro Cosmic Orbit**, how you go from your nose to the floor of the torso (perineum), is also not important. You can go at any pace you would like, whether it is sudden or in increments.

Step #2 at Point #2, the floor of the perineum, the floor of the torso, is one of the primary points in practicing **The Micro Cosmic Orbit**. So Steps #3, 4, & 5 are done at Point #2.

Step #3 is, go down to point #2, pass right through the sternum (Point #1), down to the floor of the perineum, on the inhale and squeeze your urinary and anal sphincter muscles. Notice all the air is going in from all directions in toward the center. This time "up and down" are included. Do not be concerned with "how to bring the energy up and out again." Right now, all that is important is going down the tube as fast as you can get there while contracting. Squeeze your urinary and sphincter muscles and contract into the floor of the perineum, the point between your genitals and your anus. Men and women contract into the same spot.

Special note: remember, you will never squeeze your urinary and sphincter muscles on the exhale.

The Micro Cosmic Orbit: The reason we don't exhale out of our mouth is because if we do that, our energy will go "out" as opposed to "down" into **The Micro Cosmic Orbit** and return to Tan Tien.

The Micro Cosmic Orbit: Going up the spine is natural. That we can do almost innately. What is not natural, but requires skill or learning is "running or dropping the energy down the front of the inside of the spinal cord." In Kundalini Yoga, they bring their energy up, but they never concentrate on moving it "down" again. <u>In Chi Kung, we direct the energy up and direct the energy down also.</u>

Layered Condensing - Fitting In More Than Will Fit: Everybody understands the concept of the onion and what "pulling off" one layer after another means. This principle is the reverse of **Layered Condensing**. This is as if, <u>in the same amount of space, you can suck in more and more, but the actual size does not expand, only the density.</u>

While practicing "Layered Condensing," you suck in as much as you can possibly suck into Tan Tien (3 inches below the navel and 2 inches in) and then you continue to suck in more and more and you continue to squeeze and pump your sphincter muscles until you're full. As "full" as you can possibly get. After you have filed your vessel, then you exhale and empty out and fill the whole universe.

Then suck more and more and more and more, all on the same inhale. It is a smooth inhale but you can "pump" your sphincter muscles, as a way of "rooting your mind in your body."

Then, on the last inhale, you suck and everything goes in. On the last exhale <u>keep the energy in and only let out the air you're breathing</u>. You don't expand, you just "leak your air out," and keep everything inside. Then you're done. **This is the final exhale.**

The Daily Practice Routine - 40 Minutes That Will Change Your Life:
Condensing Breathing - 3 minutes, Basic Path Training - 6 minutes, Inside Air - 1 minute, The Sitting Form with The Mind Training - 10 minutes, Palms on Knees Meditation - 2 minutes, The Micro Cosmic Orbit - 5 minutes, Heaven and Earth Meditation - 3 minutes, Your Daily Affirmations - 3 minutes, Projecting / Impregnating the Universe - 5 minutes, The Bone Marrow Exercises - 2 minutes (for stretching purposes), **TOTAL TIME = 40 MINUTES.**

ADVANCED TRAINING: WORKSHOP II.

1) CIRCULATION ACCELERATION

2) CHI IN VOICE AND ACTION

    A. TAO MEDITATION (STANDING)

    B. 4 DIRECTIONS (SITTING)

3) MOTHER MEDITATION

4) PULSE COORDINATION MEDITATION

5) TAOIST LONGEVITY EXERCISES

6) COMBINING HEAVEN AND EARTH MEDITATION

7) TAO KUNG, SITTING

8) FREE-STYLE CHI KUNG

9) NEI KUNG/STANDING

CHAPTER #4
CONCERNING PEOPLE

THE SUBJECTS HIGHLIGHTED IN PERSONAL POWER TRAINING™

LEARNING TO ROAR
BODY LANGUAGES
SELF-DEFEATING ATTITUDES
RETRACING/RELEASING
DEVELOP A WARRIOR SPIRIT
CINDERELLA/CINDERFELLA ILLUSIONS
RELEASING ABUSE
IMPROVING COMMUNICATION SKILLS
SUCCESS & PROSPERITY TRAINING
WHY BE LAST IN LINE
DON'T ROCK THE BOAT
PARENTAL DE-PROGRAMMING
VICTIM/SAVIOR ROLES
SEQUENCE PATTERNS
SELF-ESTEEM DEVELOPMENT
DEVELOPING PERSONAL SPACE
ADDICTIVE PERSONALITY TRAITS
ASSUMING THE SALE
RELEASING PHYSICAL VIOLENCE
POLITE/IMPOLITE TRAINING
MONEY'S NOT DIRTY TRAINING
BE NICE TO YOURSELF
I COME FIRST, NOT LAST
GUILT/DENIAL COMPLEX

PERSONAL POWER TRAINING™ SUBJECT DEFINITIONS

Section I: The technique. Energy cultivation exercises that propel you to cultivate, accumulate, rejuvenate, and circulate your newly developed internal power. No previous experience is needed to perfect this system. 80% mind training and 20 % physical.

Section II: Determine and harness your vehicle using the following subjects. **PERSONAL POWER TRAINING™** creates clarity and strength to obtain your desired results. Listed below are the topics covered in **PERSONAL POWER TRAINING™**.

LEARNING TO ROAR - Talk with physicality, talk so people respond.

BODY LANGUAGE - Connecting body movements to what you are saying. Correcting your problems of uneasiness, fear, frustration, and anxiety through your physical and vocal movements. Like; laughing on certain words, covering your mouth with your hand, looking away instead of communicating directly.

RETRACTING/RELEASING - Get to the core of your beliefs, are they still valid? Re-experience the original incident and let it go.

DEVELOP A WARRIOR SPIRIT - The tenacity to go beyond your natural limits, and retain your ability to evaluate if the direction is productive.

CINDERELLA/CINDERFELLA ILLUSIONS - Eliminating the fallacy of waiting for the right man or women. Compromise in your relationships, appreciate what you have, or find something better, but know what you want.

RELEASING ABUSE - Physical, Sexual, and/or Emotional abuse. The abuse of being ignored, repeating the pattern of picking the people that cause the abuse. Why? Lack of discipline, develop it, and change. Don't allow people to abuse you, and they won't.

IMPROVING SALES PRESENTATIONS - The ability to read people and present in their language, not yours! Pre-program through your languaging so prospects will respond immediately.

SUCCESS AND PROSPERITY TRAINING - Look at your world from a prosperity attitude through personalized affirmations that will be of your own creation.

WHY BE LAST IN LINE - You will answer the questions, "what's more important me or my environment, and why do I always let other people get ahead of me?" Claim your rightful place!

DON'T ROCK THE BOAT - Conquer the fear of speaking up, and the consequence that will follow.

BEYOND SELF-HELP: MASTERING PERSONAL POWER™ by Gary J. Clyman

PARENTAL DE-PROGRAMMING - Look at the rules you live with, and recognize where they came from? Go back to their origin and re-create new rules that fit your life today. Disempower the people that make your life miserable.

VICTIM / SAVIOR ROLES - You pick your position then find someone to play opposite. So you're always saving someone or being saved. You always pick the same kind of person to feed your neurosis. You will stop doing this immediately.

SEQUENCE PATTERNS - Look at the insanity of how you think things have to be done. If you're not getting results, why aren't you? Are you making life too complicated? See the simple in the complex.

SELF-ESTEEM DEVELOPMENT - Low energy and low self-esteem are a reflection of each other. Discover why you don't have self-esteem and how to get it.

DEVELOPING PERSONAL SPACE - Develop a buffer zone between you and your environment. The key is to develop internal consistency on a daily basis. This is tied into developing the ability to 'be alone' instead of 'being lonely'. Prevent invasion of your personal space.

ADDICTIVE PERSONALITY TRAITS - Realize your compulsions, then make the choice whether it's good or bad for you. Make better choices!

ASSUMING THE SALE - Program Success. See the mental picture of the success before the physical act is accomplished. The mind does it first then the physical follows.

RELEASING PHYSICAL VIOLENCE - Release the stored physical violence from your body, and experience the change in your being when it's gone.

POLITE / IMPOLITE TRAINING - Why suffer with a smile on your face? Recognize it, feel it, show it. Make it be real.

WIPE THAT SMILE ON YOUR FACE - Putting a false smile when you are miserable. What was the original reason, and why do you continue to wear it when it is not true?

MONEY'S NOT DIRTY TRAINING - Are you paid what you're worth? Probably not. Learn how to effectively ask and get what you want. You're worth it.

BE NICE TO YOURSELF - Why punish, beat, and torture yourself. Break your patterns. Enjoy the small accomplishments and you'll be better able to produce results on a larger scale.

I COME FIRST, NOT LAST - Visualize the outcome of any event, before it happens. See if it feels good or bad. If it feels bad don't do it, if it feels good, proceed.

BEYOND SELF-HELP: MASTERING PERSONAL POWER™ by Gary J. Clyman

GUILT / DENIAL COMPLEX - Depending on your background, you have certain characteristics. Feeling guilt about things you've done or haven't done? Quit re-thinking old choices. Live in the now. Avoid the could have, should have, would have syndrome. Haven't you denied enough? PERSONAL POWER TRAINING™ is the answer.

RESULTS OF PERSONAL POWER TRAINING™ ARE OBTAINED IN THE BEGINNING AS WELL AS AT THE END.

MISCELLANEOUS CASE HISTORIES

Due to the diversity and differences with each person that I work with I have included many perspectives from many different kinds of people. These perspectives reflect some major portions of the population in the way people think, what they do for a living, and other attitudes. Some will apply to you directly, more directly than others. Some won't apply at all and some will be like it's yourself reading something that you wrote.

A CASE HISTORY BY GAYE LINCH

We were delighted with the "hopes" of a second child, but when I first became pregnant, I knew from the very beginning that this pregnancy was "in trouble." It just didn't feel right. I was very ill, not like "morning sickness" but the kind of sick I had experienced with a miscarriage years ago. We tried everything possible to give it a chance, which included the better part of 4 months in bed and several hospital trips. Then at 4 months their was "no fetal heartbeat," but I didn't spontaneously miscarry. So I went under a general anesthetic for a D&C and what was to have been "a couple of hours" turned into a frightening overnight experience.

In spite of all the disappointment, illness, and fright, I came home <u>knowing</u> full well that I had been lucky and that things could have been a lot worse. A friend had just lost a pregnancy that was several months further along and another friend had just lost a full term baby several days after birth.

I felt that what I needed to do was to be as supportive of them as possible and simply get back with the program. What I didn't expect was how tired I felt all the time and the apathy I was experiencing.

Gary was doing a workshop in town with Dr. Whitley as a participant. A mutual friend had to literally drive me to the workshop amid much protest because I simply didn't feel up to dealing with any of it.

Gary helped me understand and accept the denial and depression I was experiencing and then he and Dr. Whitley worked with me to balance the hormonal changes my body was going through. There was "Shock" as they began working and then I don't exactly remember the details about what followed. When they finished, I must have gone to sleep because I remember waking and experiencing "incredible physical sensitivity." We were several floors above ground level and I actually experienced pain when the building shook, as traffic came and went with the signals. I could not hear the traffic but I could feel it. At that time, I was taken home because I was so physically sensitive I could not handle being there.

By the next day, some of the "acute sensitivity" had passed and what I was experiencing was a feeling of "incredible well-being and happiness." When I went into the workshop, we talked about the hormonal changes involved in pregnancy and the physical confusion my body had been experiencing because I had not actually miscarried and on top of that was the anesthetic, disappointment, and stress.

What Gary and Dr. Whitley had done by balancing my hormones was to help me physically complete the birthing cycle and in so doing, to released both the physical and emotional imbalances that I had been trying to cope with.

I know that my entire outlook on life then changed. I felt wonderful, full of energy, at peace, and incredibly thankful for the support that I had been given!

A few months later we "tried again." I conceived easily, had a good pregnancy, and we now have a "wonderful little lady" who has joined our family. Gaye Linch, Portland, OR

A CASE HISTORY BY DOUG CARTER

After spending 8 years as an instructor in a well known public speaking company, I have heard over 60,000 talks. Many of these talks have been extremely emotional, and cathartic experiences for the participants. As the instructor, it is my responsibility to the class members to always be in enough "control" to respond to the class member in a very positive, supportive manner, and I was good at it. As time passed, I got to be an "expert" at controlling my emotions. I developed an "impassive facial mask" to hide my own emotions so I could always be in control when it came time to make a comment to an emotional class member. I was used to being the leader; the person who could objectively set the tone for meeting and seize control in an emergency. Still, I was pretty unhappy because "I felt like I was missing something."

When I first walked into the room for the Personal Power Training™ Workshop, Gary and I looked at one another and I realized that we would work together extremely well. I didn't realize how well until much later. As with every seminar it started with "who are you? what do you do? and, why are you here?" Naturally, "leader" that I was, I volunteered to go first. In my best "objective" style, I stated my name and my position in my current company. As I began to talk about why I was here, I heard this voice, Gary's voice, saying, "Stop, Stop, Stop, Stop... Stop!" I turned to him, he turned to the class and asked, "How many of you, has this guy already lost?" To my surprise, every hand went up! My most immediate thought was, "treachery! All these people have teamed up just to set me up!" I now realize that was "a typical reaction" I had to a lot of things.

I'll never forget Gary's comment, "Look at you! The only thing moving on your face is your lips!" I had become an "emotional robot!" And so, we began the process of breaking down some of those barriers. In the first exercise I really struggled. I struggled because besides freezing up my face, I'd managed to freeze up my hands, arms, feet, legs, head, neck, back, chest, lungs and anything else I could. Most importantly, I'd frozen up my heart. My heart and my freedom. As I began to free up different body parts and stretch them out, I began to free up my emotions and my feelings. You know something? It feels good to let go of all that garbage. Less than 6 hours later, I looked at myself in the mirror and could barely recognize myself. People like me hang onto things that won't hurt us and it's like having the tail of the tiger. What I now know is that "people can never be free from something if they won't let it go." Gary Clyman's Personal Power Training will help set you free. Doug Carter, San Diego, CA

A CASE HISTORY BY MARGARET DOERSCH

The Chi Kung practices that Gary has taught me has changed my life. Before taking Gary's workshop, I had been struggling with depression and a near nervous breakdown. Many everyday events seemed to easily "get through" to me as if I had a lot of "holes" in my protective cover. I was easily devastated. Chi Kung has strengthened what I call my "boundaries" by making me more solid.

His system seems so simple, yet is so deeply powerful. With minimum daily practices of 15 minutes, I can achieve major increases of energy. Since I took my first PERSONAL POWER TRAINING™ WORKSHOP with Gary 2 years ago, I've also noticed a gradual overall shift in my "presence" in the world. My appearance, self-confidence and communication have all positively changed; as if there is more of me. People notice me and pay attention, and I "care less" if they do. I find that subsequent workshops update, fine tune, and accelerate my process of "Chi Development." Thank you Gary. Margaret Doersch, Portland, OR

BEYOND SELF-HELP: MASTERING PERSONAL POWER™ by Gary J. Clyman

PERSONAL POWER TRAINING™ PERSONALITY PROFILE I

This Self-Evaluation & Empowerment Form should be filled out periodically to gauge your own progress.

Use a separate sheet of paper and keep your scores.

> Please rank these items using the following numeric code.
>
> 10 Points = Important, I want immediately
> 5 Points = Important, but secondary
> 0 Points = I possess satisfactory skills

___ Develop more energy in daily life.
___ Develop more self-confidence.
___ Develop more WILL power.
___ Develop more self-discipline.
___ Develop stronger and longer concentration abilities.
___ Develop dynamic public speaking skills.
___ Become more self-expressive.
___ Become more spontaneous and direct in communication.
___ Control bad habits.
___ Break the worry habit.
___ Develop leadership qualities.
___ Develop executive qualities and traits.
___ Improve my memory.
___ Develop better study habits.
___ Achieve my goals and objectives.
___ Become enthusiastic about my work.
___ Become more creative and expressive.
___ Save energy and become more efficient.
___ Become more convincing in selling my own ideas to others.
___ Put an end to procrastination.
___ Develop a prosperous attitude.
___ Control my addictive personality traits.
___ Honor and follow my word.
___ Practice what I preach.
___ Improve my self-destructive personality traits.
___ Develop more personal power.
___ Stabilize my emotional states.
___ Improve my negative viewpoints.
___ Become less superficial and see more deeply.
___ Be more committed to good health.

_____ Stop being suppressed by other people.
_____ Stop being controlled or intimidated by other people.
_____ Improve my love relationships.
_____ Transform my poverty attitude into a prosperity way of thinking.
_____ Stop resenting the opposite sex.
_____ Lose weight and keep it off.
_____ Be more gentle with myself.
_____ Be more firm with myself.
_____ Make more money.
_____ Be more consistent.
_____ Become more responsible for my actions.
_____ Start a regular exercise program.
_____ Improve my daily diet.
_____ Be more gentle with other people.
_____ Be more firm with other people.
_____ Retrace and release old experiences.
_____ Decrease parental programming and influence.

_____ Total Points

Circle your 3 most important items on the above list for Immediate Life-Changes.

copyright 1985 Gary J. Clyman

BEYOND SELF-HELP: MASTERING PERSONAL POWER™ by Gary J. Clyman

PERSONAL POWER TRAINING™
PERSONALITY PROFILE II

List 3 things you **HATE** the most.
1) _____
2) _____
3) _____

List 3 things you **LOVE** the most.
1) _____
2) _____
3) _____

List 3 things that would exist if you could push a button and make them happen.
1) _____
2) _____
3) _____

List the most important events in your life - Good and Bad.
1) _____
2) _____
3) _____
4) _____
5) _____
6) _____
7) _____
8) _____
9) _____

How do you feel about money? _____
How much money do you **WANT** per month? _____
How much money is "a lot of money" to you? _____
On a scale of 1-10, internationally, how do you rank in what you do, ? (10 being the highest) _____, Why? _____

---

copyright 1986 Gary J. Clyman

BEYOND SELF-HELP: MASTERING PERSONAL POWER™ by Gary J. Clyman

HANDS ON, TRANSFER OF POWER™

EXCHANGE OF TRAITS

PAST / CURRENT   **NEW / REVISED**

GOALS:_____
_____
_____
_____
_____
_____

SUPPORTIVE AFFIRMATIONS:_____
_____
_____
_____
_____
_____
_____

MISCELLANEOUS:_____
_____
_____

copyright 1987 Gary J. Clyman

NOTES

BEYOND SELF-HELP: MASTERING PERSONAL POWER™ by Gary J. Clyman

PERSONAL POWER TRAINING™
LIFE-CHANGE SHEET

IMMEDIATE   **SHORT TERM**   **LONG TERM**

MAJOR PURCHASES   **MINOR PURCHASES**

BEYOND SELF-HELP: MASTERING PERSONAL POWER™ by Gary J. Clyman

PERSONAL POWER TRAINING™ PERSONALITY PROFILE II

BELIEF SYSTEMS

I am:
unworthy
unattractive
inferior
unlovable
incapable
powerless
incompetent
unproductive
undeserving
victim
trapped
punished by GOD
alone
burden
I am generic
bad
must be the best in everything
vulnerable
I have no identity
GOD doesn't love me
separated from GOD
unwanted
ridiculous
I have no soul
I am my mind
perfectionist
life is a struggle
money is dirty
I am worthless
I am persecuted
I am fragile
I am unappreciated

FEELINGS

lonely
isolated
rejected
abandoned
angry
sadness
ignored
resentment
bitterness
discounted
desperation
inadequate
hopelessness
failure
depressed
self-righteousness
useless
overwhelmed
burden
helpless
terror
rage
panic
doomed
fear
forgotten
confusion
grief
mediocre
compulsive
unforgiven
misunderstood
unhealthy

BEYOND SELF-HELP: MASTERING PERSONAL POWER™ by Gary J. Clyman

NEGATIVE WORDS

- panic
- fear
- guilt
- unworthy
- abandonment
- rejection
- struggle
- separation
- failure
- confusion
- control
- grief
- impatient/impatience
- exhaustion
- struggling
- sadness
- sorrow
- past
- denial
- hopelessness
- helplessness
- despair
- lack of
- scared
- self-pity
- depression
- victim
- resentment
- persecution
- bitterness
- trauma
- terror
- anguish
- I am generic
- arrogance
- selfish
- self-destructive

PAYOFFS

- no commitment
- panic
- security
- no responsibility
- permission
- control
- don't have to love
- avoid suffering
- detachment
- no rejection
- get to be right
- no decisions
- no choices
- don't have to try
- sympathy
- martyr
- freedom
- physical pain
- superiority
- don't have to listen
- manipulation
- attention
- just getting by
- identity
- not vulnerable
- don't grow up
- compulsive
- get to act crazy/reckless
- not face things
- get taken care of
- safety
- judgment
- denial of: aloneness
-   emotions
-   fear
-   self-esteem
-   confidence

BEYOND SELF-HELP: MASTERING PERSONAL POWER™ by Gary J. Clyman

This is a new presentation of old material. I am not the creator of this material, only the presentor of this traditional material in a new, easy to use and understand style.

Many people have benefited from the use of "The Five Element Theory" over the last few thousand years. This is at the heart of acupuncture, The Macrobiotic Diet, and runs deep in traditional Chinese medicine.

Many of us already recognize a connection between our emotions and our bodies. What many of us have not experienced is the direct connection with past emotional experiences and our present health status. The term "dis-ease" denotes a state of uneasiness or lack of abundant health.

In Chinese medicine, a person can be afflicted with an illness with many origins.

MORE CONCERNING YOUR EMOTIONS

Part of applying Chi Kung as an emotional cleanser or a method of flushing out old emotional things whether related to injuries, incidents, traumas, or feelings, your emotional states could change very quickly.

EMOTIONAL VISUALIZATIONS WHILE SITTING

When you sit and practice The Micro Cosmic Orbit many of these emotional surges flush out on their own. When I was a student many, many times I would laugh and cry, laugh and cry, and fall off my cushion and laugh and cry. I had all kinds of insane picture and visualizations come up while I was sitting. These pictures were part of the cleansing process of letting all these things out.

This is normal and can happen when you begin to still your mind. If this happens to any of my readers, it is important to not become alarmed or scared, but rather to allow these pictures to come out on their own. I call this "Retracing and Releasing." "Retracing and Releasing" is part of becoming objective and empty.

Anytime you practice these techniques you can use them for anything. The applications are totally unlimited. There is no specific application that is restricted to a certain thing. If you want to use The Micro Cosmic Orbit for burning the old experiences out of yourself, go right ahead. My favorite technique for burning out these old experiences is Heaven and Earth Meditation. You can give up more and more. As soon as you realize that you are not giving up enough, you can give up more. This is not in a religious sense, this is more in an emotional or psychic realm.

FAMILY APPLICATIONS

I have discovered and seen many times in my clients and students, that when my male clients are starting to progress and change the traits that they don't like and that really don't work for them, many times as these changes are going on something happens inside of their wives. It appears as their wives become upset because they can not control their husbands any more as before, or their afraid because they don't know where their relationships and marriages are going to go.

Many times in the beginning, my client's wives encourage their husbands to work with me, then suddenly when these men begin to show changes for the better, (i.e. independence, the ability to make decisions, recognizing how other people control them) their wives want their husbands to stop practicing Chi Kung or stop meeting with me. Somehow, they try to prevent their husbands from becoming who they want to be. They are threatened by their husband's new traits and added independence.

Something that I say to my clients quite frequently is, "when you start to change for the better, the people that say they love and support you, and care about you the most, are the ones that will try to hold you back." I have seen this over and over again with many of my clients.

Many of my clients relationships and marriages have been reproduced from the kind of relationships their parents had (insensitive husbands and fathers, domineering wives and mothers, second and third generation child and emotional abuse, etc.)

FRESH BLOOD IN OLD RELATIONSHIPS

Marriage to some people, both men and women, represents prison or lack of freedom. However by utilizing the principles from Personal Power Training™, you can convert a "dead marriage" that has no sensitivity, inspiration, sharing, or communication into a "new marriage," without actually choosing a new partner or breaking your old relationships. Now you will break old relationships in one sense of the word because you will not tolerate your "bad marriage" the way it had been, whether it's 10, 20, 30, or 40 years of it. In other areas of my book I've mentioned, "you don't fit Chi Kung into your life, you fit your life into Chi Kung." This is one reference to that.

Many times the spouses of my clients have trouble fitting into the life of my clients. This is because they've been in a stagnant relationship anywhere from 10-50 years. What happens is after one of my clients changes and goes through the necessary transformations, their spouse has trouble associating. This is very common. Lately, the spouses of my clients have been coming to me to become my clients also. They want to take a more active role in creating these new marriages that are born from the old ones. Changing one partner in a relationship is a major part.

The secondary part is then helping the second person in the same relationship attain what they want from their life. When two people are attaining what they want from their lives, this usually improves their marriage. There always is a chance, when you improve your life, you won't want your partner with you because of some deficiencies or inadequacies that will then show up. The cloud or the haziness related to not knowing what to do or who you are has been lifted. After this haze has been lifted, you will clearly see who you are in relationship to your marriage or relationship. That's why there is so much trouble from your spouse. They want to hold you the way you were. So figure, if your wife or your husband has been in a position of dominance for many years and you all of a sudden declare your independence without breaking the relationship, there will have to be alterations in the relationship. So one of the techniques or applications of Personal Power Training™ is to be able to negotiate and get what you want.

These negotiation skills are applied to business, relationships, etc. This has been true with my own relationship with my fiancée. She has gone through five or six different "levels of transformation" so far, either because of getting worked on by Dr. Gary Whitley 2 or 3 times or getting worked on by me, 2 or 3 times. The material that my fiancée is living with or the emotional incidents that have shown up have been primarily erased. In most cases they do not resurface. This is true for many of my clients, almost all.

So, as each level of emotional distress has been removed, you are left a different person each time.

EMOTIONALLY DYSFUNCTIONAL FAMILIES ARE VERY COMMON

Coming from an emotional dysfunctional family and growing up in the 50's and the 60's is not as rare as some people might believe. The symptoms are too numerous to go into in this book, but those who have experienced an emotional dysfunctional family will understand exactly what I'm talking about.

Emotional dysfunction in families is extremely widespread. This shows up as many forms of child abuse, ranging from being ignored to being raped by your father. This problem ties in with alcohol and drug abuse, but is not restricted to these avenues. Only lately, say over the last 10 years or so, has the psychology community concentrated on this once unspoken and unrecognized problem.

KEEP DRINKING & KEEP MISSING THE BOAT

As long as a person is drinking alcohol or taking drugs, they can never tell exactly what their problems really are. They can always blame their misfortunes and recognition problems on their indulgences. When a person that practices Chi Kung abstains from drugs and alcohol, only then can they discover and realize what the causes of the problems are. Alcohol and drugs can and do quite often mask a personality trait such as laziness, anger, depression, etc. Only by quitting can you begin to see clearly what the reasons for your life's manifestations are.

WHY DID WE DO DRUGS?

A great deal of people my age have taken drugs that grew up in the late 1960's. A more important question is "why did they do drugs?" not if they did. The answer to this question is quite diverse, however in my opinion, there are certain specific similarities in many of these reasons. From my perspective, people do drugs to create a physical identification with their bodies to develop a relationship. So if someone is taking drugs and they are having good or at least some physical sensations, many times these sensations are identified as physical presence, where as by using Chi Kung, you can establish a better relationship with your body without any of the harmful side effects. Chi Kung is "The Perfect Positive Addiction."

IDENTIFYING WITH PLEASURE INSTEAD OF PAIN

Most people associate having a body or identifying with their bodies usually under painful circumstances (i.e. a speck in your eye, back pain, or sore feet). By practicing Chi Kung, each person can develop a new relationship with your own body. It's as if pain gives you a physical focus and without pain, your awareness declines. Chi Kung can and will give you a "pleasurable body identification."

JUST SAY "NO" TO DRUGS, BUT "YES" TO CHI KUNG

Many people ask me the question, "How come I don't feel good when they don't practice and I feel so good when they do practice?" The answer to that is very simple. The reason they feel good when they practice is because they practice. The reason they don't feel good is because not feeling good is a natural state and the only reason they don't feel good is they now have something to compare it to. That's why you should practice on a regular basis. It takes work to feel good. It's natural to feel as good as you can when you practice Chi Kung. Chi Kung is very addictive, but so is feeling good, so you have to choose your addictions carefully and this "The Perfect Positive Addition."

CHI KUNG IS "THE PERFECT POSITIVE ADDICTION"

The sense of wholeness that can be cultivated through the practice of Chi Kung can be the perfect antidote to a life of pain and suffering related to this problem.

The application of these techniques can create a feeling of aliveness for you. Since so many people nowadays have addictive personalities, Chi Kung can fulfill your needs and become the perfect positive addiction. The feelings derived from your Chi Kung practice can be stimulated in many people in less than 30 seconds. There are no harmful side effects that are always associated with taking recreational drugs. Practicing Chi Kung will immediately give you the power over your own mind to change your mood to a more positive one. If I had to compare Chi Kung to any drug, it would probably be morphine, without the harmful side effects.

CHOOSING BASIC PERSONAL RULES

There comes a time in your life (with luck, very early), when you make a decision that you want to be who you want to be instead of just sort of floating around, or wanting... It's almost like, the difference between wanting to be somebody is the exact opposite of not wanting to be like somebody. Most people that I have seen don't concentrate on what they want to be, who they want to be, or what traits they want, but they would rather avoid what they don't want to be. Does that make sense to you? In the book I said, "There's a difference between being celibate and running away from sex, and being celibate and running towards something else." Well, in developing your personality, which can happen at any time, or even a couple of times, you have to pick traits that you want to live with and the rules you want to live by.

I've mentioned before, "Personal Rules." Some people don't have any. Well here we've got instead of "Personal Rules" as the topic, we're talking about Personal Traits, characteristics and just ways of being. This is a very common problem. I can only give it to you in how it happened to me.

When I was about 21 or 22, I didn't have any positive traits. I was just a fat slob that was drinking alcohol all the time and just liked running away from everything. I didn't want to go to college, I didn't want to be a doctor, I didn't want to be a dentist, I didn't want to go in the army, I didn't want to do anything. So what did I have? A lot of nothing. And what I didn't have was everything I didn't want. And I wasn't anybody because I was avoiding being anybody, and living in denial, like an alcoholic. It's kind of complicated. So when I was 22, I had a friend who was a professional athlete and a musician in my band. He was not a real good musician, but he was an excellent athlete. I asked him. He had no structure in his life at all. He had many girl friends, he had kids all over the place, but I asked him "what do I have to do?," because he was an expert athlete. He said just, "Pick 3 things you care about and don't worry about the rest." For lack of another approach, I made my basic choices.

What I picked was sex, martial arts, and making a living. I didn't care how I made money (at the time I was in the optical business) and I didn't care how I had sex, but I did care about my martial arts and my martial arts is what pulled me out of the gutter that everybody else was in and helped me specialize and become a "specialty person."

Client: How do you become a specialty person?

GJC: This question often comes up.

Client: O.K., I'll pick one.

GJC: Name a specialty. Let's first start by eliminating what you don't want.

Client: Because I have no idea?

GJC: Yes. You can't live your life by eliminating but to come up with the end result, we should eliminate the obvious. So, what don't you want? You can just start with anything and as long as it's not wrong, and as it gets better and as you get more clear, then you tailor it. Make a list of things you don't want to do and things you might want to do. A saying I use for this is, "it's easier to steer a car that's rolling than it is to steer a car that's standing still."

MORE ABOUT BELIEF SYSTEMS

Working within your own belief systems in relationship to the practice of Chi Kung at taught in PERSONAL POWER TRAINING™ is a very, very important part of all this. If you believe a certain way and you are living outside of those beliefs or in conflict with those beliefs, the symptoms of this show up in many ways. Unhappiness, obesity, depression, feeling like something's wrong all the time, and others are some very common examples.

So, what you are facing is a daily challenge to do and be the best you possibly can, the way you want to be. Life throws a lot of targets in front of us we have an opportunity to either "shoot" or let them fly by. The more targets you "shoot" and hit, the more this supports your purpose in ideal life. If you hit enough of these targets (the number is not important), this effects your confidence levels in a big way.

RECOGNIZING YOUR CAGE

Most people are trapped and have no idea that they are or that the trap exists. The condition of most people is being "in trouble and miserable" and not knowing it. This sounds grim to say the least, however, if this condition can be realized, it can be used to propel you forward, up and out of your trap, to freedom.

EXPANDING YOUR CAGE

When animals are born and raised in a zoo, they lose much of their instincts. These "domesticated" animals even though they still have the "genetic link" to their blood line, don't express and utilize their traits as though they were in their natural environments. Imagine a lion being raised with a flock of sheep, would the lion think he was a lion or a sheep?

People can have the same tendencies. If a child is raised in an "abusive environment," how can this child know the difference? Only by going outside of your present environment, can you understand your human possibilities. Using Chi Kung can and will help you push beyond your comfort zones in many areas. Most people that work with me, discover how limited their "closed environment" really is, but by doing Chi Kung on a fairly regular basis, these natural limits can be expanded and eventually removed.

Animals and people that are raised in closed environments. They don't have any other perspective than the one they have been exposed to. Unfortunately, this "limited exposure" leads to the reproduction of many environmental and generation-passed dysfunctions. The major categories of these "inherited traits" show up in the areas of child abuse, drug abuse, alcoholism, emotional abuse, and physical violence.

WHAT GETS IN YOUR WAY?

In doing this work we call getting ENERGY FOR LIFE, people will create any excuse to prohibit themselves from having life the way they want it. Excuses show up as health problems, not feeling well or even more serious diagnosable problems. They show up as having circumstances in your environment crop up to prohibit you from having life the way you want it. These excuses are used most frequently by people who have addictive personalities or substance abuse histories.

PERSONAL APPLICATIONS FOR STABILIZATION

Chi Kung as taught in PERSONAL POWER TRAINING™ can be used to stabilize each practitioner on a daily basis. When you hit lows, regardless of the type, practicing Chi Kung enables you to pull yourself out of your slump. It induces objectivity and hope into your daily life so you can see that this won't last for long.

SPONTANEITY WITHIN REASON

A certain amount of spontaneity is important but to be totally spontaneous is to have no control of your life and have a lot of trouble being constructive and productive. Structure can be one of the most important ingredients in life.

THE ENERGY CRISIS OF THE NEXT CENTURY

"Our country is suffering from a National Energy Crisis. Practicing Chi Kung can solve your Personal Energy Crisis." GJC

Many people have conversations with me during their initial consultation concerning what I call "The Commodity of Energy" or ENERGY FOR LIFE™. Many of my clients have many of the worldly things that seem to make many people happy. However, after careful investigation into their lives, personalities, spirituality, and all these other aspects, it turns out that having these worldly things does not actually bring them happiness.

Now, I'm not saying that they must give up worldly things to attain happiness. I think that's a bunch of hogwash. "Having" is a lot more fun than "not having." "Having" is a lot easier on your system than "not having" and "having" is definitely better than "not having." If you are wealthy and have a lot of worldly goods but you don't have "wealth of self" or this commodity I call ENERGY FOR LIFE™, what's the point? So, I teach you how to develop "The Commodity of Energy... ENERGY FOR LIFE™." This is independent of your financial status and other important material things in your world.

ENERGY STABILITY IS POSSIBLE

One of the things you'll want to do as you begin to practice Chi Kung is to try to stabilize yourself which means to keep your energy levels above a certain point. In order to do this, you must do your daily practice in the morning and all day long continue to practice, a little bit here and a little bit there, to stay stable. Depending on your maturity in Chi Kung and the amount of years you are able to do this, you will derive many benefits in the long run for the rest of your life.

CHI KUNG HEALING: THE WHOLE PIE

If there was such a thing as a Chi Kung doctor, I would have been one a long time ago, but there is no recognition for this particular ability, just the need. Many people I have met have a need for someone to either correct their personal meditation or teach them a better way so they can practice unencumbered, on their own.

Nowadays people go around saying they are healers. Many new healing systems have surfaced in the last 10-15 years. Chi Kung is the best because of it's direct use of accumulated personalized energy. From my perspective, many of these other healing systems are only fractions of what Chi Kung is and has to offer. If these other practitioners would learn Chi Kung, first it would help them perform their healing duties better and more efficiently and they would immediately see what is missing in their own system. The use of energy in Chi Kung is like no other system. "The storage factor" is what makes Chi Kung better than all the rest. You must heal yourself before you can heal anybody else, and that's exactly what you will do. This is the unique and distinctive difference.

THE 6 LEVELS OF HEALING

The first and highest is level #1, Chi Healing, then comes level #2, Acupuncture, Chiropractic, and other modalities, then comes level #3, Nutrition, then comes level #4, Herbs, then comes level #5, Drugs and last but not least comes level #6, The Knife. Look at how our modern civilization has it stacked!

THE INVISIBLE GAP - THE BODY/MIND SEPARATION

This work, Chi Kung as I teach it in PERSONAL POWER TRAINING™ is bridging the gap between body and mind which is an artificial gap in the first place. Our Western culture, over the last 300 years teaches us that the body is separate from the mind. This separation or gap is responsible for many modern day psychological problems. These 2 parts of our being are actually united and you do not have to treat them as separate entities.

The merging of these 2 parts, the body and the mind, will reduce your fragmentation and pain which manifests on both the physical and mental plains. This principle, "the merging" not only has been absent from our western culture, but has been magnified as much as possible. If you look at religion, psychology, medicine, exercise, diet and nutrition, interpersonal relationships, or any other subjects, you can see the results of this separation.

Just look at the treatment of modern chronic degenerative diseases and you will see evidence of the fragmentation.

THE PROBLEMS WITH "ASTRAL PROJECTING"

Many years ago I had an "out of body experience" that was the beginning of my journey on the path. I had been astral projecting since I can remember as a child. I used to astral project and get stuck in the walls on the way back in. I remember soaring or flying in my dreams. Many people do, this is very common phenomenon. The pictures in these "trips" were usually very vivid. When I would try to "return home," I would quite often get caught in the wall of my house on my way back in. My mother would wake me up for school and I never wanted to wake up. I always wanted to wait for my spirit to get back into my body, most of the time, it never did get back in and I would go to school only "half there," like a zombie. I believe most people live their lives this way, being "half here." This body does matter and this time around is all you really have.

STRANGER THINGS HAVE HAPPENED

Auto writings and auto paintings have apparently been happening to many people over the years. Some of them have been misunderstood and thought to be "crazy." I'm sure there have been artists throughout history that have experienced strange phenomenon like this. It also happens through me, but it doesn't come out in paintings, writing, or music. It comes out in advise I give my clients. And when this advise is given to individuals, it can help change their lives. You really can't help or change the world until you have your's together, but you can change your life, in an unbelievably short period of time. I help people peel off their "onion skin," the various layers that prevent them from operating at their fullest. Some people might call this Karma. I do remove other people's Karma.

DUMPING YOUR KARMA... HOW?

The unique thing about this process is "I don't take on their Karma because they do it and I don't, they eliminate their own Karma, not me doing it for them. This does not relate to the Hands On, Transfer of Power™, but you have to do your own homework long before (when I say long I mean a few weeks) I actually do the Hands On, Transfer of Power™ process. But if the advise is followed to a great extent and the Hands On, Transfer of Power™ is performed, you will be different. This can induce spiritual growth or more specifically, "spiritual switching or transformation."

MORE ABOUT KARMA

Most people are very concerned about Karma who are on some sort of spiritual path or development. They think they have to "burn off their Karma," they think they're a prisoner of their Karma... etc. If someone would merely practice Chi Kung and develop the internal energy they can cultivate from their practice, they can actually dissolve their Karma instead of being a prisoner of it. When I do a Hands On, Transfer of Power™ on some of my students/clients, what I'm actually doing is dissolving their Karma related to that specific "original incident."

YOUR RESULTS EQUAL YOUR WILL

This even showed up when my dog died in March of 1986. She had been with me since the year after I graduated High School and within 9 days, I had found another dog exactly like her with the same body, but slightly larger and the old dog's spirit moved into my new dog's body, because she was only a puppy. Basically, this dog has been with me over 20 years. And now, she's only 3 years old in 1988. So, I'll have this dog with me for another 15-20 years and the decision to replace her will be made at that time, again. By then, I'll have children, because I am getting married on June 4th, 1989. I'll make a decision whether I'll want another dog for another 20 years at that point.

The point is "you can really have what you want, even if there is no logical basis for getting it." That's what we're talking about when I explain "The 3 Ingredients of Change" in a few different places in this book. These are very important principles.

BEYOND SELF-HELP: MASTERING PERSONAL POWER™ by Gary J. Clyman

YOU CAN GET WHAT YOU WANT

"You can have what ever you want, if you really want it bad enough." If you don't know what you want, and most people don't, you won't get it. There's no mystery why people are unhappy. There's no mystery why they never seem to have things work out "the right way." It's obvious. If you don't know what you want, why should you have what you want? The important part in "Creating Your World" is called Shen, that's Spirit. I've said this before, first comes Shen, then comes Chi which is the energy of the mind or the steps in the process of creation, then comes Jing which is the physical, cultivated sexual energy, the actual movement toward you want, the actual physical manifestation. First Shen, then Chi, then Jing. You can have your world the way you want it, when you want it bad enough.

FOUND BAREFOOT IN THE SNOW, AGAIN

I've been talking in my sleep since I can remember. Probably this sleep talking and I believe before that it was sleep walking on a grosser level, where I used to find myself outside in the middle of the night, dressed in my Karate uniform, in the middle of winter, in my bare feet, walking around outside in the snow. This used to happen to me on a regular basis.

I had roommates that used to go out and look for me in the middle of the night. They heard me leaving or something, I don't really know, it was pretty unclear at the time about what was really happening. I was not aware at the time as to what I was doing, but I believe this talking in my sleep can be considered auto-talking, which was my ability developing its way to the conscious realm of usable tools.

Now, with all my work in my past, I am able to auto talk to my clients. This again is one of the things that is so unique about working with me. You being a substantial person, not some "airy-fairy," can get the benefit of having advise come from another source. The source is me, and it vehicles through me.

MORE ABOUT THE INVISIBLE GAP

Unless you have some sort of technical system that enables you to make sure you are in their body, you probably are not. It is not a natural phenomenon for you to be "in your body." The way society has pulled everything apart, religion is in one place, the mind is somewhere else, the body is somewhere else, exercise is something separate, sex is isolated, and you are lucky if "love" and "sex" are in the same person. Everything about humans is "pulled apart." That's the nature of what's going on with humanity now a days, "separation."

Why is it so surprising and curious to find out "nobody has their shit together." Reflecting on this, when kids are daydreaming in school, they could be anywhere. But now that they are not kids any more and they are in their 30's, 40's, 50's, they still have the same problem.

Nobody talked about "astral projecting" when I was 6 or 7 years old. How many kids were taken to psychologists and psychiatrists to find out what was wrong? How many kids where labeled "slow learners," "learning disabled" or diagnosed as having "concentration problems" when in reality they are not present. Some of these "labels" have stayed with us as adults. I have seen exceptionally smart people with these "old labels," and have seen these "old labels" deeply effect confidence levels in adults.

So one thing led to another and in 1977, I had a conversation with one of my Tai Chi seniors concerning "astral projection." I told him about my willingness to "astral project" and he advised me to "stop it immediately" and showed me how pointless it was to try to connect body mind and spirit while consciously "sabotaging my convergence."

So back to my original "astral projection" decision. My question was do I want to live or do I want to die? I did not want to kill myself because it was too sloppy, but I didn't see anything wrong with just laying there and "leaving my body" for the last time. I could have died and no one would have found me for at least a day or two. But I made the decision to continue to live. I popped up and landed 6 or 7 feet away from where I was lying on the ground. I don't remember how I got up. I just popped up and the next day I was determined to do something, so I ran 8 miles. I was sick for two weeks after I had run that far because I hadn't run for many years. I knew I had to get in better physical shape because I was an "obese pig." I was as bad as anybody I have ever met. This experience led to me beginning my martial art path shortly thereafter.

AN INTELLECTUAL'S VIEW OF THE BODY

In having a conversation with a "pure intellectual" with practically no aspects in "the physical," he described his relationship with his body as "owning or renting a house, and rarely, if ever having a necessity to go to the basement." He actually said, "why should I go in the basement?" as if there was no reason to even dwell in the body. I told him, that if he worked with me, 2 months from now, he would absolutely understand what he has been missing all these years.

ARROGANCE VS. SELF-CONFIDENCE

Arrogance and self-confidence are both in the eyes of the beholder. I believe that if someone is self-confident, they can be interpreted as being arrogant, without actually being that way. It's sort of like walking on the sidewalk and scaring pigeons, I guess it's O.K. When I was coming up as a Tai Chi student, I was having trouble with many other students. They were always crying and complaining about how I was acting and my Tai Chi practice. They were jealous because I was more serious then them and was practicing all day long. It showed.

I asked my Tai Chi master what he thought the problem was, he asked me this question, "when you are driving cross country and you run over a small rock, do you get out of your car and check if the rock is alright?" This question saved me a lot of unnecessary worrying about pleasing other people. Just please yourself, that will be hard enough.

THE EGO VS. SELF-CONFIDENCE

Concerning the defense mechanism of the ego to defend itself: I rarely get any clients that come to me with the traditional Zen attitude of the uselessness or the fruitlessness of the ego (fruitlessness can be changed to a different word). What this means is, the ego takes an "all important control" of the personality, thus not allowing the person to change specific and important characteristics because of the relationship the ego has with these characteristics. This rarely comes up, but every once in a while, I run across somebody who comes in and thinks the ego is bad. This is usually a person with very low self-confidence levels who believes, and has been told for many years that he has "an ego problem."

By careful analysis of what the ego really has to do with the whole person, many times the ego can be retained, if there is in fact an ego. This is related to a self-confidence/arrogance vs. ego relationship. A good ego is an important and necessary attribute to have in this world. However, when the ego is just an image of self and not truly self-confidence, this is a serious problem. As I said before, very few of my clients actually have ego problems, but every once in a while I run across one.

SELF-RESPECT BEGINS WITH SELF

Having self-respect is not the same as thinking and acting like "your shit don't stink." This second attitude does have negative connotations, but true self-respect can be one of your most valuable assets.

If you don't respect yourself, how can you expect anyone else to? This is a disturbing question to many people, especially since our society has put so much emphasis on "helping others" and "doing for others." Without an "inward focus," there can be no "true and permanent" self-improvement. I am not talking about "a bandaid or quick fix," I mean "real change." I believe our society has created so much "outward focus" that the "return home" has become almost impossible. Chi Kung, the way I teach it, will heal this wound.

Self-respect is something that everybody needs but very few people have. If you have self-respect, that is respect yourself, then the world will show you and treat you the way you deserve. Many people lack this valuable ingredient to happiness. All the seminars, therapy, and self-improvement work will not give you self-respect. However, by practicing Chi Kung you can obtain this important, missing personal trait. If you treat yourself like you are "worthless and undeserving," how can you expect anybody else to treat you better?

When your level of self-respect increases, the changes are very subtle and nearly hidden. You will notice that many people tend to regard you in higher view. This will be confusing when lit first starts to show up, but it will show up, and it won't take very long. Sometimes within hours of beginning Chi Kung with me. That is because when you do Condensing Breathing and begin to become the center of your Universe, your Universe begins to respect you automatically. Many people are shocked when they first see people they were previously nervous around or even afraid of, treat them differently. Self-respect will show up in your relationships at work, your marriage and relationships with friends, and most importantly, in how you treat yourself. I guarantee it.

In the way you treat yourself applies also to making money and your attitudes about prosperity. A common result of working with me is that your life becomes a better and happier place to be. This is primarily because of the "inward focus" derived from the practice of "Condensing Breathing." Carefully examine my logo. This exemplifies this "inward focus."

Self-respect is directly related to what I mentioned earlier as "commanding respect vs. demanding respect."

MORE CONCERNING SELF-ESTEEM

Some people carry an automatic smile on their face at all times. This silly, retarded fake fixed smile shows up on people more than you would imagine. In fact, if you have one on your face, you might not even be aware of it being there. I have found this fake smile on people that have severe self-esteem problems, whether men or women. I have tracked this to childhood as an alternative to appearing severely depressed. Recognizing its presence, then finding a Chiropractor who knows what to do for this is the easiest remedy after releasing the emotional blocks associated with this symptom.

This fake or fixed smile is related to covering up your misery. Sometimes this smile is a sign of emotional unconsciousness. These strange facial expressions are related to wanting to look good, or responsive.

TAKE OFF THAT "HAPPY FACE"

This portion is concerning a very strange condition that many people carry in their face. It's called an "Unconscious Fixed Smile." The origins are many but usually stem from childhood. Many children were expected to appear happy when they were not. Over the years of "faking happiness," some people have learned how to fake a happy face, at their own expense. This is a very serious problem in the long run.

This "Unconscious Fixed Smile" keeps many of its owners from achieving all they can and from being all they can be. Some of it owners do not even realize they are not happy at all. They have fooled everyone including themselves. They forgot they were "faking it" since it has become second nature over the years.

VISUALIZATIONS RELATING TO SELF-ESTEEM

The way we speak and see ourselves makes all the difference in what kind of results we get. If you have difficulty seeing yourself a certain way, you can bet your life that you will have many difficulties becoming that way. Here's where your Shen fits in.

In order to raise your level of self-esteem, two working definitions are important to understand. The first definition is for self-confidence and the second is for self-esteem.

Self-confidence is your level of performance.

Self-esteem is your level of deservingness.

Nearly always, these two definitions are misunderstood. You can not raise your level of self-esteem unless you have a clear concept of what self-esteem truly is.

Self-esteem is the end result of our life-time punishment. Our level of self-esteem is a reflection of how much punishment we accept and claim ownership to.

The way I lift a person's self-esteem to a higher level is through the practice of "forgiveness." Self-confidence and self-esteem go hand in hand. Self confidence is our ability to express outwardly; self-esteem reflects how we treat ourselves, inwardly. Yes, you can have high self-confidence with low self-esteem and high self-esteem with low self-confidence.

YOUR "FILTER" VS. YOUR "RULE"

Your "filter" is the composite of belief systems that has been dumped on you and accepted from many sources usually beginning as an infant, to create "the way you look at things in the world."

Your "rule" is something you took directly from somebody else and you incorporated into your person so that no matter what you do or you're about to do, your "rule" limits you. Your "rule" is something you got directly from somebody else where as your "filter" is your own creation. I determine a persons "rule" or "filter" both in groups and also privately. These "rules" and "filters" run your life. Another commonly used "filter" is "If I'm not aware, I don't have to be responsible." Many "smokers" and "drinkers" live with this "filter." This is related to "the comfort of confusion" which I have explained elsewhere in my book.

If you are aware, then you have many decisions and options and possibilities. So this is related to something I call "The Comfort of Confusion." This is not an intellectual problem. It's an act. Keeping in mind that your "rule" or "filter" runs your life, this is responsible for many long term ongoing problems that many people have. Some of these problems are: eating disorders, gambling, adultery, and many other common compulsions including sex and drugs. Many people have combinations of these compulsions. It's like your trying to fill the "black hole," a void that can never be filled. This "black hole" is responsible in many people for the appearance of "working on the problem."

How sneaky and sophisticated a person is will determine the contents and appearance of there "rule" or "filter." Some of these aspects of your "rule" or "filter" can be defined very clearly, while others remain very obscure and hidden. Different aspects of your "rule" or "filter" fall outside of your range of communication and your range of control. With some of these aspects there is nothing you can do.

HOW DO YOU SEE THE WORLD?

One of my favorite portions of PERSONAL POWER TRAINING™ is helping people to define what I call their "rule" or "filter." The "rule" is directly dumped on us by other people. This means we accept their belief system. Our "filter," however, is a combination of our experiences and conclusions we have drawn from them. Look into your own life and see where your basic belief systems stem from.

Examples:

"I am fragile and could lose everything at any time" (this is for a man or woman). This is a common "rule." The origin of this "rule" in this particular case history was given to a boy by his mother over 30 years ago. This man is vision-impaired and was treated as a wimp throughout childhood.

Another common rule/filter for women is: "I am not _pretty_ enough, I am not _smart_ enough, I am not _tall_ enough, I am not _thin_ enough, I am not _short_ enough, I do not _deserve_ enough." Get the point?

This is very common (underlined). This belief system causes more pain and difficulty to women than any other I have found. The reciprocal for this is the use of specific personalized affirmations--of course, after careful investigation is taken place. The cause of this is so obvious it is simple.

ABANDONMENT IS WIDE SPREAD

The "abandonment issue" is reflected in many of my clients, depending on the age of the "original incident" related to your abandonment issue. This reflects your level of "hopelessness and helplessness." Part of the way of getting out of the effect of your "rule" or "filter" is by receiving a clear explanation of how it effects you. These explanations do not usually come from within you and must come from an external source. The decision to go back to the most painful experience of your life is a serious, scary as hell decision, especially because you don't know what your going to find when you take a look.

BEYOND SELF-HELP: MASTERING PERSONAL POWER™ by Gary J. Clyman

WOMEN AND SELF-CONFIDENCE

Many women have been raised in this day and age to believe that they are supposed to be the support person--the secondary person, and the man is primary. This doesn't even work in marriage let alone in other aspects of life. This rule/filter is almost as prevalent with women as "I am not **BLANK** enough." This is a belief system that many women carry which leads to great unhappiness, lowered self-esteem and self-worth, and can lead to non-specific depression.

It doesn't matter what you do; what matters is how much guts/internal fuel you have. It is the same issue for men and women. Whether it looks like talking and not being listened to, being in a relationship and not having your feelings matter, being abused by the people we love and supposedly love us, or being "shit on" on the job. The problem is not theirs; it is ours. It is our discipline problem that we accept things that are not acceptable. This issue I call "commanding respect vs. demanding respect."

True leaders and other people that have sufficient levels of self-esteem and discipline are respected without asking, automatically you might say; whereas, people with low self-esteem do not command or take responsibility for the kinds of communication given to them. This is a serious problem.

Question: Are you telling me that I have something to do with the way people treat me?

Answer: You only get what you accept. If you are satisfied with people treating you like "dog meat," people will pick up on it and give you what you ask for. All the screaming in the world isn't going to change that, but if you have an internal conversation with yourself and decide that you are only willing to accept communication above a certain level and not lower, those same people will give you what you ask for.

DECISIONS AND SELF-CONFIDENCE

One of the important things with having self-confidence is also having the balls to stand behind the decisions you make and to know that the decisions were based on all the available information you could possibly have had at the time. People have trouble because they don't want to make decisions and always feel they don't have enough information to make an accurate one. Your ability to make decisions reflects your self-confidence levels. It has nothing to do with the actual decisions.

WOMEN AND FOLLOW THROUGH

Many women that I have interviewed have proven not to have what it takes to do this work. I don't mean that they're not smart enough, but they have this "undeserving issue" to the point of destruction. That's how they disqualify themselves. They create all kinds of reasons. They have all kinds of answers why they can't do this now, and these are usually fat women. They first say, "this is exactly what I'm looking for." "I really want to do this," or "I'm going to do this." The next thing you know, they're calling up to postpone their interview appointments. The next step is they start postponing their starting date and then the last step is because they don't know how to make decisions yes or no, is to postpone, to stop and just out and out cancel doing it at all. So what that essentially means is they're just trapped. They stay where they are and there's nothing I can do about it. If someone is not willing to work with me then I can't help them. It's as simple as that. This "undeserving issue" that women have gets in their way so they cannot change. This is why most of my clients are men.

PROBLEMS WOMEN HAVE MORE THAN MEN

I believe women have more other problems that are even more serious than the lack of the sense of urgency. This relies on self-esteem, self-discipline, and self-confidence. That's why what I call what I do "Success and Prosperity Training."

PERSONAL PRESENTATION & SELF-IMAGE

Personal presentation is very important. This world judges us by how we look, unfortunately. If we don't care about our appearance, nobody else will either. We get treated the way we appear, and the way we accept being treated.

The simple action of "tightening your belt" will do wonders for your self-image. I interview many people as clients who are walking around with their pants falling down. What kind of physical presence and awareness can this create when you're having trouble keeping your pants up? All it takes is making your belt a little tighter. This does give you some sensitivity in the lower part of your body, primarily around your waist, not your groin, and this adds to your self-esteem and self-confidence. This is important. If you're walking around sloppy with your pants falling down, please pay attention and fix this.

TEACH 100 DOCTORS, HELP 10,000 PEOPLE

Teaching Chi Kung in PERSONAL POWER TRAINING™ was an important decision for me because I was planning to become a Chiropractor. I made a decision a few years ago to give up a Chiropractic study and career, which I hadn't completed yet, to bring Chi Kung to the masses. My decision to teach Chi Kung instead is based on my belief that if I teach 100 Chiropractors how to use Chi Kung in their practice, I will help many more people than I possibly could by myself. So that decision was made when I withdrew from college to do this exclusively. My decision was right.

Helping people by teaching them Chi Kung has proven to be more valuable to my students because they keep their benefits forever. There are many other people who who can help people by using Chiropractic.

ABOUT CONCENTRATION

Many people are under the misconception that they can concentrate for short periods of time. A short period of time might be considered from 15 minutes to an hour. The truth is most people have never concentrated in their entire lives. Concentration is the ability to "be present" on command.

There exists a methodical way of realizing and developing these concentration skills. "True Concentration" resembles a clock with each minute representing an interval. A process of developing concentration that I teach my clients is to concentrate for 10 seconds and then distinctly not concentrate for 10 seconds. Realizing and developing the ability to turn it off and on gives you a handle on internal control. After this practice has been developed to a small extent, the next step is extending your concentration abilities for two intervals followed by a one interval rest period. This method works.

Practicing this technique I call "The Anatomy of Concentration," will give you, the practitioner, the necessary sensitivity to concentrate at will and to be able to distinguish the difference.

Many people suffer from not being able to concentrate but few realize the problem even exists. People only operate at 20-30% of their capacity at the most. Obviously there are other factors involved: enjoying what you do, doing the right thing, and many other variables. I am talking about dealing with the ability to concentrate, which is directly related to choosing what you decide to concentrate on. This is concentration at your peak.

Many people spend most of their waking hours trying to not be where they are because they don't like what they are doing. Concentration, however, is the opposite. That means you are spending your time becoming physically present and aware, being _more_ where you are.

RELIGIOUS CONDITIONING AND DEPROGRAMMING

For all practical purposes this material will be divided into three basic categories:

1. Protestant Influences
2. Catholic Influences
3. Jewish Influences

PROTESTANT INFLUENCES:

The first thing we will talk about is the "Protestant Influences" and it doesn't mean you have to be Protestant to have this; you can be Catholic, you can even be Jewish. What you really are won't make that much difference; it might shade or flavor the problem but it doesn't change the category of it.

Protestant conditioning -- the basic rule to recognize this is -- "if it is easy, it is wrong." This has many other implications relating to money, work, and being natural. Having fun and being happy are also effected.

"The Protestant Work Ethic" and applications of it are the most prevalent problems related to this particular branch. Many of my clients come to me feeling guilty unless they have suffered enough to deserve something. There is no real cure to this -- just what I call "reframing." Part of reframing is to recognize whether this particular trait is a member of a category of traits or is personal like a possession, a personal trait. When I help my clients and students deal with this particular problem, it is done on an individual basis. However, after the problem has been "Reframed" or dealt with, many of my clients recognize it as a common problem. Prior to working with it and dissolving it, it looked totally isolated, individual and unrelated to anybody else's issues. This is very common.

CATHOLIC INFLUENCES:

Christianity has given us many beliefs. For example: "it is easier for the poor man to pass through the eye of a needle than it is for a rich man to get into Heaven."

This single quote has caused more problems in relation to prosperity than I have seen anywhere else. This quote has affected people and successfully motivated them to sabotage their own personal success. Another common belief related to this, is "if you make a dollar, you had to take it from someone else."

This also runs deep in preventing people from accepting their God-given riches.

"Catholic Denial," and many variations of it, prevent many people from action -- positive action. "Catholic Denial" shows up in many of my clients as an underlying belief that they don't deserve it, so they don't get it and they are unhappy because they don't get it, yet they sabotage themselves in advance. So one of my goals in working with my clients is to show them and dissolve these negative belief systems.

JEWISH INFLUENCES:

Dissatisfaction is very current; so many of my clients are dissatisfied with life. Dissatisfied doesn't mean they are poor or broken, dissatisfied means they know they are not performing to their full potential, whether they are commodity traders, Chiropractors, attorneys, people managers, executives, artists, musicians; they are not doing what they are supposed to do, so they are not happy.

JEWISH GUILT AND CATHOLIC DENIAL:

Jewish people have a trait that is rarely found outside of Jews. Fortunately, this trait does not prevent them from getting something accomplished, and achieving their goals; however, the punishment associated with achieving their goals which appears as "Jewish Guilt" is sometimes a serious drawback. "Jewish Guilt" is quite different than "Catholic Denial." The joke "the Jews created guilt, the Italians perfected it," is quite accurate. Most Jews do not suffer the same malady as their Catholic/Protestant counterparts.

The remedy to all negative belief systems in my work is what I call "Illogical Logic" or "The Task-Reward Ratio." "The Task-Reward Ratio" helps many of my clients come to grips with many recurring responses. These responses can look like feeling bad about something good, feeling good about something bad, or feeling more justified to fail than to succeed.

These tasks are so simple, they are guaranteed to be successful. By picking the correct task and tying it into the reward, success is assured. The reward can be being happy, feeling successful, losing weight, not being depressed, making money, and/or having fun. The ratio between the task and the reward is tremendous. Remember, we are purposely picking a task or homework assignment that is guaranteed to succeed.

At the completion of this task or homework assignment, the client deserves the associated benefit. Ridiculous as this may seem, it produces great results. I will now give some examples:

One of my clients is wealthy and was chronically unhappy. Upon investigation of his unhappiness, we, he and I, found that he had no reason to be unhappy so I had him pick a task that, upon completion, would allow him to feel he deserved and earned happiness. The task in this particular case was to drink a cup of decaffinated coffee -- one cup, one time. His happiness lasted for months.

Example 2:

I had a psychiatrist as a client one time who was chronically 10 minutes late everywhere he went. So, for being 10 minutes late everywhere he went, he felt bad for hours (guilt). So on my first confrontation with him, my homework assignment was to leave 15 minutes earlier than he ordinarily would to be anywhere. In the process of leaving 15 minutes early, he was arriving 5 minutes early. Everybody he worked with wanted to know what was wrong. He didn't answer them. A week later at our 2nd consultation, he felt "Great," but still was unhappy. He felt residual guilt because he had been that way for so many years that the change was hard for him to get used to. So his homework assignment, (the task) was to feel O.K. about not being late any more. He chose to do two push ups. Upon the completion of his two push ups, he was truly better.

GARY'S EVALUATION OF EVELYN'S STORY:

Evelyn's story is classical, classical abandonment. The original cause was due to her parents being killed in a car accident when she was only 4 years old. She was raised by her relatives and all the rest of the children in the family. She was forced to share what she had with everybody else because she had more. This original cause set her up for a lifetime of unhappiness.

EVELYN'S STORY:

I initially started PERSONAL POWER TRAINING™ because I was not accomplishing my goals, my relationships were failing consistently and something kept getting in the way. It was a fear that if I got involved that person would leave, so I created relationships that would fail over and over again and I didn't know how to stop it from happening. As I got involved with working with Gary, I started to realize the pattern I had established and how it was effecting my body. Through doing Chi Kung practice and the body work, it helped eliminate the fears I have with encountering new relationships. I am more objective and I won't die if the person leaves me. I feel I can go on with my life now.

It still effects other areas of my life. My friendships with other women were not satisfying. I was able to let go of some of the ones that were not good for me. I used to just hang on to them.

What it looked like is a terrible fear of being alone, abandoned and even though I tell myself I enjoy being alone, I was so miserable and every time I got around people I always felt I had to do something to keep this person in my life to make them accept me. To make them want me and I had to be more than just Evelyn--I had to be something else to keep that person there in my life and was not letting that person be who they are, but treating them like a possession, an object and what they could do for me and so far as fulfilling my needs. I felt other people had to make up for what was taken away from me as a child. Other people had to make me feel loved because I lost my parents at 4 years old.

I didn't know how much of an impact had on me until I saw a pattern in my social life. I could not get past the fear of somebody leaving me or me not being enough for them to stay in a relationship with me or not being enough to do a good job, establish a new business. Also feeling like I had to fill myself up with food, alcohol, smoking to feel I had something I could control that wouldn't leave me be alone. I tended to indulge in things. I would go on drinking binges at times.

It's changed to the extent that my awareness has increased and my ability to say no to my cravings and urges to compensate has gotten better in that I feel that I can be myself. I don't have to fulfill another's needs so they will have me as a friend, lover or employee. I can be me with what I have to give and feel more confident in that. It looks like I am loving myself more and putting myself before in the sense that I am not looking to please other people so much. I am looking to please Evelyn. I want Evelyn to be taken care of. I don't want Evelyn to be hurt again and my awareness is considering me now when before I wasn't. I was only looking how the other people were reacting to me.

BEYOND SELF-HELP: MASTERING PERSONAL POWER™ by Gary J. Clyman

I would say about 60% is gone now.

How much of your improvement is personal advice vs. the practice? I would say 50/50.

CONTRIBUTIONS BY DOUG CARTER

MORE ABOUT ABANDONMENT

One of the biggest problems that I think people run into is they get caught up trying to do what's right. They get caught up trying to do what they think they're supposed to do rather than what they really want to do and even though what they think what they're supposed to do is not necessarily the right thing or the best thing for the other people that are involved either and it's certainly not right for them. In fact, I was driving down the road the other day and one of the things that came up for me was values and where values come from. I know that everybody's got a set of negative and positive values.

You can rank them in order of what's most important, what's second most important, etc. I found out that the values that we hold dear are the things that we were "accused" of violating when we were younger. So for me, my biggest value is "integrity." Doing what's right. My second biggest value (well, it was, it's not any more) is honesty and then trust. And the reason, I found out, you know the things that drive me crazy, is when people don't do what's right, or when people aren't honest, and you can't trust people. You can't find anybody you can trust. That kind of stuff. And yet, in reality what was going on for me is that I was afraid that I wouldn't do what was right, be honest, or that I wasn't trustworthy. Where did all that garbage come from? The things I was accused of by my parents, specifically my father. And God! I mean some of that garbage has been with me for years.

Now it's coming up and I say "well gee, if that's where my values came from, they came not from a positive perspective but a negative one. Maybe the time has come for me and I don't know how to do this yet, but maybe the time has come for me and a whole bunch of other people to take a look at ourselves and say, "O.K., what is really right? Who are we really and what is really important to us?" Not because somebody else told us who we were "supposed to be" but because it really is important to us.

GJC: So, you've never really created who you are supposed to be?

DC: No, I've always been living by other people's expectations or what I thought other people's expectations were...

GJC: And not really what they really were either!

DC: No, it was an interpretation.

GJC: Right!

DC: And it was an interpretation of events that occurred when they were emotional. I mean, it wasn't even something accurate for them because they weren't always emotional. It's like this one time when I was about 12 years old, my dad got real upset with me and just yelled and screamed and said... I don't even know what he said but this is the "original incident" that came up the last time that Gary and I did "Hands on, Transfer of Power."

GJC: With the shooting incident?

DC: Pardon?

GJC: With the shooting?

DC: No, no, this had to do with cleaning the back yard. And, uh... he'd asked me to clean the back yard two or three times and you know, I was only a 12 or 13 year old kid, so I kind of half-heatedly put the thing together. I didn't want to be out there, it was cold! And so on Saturday, my father comes along and says, "I thought I told you to clean the back yard?" I said, "well, I... I did," and he said, "Bullllllshit!" And so he went out and grabbed the rake and started to clean the back yard. So I go out to help him and I'll never forget this. He looked at me and said, "what are you doing out here?" I said, "well, I'm helping you clean the back yard." He said, "I don't need you." He said, "you had your chance. If I want it done, I'll do it." He said... "Get outta here!" And so I did.

I went back on the porch, and the porch is covered with plastic so the wind wouldn't blow through and I remember standing there, looking at him through the plastic and it was all blurry and such. I started to cry. My whole life, all I ever wanted to do is be a part of my dad's life. And that was the last time... right there... and we never really got along from that point on.

Until just recently and the reason was because in a moment of acute stress, I mean he had so much stress in his life, from a moment of stress for him, he reacted to me - not because of who I was, but because of the things going on in his own life, you know - his own garbage, but I didn't know that. And so I have "owned" that as being my problem, what I thought his expectations were and they weren't. Does that make sense?

GJC: Yeah!

Connie B. Kroft was my typist: (CBK) Oh yeah!

GJC: So, can I put that in the book?

DC: Sure, it will probably help other people with this issue.

GJC: Can you resolve it?

DC: Well yeah. What I did already was I called him and I told him, I said, "I've had some stuff come up for me and you know I've always been real logical, and I've had some stuff come up for me and it's emotional and I'd like to talk to you about it." And he said, "yeah. What was it?" And I told him about it, about feeling like I was "abandoned," feeling like I had never been good enough.

GJC: So this is directly related to the issue of "abandonment" with you.

DC: Oh yeah, yeah it is. And it all started in March, when you were here last.

GJC: So the Hands On, Transfer of Power™ last time actually brought this one out.

DC: No actually it came out in between, but the Hands On, Transfer of Power™ resolved it.

GJC: O.K.

DC: The last time. The Hands On, Transfer of Power™ in March, when you were out here is what brought it up.

GJC: O.K.

DC: And in the meantime, when I started to resolve the process and when I was with you the last time, one of the reasons was because logically, I had already dealt with it.

GJC: But you didn't get it out of your body yet.

DC: I didn't get it out. I couldn't let go of it.

GJC: Did you get it out last time I did the Hands On, Transfer of Power™?

DC: Must have, because in order for me to talk about it and not have a big emotional reaction to it...

GJC: Great.

DC: About as gone as you're gonna get.

GJC: Can I put this in the abandonment section?

DC: Sure.

GJC: O.K., because I have a place for it.

DC: Sure put it in there. Anyway I talked to my father and you know what happened? I told him, "you know I had all this stuff come up for me and I said logically I know that that's not true. You know, logically I've got it all handled, but you know emotionally it's a mess." And he said, "you know, I was always afraid of that." Now we never talked about that specific incident, but we talked about that specific time period and we talked 45-50 minutes - something like that.

GJC: Well he was afraid he screwed you up as a kid.

DC: Yeah!

GJC: And he was right.

DC: Well he was right.

GJC: He did.

DC: And you know what's real interesting is that our relationship has been so much better since then. Since our discussion about it.

GJC: That's really exciting.

DC: It's been incredible. You know, I told him, "you know, next to my daughter, you're the most important person in my life. You always have been." And what's sad is that we hardly talked from the time I was about 11 until I was about 21.

GJC: Well, fathers don't have much to say to kids until they're about 21 anyway.

DC: Yeah, well I left home.

GJC: Well congratulations.

DC: Hey, such is life. Thank you. Not thank you for saying congratulations, but thank you for your help and support.

GJC: You're not done yet...

DC: Yeah I figure that one of the things that is gonna happen is that between you and I, we're gonna plow into the ground here.

GJC: We'll do what?

DC: We're gonna plow it into the ground. I mean, we'll do stuff that nobody's ever done before.

REGARDING CO-DEPENDENCY

Doug Carter: Co-dependence, the modern therapy of Co-dependence goes much deeper than what happened in like "Alcoholics Anonymous" and other addictive consciousness. I'll repeat this. It doesn't make any difference whether it's food, or alcohol. Whether it's chemical dependency, sexual dependency, or whether it's relationships, and it doesn't make any difference - it's all part of a bigger addictive process.

CBK: Co-dependence?

DC: Yeah, with a lot of people, what will happen is that they'll kick alcohol or they'll kick something else and they don't...

GJC: They pick up something else.

DC: They just change it. They stop drinking alcohol and so what do they do? They start smoking more, or again, or for the first time and they start drinking coffee and stuff like that, which AA condones because it's a "slower death," but it's still part of the addictive process. And the way this is manifested is. We learn a lot of our co-dependency from our parents and our parents learned it from their parents and their parents learned it from their parents, etc... I mean, God there are cases right now where what people are dealing with is healing a family and healing a family tree, because you can go back six or seven generations and find somebody that committed suicide because they couldn't deal with the addictive process, and what happened is that their kids picked up their same mannerisms and their kids picked up their same mannerisms and things like that.

What happened for me is that I was lucky in that in that I recognized early enough that there something wasn't right in the way that I was treated and in the way that I was treating people. So my relationship with my daughter is really pretty good. Well she's got some stuff... some co-dependent behavior.

CBK: Wait... Can you specifically state something, like what "type?"

DC: Yeah, eating.

CBK: Eating too much. We all eat. Some addictions are healthy... you know.

DC: So, that's a co-dependent behavior. It has nothing to do with being hungry.

CBK: O.K.

DC: For her it has to do with being lonely, and being bored, and to a certain extent it has to do with fear associated with being left, with being abandoned.

GJC: Oh, it's basic Bulemic characteristics, but without the vomiting part.

CBK: Well, what would you call... Would Co-dependence then... Could you... Could you say it was not taking care of your own basic needs directly but finding an alternative?

DC: Yeah... subterfuge. It ties into there not being enough of something and so it's an overcompensation. It's like any impulsive/compulsive behavior is a symptom of co-dependency. And for me, personally, you know I've gone through a lot of different things, but the thing that I'm dealing with right now is in relationships. I'll go through relationships and relationships and relationships... I'll meet new people and I'll be with them and all of a sudden they're no longer exciting and it goes on and I'll find somebody else. I'll give you a better example of Co-dependency... Drugs... Adrenaline. You know... Do you ever procrastinate?

DC: Well procrastination is a good technique to all of a sudden have to do something, to... Oh my God! I gotta do this, and we run around here and we run around there...

CBK: That's why I'm late all the time!

DC: Yeah, and what happens is...

CBK: The adrenaline rush that I'm gonna be in trouble... I bet.

DC: Anything like a shot of alcohol, or a shot in your arm. Adrenaline is the most powerful drug that we have. Another one is endorphine from runners. All that is Co-dependency. It's an addiction.

DC: Well I figure... God Gary it's sad... I figure that probably 95 to 98% of the population in the United States is co-dependent to one degree or another.

GJC: And in the book I also have a section that says Chi Kung is "The Perfect Positive Addiction." That's where it will go.

CBK: Why do you think it is from our society, that we have such a large populace that cannot meet it's needs directly? Because you said it was from having an abundance... a heirachy of needs that weren't fulfilled, but it's like all societies... All children need things; to grow and to live, but what we've used as, what did you call it subterfuge?, We've... It's a big enlightenment process when we call somebody up and say, "hey, I'm lonely will you talk to me?," instead of feeling lonely and eating the chocolate cake in the refrigerator, or whatever the other co-dependent kind of behavior would be.

DC: Let me answer the first question. Let's get back to if this is in fact hereditary, not from the genetic standpoint, but from an environmental standpoint?

CBK: Uh huh?

DC: Where did most of the people in the United States come from? They were the disenfranchised, the disenchanted people of Europe and the world.

GJC: Cast offs and rejects.

DC: Yeah. They came because they were either driven out or they couldn't get what they wanted in Europe, so they moved but a lot of them came because they were driven out. And when they came here, what they did was they took a peace-loving people, the vast majority of native Americans, who may or may not have been co-dependent under the current terms that we're using, and forced them out. And so generation by generation by generation, you know... we build it in. We've got co-dependent organizations and the work that I'm doing now has to do with healing organizations. Because you figure if 10% of the organization, the right 10%, if they are in fact co-dependent, they will have mannerisms and management traits that will carry off into the entire organization making the entire organization dysfunctional. How's that?

GJC: Pretty cool.

CBK: That's real interesting and I've always thought that sanity was a matter of majority rule. If 97% of the populace is co-dependent, then the 3% that is "normal," what do you call that? Wouldn't they be considered strange?

DC: Well yeah. Well, I don't know any of them.

GJC: I don't know any of them either!

DC: A lot of this is really...

CBK: Where do they live? Out back in Wyoming? (laughs)

DC: No, they live all over.

CBK: Uh huh.

DC: But these are the people that don't get caught up in other people's garbage. To give you an example; One of the techniques that you can use to get out of co-dependency and that is to "draw the line," and I'm working on it myself. I had a conversation with my wife's boss today. Actually, he had a conversation with me and he started talking about how we need to this, in his company, they need to do this, they need to do that, they need to do something else, and he said that he needed to talk to my wife about... and he mentioned two or three things, so he was looking to me, to help him, tell her...

CBK: Uh huh.

DC: How she needed to make a behavioral change. And I said, well Kevin, I'll tell you what, the first thing you need to do is to talk to her and not to me.

CBK: Right, draw the boundaries... find your own boundaries.

DC: Well yeah. It's not my problem. That's the first time in my life I think I realized that I can say, "that's not my problem" and not feel responsible and guilty about it. Because it's not my job, it's his job. He's the owner. She's the manager. If he's got a problem, he needs to go to her, not to me. He doesn't pay me, he pays her.

CBK: Uh huh.

DC: It's amazing. You should have seen the shift occur in him and he changed.

CBK: And in the past you would have unwittingly or unconsciously taken that on, gotten real... uh, soap opera... right in the middle of it.

DC: Of course. I would have said, "let's take a look at this, let's see what we should do.."

CBK: And probably have been flattered that you were asked.

DC: That's it, and that is a symptom of...

DC & GJC simultaneously: CO-DEPENDENCY.

DC: Co-dependency is when somebody needs you, you have a false superiority/inferiority...

GJC: Or it's like the victim/savior roles.

CBK: Uh huh... that makes sense.

DC: Anyway, Connie, I gotta tell you, you came to the right place. This may not solve all the problems you'll ever run into in your life, but it will sure clean up a lot of old ones.

CBK: Right, well it's been a lot of fun so far. Yeah, well I feel like we're old friends in a way.

DC: Remember what I said was that my whole body was frozen up and the reason is because people tend to store emotional feelings in their bodies, specifically in organs. Some people will transfer from an organ to different muscle groups. I don't know exactly how it works, but it seems to work that way. There are different organs that seem to store a specific type of emotion or feeling.

BEYOND SELF-HELP: MASTERING PERSONAL POWER™ by Gary J. Clyman

GJC: Organs or body areas.

DC: I know that for me "abandonment" is right at the bottom of my sternum, right in that area. All of the surrounding area has to do with loneliness, fear, rejection, a lot of that for me is in my fat. "Guilt" is a lot lower down and for me, it is in my groin area. The way that you check is real simple, with medium/mild pressure, like tapping of a finger or thumb and if pressure on that area elicits pain, you know, if it hurts, if it's real sensitive. The only way it hurts is if you're resisting. Does that make sense?

CBK: Yeah.

DC: So, if you're resisting and you put pressure on it, it's gonna hurt. If you aren't resisting it just gives. And as long as it resists, you've got something in there. That's emotion or memory there. I said memory, I meant memory. What happens is that emotion is typically tied into memories that you didn't deal with completely. So because of that, as the body part is being softened up, you'll have the emotions. They will become elicited and you'll start to experience those more fully and as you do that you'll, most people tend to have memories, the vast majority in pictures, some people will have in sound connotations, you know things like that, but the vast majority are pictures and you'll have experiences out of your life come up that you didn't even know were there. So it actually is "buried." You "bury it" in a body part. It's like all of sudden you get scared and your shoulders draw up... like that kind of response.

CBK: Uh huh.

DC: Well what you're doing is preventing that emotion from being fully experienced and you've stored it. Almost guaranteed that you've stored it some place.

CBK: Uh huh.

DC: Does that make sense?

CBK: Yes, it does.

DC: That's how he does it. By touching different body parts and Gary...

GJC: That's what I do on everybody when I do the Hands On, Transfer of Power™.

DC: That's basically in a nutshell what Hands On, Transfer of Power™ is all about. At least the first part of it, to help you break loose, those emotions in those parts of your body.

GJC: I'll put this under the "Abandonment" section.

DC: Great Stuff!

NOTES

BEYOND SELF-HELP: MASTERING PERSONAL POWER™ by Gary J. Clyman

INSIDE KUNG FU MAGAZINE APRIL 1987

AN INTERVIEW WITH GARY J. CLYMAN

This interview was printed in part in the April 87' Issue of Inside Kung Fu magazine. This interview was between myself and one of my students, Mr. Dennis Franke R.N. The response to this article gave me a national and international reputation and visibility. Since this publishing, clients and students of all levels have come to study with me from all over the country for my special Two Day Private Instruction Format. This is that article in its entirety.

Gary J. Clyman is director of the Chicago Wholistic Health Center, a unique clinic where the ancient arts of Taoist self-cultivation still live - 20th century style. Clyman's practice is one of Bio-Mechanics, Spinal Touch Treatment, Orthomolecular Nutrition, Muscle Response Testing, and PERSONAL POWER TRAINING™. But behind this modern terminology, and the doors of his downtown loop office, hides the Chinese arts of Tai Chi boxing, Tao Yin corrective exercise, An Mo massage, Wai Tan alchemy, and Chi Kung meditation - practices of Chinese Taoism shrouded in secrecy and rarely practiced today as a unified self-healing system. In each of these arts Gary J. Clyman is an expert, a modern Master.

Ever since the age of twenty he has been studying, cultivating, refining, and teaching the arts of Yang Sheng - Taoist practices for the "nourishment of life and the strengthening of it against disease." A life-long Chicago resident, he is a senior member in the city's martial arts, macrobiotic, and Wholistic health circles. He has appeared on numerous T.V. and radio shows; twelve of the latter with his friend and mentor Dr. Robert Mendelsohn (deceased April 1988). And in an ever-continuing effort to spread the Illinois Wholistic Health Network: a forum of health care practitioners dedicated to the education and promotion of Wholistic healing in the greater Chicago metropolitan area.

If there's still meaning in the epithet, "a self-made man" then Gary Clyman embodies that ideal. All of Clyman's training as a Wholistic health practitioner was secured by direct, one-on-one apprenticeship and thousands of hours of intense, disciplined practice. The adventure began in 1974.

After a year and a half of studying the Korean fighting art of tae kwon do, with Master Han Cha Kyo, and enlightened by the new Feng and English translation of the Tao Teh Ching, he went in search of a martial art that could offer more than just fighting know-how. He wanted to develop vitality, assertiveness, self-esteem, and character. Han thought him "so strange for an American to want to be Philosopher?" Eventually, Clyman discovered Temple Style Tai Chi Chuan and the city's premier Tai Chi Master, Waysun Liao; and for the next six years he studied full time with Liao and his two branch school instructors. It was during the period with his second Tai Chi instructor that he immersed himself in the Nei Kung - to develop the self and cultivate the Three

BEYOND SELF-HELP: MASTERING PERSONAL POWER™ by Gary J. Clyman

Taoist Treasures of Jing, Chi, and Shen.

To cultivate his Chi, his inner energy, Master Liao put him on "the monk's diet": a regimen of grains, beans, vegetables, and seaweed. Living the Monk's life, he ate the diet, became celibate, and practiced Tai Chi from six to ten hours a day. To learn the classical Taoist path his textbooks became the Secret of the Golden Flower, Charles Luk's Taoist Yoga and Secrets of Chinese Meditation, and the tenth-century Ishimpo: Tao of Sex.

In those early days when Liao's was a center for imported Chinese talent, Clyman had the opportunity of being exposed to Chinese wrestling, Shuai Chiao, with the Grandmaster of the art, Chang Tung Sheng, who died April 1987 at 78 years old. Acupuncture was exposed to Clyman in 1975 as he received his first lessons in natural healing. And of course, Master Liao opened the door to the inner workings, the temple secrets, of Temple Style Tai Chi and Chi Kung.

In the fall of 1979 Clyman attended a Chiropractic seminar as the assistant of Dr. Ineon Moon, his acupuncture teacher. The lecturer was Dr. Lamar Rosquist from Salt Lake City, and he was teaching the original John Hurley D.C. technique under the name of "The Spinal Touch Treatment," a non-force, gentle, soft tissue technique that works by releasing hypertonic muscles that misalign the spine and pelvis, he had found it the most helpful technique in his large Chiropractic clinic.

Gary immediately sensed that "The Spinal Touch Treatment" was after the same results as Tai Chi - perfect alignment of the spine through "hanging by a string at top of head" and "tucking the pelvis under." He saw that The Spinal Touch Treatment's goals of proper body mechanics and unimpeded neural flow were the same as those of An Mo massage with its manipulating of the sinews and stroking of the Chi tracts. He added it to his repertoire of natural healing arts and it soon became the center of a successful Wholistic health practice.

Gary J. Clyman is an imposing, fiery personality. He often comes on too strong, with his ever-present handshake and booming smile, that new acquaintances are hard put to peg the man. And so they should be -- because Gary Clyman is one of those rare spirits totally enmeshed in the joy of living. If his sense of life could be labelled I'd call it Yang Chu hedonism, after the fourth-century Taoist, because he finds real joy in every action and endeavor, whether it's doing the Tai Chi form, meeting a new client, sparring with a parking lot attendant, or yes, even jostling a drunk driver from his car to perform another citizen's arrest. Optimism and vitality are his trademarks. The years of Tai Chi practice show in his military posture, erect and buoyant, yet still pliable and rooted in his every move. He uses and somehow remanufactures more energy in one day than most of us do in a week, and it just may be that his daily Tai Chi and Chi Kung practice has something to do with it.

In his interview he shares the secrets of Chi Kung meditation, the central practice of Taoist Yang Sheng without the mysticism, which is the foundation of his PERSONAL

BEYOND SELF-HELP: MASTERING PERSONAL POWER™ by Gary J. Clyman

POWER TRAINING™ Workshops.

IFK: Just what is Chi Kung meditation?

GJC: Chi Kung is an ancient Chinese Taoist method for rejuvenating your internal energy systems - your Jing, Chi, and Shen. It's done using various postures and different kinds of breathing, but it's the internal exercises behind these outer movements that's important. So right here it's different than say Hatha yoga or Chinese calisthenics, which it can look like; plus, the postures aren't for stretching. Traditionally, it's part of Taoist yoga - the practices of the Taoist monk's. Today, it's the backbone of the internal martial arts of Tai Chi, Hsing I, and Pa Kua. (If it's taught that is!) Right now in China, a popularized version is getting attention as a kind of cancer therapy (see Chi Gong: Chinese Cancer Patients Exercise their way back to Health in East West Journal, March 1983. Ed.) There are similarities with Tantric yoga, but the language, exercises, and objectives are different. What makes Chi Kung unique is the conscious directing and use of the energy. So, it's really a meditation for self-development, for creating change in your life; and it can be done by anyone. I've had doctors, Chiropractors, commodity traders, attorneys, housewives, teachers, and business people do this training, and everyone has experienced important, positive changes in their life.

IFK: Many articles are now appearing in martial arts and new age magazines on Chi Kung. With your busy practice, have you had a chance to read them? And if so, what are your conclusions?

GJC: All the articles I've read have been too superficial to do justice to this Nei Kung practice, so deep-rooted in Chinese culture. People have been led to believe that if they sit in the lotus posture and stretch one hand over their head and hold the other at tan tien while they abdominal breathe, that's Chi Kung. No way! Chi Kung means internal energy work, internal training! And it's tied into the oral secret teachings of the Taoists, and martial arts Masters. What we're talking about here is a sophisticated inner science involved in this art. People have spent their entire lives doing this and never moved off a cushion. I mean, if they're doing - why the superficial material? But there is always a purpose in putting something forth: they've prepared the public for what's to come.

IFK: Many of these articles describe "abnormal reactions" or "danger signals" occurring as a result of practicing Chi Kung. Have you seen these reactions in your students?

GJC: I don't know why these reactions are being called "danger signals"! If you're a body builder you're always at risk of hurting yourself somewhere along the line. If you're a surgeon, work in the operating room is one big risk! If you want to be good at anything in life you must develop the warrior spirit to handle the so-called "dangers"; which, by the way, I still haven't acknowledged - and it's been over eleven years now. You have to look at the American people and the prevalent attitude. If they don't get it in five minutes, it's not worth working for. Everyone has to understand that when we're talking about Chi Kung or internal Kung Fu training, this stuff takes awhile to learn. No, I don't mean they should get ripped off by thinking that it will take ten or twenty years. If a student has the right teacher, the right material, and is really motivated, then he can excel in a relatively short time: say, from six months to two years. He doesn't have to sit on the doorstep for five or ten years before the "venerable Master" decides to share a secret or two. So, you have to listen to where the articles are coming from. Does the person giving the warnings really know what he's talking about? Usually the warnings are coming from a place of fear, of trying to protect the system.

IFK: But isn't there a kernel of truth in the articles regarding headaches, ringing in the ears, dizziness, and emotional catharsis that might be triggered by this meditation?

GJC: Yes, but these aren't problems to worry about or to deter you from practicing Chi Kung. The more of these symptoms that a student has when practicing, the better, because as they figure out how to work through all these little bumps on the road, they're going to become masters, powerful, fearless! My advice is "do not worry about these reactions. No pain, no gain, no risk, no nothing!" Years ago in the heart of my Tai Chi training, I learned a valuable lesson applicable here. I'd often see my Tai Chi master whenever I had a problem with another student, a problem at work, or a problem at home. I'd go to him and ask: "What should I do about this?" His standard answer to reduce it's importance was: "When you're on a long road and you run over a little rock, do you stop to see what's happened to the rock, or do you just continue on, more concerned with the actual journey?" That's the approach I use with my students. When a student calls me up and has a problem and says: "What about this. I feel like..." Whatever it is, I say: "O.K. Don't worry about it. If you just sit it out, you'll get through it" - because the human body is amazing. Look at what we've been eating and breathing all these years, so for a little while you'll be uncomfortable, big deal. Just take a break and come back with a different exercise and slow down." This kind of reassurance is usually all that's needed.

IFK: One last question about "danger signals." Quoting a popular author here: "Another common sensation is shaking or trembling. This is most pronounced in static postures, but may also be experienced in moving forms such as Tai Chi Chuan or Pa Kua Chang. Trembling may be in the joints, particularly in the wrists and knees, or even internally, in the abdomen. Shaking should be neither resisted nor encouraged. It is caused by a blockage in Chi flow."

GJC: Only 50% true. First of all, when practicing Tai Chi or sitting in a Chi Kung posture that you're not used to and you start shaking, that doesn't mean there's a "Chi blockage." It means your sinews, that is, your connective tissue, tendons and ligaments, and your muscles too, aren't used to working in these positions. From a Tai Chi point of view, if you look at the way most people move and the way they sit, they sort of jerk around from one position to the next. Look at our favorite Western sport, Baseball. If a baseball game lasts for three hours, are the players exercising for three hours or is it really for only maybe 30 minutes? However, when you're practicing Tai

BEYOND SELF-HELP: MASTERING PERSONAL POWER™ by Gary J. Clyman

Chi or Chi Kung, it's a continuous thing. So, yes, you're legs and arms will tremble. In fact, I'd say that if somebody learned from me and they didn't tremble or shake, they weren't doing something right: either not working hard enough, not standing low enough, or they were just day dreaming. So, its no big deal, and it's certainly not a "danger." But! With the experienced student who's trained well and who has vibrations in the abdomen or up the spine during meditation, that's what he's been chasing after! He should be excited and grateful about it! It's just here that the student needs an understanding of the traditional Three Treasures so he can make sense out of what's happening, and what's in store for him too.

IFK: So you consider exposure to the "Three Treasures" theory important for success in Chi Kung? What about elusive concepts of Chi, Jing, and Shen?

GJC: Most books confuse this and make it impossible to understand. I'd rather give the student four or five sentences he could relate to and say: "I know what he's talking about." And even taking the risk that the concept he gets is incomplete, at least it's a beginning that he can build upon during his training. It's best to look at Chi, Jing, and Shen as levels. On the deepest somatic (body) level is Jing - sexual energy. When you're sexually attracted to someone, or when sexually aroused and you have an erection, its the energy of raw Jing surging up within you. To harness that energy and work it into a purified form, to cultivate it for purposes other than the sex act, say for fighting or personality development - that's the motivating fiber of Chi Kung meditation. As the student uses this concrete idea to guide his practice, and as begins to understand my Wholistic health orientation, with the emphasis on diet, nutritional supplementation, and proper body mechanics, it's not hard for him to expand this idea into the more abstract one of seeing Jing as the organism's generative and regenerative energy system, a power source that at conception activated cells, and then tissues, organs, the mind, the total person, and now - repairs them too. So, the vibrations then are cultivated Jing. Going back into my own Tai Chi training, I remember my first intense vibrations and having my Tai Chi brother touch the base of my neck to see if he could feel anything. He couldn't feel a thing, but to me I was on a roller coaster. I wasn't afraid though. Remember, there's two attitudes you can take: "Oh my god what's happening to me"! ,(wimpy way) or "Oh boy, here we go! This is what I've been working for all those months" (warrior way). So, when my students have their first vibrations they're very excited; they think it's great.

IKF: So how does this contrast with the famous "Chi" or "ki" so often written about?

GJC: With Jing you can transmit its energy, or the manifestation of your internal development, to another person and they can feel it. So here, if I hold both of your hands and decide to give you a shock, the feeling you can get from my cultivation of raw Jing, and its release, the fah, is pure Jing. "Fah Jing" is the "mysterious" power of the great Tai Chi Masters. It's sometimes labelled "Fah Jing." Jing can be transmitted for healing purposes also, but when we're talking about Chi, the energy of Chi can manifest as a sensation I feel that has nothing to do with the vibrations I can transmit to you. Chi energy (internal energy) has a completely different vibratory frequency. Chi vibrations are in the next level and are shorter, smaller, and faster vibrations. Jing vibrations (internal power) are more guttural, more physical, and a slower. Chi of course, moves the entire universe, and is in all of us from our first embryonic breath as the source of organic change and movement, of breathing, eating, walking, fighting, thinking, and even aging too. But to sense it and use it with purpose takes technique, practice, and work. An analogy is helpful here to my students. An internal combustion engine must have an energy source, gasoline, and a method of igniting the energy, the ignition system, into the more usable form of energy, horsepower. For us, Chi is the energy source, Jing is the power, and Chi Kung is the method of transformation.

IKF: So how do you put this mechanism to work? How do you harness the Chi and make it work for you? What's your basic approach here?

GJC: The concept that cuts through the fog of ignorance and secrecy, the concept that allows the student to use Chi with purpose, to cultivate Jing, to develop and "burn" it into form, to become a dynamic self-powered individual is "The Condensing Principle." "The Condensing Process" is one of creating an inner vacuum with Chi, Jing, and Shen all at the same time. It's the process of packing the essence of things into every thought, intention, and action. Here's one basic condensing technique for developing Jing: whatever the posture, on the inhale focus on the body to expand, and at the same time focus on the inhaled Chi to contract, to condense, into the core of the body; then, on the exhale focus on the body to contract, and at the same time focus on the inhaled Chi to expand. On each inhale and exhale there is a simultaneous mental focus to expand and contract. This particular technique does two things: first, it sensitizes you to where you are in space as a physical, material body, and second, it introduces you to the first glimmer of Chi sensation, so much used in later training. This is just step one. As we go on and on, what we're doing is refining this same basic technique to the point where it goes from as gross as the body contracts, to where all the molecules in your body condense into one single atom.

IKF: I understand that your Basic Path Training and The Sitting Forms make use of many postures and coordinated movements. What's the idea behind the variety?

GJC: Basically they all accomplish the same thing - to help the mind direct the Chi and Jing through the auxiliary Chi tracts. It's like dancing: when you're studying it, you have to learn more than one step. A similar problem exists here as in Tai Chi. Many students base their choice of a system or the quality of their chosen system on how many movements there are in it. "Oh, my form has 108, his has only 68, but I know of one that has 138." This is an attitude conceived in ignorance.

What's important is, at the end of the training, what does the interpretation look like, not how many movements there are. In Tai Chi there's only thirteen forms anyway, no matter how you count them: ward off, roll back, press, push, elbow, shoulder, roll/pull, split, and the five style steps or the four directions and center. So, no matter how you concoct the name, the form is still only going to be a combination of "The Original Thirteen Forms."

BEYOND SELF-HELP: MASTERING PERSONAL POWER™ by Gary J. Clyman

In my Chi Kung training, I've used "The Condensing Principle" to condense all the material into something that makes sense, and that can save the student years of struggle. Four standing forms in Basic Path Training and "6 Forms and 7 Circulations" otherwise known as "The Sitting Forms with the Mind Training" is the result. More important than the Chi pathways used during the movements is the specific emotion that becomes associated with that movement for each student. They get angry with one movement, they laugh with another, get depressed or excited with another. The forms initiate a real, observable cleansing process, what I call "Retracing /Releasing." For example, if a student has a history of physical violence and was abused as a child, when practicing "The Sitting Forms with The Mind Training," they get in touch with the emotional trace of that experience held in the body tissues by the Jing Chi "burning" it out. Such a history manifests in bursts of crying with one form, anger with another. Its different for each person. So when the material base for the emotion is destroyed and the emotion is reexperienced, they release this pent-up energy. They set themselves free of the past and come to live more "in the moment." A new, clearer vision develops. "The Sitting Forms with The Mind Training," especially help "burn" the way through whatever trace is holding back their development, whether it's in muscle tissue, nerve tissue, Chi tracts, psychic blockages, whatever. This is the "secret" Taoist process called "transmutation of energies."

Chi Kung is such a great system of meditation, and coupled with Tai Chi, its the ultimate. I'd say it's the "Grand Ultimate." (Tai Chi Chuan is translated as Grand Ultimate Boxing. Ed.)

IKF: In most meditation the mind is calmed and it simply registers the flux of consciousness to naturally reach a state of pure awareness for eventual union with the absolute. In Chi Kung however, the mind seems to be very active and directed.

GJC: It's active, but it's also concentrated, that is, focused. The mind is active only in the sense of "guiding the Chi," not thinking. This is called "Hsing Chi" and it means "wherever the mind goes, the Chi follows." Most meditation restricts awareness to mantra, a mandala, a chant, or the breathing. Most articles treat Chi Kung as a form of visualization - wrong! This is not. My concept of visualization is something created in imagination, something not existing, or not yet existing, like in the method of Creative Visualization. In Chi Kung you're not visualizing Chi condensing, circulating, or dispersing through the use of images, you are actually doing it, physically.

The proof is that you can feel the forewarned effects, and later, the personal power is there and you feel it. When using Tai Chi in a martial application, someone else feels it. This is not like other meditation systems in which consciousness is worked at the expense of the body. In the Taoist view, there is an innate Wholistic union of Chi, Jing, and Shen. Whenever one is being exercised, the other two are right there getting worked also. The Taoists wanted us to develop all our innate capacities so we could experience the joys of living here on earth for as long as possible. In Chi Kung, the person develops as a total unit, more fit for living.

BEYOND SELF-HELP: MASTERING PERSONAL POWER™ by Gary J. Clyman

IKF: You've talked about Jing and Chi, the basic concept of condensing, and a few other techniques, where does Shen, the third "Treasure," fit in?

GJC: Well, how do you take all this, the whole system of Chi Kung, and use it in your daily life? That's what Shen is about. When you develop the personal power of Jing you have to express this excess of vitality in some way. Since you've released latent Jing energy stored in armored muscles, tendons, and ligaments and added it to your pool of retained sexual energy, you're no longer a composite of everything that's happened to you in the past. You become "in the moment." You're not distracted by what happened last week, or six months ago. Now you can focus all the energy that you are on something new, on new goals, on a new direction for yourself. What I see in my classes is my students and clients developing the ability to recognize events for what they are. They make decisions more quickly and confidently. Their lives become simpler, less cluttered with emotional baggage, and the fear of doing new things disappears.

The cultivated Jing manifests in their physical presence and awareness, the Chi, in their ability to think more clearly, to make up their minds and not be distracted. The Shen is their ability to "follow through" on what they've decided upon. "Shen is the way you can manipulate your universe to be what you want it to be. Its your outlook on life - the way you work in the world." That's my understanding of the "Three Treasures." It grew out of my Kung Fu training, not out of the philosophy books.

IKF: Give me an idea of the energy paths your students use in your PERSONAL POWER TRAINING™.

GJC: "Basic Path Training" makes use of the basic forms from my Temple Style Tai Chi System. This is a non-moving standing meditation where the Condensing Principle is integrated into Upward and Downward, Inward and Outward, Holding Tai Chi Ball, and Raised Hands and Stance. In The Sitting Forms with the Mind Training, they learn the 'well points' for drawing in and releasing Chi, how to circulate along the Chi pathways, The Micro Cosmic Orbit, and the seven subtle tao yin forms. Breath training exposes them to the different breathing methods, and sphincter training helps the student comprehend how to pump Jing, and it prepares them for the advanced Taoist Sexual Technique. And Tai Chi Chi Kung is another advanced course where all basic concepts and techniques come together using moving Tai Chi forms. Many students then decide to take my Temple Style Tai Chi and over a longer period learn the principles of proper body mechanics, how to transfer Jing, and of course my favorite, self-defense.

IKF: Isn't Chi Kung usually taught as part of Tai Chi training? At least isn't that the martial arts tradition?

GJC: Yes. But in my Tai Chi classes I was rarely able to teach this to any of my Tai Chi students - they had to be around for two or three years first and complete the Tai Chi System. The chances of a student surviving my Tai Chi system were about two in a thousand. The training I give is like being in a monastery. It's as if you signed yourself up for five or six years in Taiwan or China and said: "don't let me out until my time is up." This is the intensity of how I teach in Chicago. So to share these secret oral teachings, and to help people with physical or emotional problems take an active role in their own well-being, I've set up the training so I can take someone with no background in internal Kung Fu, and I teach them the basic concepts of Chi Kung, the basic techniques, and the practical application for modern, high-intensity living. When they work hard, they receive the personal power benefits of Chi Kung, as if they had studied Tai Chi for ten years. Traditionally, Chi Kung was taught only as an extension of Tai Chi training, only after however long the teacher wants to keep the student on the hook. If the teacher even knows Chi Kung, that is. I'm not doing that. This material is too valuable to keep a secret any longer.

IKF: The basic premise of your work then is that Chi Kung and Tai Chi offer a comprehensive program for optimal health?

GJC: Right! But it even goes beyond that and introduces the element of longevity into the students life. All we've discussed thus far is part of the Taoism Nei Tan program of internal transformation, what I call PERSONAL POWER TRAINING™.

Natural diet is important too. It's from our food and air that we receive the Jing and Chi components to manufacture new raw Jing energy for later cultivation in Chi Kung. The more pure and balanced the diet, the better the Jing production. That means basically a macrobiotic diet of grains, beans, vegetables, and fruits. Scientific research is showing that a low-fat, high complex carbohydrate diet like this can zap degenerative diseases and extend the life-span. Even here the Taoists had another trick up their sleeves. Their Wai Tan program of external elixirs was an attempt to create anti-aging medicines so they could experience life with the intensity of the Hsien Immortal - "to fly on the clouds," as Chuang Tzu said. This idea, that certain chemicals could extend our life-span, lives today in gerontology research labs. Scientists like Leonard Hayflick and Roy Walford have written that using vitamin and mineral supplements to neutralize cellular oxidants may be the best method to retard aging and extend the life-span to 120 years. Not quite enough time to become a Hsien Immortal, but good enough for we modern city folk!

IKF: So, as a Wholistic health practitioner you've found that changing to a natural diet is pretty important for creating more energy and power in a person's life?

GJC: Of course, but since our farm soils are so over used and crops are force-fed with growth-stimulating fertilizers, its not enough to rely on just the nutrients in foods to supply the needs of a modern people. What's needed is a reliable quick method to check our low energy states and the deficient nutrients that may be responsible. Only then can a wise choice be made in choosing "the right supplements," if they are needed. And its just here again that the Taoists and acupuncturists were close on the track of how to monitor out own nutrition. The acupuncture tracts and their Chi circulation can now be tested using Applied Kinesiology, or muscle response testing, to discover low levels of molecular vibration and the corresponding nutrient deficits. We're all heirs to this tradition and its modern application.

CHAPTER #5
CONCERNING EMOTIONS

MY VISION AND PURPOSE

"Masters are meant to free students, NOT imprison them." GJC

FREEDOM VS. BONDAGE

Many, I might even say "most" other spiritual systems lead the follower further in, on the path. The Clyman System™ however has very specific directions; to set yourself free. Following this path, leads you to your own "true path," not mine. When you practice Chi Kung, you will do exactly what you are suppose to do, "the right thing." My system concentrates primarily on "Strengthening your WILL."

An important saying is, "It's with the mind, not in the mind." Many people have the misunderstanding that all things in Chi Kung are done "in the mind," this is wrong. Many things are done "with the mind." This one word change is said to represent the "one inch off that leads to a mistake of 1,000 miles." Don't make this mistake.

HANDS ON, TRANSFER OF POWER™

Now my work has become very strange. I have developed the ability and spiritual strength to walk in multiple worlds, at the same time. As of late, I can be in the spirit world which involves communicating directly with people who no longer live physically on this plane, as well as being able to retrace with my friends and clients at the time and age that their original incidents took place. I can now recall their wounded spirits, speak directly with them, and bring about the necessary healing whether it may involve forgiveness, resolving problems is relationships, or any other necessary resolution or closure that may be needed.

I just realized what I have been doing, and why I have not been practicing Tai Chi as in the past. My Tai Chi has given me the skills and strength to communicate with other spirits and entities that no longer are living on this plane. My Tai Chi has contributed to my constitution and given me the spiritual strength to perform this needed work without any side effects related to living in this world and any other I may need to visit. My Tai Chi is and remains the secret to my success in my intuitional skills.

I have hit my writers block and am now stepping through it. It is very scary, but I know my work is important to mankind as well as my own personal, spiritual growth.

My father, Dr. Clyde Clyman, who died in 1968, is alive in my spirit and is pulling my strings in that I always seem to know what my friends and clients need to do.

My "Hands on, Transfer of Power™" is this work in action in this present, living world. Wilhelm Reich made his important contribution to the world and now my time has come. To heal the wounded souls of the present by re-writing the original incidents of my friends and clients over again. Yes, these new understandings are incredible and very freaky as well as scary to me, but the next stage of my work must go on.

My work has now gone beyond the restraints and limits of time and space. I have thought and wondered about this ability for over 10 years, but never knew what to do to move in this direction. I have now developed these skills and abilities without trying.

The major work ahead of me is to develop my concepts that can be readily communicated, accepted, understood and utilized by main stream humanity in this world of the 1990's.

REACTIONS DURING "HANDS ON, TRANSFER OF POWER"

While the "Hands on, Transfer of Power" is taking place, some people have very clear visualizations about what there "original incidents" are while others have feelings or hear voices. A very small percentage of my clients don't experience anything. Just because they do not experience anything does not indicate that nothing is happening. We, my client and myself, usually figure out what effect the "Hands on, Transfer of Power" has had on them a week or two later.

"HANDS ON, TRANSFER OF POWER" IN A NUTSHELL

This is how I would explain to you the "Hands on, Transfer of Power" procedure. First I energize the areas that are related to the "original incidents." After these areas have been energized and the "original incidents" are back on your screen or in view, I help my client encapsulate them so he can excrete these "original incidents" or so I can take them away, or vacuum them out. Next I actually pluck it like a grape. The final step in the "Hands on, Transfer of Power" process is I comb for any remaining particles of the old experience.

THE DIAPHRAGM

Many people have immediate associations when the word "diaphragm" is mentioned. Please put your preconceptions away for now. The diaphragm is the place I start when performing the "Hands on, Transfer of Power." The diaphragm in this instance has nothing to do with diaphragmatic breathing. I discovered this important technique almost by accident many years ago. I believe other people will be able to perform part of this valuable technique by learning from this book.

The diaphragm is a very important part in the "Hands on, Transfer of Power" process. I believe that this process is revolutionary in that the simple procedure of doing the technique itself can be performed by many different people without any serious "internal training." However, the "combing" part of the technique, does require a high level of internal energy development. I have seen some people that I have instructed, use it on their friends and family and actually be able to pull some of the same kind of results out that I am able to get.

I am not saying that many people can do what I do. I can't do it because of my tremendous amount of accumulated internal energy. There might be others out there, but I have yet to meet any others.

I have created the procedure "Hands On, Transfer of Power" in a very structured and technical way. I have seen problems with being unable to move the diaphragm that are related to a divorce that happened in the family when the client was between the ages of 6 and 11. Almost 100% of the people I've worked with that have had this "frozen diaphragm" problem to the point that they could not get it to move in the technique of "Inside Air," have come through a sever family trauma between these ages of 6 to 11.

After freeing up their diaphragm with the "Hands On, Transfer of Power" technique, many of these people have visions of what the trauma of the "original incidents" were that created this "frozen diaphragm" problem.

Many times while doing the "Hands On, Transfer of Power," their voices, faces, and body language changes to reflect the age of these "original incidents" whether they were experienced at the ages of 4 or 8 years old. When these changes happen, it is truly amazing. The client can then realize what happened and can now "re-write" what originally happened. This is like changing a computer program and having it affect your life (program) everywhere else. It is wiped clean, forever. This is a very "freaky" but real phenomenon, when it happens. And it does happen, on a very regular and predictable basis.

"HANDS ON" IS NOT FUN, BUT IS VERY HELPFUL

O.K., the "Hands On, Transfer of Power" can be very painful, depending on the person receiving it. Not that the physical technique of having it done to you is that painful, but what it brings up, the old experiences and the "original incidents," the rage, the anger, the guilt, and the abandonment. That's painful, but if you go through 10 or 15 minutes of mostly emotional pain, you're free of the "original incident" that "runs your life" and causes you pain everyday, on a daily basis anyway.

"Hands On, Transfer of Power" is not role playing. It relates to the actual "original incident" itself. I cannot stress this enough. You're not going back to "recreate the experience." We're not talking about recreating an incident or a problem. When I do "Hands on, Transfer of Power" you are actually there. Many people go back 20, 30, even 40 years while we're doing it. Say you were 4 years old and your father was leaving your mother and you knew it, but you couldn't even talk yet, you have this picture of your father leaving. During a "Hands On, Transfer of Power," you are seeing him leave and then you get to talk and say you don't want him to go. That incident is what started this long chain of recurring events in your life related to your "abandonment."

Remember, we're not talking about recreating a problem, we're talking about "being there." So, a question comes up: Is this result reproducible? Is this scientific? My answers in response to these questions are "depending upon what you mean by scientific." Can I stand up to a double blind study? Can what I do be explained in a human way, so that people with no previous understanding can understand it and is it reproducible? Yes. Is it reproducible 100 percent of the time? No, but very few things are. I have standardized the areas that I find these specific emotional issues. They are almost always the same general areas on all people I've worked with.

But, someone who has "abandonment" has it in the same place as everyone else. That doesn't mean that all people have "abandonment." Someone that has "anger," has "anger" in the same place as everyone else, but that doesn't mean that everyone has "anger" either. "Guilt" on a man is in a different place than "guilt" on a woman. "Guilt" on a woman is right over the ovaries. "Guilt" on a man is just by the inguinal ligament, which is just outside the testicles on the torso, not on the legs, not on the genitals but right on the torso next to the testicles. That's where I've found "guilt" to be on men.

Then you've got "Bitterness" which is mid-way between the naval and the Xyphoid process, right in the middle. "Bitterness" I found more recently than the other emotions. "Anger" and "depression" are in the same spot over the liver. "Rage" is in the gallbladder, which is slightly back from the liver. "Fear" is right over the kidneys, near the low back. "Fear" is very rare to find. Like I said elsewhere in the book, this is a lot of "Five Element" related material yet it's quite different. Many of these emotions work in pairs as in "Five Element Theory."

VARIOUS TISSUES EFFECTED

The practice of Chi Kung effects many different kinds of tissue in the body. The first to be effected is the marrow in the bones. The bone marrow is important in that this is where the blood is produced. The second area of effect is the nervous system which controls all the various functions either directly or indirectly throughout the rest of the body. In the fetus, the nervous system is the first to develop. The third is the flesh and inner organs with their various responsibilities and functions. Finally the skin develops. The final function of Chi Kung in relationship to the tissue is that it balances the entire body.

USING THE HANDS

The hands are wonderful tools. They can be vehicles for moving energy around. They can be physical tools for moving bones, relieving tension, again moving energy, but in a much slower pace. The hands can also be used for passing "Spirit" from one person to another.

TOUCH WITHOUT TOUCHING

Development of using the hands has many levels. These levels can go all the way to passing energy across a distance and manipulating or moving another person's body, out of that person's control, with the mind through the hands. This as far as I know, is as far as it can go.

When I move somebody using what is called "distance power" through space, it actually feels no different than when I was doing my regular practice. However, the other person experiences the sensations, the movement, the pull, the feel, and the power.

When this happened to me in 1987, I could not believe it myself. So I tried to do it again and I had my video man there to record it. We captured it the second time on video tape.

The person I performed "distance power" on, and I have done it to a few, but none ever to this extent, was a black man who was a sailor with no previous experience with Chi Kung or Tai Chi except through taking my weekend workshop with me. What I was able to do, was energize him or create a sensitivity from doing "Hands On, Transfer of Power" to him. His experience related to his father's death when he was only 4 years old.

Immediately after that I was able to move him through the room, bounce him off the walls, make him do summersaults, while even through the doors and walls the energy passed. Eventually within a 2 hour time span, I was able to move him without using my body, just by using my mind. I have this on video and it is documented with five or six witnesses who were there through the whole time.

This made me very, very excited. The possibility of doing something that I had never seen before was a high point in my practice.

Now, how does this apply to you, the reader? I'm telling you this so that you can desolve your own barriers and go through life doing things that you didn't think were possible.

What we are talking about here is the same energy that you develop, cultivate, circulate, generate and move around inside your Micro Cosmic Orbit, except that in my case, since I have been doing this for so long, and so intensively, I am able to move it outside of my body, and communicate to another person, without words.

Yes, this is a very strange phenomenon, but what the hell, life is full of strange things.

TAI CHI TRANSFER OF POWER

You see, "Transfer of Power" is a traditional Tai Chi phrase referring to releasing your internal energy, vibrating your skeleton, and what's called bouncing another person off a wall. Of course, you are touching, but you are very gently touching the other person.

The principle behind this is that you very gently touch somebody and you are able to "zap" yourself. It's almost like a bolt of lightning. Your spine and skeleton moves like a bolt of lightning and the other person has absolutely no sensitivity to the point that they fly as if they're weightless. This has been done to me many times as a student and I have done this many more times as an instructor.

The sensations felt while doing this to another person are no different than when you are doing your regular meditation practice. And when I say "meditation practice" I mean your "Tai Chi Connective Meditations." I don't mean Chi Kung.

The difference between Tai Chi Connective Meditations and Chi Kung as you can tell by an article explaining Temple Style Tai Chi, which I wrote for Inside Kung Fu Magazine (April 1989), is included in this book. "Tai Chi Connective Meditation" is done actually using Tai Chi forms and imposing "The Mind" on top of the actual physical movements, with the linkage to the ground and everything else.

Chi Kung does not have this physical structural relationship to everything else as does Tai Chi. Chi Kung is physical and yes, it's in the body, but Chi Kung is not as grounded, rooted, and linked so that one cell relates to the next in a way like "a string of pearls" as it is in Tai Chi.

Emotional stripping away of defenses and pretenses combined with a drive toward achieving an insight produces results. Together this combination is very effective. This approach does not allow a space for resistance.

I don't pick up the energy from the other person even though I directly vacuum it off.

STRING OF PEARLS?

A string of pearls is more symbolic of how Tai Chi works than Chi Kung. Chi Kung does not really carry the power in the same way because it's not the most important principle. You do Chi Kung to develop the power of the mind and your WILL. You do Tai Chi primarily (80%) to change the physical structure, the skeleton, strengthen the legs and the lower half of the body, and loosen the upper half of the body, etc.

HOW I DEVELOPED MY ENERGY PROJECTION ABILITY

Many years ago when I attempted to use my hands for using energy outside of my own body I practiced with plants. We're going back to 1976. I originally got the inspiration outside of what my mind had seen or what I thought was possible. I was actually able to make the plants wave from 6-7 feet away. These experiments were very exciting and inspiring. This was the beginning. Now that was in 1976 and I hadn't been able to move my first person until 1986 and the video event that I mentioned previously happened at the end of 1987. So it does take a long time to develop these kinds of powers.

RULES AND SUGGESTIONS

The larger the physical movement, the smaller the internal circulation. The smaller the physical movement, the larger the internal circulation. This means if you are physically moving, your mind cannot concentrate on the internal circulation because the body is the distraction.

That's why somebody who practices Karate really cannot be internal, because they are solely external. Yet somebody who is barely moving can have a large mind circulation movement. This is at the heart of Tai Chi. Very small movements with sudden change. Inaction to action equals Yin to Yang.

"You want what you deserve... etc." and you deserve more than what you want can be used to break through your own comfort zone.

Without this body, there can be no Tao. Lao Tsu

When doing "The Chi Circulations," the body does not matter!!! "The Chi Circulations" are the only things that are important. In Tai Chi Ball, the arms serve as a bellow to aid in sucking in through the knees.

Use the principles obvious in Nature when practicing. If it seems wrong, it probably is.

Never condense on the exhale, **condense on the inhale ONLY**.

When exhaling, don't be concerned with the pathway of the exhale, let nature take it's course.

If you think you can't do it, you're right. What you crave the most, is what your body is expelling during detoxification. Not eating Red Meat increases your internal sensitivity development.

GARY'S HEALING STORY

A question that comes up very frequently is where did I develop the healing powers that I use to help people get better fast?

A.   A few important experiences led me to learning how to be a healer. I already had it in me but had no idea what to do with it. I started out, believe it or not, by trying

BEYOND SELF-HELP: MASTERING PERSONAL POWER™ by Gary J. Clyman

to help people in the street. Many many years ago I found an epileptic lying on the street having a seizure--I helped him and within a year or so after that time I began martial art.

My first experience with healing was with a fellow student who had been kicked and fell and hit his head on the concrete floor. With no training whatsoever I did what came instinctively. All the students and the teacher in that class became hysterical because this student was convulsing. His head and neck were the same size. He stopped breathing; he was turning purple and I did the only thing that seemed to make sense--I pounded on his chest, which in reality was CPR and the following day the paramedic that removed him from the school came back and told my teacher that the person that worked on him the day before, which was me, saved his life. That was the start of my healing career.

Shortly after, I started Tai Chi. Within a year or two of starting Tai Chi, I returned to my first martial art teacher because I knew that he knew an acupuncturist who was teaching students.

Acupuncture was kept "secret" in those days and my acupuncture teacher made me promise I would use what he taught me "professionally." After careful questioning of my character and intentions, my acupuncture teacher started studying Tai Chi with me and a year or so later, I started studying acupuncture with him.

Then in 1979, a few years later, I learned one of the early Chiropractic techniques from a famous Chiropractic teacher named Dr. Lamar Rosquist from Salt Lake City, Utah. He took me under his wing and taught me orthomolecular nutrition, muscle response testing (Kinesiology), Chiropractic manipulation and many other diversified techniques.

When I met Dr. Rosquist, I was already practicing acupuncture and teaching Tai Chi for a living. I was able to infuse my newly learned technical training into my patient treatment repertoire.

Through Dr. Rosquist I was introduced to his partner of many years, Dr. Gary Whitley, the best Chiropractor I know. Dr. Whitley is a "genius" and a "true healer." He is as proficient in his art, Chiropractic, as I am in mine. Dr. Whitley has become one of my best friends. Gary Whitley tries to teach me to be compassionate whenever he gets a chance--we're both winning.

I retired as of November 1985 from the healing profession and no longer accept or treat patients or clients. I now help people in much larger ways than before. I now specialize in my "Energy Work." Teaching through PERSONAL POWER TRAINING™ enables me to help people in more important ways than if I were a Chiropractor. With every Chiropractor that I train in my art (Chi Kung), I can now indirectly help thousands of other people. This is more important.

BEYOND SELF-HELP: MASTERING PERSONAL POWER™ by Gary J. Clyman

MEDICINE MAN MEETS MEDICINE MAN

In September on 1979, on an Indian reservation called the White Mountain Fort Apache Reservation, in a town called Cibecue, a senior Medicine Man of the Apache tribe named Nick Thompson, age 69, suffered a stroke leaving him paralyzed on the right side. He could not walk, could not see out of his right eye, and had a "total sensory deficit" on the right side.

About two weeks after he suffered the stroke, a friend of Nick's, a white man, went home to visit his family in southern Illinois. He then spent some time in Chicago visiting a friend who was a student of mine at The Chicago Tai Chi Academy, where an ancient Chinese martial art for health and self defense is taught. While here, he asked me, because of my experience in acupuncture and other healing arts, whether there was any hope for the old man. There were no promises given, but arrangements were made for me to travel to the reservation to spend possibly up to three weeks with Nick. I left right away and spent two and a half weeks living on the reservation, treating him daily.

When I first got there, he was just coming down with what appeared to be pneumonia. So the first thing I had to do was alleviate the threat of pneumonia, which would complicate things considerably if allowed to continue. After a few days, the respiratory problem cleared up and muscle testing and other diagnostic techniques were begun to determine the cause of the stroke. According to acupuncture theory, there are about 18 possible categories of stroke. Nick's symptoms fit a "classic" type. From conversations with his family, it was clear that Nick had a liver and heart related stroke. This was confirmed by pulse diagnosis (not the same as Western medicine), indicating excesses and deficiencies in each acupuncture meridian, 14 in all. First, I applied an "emergency treatment" to balance his body and open channels for treatment to occur more efficiently. After that, I treated specifically for the type of stroke that Nick had. After about five of six days, Nick began to show slight movement in his paralyzed leg. Within the first week, we helped him walk, supporting him on our shoulders.

The treatments were composed of daily massage, acupuncture treatments and therapy to increase his activity, circulation, and range of motion. The second week, his sense of humor improved and his strength increased. Sight returned to his right eye, swelling at the side of his head disap-peared, he was able to hear more clearly, and he was able to speak understandable English. When I first arrived, his own family could not understand him when he spoke Apache, let alone English. Toward the end of the second week, he promised me that in two days he would be walking alone, without assistance. A couple of days before this promise, his wife had to come and get me early in the morning to get Nick up off the floor. He had been practicing walking with his cane, fell down in the middle of the room, and was unable to get up. His wife was unable to lift his 175 pounds and I had to struggle to get him back to bed.

Because of their poverty, people on the reservation have a diet consisting largely of white flour, white sugar and corn meal. Most of them were extremely overweight and had many health problems. I was able to influence some of Nick's younger relatives to improve their diet, but not Nick himself.

Two days after his promise, Nick walked on his own with a cane. I was scheduled to return home in two days after this. The day before I left, I gave Nick the final treatment. This consisted of touching with our hands important points on each of the acupuncture meridians, all at the same time, with the help of eight of Nick's relatives and friends, with the intention of "pooling and transferring" their energy into Nick's weak body so that his progress would continue after I had gone. At the time of the last treatment, he had become strong enough and independent enough to resist us. After some convincing on my part, he accepted the treatment from myself and his relatives.

Arrangements were made for me to fly back for three days of treatment in the middle of January 1980 to continue his recovery. Shortly before I was to leave, Nick's son told me by telephone that it was not necessary to make the trip because Nick had regained use of his paralyzed right arm. This was the goal of the cumulative acupuncture treatments.

While I was there, I also treated other members of Nick's family. One was a 16 year old girl weighing 260 pounds. After two treatments with instructions on self treatment using her own hands, she lost about 30 pounds by January. Her father, who had been severely burned on his arm and hand from insecticides five years earlier, received two treatments and reported in January that the residual rash from these burns had completely been alleviated.

Many of the Indians were afraid that I was practicing magic or witchcraft and a lot of time was spent with them explaining what acupuncture was and how it can work. They expected that an old Chinese doctor was coming to heal their medicine man. Boy were they surprised to see me!

It was a most rewarding experience to be accepted and trusted by an Apache family in such extreme conditions. Nick told me that I was closer to him than most of his relatives, because I came such a long distance to try to help.

At the time of the last communication with Nick's friends, Nick was riding his horse again as of early 1988.

INTRO QUESTIONS

Please list 3 things you LOVE the most.
Please list 3 things you HATE the most.
Please list 3 things that would exist if you could push a button and make them happen.
Many books use a format that is very difficult for people with little experience to utilize.

THE 4 CATEGORIES OF A STUDENTS SERIOUSNESS

1) A Passing Fancy / Somewhat interested
2) Serious Intenders / With No Follow Through
3) Accelerated Beginners
4) The Long Hauler / With Action

LEARNING HOW TO LEARN

Most people are so unstructured in their lives that learning how to learn is extremely important. This ties in with internal discipline. The side effects of living an unstructured life are unproductive and dangerous, and lead to your life being one long rollercoaster ride. Learning Chi Kung the way I teach it, will teach you how to understand the workings of your own mind. This understanding I call "learning how to learn."

It's very difficult to apply discipline to your profession, where it counts. It's much easier and more practical to "learn how to learn," take your "new disciplines" and use them as your professional applications. These applications are used not just in your profession but in your relationships, and in the way you think about and treat yourself.

Examples:

Many commodity traders require the ability to "think on their feet," to know where the market is going, to have some idea and to possess the discipline skills needed to perform what your mind tells you. Applying internal discipline to trading is one of the most difficult and important things a trader has to do. The question frequently comes up: "How do you apply Personal Power Training™ discipline skills to trading?" Unfortunately, there is no simple answer to this question because all traders are different.

Individual characteristics determine this. This is where we must determine what attributes need to be improved (self-confidence, self-discipline, or just plain market knowledge). I work best with traders that possess market knowledge that exceeds their ability to act. The results most of my traders experience begin to show between 3-5 weeks. This is remarkably fast when you consider how long some of my clients have been trading, before they came to me. I make sure they do what they say they want to do. This goes for everybody, not just traders... just 3-5 weeks.

YOU CAN MASTER ANYTHING

Remember, "Masters are made in the beginning, not at the end." When I was a Tai Chi student, I observed other students practicing Tai Chi with the attitude that someday in the future they would be good at it. My attitude always was different. I knew that even though my knowledge was limited at the time, what I did know was already very good. Persistence will pay off for you also. You must truly love what you choose to do.

Quality is more important than quantity. If you apply, learn, and train with the attitude that what you're learning is good, then and only then, are you going to end up being "great." If you think that some day you're going to go from being "shitty" to being great, forget it. That is not how the world works. The trouble that most people have with this, is that they have never been really good at anything, so they have no concept of what it is to truly excel at something. This is being dominated by negative belief systems.

Since I became so good at Tai Chi because of the way I was, that I learned how to learn, so that when you learn something other than your specific specialty, whether you're a lawyer, a commodity trader, or a Chiropractor, and you didn't learn in this same kind of organized fashion, you never developed the self-confidence that goes along with becoming an expert.

There are a lot of "experts" that have kept their bad attitudes, their low levels of self-esteem and self-confidence. However, if you learn the way I'm describing, your self-confidence levels elevate at the same rate as your proficiency levels. That's what this work, Chi Kung, is about, "Learning how to Learn."

SOMETHING ABOUT WIMPY MEN

There exists a very strange phenomenon that I have witnessed many times over. It shows up in men more than women. I call it "men that are wimps but don't look wimpy." What I am describing is your relationship with yourself. It's as if you are always a little <u>too nice</u> and you are always willing to give away too much. You just never put any boundaries for yourself. This shows up frequently in my sessions with my clients. It's like the phrase, "nice guys finishes last" is actually true. These men are joined in spirit, or lack of it. When they talk to each other, they know exactly what each is feeling. They share the same lack of heart. These men appear and sound successful. It's as if they have learned how to carry the facade of success, but deep down inside they know they are not truly successful, that something is missing.

With this kind of man, I can work wonders and perform miracles.

WIMPY MEN & AGGRESSIVE WOMEN VS. WIMPY WOMEN & AGGRESSIVE MEN

Unfortunately, a problem I've noticed with women is that their level of commitment is much lower then most men, at least in the Chicago area. This is the opposite in Portland, Oregon where the women are very aggressive and many of the men are "wimps." Here in Chicago, the women are very wimpy and the men are very aggressive. Why? I don't know, but I have noticed this for many years.

As a matter of fact, it's as if the women in Chicago, if they want to work with me, just can't figure how to do it. They usually don't begin immediately, or at least they rarely do. No matter how strongly they feel about something, many women just don't have the follow-through. They don't just do this with me. They usually act this way with everything. This relates back to their childhood and the limitations with which they were raised. If they have an undeserving attitude, it will usually show up in these situations.

When I'm referring to an undeserving attitude, I mean they just don't have the WILL or drive to break out of their shells. They actually act as if they need someone to give them permission. Not only do I show you how to "crack" your shell, but I show you how to recognize and dissolve it forever.

SUCCESSFUL PEOPLE FROM ALL WALKS OF LIFE

What about your really successful businessmen who have "made it?"

There is no stereotype for that because when they come to work with me, regardless of how successful, happy or prosperous they appear on the outside, the side they show to me is the side they actually want healed.

Whether it's feeling complete, self-contained, deserving, more masculine, or truly accepted by themselves, their wives or in their primary relationship, these men always get what they need from me. These men appear O.K. on the outside but all people have needs, and these men, though they appear more sophisticated or complex than the average person, do benefit greatly when they work with me.

CHAPTER #6
HUMAN POSSIBILITIES

CASE HISTORIES AND TESTIMONIALS

These case histories and testimonials are signed by their contributors. They have been included to explain and show the changes and transformations many of my clients and students have undergone. These case histories were collected shortly before the publishing of this book. Many of these transformations are still in progress at the time of this publishing. I wish to thank all my clients and students for their inspired contributions, from the bottom of my heart. Due to space limitations, many contributions were not included. For this I apologize. Maybe they can be included in my next book.

"REAL PEOPLE" TESTIMONIALS

"Working with Gary Clyman has given me the ability to focus on a problem, visualize the solution, and go in a direct line to bring about the necessary change." Daniel Garvey, (DN) Commodity trader, The C.B.O.T. Bond Pit. President, Inland Trading Company. Chicago, IL

"Gary Clyman's PERSONAL POWER TRAINING™ is one of the most relevant, important and unique trainings offered. It cuts through the crap and saves me a lot of time. I learned in two weeks what would have taken me five years to get elsewhere." Dr. Mark R. Marquart, Naperville, IL

"Gary is great - I feel stronger & more secure in my own energy flow. He can be of help in any professional or business setting. There is nothing like this that you can obtain elsewhere. Although I have been practicing for only a few months, I have seen great success already." Harvey Waller, Tax attorney and commodity trader, Chicago, IL

I'm not too good at giving testimonials but I know I should let people know about the experiences I had and things I learned while I was your student. You are a "progressive pioneer" in understanding that which is "intangible" in people.

Your unselfish willingness to improve people through their mastering that which is inside them, in ways that I don't understand, yet I know are extremely effective, should be made public. There are things in this world that are genuine only if believed in and people should not to be critical and cynical about things they don't understand.

I hope your book becomes a big success. Thanks for everything you gave and taught me when I was your student. George Larson, U.S. Navy

BEYOND SELF-HELP: MASTERING PERSONAL POWER™ by Gary J. Clyman

"When I originally interviewed with Gary Clyman, I was as skeptical as the next guy. What he said made sense, and I figured I had nothing to lose. I made "the right decision." I received major results in the areas of self-respect and self-confidence.

Clyman's PERSONAL POWER TRAINING™ has helped me to accept respons-ibility for what happens to me instead of projecting and creating future problems. Taking responsibly for my own actions made a world of difference in my life, my relationships, and most important, my trading." I never thought I'd give Gary Clyman a testimonial, let alone ever say "he doesn't charge enough." Wayne Hendricks, (WCH) Commodity trader, The C.B.O.T. Bond Pit.

As for contributions to your book, most of my Chi Kung practice tends to be at night because of my work schedule. It is not uncommon that by the time I finish practicing, I am so energized, I can't sleep at night. It's as if I could just skip sleeping and go right into another day of work. David Cheffi, Elmwood Park, IL

I just felt like I had moved very, very fast toward where I was heading on my own except I was plodding along, and it was painstakingly slow. You just gave a boost toward where I was going and my focus widened so I could see more possibilities. I now have more energy, which is great.

You attract people that can do this work and you provide "profound enthusiasm for life." I've never met anybody like you. The very thing that I was scared of originally, is the very thing that I'm now drawn to; the reason I want to work with you. Your "knowingness" and confidence levels are contagious. Sheila Rubin, Portland, OR

The main reasons that I found PERSONAL POWER TRAINING™ helped was that it helped me, first of all, identify some of the origins of my frustrations and secondly, it restored some confidence in myself as a person.

The actual daily practice, which from my point of view, is only a small portion that probably could be done, has helped me focus in on the day when I do it early in the morning. It has helped me improve my awareness and I believe that's been very helpful.

I'm a commodity trader and I do customer business as well as trade for myself. During those months that I was very frustrated with the whole situation, PERSONAL POWER TRAINING™ helped me calm down and restore confidence in myself. This is important because most of "The Game of Trading" is a test of confidence. Paul Kram, (PKL) The C.B.O.T., Chicago, IL

"Now I have a higher tolerance for dealing with life's frustrations and less of a tendency to indulge in extremes... like food." Elyse Green, School psychologist, Chicago, IL

"I have been using the ideas and internal energy cultivation exercises taught by Gary

BEYOND SELF-HELP: MASTERING PERSONAL POWER™ by Gary J. Clyman

Clyman for the past 5 months and the results have been phenomenal. My practice is growing and my daily life is filled with greater amounts of energy and joy. The increased inner power I feel helps me turn conflict and problems into solutions. I can be a tiger when the situation calls for it. Peace of mind feels GREAT. Thanks Gary." Dr. Gary Whitley, Chiropractic Physician, Salt Lake City, UT

"Gary is gifted with the 6th and 7th senses about what truly afflicts people, and how they can heal themselves." Joseph Mill, Psychotherapist, Chicago, IL

Gary, I just want to briefly share with you what Chi Kung has done for me. The major benefit to me may also be the most basic benefit. Chi Kung has taught me how to breathe. As a childhood asthmatic, I was always a "chest breather." To this day during times of stress and anxiety, I still breathe shallowly. At this point, I use some of the techniques you taught me and in moments my breathing is back to normal.

The second benefit I have derived from my Chi Kung practice is a presence I feel, the way I feel within my body, the way I am aware of my extremities. I get a feeling of total presence. Thanks Gary. John Goodman, Chicago, IL

"I've been with a Chiropractic management firm with moderate growth for 2 years, but with Gary's coaching, the increased growth has been dramatic and accelerated. This is the perfect adjunct to any professional Chiropractic management program. My self-image has improved greatly... When I look in the mirror, I now see a successful doctor. My technical skills have gone beyond technique. Cultivating internal energy really makes a difference."

I used to ask myself, "How can this work?" I don't anymore. Gary's methods are unorthodox, but so effective, I just do it and the results follow. My business has grown and I am very grateful for that. Gary does just what he says he'll do. Dr. Joseph Kalal, Chiropractic Physician, Chicago, IL

"I find I'm more outgoing... I've become more aware of how I function... The most important thing to know about PERSONAL POWER TRAINING™ is... It Works!" John Packel, Commodity Trader, Los Angeles, CA

"After experiencing only a third of the first day of the two day weekend workshop due to a family emergency, I noticed major changes immediately in my negative belief systems. I can hardly wait to complete the workshop after participating in just a fraction of it." Larry R. Michalski, Des Plaines, IL

"My experience in taking PERSONAL POWER TRAINING™ with Gary Clyman was unique. It opened many doors that were previously closed to me. The training helped me physically, mentally, and spiritually, and in witnessing myself with new understanding and courage. These experiences helped release much of the stress and blocked energy I was holding onto. Being with Gary was truly part of the training for he showed me that "a person can be what his words are all about." It is truly a

BEYOND SELF-HELP: MASTERING PERSONAL POWER™ by Gary J. Clyman

worthwhile experience for everyone. It teaches you to be one with yourself." Joseph Bruno.

I have more energy than I've had in my whole life and I feel better than I ever have, too. I feel I can handle anything that might come my way. So much of what I feel is emotional - it's hard to put into words... but if I had not done PERSONAL POWER TRAINING™, I would surely have ruined the current relationship I'm in.

People notice me now when I walk down the street. My confidence has been elevated to a new height... My goals have changed and the motivation behind them is stronger, so I'm looking toward the future in a totally new light.

The energy and improvement come from within yourself. You're not putting yourself in anyone else's hands to cure you or to heal you. It all comes from within!" Theresa Williams

PERSONAL POWER TRAINING™ helped me become more active in applying everything I know to whatever I want to do. Things are clearer for me. Each time I do my daily exercises, I feel more attuned to the energy in my body. I'm using the training techniques in every area of my life. PERSONAL POWER TRAINING™ has given me a place from which to focus.

Now I have a way to focus and concentrate that is relaxing, but not boring... It's a catalysis to energize myself. PERSONAL POWER TRAINING™ has helped me improve my relationship with myself... my self-esteem has been enhanced; and it has improved my relationship with others as well.

PERSONAL POWER TRAINING™ has helped me become much more aware of breath control, concentration, and my sense of power. It has helped me to organize myself internally. I have never felt better in my life. PERSONAL POWER TRAINING™ is a catalyst for change... it gets things done! Andy Roth

PERSONAL POWER TRAINING™ is the most honest and straight forward course I've ever taken. It's taught me to recognize that I have an emotional side, and not just an intellect and a body. It's made me more spontaneous of stature, and I realize that life doesn't have to be so serious! Andy Welter, Chicago, IL

Gary Clyman not only teaches unique exercises, but he also teaches how to make changes in your life. Gary will help you decide on your goals if they are unclear, and he'll assist you in being specific on just how to attain them. He supports you in taking action to make the changes you want. There's no hiding from your own greatest potential when you work with Gary. I now have more confidence and greater energy. If you decide what you want when you begin PERSONAL POWER TRAINING™, you'll get it! Everyone wants something different and that's what you get... the things that satisfy you the most! Manuel Mendez, Chicago, IL

BEYOND SELF-HELP: MASTERING PERSONAL POWER™ by Gary J. Clyman

"I took the PERSONAL POWER TRAINING™ because I wanted a non-intellectual, no-nonsense experience of my body. Clyman delivered. I got breakthroughs I came in to get, and more besides. I quit trying to protect women from my physicality as though it were evil and would hurt them. They loved it! (So did I!) Where had I been all these years?

For the first time in my life, I sang alone before an audience--and kept going back for more. I learned to catch myself doing projects and the hard "get ready to do it" way instead of just piling in and getting things done. And one day I suddenly realized how silly of me it had always been not to use the status power available to me through dressing in fine, fashionable clothing that I could long ago have afforded.

Probably best of all, I quit being a "Care-Taking Machine," patronizing people as though I were smart enough to take better care of them than just being my "raw self" would accomplish. Me, just the way I am--I'm really great! Being physical has released my love and my work energy without any need to "be figured out" in my mind. I'm living right out of the center now. I found the groove. I didn't think it would ever happen!

Clyman knows how to catalyze things like these for people, and he knows what it means for them and their lives. It's clear to me that love is what has him motivated to focus his life's energy around setting people free. He needed to share this practice with me, and I needed to get it. Don't YOU miss it! Robb Murray, Chicago, IL

PERSONAL POWER TRAINING™ has given me just that - more Personal Power! It gave me the Personal Power for "me to be me, without apologizing!" I was always taught to be "a good little girl" and not make waves! That meant to allow myself to be pushed around and not speak up when I was hurt. I always felt intimidated.... especially in relationships with men or with anyone more intelligent than me. But not anymore! I figure the only difference between a so-called authority figure and me is a little bit of knowledge. That I can get! What no one could give me was my self-esteem. I have that now and much, much more.

PERSONAL POWER TRAINING™ helped me in being "ME"! No one can ever give me that! That's something I gave myself. What PERSONAL POWER TRAINING™ does, through Gary Clyman's guidance, is it gives you the tools to work with yourself daily so you can fully live life without feeling intimidated! Life is a JOY rather than a burden! PERSONAL POWER TRAINING™ is worth every minute and every penny I spent on it. Thanks Gary, for creating PERSONAL POWER TRAINING™ and for being so committed to people.

PERSONAL POWER TRAINING™ allows you to be yourself, naturally, and what it is that Gary Clyman does encourages you to be MORE of yourself, naturally, and have fun with it. Gary Clyman extracts and expands the positive qualities of each person. I've seen him do it with nearly everybody he comes in contact with. Barbara Tomzack, Chicago, IL

BEYOND SELF-HELP: MASTERING PERSONAL POWER™ by Gary J. Clyman

PERSONAL POWER TRAINING™ gave me a much richer and deeper appreciation for relating to my body and body sensations. I learned flexibility and being able to tap into my internal energy. It has helped me with my coordination, my diet, and has given me a new understanding about internal meditation through the Tai Chi exercises. My purpose for doing PERSONAL POWER TRAINING™ was to support me in understanding myself as a physical being. I feel that in the well rounding of an individual a person needs to have his physical life together as well as the mental, emotional, and spiritual.

Gary works with people right where they are... He's in perfect dance with each individual who goes through PERSONAL POWER TRAINING™. James McClenahan D.D.S., Homewood, IL

In terms of personal power, I have been able to tap into doing PERSONAL POWER TRAINING™ exercises and re-energize myself during the course of a busy day, and it will lift me out of my fatigue.

It's given me the ability to blast through resistance from both other people and my own as well, in business as well as in inter-personal relationships.

Within six months after doing PERSONAL POWER TRAINING™ my energy began to soar. I was able to complete a music videotape, I wrote a lot of music, and I elevated the level of my performance ability as well. I've also utilized a lot of information from PERSONAL POWER TRAINING™ to improve my personal self-image.

PERSONAL POWER TRAINING™ has opened up my awareness and led me to other avenues of personal power. It has also expanded my financial horizons. Oliver Williams, Psychotherapist and musician, Chicago, IL

PERSONAL POWER TRAINING™ not only gave me more energy, it also gave me an awareness of what is available in life at any moment. By available I mean, for example, if I feel resigned, I know at any moment I can go into the energy focus Gary taught me and come out of it with a feeling of high energy. It has given me a powerful distinction in relation to myself and others around me. I have an awareness of people not using their power. When I have the energy, I see the lack of it in other people. Russ Taylor, San Francisco, CA

I notice that I have more mastery over myself when I have the energy. After I do PERSONAL POWER TRAINING™ exercises, things are more easily accomplished. The energy is powerful but it doesn't "wire" me, or make me anxious... it's really very nurturing. I feel more joyful - things are more colorful and life looks brighter. I am more assertive in all areas of my life, for example with women in relationships. I'm more out in the world participating in every area of life.

Since I did PERSONAL POWER TRAINING™ two years ago I started a business which has become very viable. Also, a lot of who I am is a dedication to physical fitness, and

BEYOND SELF-HELP: MASTERING PERSONAL POWER™ by Gary J. Clyman

it is the way that I see the world. PERSONAL POWER TRAINING™ has assisted me in both of these areas. I now have more energy to do a better job at work.

Being around Gary is very empowering. I wouldn't do the course unless I wanted to be confronted and play full out in life. I find Gary very inspiring and powerfully committed to what's possible for each of us. Who he is, is about using what the Universe has to offer to empower us and for us to grow. He knows a lot about using universal energy and teaches his knowledge to others. I think he's an extraordinary person - a very, very unusual man. A Mystery Supporter, Chicago, IL

I have a new job, new apartment, and a new lifestyle, and I couldn't have done it without PERSONAL POWER TRAINING™. Joseph Arnswald, Chicago, IL

I have gained more clarity in the past week. I'm also approaching problems as they occur rather than putting them off till later. Fred E. Estey, Chicago, IL

Gary's vision and presence were "tailor made" for the times and world we live in. This is a very aggressive, demanding world and Gary has taught me not only how to cope, but even to prosper in it. Thanks Gary. Edward Gallagher, Chicago, IL

Gary's strength and clarity becomes contagious when you work with him in PERSONAL POWER TRAINING™. Anne Surowski, Chicago, IL

Acting is probably the most stressful profession there is. Every job you get, you're going to lose. In 90% of the auditions you get rejected. This takes a tremendous toll on your personal energy stores. PERSONAL POWER TRAINING™ continues to help me to overcome this stress and gives me the personal magnetism necessary to excel in this very difficult field. Kurt Johns, Professional Actor, Chicago, IL

PERSONAL POWER TRAINING™ helped me keep myself in front of my typewriter, so I could start my new career as a free-lance writer. Dennis Franke R.N., Self-Care Associates, Chicago, IL

RESULTS AND BENEFITS DERIVED FROM PERSONAL POWER TRAINING™

1) Your confidence and self-esteem levels will be increased affecting your creativity.

2) You will discover, uncover, and de-program negative behavior patterns and personality traits.

3) You will have an abundance of energy and be able to harness it at WILL.

4) You will require less sleep and get more out of your day.

5) You will have an expanded sense of freedom in all areas of your life.

6) You will become more expressive of your own sexuality.

7) You will develop new sources of income from your present environment.

8) You will recognize how you regularly abuse yourself and put a stop to it.

9) You will become independent from what has been holding you back.

10) You will choose to create new relationships from your present ones.

11) You will release many of your negative attitudes and beliefs concerning money and adopt more prosperity and success in your life.

12) You will "choose" to be different after you complete PERSONAL POWER TRAINING™.

13) You will learn to make better choices with your own benefit in mind.

14) You will give up anger, rage, fear, abandonment, resentment, guilt, indecisiveness, and procrastination, and learn to trust yourself.

REASONS WHY PERSONAL POWER TRAINING™ HELPS MANY PEOPLE!

1. I help people focus energy to make positive behavioral changes.

2. I help people utilize their knowledge and business skills to the best of their ability.

3. I help people identify their own strengths and weaknesses.

4. I teach my clients how to monitor and master the workings of their own minds.

5. I instruct the discipline skills which directly lead to higher levels of self-control and self-confidence.

6. I help repair damaged self-esteem levels.

7. I teach Internal Energy Cultivation Techniques that raise each person's physical presence, self-awareness, and aliveness.

8. Working with me is as much FUN as it is productive.

9. I restore "the eye of the tiger" that is required to be successful in all endeavors.

10. I teach you how to reduce the harmful effects of "daily stress" by performing more effectively, thus helping you become more consistent, productive, and happy.

BEYOND SELF-HELP: MASTERING PERSONAL POWER™ by Gary J. Clyman

MOTIVATIONAL SAYINGS AND QUOTES

My teacher's generation got its power from controlling information and distributing faulty information. My generation gets its power from distributing correct information and correcting past faults.

We don't dwell on problems, we work toward solutions.

"It is easier to steer a car a that's moving than it is to steer a car that's standing still" GJC

If you <u>practice</u>, you only have to know a few things. If you <u>run through</u>, you can never know enough. GJC

You don't want to make your Tai Chi and Chi Kung practice so important that it becomes more important than the reason you're doing it (i.e. to be a good husband, father, trader, doctor, etc., whatever you are). This is my modern application for Chi Kung, to have a better and more fulfilled life.

Man, the living creature, is more important than any established style or system. Bruce Lee

There's a difference between being limited and being controlled by other people. Being "limited" is being judged and not being given something by other people while being "controlled" is being manipulated or dominated consciously or subconsciously by another.

Living the way you've been living is a lot harder than living the way you're going to live.

There is a saying related to students staying with the same master. Good ones graduate, the bad ones never leave.

Efficiency in action is more important than effort.

"The only way to it is through it." F. Lazerson

Quantity never makes up for quality.

The reputation of a great teacher should be judged by the results of his students.

The market's never wrong. There is "no karma," only good technique or bad technique and discipline.

WORKING WITH YOUR AFFIRMATIONS

PERSONALIZE YOUR AFFIRMATIONS

I have found the use of affirmations to be an excellent tool in conjunction with your daily Chi Kung practice. The affirmations that I am talking about are dealing primarily with "undeserving issues," self-esteem, self-confidence, and discipline which are the basic themes of my work with my clients and students.

Incorporating affirmations into this work, not counting "Hands on, Transfer of Power," is a very specific tool. Each person should choose the affirmations that best suit his situation and his personality.

I will list many of the affirmations. Some of these are very generic for very specific problems. In making the list, I have tried to keep them relatively general so the major readership of my book can actually use them in the format that they are presented.

AFFIRMATIONS ARE LIMITLESS

When using affirmations there is no limit to how many you can use. I do suggest four to six different ones. If the affirmation does not suit your needs, tailor it, change it, drop it, or just adopt a new one. Your affirmations usually need to be updated on a frequent basis.

Some people actually think there are rules for how to use affirmations. If you think there are rules for this, you should look at your belief systems because you probably believe there are rules for everything, when in reality, freedom is different than having rules.

When I talk about rules I don't mean restrictions. I mean self imposed "rules for living." Many of us do have certain guidelines that we stay and work within in relation to discipline, however, some people have none whatsoever. These people are rare but every once in a while I run across one that has "no rules" for anything. These people usually have no way of doing anything that is specific. They are just sort of spontaneous, with no structure at all. It's hard to be "productive" without a structure.

THE AFFIRMATION LIST

"I am spontaneously direct." This is my favorite.

"I will be determined not to be defeated by someone else's opinion of me or my ideas."

"The secret to winning is desire."

"I am a doctor, not a janitor." This affirmation is used when a person has severely low self-esteem levels. This man has a Ph.D.

"Master the fundamentals."

"Keep life Simple."

"I am happy, healthy, skinny and wealthy."

"There is a lot of good in the world."

" I should Command respect, not Demand respect."

"I am a vicious bitch." This will help you stop taking abuse from other people.

"I am open to the abundance of the Universe to flow to me and through me."

"I deserve and shall receive the perfect relationship." Be ready for who it is you ask.

"My perfect job is now becoming available."

"I command respect from my friends and peers."

"I am happy, healthy, _____, and wealthy."

"Prosperity is my birthright, abundance is my choice."

"My WILL and self-esteem are increasing daily."

"God works through me to help many people."

"I have an abundance of self-confidence and self-control."

"First comes the action, then comes the proof."

"I am becoming stronger and stronger everyday."

"Spiritual freedom is my natural state."

"The quality of my health is excellent."

"I am full of energy and emanate self-confidence."

"This test is an automatic A."

"I have the perfect product for the perfect _____."

"I make great suggestions and people respond."

"I am doing the perfect action."

"The time for action is NOW."

"My income comes from expected and unexpected sources."

"My healing ability helps thousands of people

"I forgive myself. I trust myself. I love myself."

CHAPTER #7
LIVING HEALTHY

THE 7 BASIC PRINCIPLES OF WHOLISTIC HEALTH

Are you destroying your most prized possession? When I am talking about the most prized possession that we could ever hope of having, what could be more valuable than our own health?

Of what value is having all the riches in the world, if we don't have the vitality and well-being to enjoy them? What about the common practice of successfully accumulating many different forms of riches, (money, real estate, etc.) but to have them wiped out during a brief stay in the hospital, at about $1000 per day and rising. Would it not be better thinking in advance of cultivating our health resources and actually own up to taking responsibility for our own health and financial future.

What I, as a wholistic health practitioner (Retired-1985), am going to give you, is what I call **"The 7 Basic Principles of Wholistic Health."** These concepts are given with the intention of saving you much of the work that has been painfully undertaken by many people that have made a conscious decision, that they are not willing to follow the same "path of doom," that their parents and relatives have followed before them.

I would like to give you a bit of my own personal history. I was living under the illusion that modern medicine had an answer for everything and at the appropriate time would mysteriously appear. At that time, my favorite uncle was using one of the wonders of modern medicine, insulin, ignoring his own diet, weight problem and smoking cigars. Little did I know that that was not the end-all answer to all of his problems. He had been a diabetic for many years, and who, in those days, would have ever thought that to be unusual. However, with his diabetes and some additional stress, he had a massive heart attack and died in the presence of the doctors, hospitals, and all their equipment couldn't put Uncle Joe back together again.

So are you wondering what my story has to do with wholistic health? Hold on, we're getting closer. Nine days after my uncle had his heart attack, his closest brother, my father, had his heart attack and died within hours. This you see, started me thinking, my father had gone to the hospital just a few days prior to having his heart attack, and was given a "clean bill of health." So let us look at the daily stressors that led up to this tragedy. The stress of their mother dying of cancer, with the additional stress of a tormented neighborhood in 1968, the undue influence of the terrible America diet, and smoking 3 packs of cigarettes daily. Does this sound like a common situation that you have seen in your family? If this had never happened, I probably would have been a quite successful dentist by now, and followed another path. However, how could one ignore such a "calling," when there was such a need to discover and educate other people in "the ways of health." For this reason, I made a conscious switch of paths, from the path of illness, to the pursuit of health.

When you look at the general health of the people in one of the richest countries in the world, and see what the average person is suffering from, how can you but wonder, what influences can contribute to the depletion of such a rich people and their most valuable possession? I have been in the "people business" for over 10 years. Many traits come to mind when looking at the general population. Please inspect these ideas and take from them the strength and understanding available to you.

PRINCIPLE #1. The body possesses the natural ability to strive towards achieving "perfect health." If this ability is recognized, then it makes our wish to obtain "perfect health" much more realistic. If the proper steps towards replacing illness with health are taken, then prevention and normalization of many disease processes can begin. This means that we as individuals must take personal responsibility for our own "health status," and only when we do this, can we enjoy the pleasures of abundant energy, an the attitude that we can produce our wishes for the future.

PRINCIPLE #2. The structure of the body is directly related to its function. By this I mean that any changes which are made in the outer or physical body will affect a direct corollary change in the spiritual, emotional, and mental counterparts. For instance, notice what happens the next time you are under a great deal of stress on your job. Look for associated symptoms that you would usually overlook or attribute to another cause. Look and see if you have a tendency to reach for some kind of sweet snack the next time you are under fire. There are very logical reasons that your body craves sugar at those times. When the body is under more stress than usual, the adrenal glands have to work harder to try to equalize the body's chemistry. We as Americans, due to over-stimulation from sweets, have developed what is commonly referred to as "the roller coaster syndrome." The illness that is in epidemic proportion is called "hypoglycemia," which means low blood sugar. The answer to this problem is not to ingest more sugar, but to allow the body to come off the unhealthy high many of us have been on for so many years.

If sugar was introduced for the first time today, the FDA (Food and Drug Administration) would not allow it to be put on the market. Sugar is more addictive than heroin, but due to a strong sugar lobby, it has become an accepted part of our food supply and our society. Many great books are available to easily explain this common ailment. <u>Sugar Blues, by William Dufty</u> is an excellent book that should be read. The human body is a miraculous machine, no matter how much punishment we inflict upon it, it always tries to bounce back for more.

In the old days, it was very easy to determine what our obstacles were. However, with the advent of modern fast foods, we have lost sight of our enemy. We are no longer at risk of sanitary diseases or instant death afflictions. Now we have to be aware of our new enemies. The diseases of the past used to kill off mankind at an early age, but now, since we are living much longer, we are developing chronic degenerative diseases. Old age does not cause disease, longer life spans allow for longer developmental periods. We must prepare our worn out bodies and strengthen our health reserves. Improved diet, and effective methods of reducing stress, proper rest, and sufficient exercise would be a good list with which to start.

PRINCIPLE #3. Health is the primary area to study when attempting to understand disease. If of our modern health providers would concentrate on the prevention and maintenance aspect of health, many people would look at the other side of the coin. Imagine preparing and participating in your own health future, so you could become independent of the doctors, whom so many people have learned to respect and revere. Does it not make sense to learn health-giving habits and traits that you could use for your own well being? Running off to your doctor for a pill that will cover up, or suppress, that valuable signal that your body is trying to communicate, what's the point? We should learn to listen to our own nature, because if we just let our bodies communicate with us we would understand what our body is trying to tell us.

PRINCIPLE #4. The Musculo-Skeletal System, which incorporates bones, ligaments, muscles, fascia and many other kinds of tissue, forms a structure which, when disordered, may affect the function of the other parts and systems of the body. This might be the result of irritation of abnormal response of the nerve, and/or poor blood supply, nutritional supports, and/or electrical energy to these other organs or parts. The body is and should be viewed as a complete unit. This is what has gone wrong with conventional western medicine. In Wholistic Medicine, the body is viewed as a complete unit, and each part is directly related to each other part of the whole. In China, the concept of a unified body, mind and spirit, is an unsaid law. Only in the west, do we have to actively think to try to re-unite all the different aspects of parts of our being.

PRINCIPLE #5. The body is subject to many mechanical, nutritional, emotional, and/or electrical disorders and is therefore capable of multiple corrections. Each correction may be enhanced by considering the body as "a complete unit" when aiming at normalizing and strengthening each part of the body. This would explain why you get depressed when you have a physical pain, and why you can also create a physical pain that is directly associated with your adverse emotional states. This is also why you feel better when you eat foods that are better for you.

Nutritional supplements sometimes can aid with physical problems, adverse emotional states, attitude problems, and many other seemingly unrelated factors. Imagine if there were a specific way of determining exactly what nutrients your body needed on a daily basis, wouldn't that be a great tool? That tool does exist. It is called "The Muscle Response Test" (The MRT). You might have heard about this test already. It can help you determine exactly what nutrients are needed by your body on a daily basis. When you receive this test, you can find out exactly what your body needs on a daily basis. The procedure is painless, accurate and effective and has been used by many doctors, Chiropractors, and nutritionists all over the country. There are practitioners offering this test in your area, just ask.

PRINCIPLE #6. Our bodies are constantly struggling to overcome many daily stressors. I will list the major stressors according to categories. 1) Severe exertions, 2) Immunological reactions, 3) allergies, 4) infections, 5) surgery, 6) malnutrition, 7) strong emotions, 8) environmental pollutants and food additives, 9) pregnancy, 10) severe exposures such as heat, sun, and cold, 11) unhealthy lifestyle, and 12) habitual abuses. Take a close look into your own daily life to see if your actions fit into some of these basic categories. When you have all these unhealthy factors working against you, no wonder the most commonly reported complaint in my health practice is "Low Energy." This is one main reason so many people want to learn Chi Kung.

PRINCIPLE #7. Good health is our God given right; illness and disease represent an unnatural state. To be really healthy is our Godly inheritance. That's why maintaining "perfect health" is a constant and ongoing process.

SUGAR: A HORRIBLY ADDICTIVE DRUG

The most important principle to follow is, "everything in moderation." Many people abuse their bodies one day, and then try to make up for it the next day. This is a very illogical and unhealthy thing to put ourselves through. Most people know that white refined sugar is very bad for the body. However, how many people know that brown sugar is nothing more than white sugar covered with molasses. O.K., so sugar is bad, but did you know that alcohol is even worse? The sugar content in alcohol is much more difficult for the body to metabolize, not to mention what alcohol does to our poor liver, when it tries to absorb the poisons we so joyfully ingested.

I would like to address a modern day disease that is in epidemic proportion; Hypoglycemia, alias "Low Blood Sugar." Stop, that does not mean you have a sugar deficiency. Some medical doctors are still telling their poor, defenseless, ignorant patients, that when they feel tired and run down they should eat something sweet like a candy bar. This brilliant bit of nutritional advice is equivalent to telling a fireman to go throw gas on a fire. This absolutely aggravates the situation and this is about as practical as being told to eat a well balanced diet from the 4 basic food groups. With all this knowledge available, why has the medical profession stayed with the nutritional principles taught in the 1950's? Could it be that that's when they learned? Robert S. Mendelsohn M. D. told me one time, "you can tell when a doctor went to school by the drugs he prescribes and the advice he gives."

I would like to give a practical explanation of how to view Hypoglycemia. Imagine a young child living on a very poor diet. What would that look like to you? He goes to the store everyday and buys his regular daily snacks. He eats his share of Hostess products, he fills his pockets full of "Life Savers," and enough bubble gum to last all day. He is also very thirsty, so what does he drink? "The Real Thing" of course, with approximately 8 teaspoons of sugar per 16 ounce bottle. He also eats his share of peanut butter cups because he was told that peanuts are high in protein. O.K., stay with me, we haven't gotten to lunch yet. For lunch he goes to his favorite neighborhood hamburger place for a really good and nutritious meal (JOKE). He has

BEYOND SELF-HELP: MASTERING PERSONAL POWER™ by Gary J. Clyman

been living on foods like this since he was old enough to point his finger at that pretty candy as a child. Now those are known as the developing years on his TV, so you know he is building a strong body in 9 different ways (JOKE).

So he is now in high school and has developed some very serious problems. His parents take him to the school psychologist, who of course is an expert about what children need. His parents are told he is hyperactive, so they go to their medical doctor to get the poor kid fixed. He prescribes something magical to help the child concentrate. The child has also by this time started to develop rather severe headaches and stomach aches. So the wise doctor prescribes 3 different drugs to cure this poor child. Now, a few months later, this child is starting to show other symptoms, like his inability to concentrate, severe mood swings, and bad sleeping habits, not to mention gaining 20 pounds.

Now, this poor child is about 16 years old, has been raised on this lousy diet all his life, been taking drugs for the symptoms associated and caused by eating this way, and he has just discovered something his father has been doing since he can remember, drinking alcohol. Did you know that alcohol is the most widely abused drug in this country? Of course, now he's cool, 'cause he drinks with his friends, who had good examples to follow, their fathers.

A few more years go by and he is having trouble in college. You see, he never could make up his mind and didn't want to be there in the first place. Now he finally finds the greatest, most fun thing he has ever experienced, recreational drugs; marijuana, cocaine, and speed. Of course he sees nothing wrong with taking his own drugs, after all, even his doctor prescribed drugs for him when he was in his formative years.

Need I go further? Now he is a businessman, where good judgment is what counts, except he has never never been prepared for the working world. Now this poor child is expected to be creative, productive, and enthusiastic about his new job.

What we have here is a typical adult raised in the 1950's and 60's. Give him enough rope and he has hung himself. Back to Hypoglycemia.

The body is designed to work like a finely tuned machine. The only difference is that a machine can have it's worn out parts replaced. We are stuck with what we have created.

You should understand that with Hypoglycemia the pancreas has developed a trigger-response mechanism to sugar. As soon as you ingest sugar, your pancreas secretes the hormone called "insulin" which has the job of metabolizing sugar, thereby lowering the amount of sugar in the blood stream. It does its job for as many years as it can.

Now, you learn that the way you have been eating has no future, because your parents and other relatives all have developed strange 20th century diseases like heart disease, high blood pressure, arthritis, diabetes, and many other well known

"Incurable Diseases." All these diseases have supposed unknown causes. It's as if one day they just appeared and we had nothing to do with it.

So the drama goes on, he changes his diet and is determined to follow the straight and narrow path. No more sugar, no more drinking, no more dairy products, no more red meat, no more white bread, no more of the "real thing," etc. He now doesn't feel as good as he used to. He blames it on his new eating habits. After all he should feel better, it's been two months. He now lives on salads, soy bean ice cream, and tofu. Is this your idea of a good balanced vegetarian diet? Of course not, but he knows no different. This type of diet is known as "the vegetarian junk food diet." This is almost as bad as what he was doing.

This is not what is known as "Becoming a Vegetarian." There are many kinds of vegetarian diets. My favorite is "The Macrobiotic Diet" which I have been following for the last zillion years.

BACK TO HYPOGLYCEMIA...

He now has joined the low energy, depressed, over weight, headache, back ache, wishing to take a nap at 3 p.m. or eat sweets in the middle of the day crowd. What has happened to his poor pancreas and adrenal glands? His pancreas is now spilling large amounts of insulin into his blood stream at the slightest taste of sugar. The insulin reduces his blood sugar far below normal safe levels. His adrenal glands interpret this as being a dangerous situation, so they secrete adrenaline to compensate for his excessively low blood sugar condition. More time goes by, and now he has exhausted his adrenals as well as his pancreas. By now he is really in trouble. By this time he has developed very strange sleeping habits, so he never feels quite all there, sleeping when he is supposed to be awake and vice versa. The only time he really feels alive is when he eats something sweet. And the vicious circle goes on and on.

How does this all relate to diabetes, one of our favorite and most popular diseases? <u>Hypoglycemia is the precursor to Diabetes.</u> When the pancreas has become so fatigued that it cannot do its job anymore, we now go back to that wonderful doctor for more help. Now he has us take insulin because we have destroyed our pancreas. What about the side effects related to use of insulin, the breakdown of the cardiovascular system, diabetic retinopathy, and kidney failure, just to mention a few. Does he ever ask you about your diet? Maybe, but what does he tell you to do about it? Eat a well balanced diet. And what is a well balanced diet? Eat from the 4 basic food groups. (JOKE, JOKE)

There is hope. Read as many books, talk to as many people as you can, go to somebody who follows his own advice, and take responsibility for your own health.

I would like to give you some basic guidelines to follow when improving you diet and eating habits.

1. Avoid the all white products, this includes sugar, flour and milk. Soy products are a good substitute to eat instead of dairy products.

2. Avoid red meat, pork, cold cuts, and any other kind of meat that has been either raised with chemicals or hormones in the feed, or has been injected or treated with these chemicals or hormones. If you are really attached to meat and think you really need it, go to a health food store that sells organically grown meat. The price is probably more, but it is well worth it, for your health's sake.

3. Make sure you eat plenty of fresh vegetables. Avoid canned or frozen vegetables.

4. Do not use margarine, it is very bad for your system. The melting point of margarine is 110 degrees; it only makes sense that if your body temperature is 98.6, how can it melt down margarine?

5. Introduce whole grains into your daily diet. This will give you the necessary complex carbohydrates you need to produce energy as well as give you necessary vitamins and minerals that have been removed from the other fast food, junk food you have been used to eating.

6. Read about nutrition and try to match up your personal needs. Be practical.

7. Get sufficient amounts of the right kind of exercise that suits your personality and body condition. Sleep enough for your particular body chemistry. Some people require only a few hours of sleep, while others think they need 8-10 hours. For those who feel they need 8-10 hours, you might find you require considerably less when you improve your daily diet. 6 hours should be enough for most people. In my experience over the last decade, I have seen many people lose weight as a side benefit of improving their daily lifestyle and diet.

WHAT TO EXPECT WHEN CONVERTING TO VEGETARIANISM

What to expect when converting from a traditional "meat and potato diet," to a vegetarian diet? At first, one would think the transition to a better diet would be an automatic increase and upscale in energy and the feeling of well being. Well, I've got news for you, as soon as you start to improve your diet, your body starts to discharge poisons at the same time.

This discharge comes along with many symptoms. The novice vegetarian should not become scared or upset, but should rather view these symptoms of change as a small price to pay for a large benefit.

SYMPTOMS REFLECT IMPROVING YOUR HEALTH

Some of the symptoms are many different kinds of discharges. Through your nose or mouth as respiratory discharge. This might feel as if you have a cold you never seem to get over. It is not. It is part of the cleansing process associated with improving your diet and health in general. Over the counter drugs should not be taken to suppress these symptoms. Taking these drugs will only inhibit and extend your detoxification process.

Mucus might be released through your digestive system when you move your bowels. Your bowel movements will be different than ever before. You will fill the toilet up many times and not be able to figure out where all this feces came from.

It has been stored in your colon for many years and has just recently begun to be released. Remember, you have been "full of shit" for a long time and it's about time to clean it up. You will actually have bowel movements that can weigh 5 to 7 pounds and come out all at one time. You will be shocked in the toilet at what you will find and at the huge amount. Don't be afraid. It is your body saying, "O.K., let this come out now." You might and probably will crave exactly the foods you are getting out of your system. It is not uncommon to crave chocolate and many other foods you have recently decided to give up for you health.

Even skin eruptions are common during this time. You are not having your second puberty, and it won't last for long.

When you become a vegetarian, you turn off the incoming flow of poisons and extra fats, acids, additives and many other chemicals and toxins that are contained in meat. Your body starts to work more efficiently in a more pure and refined way. It throws these poisons out of the body in a relatively high volume.

THE FOUR AVENUES OF DETOXIFICATION

These four avenues of detoxification are all our body has to deal with the abuse we have subjected ourselves to our whole life. Many variations or groups of symptoms can come out, individually or in combination with others. It is important not to try to inhibit this process by taking prescription or over the counter drugs. You must let nature take it's course. Wait it out, it is great for you in the long run.

There are only four avenues of excretion for your body to use in the detoxification process. 1) Your respiratory system, via your lungs, mouth, and nose. 2) Your digestive system via your intestines. 3) Your skin, via pores. 4) You urinary system, via your kidneys and bladder. 5) Your perspiration and body odor system, which is related to your skin, but involves other processes also.

WHAT IS COLONIC IRRIGATION?

Colonic Irrigation or "Colonics" as it is also called, can be thought of as huge enemas that consist of 15 to 20 gallons of fresh water. This water enters your "back door" (anus) 6 to 8 ounces at a time and drains out using gravity. There are a few other methods but I don't advise them at all. The gravity method is named "The Woods Method." With the bottle hanging high over head, with the intake hose leading in and the waste hose draining the water out, is in my opinion, the best. "The Woods Method" is safe. With the other methods, if you are using a machine, possibly the machine could have a problem with one of the controls or gauges. It all depends on the technician performing this service. I personally trust a natural method more than a machine for this function. They might be safe, but make your own choices.

"Colonics" flush out your lower bowel (large intestine). One important maneuver to have the colon therapist do is to close your illeo-cecal valve. It is a very simple Chiropractic maneuver used to keep water from entering the small intestine. There are a few good books on "Colonic Irrigation and cleansing your colon." You should read them yourself and make your own health improvement decisions.

"Colonic Irrigation" is an important part of discharging toxins from your body. "Colonic Irrigation" is really not to be used for losing weight, but might help in the initial stages of upgrading your diet. "Colonic Irrigation" is helpful in removing old, stuck feces out of your lower bowel which may poison your body. Everything is O.K. in moderation. Don't become a "colonic junkie."

JUNK FOOD VEGETARIANISM

I was a "Junk food vegetarian" for the first two years of my new vegetarian lifestyle. The only thing I did personally to improve my diet was remove meat from it. THIS IS NOT SUFFICIENT!!! I started this new way of life in 1973. In 1975 I asked my Tai Chi Master for some guidance concerning a diet that would help me develop my internal energy and Tai Chi ability, A.S.A.P.

Information in those days was extremely limited. "Food combining and the Natural Hygienist approach" existed, but it was too complicated, rigid, and wimpy for my personality, body type, constitution and purposes.

FIBER, THE THREAD OF LIFE

Fiber is indigestible. You eat it, it passes straight through without breaking down. However, fiber attracts water. That's why, if you're constipated and you take some sort of fiber laxative, the fiber attracts water which puts more fluid in your feces, which makes it easier to more your bowels.

Let me make this a little more clear. When you first become a vegetarian, your body is very responsive and goes through a shift where, as soon as you take the meat out of your diet, your body goes "Oh boy, freedom!" but that freedom doesn't last very long. It only lasts until you actually get the food that you have eaten out of your system. After your body gets used to the new way of eating, it will try to go back to the old way of eating. That's why you have to go on a long-term maintenance diet.

If you don't have enough fiber in your diet, you will get locked up. When you eat white bread, white rice, and the rest of the "dead white" unnutritious foods, it's like eating glue, and that's exactly what it does to your insides, binds you up. So what you're going to have to do is, get the fiber in.

On of the best ways of getting fiber in your diet is not by taking fiber tablets, which does work, but by eating whole grains. Examples are barley, brown rice, millet, etc. Whole grains have fiber in them.

Vegetables, semi cooked, have fiber in them. The more you cook vegetables, the softer the vegetable fiber (cellulose) gets. Remember, fiber is an indigestible material. It's like a course thread that runs throughout many whole foods. Fiber is like "burlap" underneath felt, if you can imagine this combination. Felt could be considered the actual nutrients whereas burlap is like the course material that holds it together.

"Colonics" really do fall into place here. "Colonics" is natural. Right about now you are probably thinking that that much water water is not natural to have in your colon. You're right, but compared to your other options, like mineral oil, water is the best way of flushing yourself out. Besides the way you had to eat to need "Colonics" hasn't exactly been the most natural way of eating. Mineral oil just lubricates the walls of your colon and does not really clean out any of the old feces. You've had "old shit" stuck in you for a long time. The water will help flush it out.

Question: Have you ever moved your bowels and felt like you never had to do it again for the rest of your life? This is the kind of bowel movement I am talking about when you finally clean your body out, as opposed to feeling like you just never get enough out.

DIFFERENT KINDS OF VEGETARIANS

In my opinion, there are a few different reasons for turning toward a vegetarian lifestyle and diet. You must make your own choices.

For spiritual reasons, because you don't believe in killing animals for food purposes. This approach sounds respectable at first but has some serious holes in it. I have seen some of the most weird and wimpy people hold these beliefs. Some people won't even wear leather shoes or belts, because the cow was killed to make them.

Next we have the vegetarian who does not like the way meat tastes. I rarely meet people who are vegetarians for this reason, but they are out there. When you meet them, you will not forget them. Don't talk loud to them or they will get scared from your aggressive behavior and go hide somewhere.

And at last, you have what I call a practical vegetarian. This type is a person who avoids eating meat, not because the cow had to sacrifice her life to feed you, or because meat tastes bad, but because meat is simply not good for your health. Learn about all the chemical additives put in the meat. All those great cancer causing agents and how they increase the taste and preserve the shelf life of our modern food. Educate yourself. You will not see this on TV for many years.

Quality is more important than quantity. I'm not suggesting that you only eat "organically grown." That is sometimes impossible as well as impractical. The cost factor I do not believe should be that important. If it is, you have more concerns than food and should take a good look at your relationship with money, prosperity and self-deserving issues.

I am this last brand of vegetarian, plus an added aspect. I couldn't care less about the cow giving her life. The Internal Sensitivity Diet encompasses the practical health reasons for becoming a vegetarian and very specific factors for helping you to develop and cultivate your internal energy through Chi Kung.

Much of this material will be explored in more detail in my next book. To include an extensive "Health Chapter" would make the size of this book impractical. My next book will go much more into detail. I will include Orthomolecular Nutrition, specific sexual techniques, and much more.

I have students and friends that I have put on the diet many years ago and their weight has gone up and down repeatedly. I have a friend that switched to a vegetarian diet and lost weight very quickly. I have had relatively skinny people with no previous weight problems or concerns lose between 20 and 25 pounds without even trying.

After he had been on the diet for a few years, he had put the weight back on in a healthy way. Instead of being very skinny with a large pooch, and looking like an over fed snake, he had filled out.

Improving your diet is an excellent step in preventative health maintenance.

It is very common to crave the foods that are your personal poisons, that you are discharging once you've stopped their intake.

COMPARING POISONS

Concerning coffee, coffee is the least of your problems. Concerning sugar, sugar is the worst of your problems, not counting drugs, alcohol, and other intoxicants. Alcohol is very bad. Alcohol offsets your sugar metabolism system as well as killing brain cells. The hang over effect related to drinking alcohol in my opinion is the sugar imbalance experienced the day after after the metabolic stress put on your pancreas and adrenal glands.

MORE ABOUT HYPOGLYCEMIA

You see, the pancreas produces a hormone called insulin. What many people do not know is that the function of the adrenal glands is to assist the pancreas in stabilizing sugar levels. Continued use of alcohol, which is interpreted as concentrated sugar by the body, leads to a very common chronic, wide spread illness called "hypoglycemia." Hypoglycemia is much more wide spread than most health care practitioners would admit.

Yes, a glucose tolerance test (GTT) would show in extreme cases of hypoglycemia, but it is very rough on your body to sit through the actual test. For all practical purposes it won't really tell you anymore than what you already suspected. You can skip the test and assume you have a blood sugar problem. There are many books on the subject. My favorite is a book called <u>Sugar Blues by William Dufty</u>. Read it, it will enlighten you to this common human ailment.

Remember, even if you have a GTT and you show a normal blood sugar curve, realize who "normal" is referring to. Many people have hypoglycemia and have no "irregularities" according to the glucose tolerance test.

Hypoglycemia is a precursor to diabetes, which is one of the most wide-spread killers of all time. One out of 7 dies from diabetes every year, not to mention the other related diseases like kidney disease, heart disease, cardiovascular disease and many more. Read and educate yourself. The books are available.

PART #1 OF THE NUTRITIONAL PIE
THE CHI KUNG INTERNAL SENSITIVITY DIET

I am a "physical" person and I work in the world as a "physical" person. My relationship with nutrition is also as a "physical" person. This is not 1973-1974. Since those days many nutritional discoveries and breakthroughs have taken place.

In 1975, my Tai Chi Master put me on "the traditional monk diet." In 1976, I discovered The Macrobiotic Diet, which was nearly the same without ginger, garlic, and onions. These spices tend to raise your sex drive which is not preferred in the very beginning when you are becoming a celebrate monk. To raise your sex drive after you have developed your Chi Kung foundation is a different story. This has been explained in another section of my book.

The Traditional Monk Diet and The Macrobiotic Diet includes eating no meat and no chicken due to unhealthy added hormones (estrogen). The Macrobiotic Diet consists of whole grains, fresh vegetables, locally grown and seasonally grown fruit, soy products such as tofu, tempeh, and miso. Seaweed is also added to the diet to help supply many important minerals. The method of cooking is somewhat important in this way of eating. Don't over cook your food.

BEYOND SELF-HELP: MASTERING PERSONAL POWER™ by Gary J. Clyman

I personally have been suggesting taking vitamins for many years because it has been proven that most of the food we have available to us is deficient in many important nutrients. I don't believe the food is enough. You must take nutritional supplements in a smart fashion.

Being on the basic monk diet combined with being celibate for two and a half years led me to developing my "internal sensitivity," which led to developing my "internal power" (Jing) and my Tai Chi / Chi Kung ability. Those years were the most important in my development and progress.

Many other teachers tell their students not to become celibate, not to become vegetarians, to eat what feels best. I strongly disagree. I just think they don't know, are ignoring their students welfare, or are just not willing to truly give their support. I believe celibacy is important for certain people, for certain reasons, but <u>not for everybody</u>. Changing your diet, however, is a very important part of the meditation and energy cultivation system. But do not become "over anxious" about your diet. It's not that important for everybody, but for certain people, who can do it, it will be more important. <u>Your Chi Kung is the first place to start.</u> Dietary improvements will come naturally after you stabilize.

Many people are afraid that they have to do everything at the same time; i.e., change their diet, give up sex, quit smoking, quit drinking, avoiding sweets, etc. This is not true. You do not have to change your diet, give up sex (masturbation <u>not</u> included), sleep only 4 hours per night, practice 6 hours per day, take ice cold showers, or quit your job. Anyone that thinks he has to do all these things, all at the same time, is not understanding what the true message is in this book. Changes are good, but only if you make choices yourself, not because someone told you to or you read it in a book. Make up your own mind.

PART #2 OF THE NUTRITIONAL PIE
PROPER NUTRITIONAL SUPPLEMENTATION

You are <u>not</u> what you eat. You are what you assimilate, and always keep this in mind as you read this chapter.

Due to space limitations and the need to explain this topic very thoroughly, I am only briefly touching on the section on "Nutritional Supplementation." I will include "Orthomolecular Nutrition" in my next book.

Because I have an acupuncture, Chiropractic, and a Tai Chi background, the applications that I will use to explain the nutritional approach connected to the practice of Chi Kung, will be quite simple.

There are two halves to the whole. The first half, and not necessarily the most important but equal at least, is your diet: the food you put in your body. Your diet has a relationship with what is actually assimilated, but the food you eat is not necessarily what you assimilate. There is a great deal of loss, depending on the quality of the food, how it's cooked, and what it is. Nutritional supplements are very important in these days of depleted food. However, I cannot attempt to satisfactorily cover this topic now. It will be included in my next book. In the mean time, read and educate yourself. If you need a referral to what companies to purchase your nutritional supplements from you can call me personally. I have a few that are GREAT!

PERSPIRATION & SHOWERS

Perspiration is an important bodily secretion. Besides it's traditional functions, such as stabilizing body fluids, temperature, and operation, it is also a way for discharging poisons from the body. Sweating is an important, yet commonly ignored function. When they begin practicing Chi Kung, I advise my students to take normal warm to hot showers followed by an ice cold showers, immediately upon rising, before starting the daily Chi Kung or Tai Chi practice.

There are a few good reasons for this. 1) The hot/warm shower starts your circulation as if you were awake a longer time, 2) the hot/warm shower gets the stiffness out of your joints so your practice can be more productive, 3) by ending your morning shower with a very cold final rinse, it stimulates your spirit and drives your internal energy into the center core of your torso, which is very similar and helpful to the results of Condensing Breathing. The obvious effects of the cold shower are it will wake you up immediately which is also a by-product of practicing Chi Kung.

Taking the cold showers in the morning is like getting on the expressway in the morning at "the speed of traffic." Without the showers, it's like creeping along like some old man that shouldn't be on the expressway in the first place.

TWO DIFFERENT KINDS OF SWEAT

Body odor is related to body detoxification. As you practice, you will notice there are 2 distinct types of sweat. The thin, almost watery type with very little odor, which is related to regulating your body temperature. The second is a more thick and smelly kind of sweat. This second type is related to body detoxification and should be washed off after completion of your Chi Kung practice. You should not take showers immediately following your practice. You will lose valuable body heat and confuse your internal energy. Wait until you cool down before taking your after practice shower. If you take a combined shower (hot & cold) before your daily practice, it will cut down greatly your accumulated body odor.

SINUS FLUSHING - BLOWING YOUR NOSE AT DRUGS

Many times sinus headaches, respiratory problems that do not involve the lungs and bronchial tubes or sinus problems show up when you change your diet. It's normal, don't worry. If somebody that has chronic sinus problems wants to alleviate the problem himself, instead of taking an over-the-counter drug or prescription for it, it would only take about 10 minutes in the beginning of the day.

This self-maintenance step is to inhale relatively warm water into your nose and gag it out your mouth. It sounds terrible but will work wonders for your chronic sinus problems. This will almost guarantee you a winter without a cold, if only done regularly. You should see results with this technique after doing it only a few times. It will seem impossible at first, be persistent. It really works, almost immediately.

ANTIBIOTICS ARE NOT "HARMLESS" OR "WONDERFUL"

Many many people rely on their medical doctors much more than they should. I have seen many instances where people catch colds, and what do they do but they run to the doctor and the doctor gives them an antibiotic and tells them that this will help. Actually, it really doesn't. The cold just runs its course. Taking antibiotics... many times upsets the normal balance of intestinal flora and friendly bacteria normally present in the intestine. Candita Albicans, a fungus normally present in the body, can multiply to a degree that can be very unhealthy, with many serious and diverse symptoms. Don't take antibiotics unless you absolutely have to. There are two books you should read concerning Candita Albicans: one is by Orian Truss M.D. and the other is by William Crooks M.D. They are both on my suggested reading list. You should also read a book by a friend of mine entitled CHRONIC FATIGUE SYNDROME" by Jesse Stoff M.D. This book is a must!

CHAPTER #8
SEXUAL KUNG FU

The sexual technique associated with the practice of Chi Kung has been kept a secret for many years. Few books have been written on this obscure subject. Most of my clients and students have little or no experience with this aspect of Chi Kung. Neglecting this aspect of the art is like "leaving off the icing on the cake."

Many years of practicing Tai Chi and being celibate for over two years taught me many things. Those two years of celibacy and avoiding members of the opposite sex, turned out to be the most productive years for my internal power and sensitivity development.

During that period, my internal sensitivity had become extremely acute. My meditations had matured and solidified, and my constitution had acquired my "Pit Bull" characteristics, which I still have.

The Taoist Sexual Technique, still quite unknown, is very closely related to Chi Kung and is a direct extension of it. The Taoist Sexual Technique is an extremely important and valuable branch of the Chinese Internal arts.

Again as stated previously, the books on The Taoist Sexual Technique that currently exist, focus their attention on form, the philosophy, and the emotional sides of the art, again missing the point. Without The Chi Circulations or The Mind Training there would be no applications.

Because of my Tai Chi background and extensive experience, I have found form to be the least valuable. The most important ingredient; Developing Your Jing (cultivated sexual energy) is usually ignored. Form is barely necessary, but Jing is absolutely necessary and should be at the heart of your practice. My presentation of The Taoist Sexual Technique will be for introduction purposes since detailed instruction might require a whole book to itself. Apply your Chi Kung while having sex and see what you discover on your own. Mail your questions to me and I will include them in my next book. Make your questions as specific as possible.

RADIO SHOW: SEXUAL KUNG FU

Good evening and welcome to Pathways. This is your host Paul O'Brien. Every week at this time we invite you for a visit with selected leaders in transformation and self-discovery. This week we have live in our KBOO Studios, Gary J. Clyman, a Tai Chi Master from Chicago.

Paul: Gary it's good to have you back on the show.

BEYOND SELF-HELP: MASTERING PERSONAL POWER™ by Gary J. Clyman

GJC: Hi.

PO: We've had you on the show a couple times and you've talked to us about Temple Style Tai Chi Chuan.

GJC: Right.

PO: Your Personal Power Training Seminar, The Inner Power Workshop, The Spinal Touch Seminars...

GJC: Yeah, we haven't talked about that yet, but that's not what we're here for.

PO: No, we'll have to do that on another show. And, in general, your business is called Energy for Life Systems. We've talked to you about quite a few things, and tonight we're going to talk about Sexual Kung Fu.

GJC: That's right!

PO: What is Sexual Kung Fu?

GJC: OK. Well first of all, in order to understand what we are talking about, this goes into learning the Internal Meditation System that I teach and adapting it while you're making love, so let me talk a little bit about how to cultivate internal energy in general.

PO: O.K.

GJC: When you practice Chi Kung, which means "Energy Work" in Chinese, what you're doing is developing and cultivating sexual energy. Now it's not normal sexual energy which almost everybody has, we're talking about something very specific called "Jing," in Chinese. "Jing" is a transformed accumulation and directed use and form of this energy so that it really is a lot different. The way that I found this, to give you a little background first is, I started Tai Chi in 1974 and in about 1977, I learned what is called "Chi Kung," after I'd been in the system about three and a half, almost four years. This is like the end result, one of the end things, the last thing that you learn in "Temple Style," the Tai Chi System that I practice. What that is, is that it's purely "internal," very little, about 20% shows up externally that you can see a movement or something. Most of my Chi Kung system is done either sitting still on a chair or on a cushion. When you cultivate internal energy or "Jing," what you're doing is, you're moving energy and you're condensing energy, when I said "Condensing," I mean "sucking energy from your Universe, from your environment," and sort of "converting coal to diamonds" in the process.

PO: O.K.

GJC: And when you cultivate internal energy, it affects you in a lot of different ways. One of the major ways and what I concentrate on in my training that I do, is I help people develop a sense of what I call "self-containment." That means the ability to be self-contained, primarily, and what that means is that they are not really reliant on things or on other people.

PO: So this is a special kind of meditation that you teach?

GJC: Yeah, Chi Kung.

PO: Chi Kung is a type of meditation that has to do with internal alchemy so to speak?

GJC: Yeah, it's not like TM, or like different yoga systems where there's stress reduction. Yes, there are stress reduction aspects, but it's not primarily a stress reduction practice. It's primarily for utilizing, cultivating and harnessing internal energy and developing your WILL.

PO: O.K., now I can see how an individual could use cultivation in terms of getting more personal power from within, and all that. What about dual cultivation which is really what we're talking about tonight?

GJC: "Dual cultivation" is the process of two people circulating their internal energy in what's called The Micro Cosmic Orbit which is taught in my workshop. When two people do it and I don't mean just sitting next to each other, I'm talking about while two people are "making love," when one or both parties circulates their internal energy, it's like meditating together but it's like a feeling that you've never experienced before. I've been doing this since 1977.

PO: Now The Micro Cosmic Orbit is something that flows between the both of them?

GJC: No, The Micro Cosmic Orbit is your own internal circulation. It's circulating energy inside the torso, up the back of the spine and down the front of the spine. Dual cultivation is doing it together.

PO: So what difference does it make whether you're having sex or not?

GJC: Well, you don't communicate with anybody when you're doing it yourself.

PO: Oh, so how does your Micro Cosmic Orbit communicate with somebody else, or somebody else's Micro Cosmic Orbit?

GJC: Well, when you're having sex, and I'm not just talking about when you're "inserted," it doesn't have to be that way. You can circulate without any sexual contact, however, you've got something called Tantra yoga, which some people listening to the program may have heard about. Tantra is a little different than The Taoist Sexual Technique, which is what I teach. The Taoist Sexual Technique allows women to orgasm and doesn't allow men to, and Tantra doesn't allow women to either. It's like you treat the orgasm as...

BEYOND SELF-HELP: MASTERING PERSONAL POWER™ by Gary J. Clyman

PO: An obstacle.

GJC: Something very very special. Well, imagine raising a dog. You get it as a puppy, you raise it, you've had it two years and then you slit it's throat. And then you get another puppy and you raise that two years and then you raise that for another two years and then you slit it's throat. So, what we do when you have an organism or we ejaculate as men, is we just completely annihilate any energy that we've been able to accumulate and build up. Now, when you practice Chi Kung and you cultivate internal energy, that becomes a very precious thing and you're not so anxious to give it up. Now most men are uncomfortable about having sexual energy in their bodies so what do they do? They do whatever they can to get rid of it. They drink or they... they do all kind of things. So what do you do when you're practicing The Taoist Sexual Technique... I'm careful.

PO: That's good. We're on the radio here.

GJC: I almost forgot... What you do when you're practicing The Taoist Sexual Technique, is you treat the orgasm like it's something extremely valuable that you don't want to have, because that same energy that you use when you're having sex is the same energy that you use to create dynamic physical presence, to be self-assured and to have self-confidence and do all the other things that make you...

PO: Now wait a minute! Wait a minute! There's a lot of men, I'm sure they're a lot of men that are confident, self-assured, etc., that still ejaculate.

GJC: Right, but we're not talking about cultivating "Jing" or cultivating sexual energy.

PO: O.K., well what is the problem that cultivating Jing solves, or addresses itself to? What is it good for really, I mean?

GJC: Well, it's good for a lot of things. It's really good for health benefits. There are a lot of people that are having all kinds of different aches and pains all over their body that if they practice Chi Kung and they didn't just lose it on a regular basis, they would just feel better. It's like they treat themselves. They keep healing and healing. This is also called "healing energy."

PO: So, is this an all or nothing proposition? I mean is it...

GJC: No it isn't.

PO: O.K. So it's kind of like regulating the orgasm is good, even if you don't?

GJC: Yeah, you can not do it at all, which some people do, rare, but some do. Or, you can use it for prolonging sex also, which a lot of men do. You know, if you go an extra two hours or so and at the end of that you decide that you want to "let it out." That's a different story. I don't do that necessarily. The book you have in front of you is called,

BEYOND SELF-HELP: MASTERING PERSONAL POWER™ by Gary J. Clyman

<u>Taoist Sexual Secrets of Love, Cultivating Male Sexual Energy</u>. That's a book by Mantak Chia, from New York and that's a whole book on what the benefits are and how to circulate this internal energy. There is also a woman's book called <u>Cultivating Female Sexual Energy or Ovarian Kung Fu</u>. They can get it at your local bookstores.

PO: Now it seems to me Gary, that a lot of men are rather attached to the feeling of having orgasm.

GJC: You're very perceptive Paul, did you figure that out all by yourself? That's because they're always trying to get rid of their sexual energy. They associate it with being uncomfortable... Horny.

PO: But it's highly pleasurable to expend sexual energy, isn't it?

GJC: Yeah, but how long do you it spend it for? About 10 seconds and then it takes about 5 days for you to accumulate it again.

PO: In the Taoist system the woman is encouraged to have orgasms?

GJC: Right, because first of all, woman are treated differently.

PO: Treated differently by whom?

GJC: In the Chinese old society.

PO: Right. O.K.

GJC: But outside of that, women can have organisms because they don't lose what men lose.

PO: In other words, it's not depleting for a woman and maybe they even pick up energy.

GJC: Right. But, men can't do that. Some men think they can, but it's really not good and you know, I'm not saying that sex is not good. I'm not saying that ejaculation is not good. I'm saying that if you're cultivating internal energy and you ejaculate, then you're losing exactly what you're going after when you practice, whether you're practicing Tai Chi or whether you're doing some sort of other meditation. You lose the electrical and chemical energy that you're starting to work with.

PO: O.K. well, what does it feel like to make love with a woman, I mean as we are both men?

GJC: You never did that before? (laugh)

PO: What does it feel like to make love with a woman and not have...

GJC: And not lose it?

PO: And not ejaculate as a man, and the woman has an orgasm, or two or three, or thirty.

GJC: Or many, many, many...

PO: What does that feel like afterwards, from the male point of view?

GJC: Well, you can get up and go run around the block without having to worry about being tired, worn out, or anything. I mean it really is revitalizing!

PO: Well what about... when I was in high school we used to hear about this thing called...

GJC: "BLUE BALLS?"

PO: Right.

GJC: No that's not it with this, because you're not just leaving your energy down there in your prostate gland. What you're doing when you practice this Chi Kung, or whatever you want to call it that we're doing here, this sexual thing, is that you're circulating it throughout the rest of your body, which is what I teach in the training.

PO: Uh huh. Tell the audience some of the effects of semen loss. Some of the adverse effects.

GJC: Fatigue. You lose you're drive in general. You lose you're self-confidence. We're talking about men now, not women.

PO: Women don't?

GJC: Women don't lose it like that. But when men do it, it's an extreme. It just wears you out completely. I was celibate for two and a half years during the time that I was practicing and learning all these things.

PO: By celibate you mean no ejaculation at all.

GJC: No sex. I said no sex.

PO: Different people mean different things by "celibate." I just wanted to know what you meant.

GJC: No sex.

PO: No sex with a woman?

BEYOND SELF-HELP: MASTERING PERSONAL POWER™ by Gary J. Clyman

GJC: No sex with anything! Nowadays that means anything. So when I was practicing Chi Kung in the old days, when I was in training full time, what I tried to do was, I tried to practice every single practice and bring it back to where it was when I quit the practice before, which is a very very hard thing to do, because I was practicing 6, 8, 10 hours a day. That's what I was doing. Most people when they asked you what you do for a living, you said you did this, you did that, I said I practice Tai Chi. They used to look at me pretty funny and say, "What are you talking about ?" Because other people practice Tai Chi three hours a week. I was practicing full time because I knew that I was going to make it and I did turn out to be the survivor of my generation.

PO: You mean your generation in that particular school?

GJC: A year or two either way. I'm the only person teaching publically that you can find anywhere. But when you practice this stuff, you just keep your energy. Now, when you practice Chi Kung, you try to develop a certain ability to be with yourself in a very self-contained way. Now if you ejaculate, you lose that self-containment. If you lose it in winter because of the nature of winter, you know, you really lose all your body heat and all your "protective mechanisms." If you do it during the spring, it's not so bad because things are growing and they're green and sprouting. Summer and Fall is not so good, but Winter is terrible and Spring is O.K.

PO: So, if you're going to ejaculate the best time to do it is in spring.

GJC: Hey, you learn pretty fast. You might as well do it in spring.

PO: According to the ancient Chinese, the Jing was considered to be your very precious thing. Can you say a few words about what they used to call "The Three Treasures?"

GJC: O.K., "The Three Treasures" are Jing (which is cultivated sexual energy), Chi (which is an electrical energy that <u>does not</u> show up as a physical vibration in the body).

PO: That's the "Chi" in Tai Chi.

GJC: Right. And Shen is like your essence, or your spiritual essence. Now, the way I teach Shen in my training is a little different because I've taken it out of a Taoist context where out of ten people only one person understands what I'm talking about. I've modernized the whole concept of Jing, Chi, and Shen in a way that when I'm talking about Shen in my training, what I mean is connecting it with visualizations, affirmations, and projections, to create the picture of your particular universe the way you want to and then it just helps things fall into place better. That's taking the internal essential energy which is our spirit inside which is different from our sexual energy and from our electrical energy. It's who we are in spirit and sort of superimposing our WILL into our environment in a way the way we plan it.

BEYOND SELF-HELP: MASTERING PERSONAL POWER™ by Gary J. Clyman

PO: So it's kind of like facilitating the creative force. GJC: Absolutely! And it's really exciting. This is probably the most exciting thing that I teach in my workshop.

PO: Oh, I see. So that's related to Chi Kung training?

GJC: Right. In my particular way of teaching. Now, what I've done is I've taken about four to five years of Tai Chi/Chi Kung training and I've created it in a way that I've recreated a system that is pre-formatted so that I know exactly what the material is that I'm going to teach. Many years ago, I decided to teach this material and I needed to set it up in a way that people could understand it without any previous experience and I did. So, I've given people all the basics that they need for practicing Chi Kung, which include some what I call Tai Chi Connective Meditations, which is not Tai Chi, but it's using the mind training, not the mind, but the mind training and incorporating it directly in with the body, so it's connecting body and mind. I've created the workshop and I just finished one today and it's really good to see what people get out of it, because they really can change a lot of things.

PO: O.K. Have you ever done a workshop on Sexual Kung Fu?

GJC: Yes, I did a couple of years ago in Chicago.

PO: Do you think there is much interest in that these days? Are people ready for this?

GJC: I think there is. However, I think the people that want to learn it don't know what they're talking about because they don't have any "vocabulary." So, when I teach the Sexual Kung Fu part of what I do, it's after they've already taken my training, The Personal Power Training and then they already have the pre-formatted vocabulary that they can understand what I'm talking about and it's a very simple procedure.

PO: So then they have a context for it.

GJC: Yeah, because without the training they don't know, they can't... It's just words, it doesn't mean anything.

PO: Your Personal Power Training then I assume contains elements of Tai Chi and...

GJC: There is very little Tai Chi in my training, however, the Tai Chi Connective Meditations, I do teach Chi Kung. The Personal Power Training is a self-contained unit that I teach in two days.

PO: O.K. What do you think the effect of dual cultivation of sexual energy has on a relationship between a man and a woman as a whole.

GJC: It really can combine them as a single unit. It's very exciting to watch people practice this. I've been doing this for a long time myself, but when a couple comes in together who are already a couple and they learn this, it's very exciting, however it's very rare to find two people who even care about it at the same time. Usually you find a woman that knows how to do it or wants to do it and a man that couldn't care less, or a man that knows it or wants to do it and a woman that couldn't care less. But when I work with a couple that really together want to learn it, it just, I mean, it's like taking whatever love they have and expanding it a thousand percent.

PO: Is it possible for couples to learn this on their own?

GJC: If they have a background they can, but usually not. Now, they can get the background from me, but they need a common vocabulary and a languaging system they can use. Like reading the books doesn't do anything.

PO: It must help a little bit.

GJC: Not much, because all it does is confuse you because you don't have a "physical anchor." You don't have any "rooting" for what the books are talking about. But when they take my training, they read the books and the books make total sense. It's very simple but the books still aren't that good, except for the book I'm writing.

PO: Do you think that this practice ever came naturally to mankind?

GJC: Yeah I do, as a matter of fact. If you were in "survival," you know, living in a survival environment in which we are, but a different kind of survival environment.

PO: You mean like a physical survival.

GJC: Right. If you lost your seed, your precious thing, you would also lose a great deal of your ability for self-defense purposes. I don't mean fighting necessarily, I'm talking about the environment. So I can tell you from personal experience, when I first discovered this, see I've been doing this a lot longer than the books. I was doing this a long time before the books were out. And what I got from practicing this and the way I learned how to do this was from practicing the internal energy cultivation standing meditation in Tai Chi that I learned in 1976 and 77. This is an extension of the internal energy work directly, because why work for years on cultivating internal energy and then get in a relationship and have sex and then lose everything that you've been working for. So this is a direct extension of that particular idea of cultivating energy and not losing it.

PO: Well, energy has to flow. Right? I mean...

GJC: Yeah, it flows. It flows inside your body, but it doesn't have to flow to outside your body.

PO: But it rebuilds itself, even if it does, doesn't it? Isn't there a natural cycle?

GJC: Yeah, but it takes too long.

BEYOND SELF-HELP: MASTERING PERSONAL POWER™ by Gary J. Clyman

PO: How long does it take?

GJC: You lose five days after and four days before of all the work that you've done.

PO: So, do you think it's natural for a man to make love to a woman and then just roll over and go to sleep? Does that make sense?

GJC: That's what is natural here.

PO: Well, I mean if he ejaculates.

GJC: Yeah.

PO: It's logical that that would happen then.

GJC: Yeah. But that's because he "lost it." But if you practice this, you don't do that.

PO: Uh huh.

GJC: At all. This is the answer to all that stuff. On top of that, I've had men take the workshop who were concerned with more sexual performance things. I mean they didn't have problems originally, but they definitely don't have problems now. I mean from practicing this stuff, it definitely changes the way you are sexually.

PO: Well what did you mean, you used a peculiar phrase "that precious thing?" What sociology does that come out of?

GJC: That's Chinese.

PO: What's the background on behind that?

GJC: Well, if you lost it, then you know what I'm talking about. If you're cultivating internal energy and you spend a lot of time doing it, "that precious thing" is the thing that means the most to you, which is your personal cultivated sexual energy which is called Jing. Now Jing can be used the same in many ways, it can be used for healing purposes. Jing is also the thing that if a Tai Chi Master touches a person and sends them flying all the way across the room. It's just a different usage for the manifestation of Jing. Now if you take my training and you cultivate internal energy, which does happen frequently, it's a different kind of cultivated sexual energy then it would be if you went through the Tai Chi system that I came from and cultivated, because when you've got a Tai Chi foundation or background and you cultivate internal energy, you also have the capability of being able to connect your internal energy to your bone structure and "BAM" that's where the explosive power comes from, which is called "Fah Jing."

PO: Uh Huh.

GJC: So when you do The Personal Power Training and you learn Chi Kung from me, you don't develop that. However, what you're able to do with your "precious thing" is that you're able to use it in business, in relationship, and in relationship to your self-defeating attitudes. You can get rid of self-defeating attitudes and you can develop self-esteem and self-confidence and all that other stuff that goes along with it.

PO: And how does this help women? How does it help women for men to cultivate their sexual energy along these lines?

GJC: I don't know what you're talking about.

PO: It is... are there any benefits for women in a "dual cultivation" practice?

GJC: Yeah. Women.... Do you mean women who cultivate for themselves, or women in relationship?

PO: With a partner.

GJC: Yeah. It brings a couple much closer together. You know, they start to think together and there are all sorts of things that happen. It really improves love relationships if they're "right." If they're wrong, it doesn't. If they're right it does.

PO: It seems to me that it really would improve the quality of the love making from the female point of view.

GJC: Sure.

PO: Now you've talked about self-containment a lot. I can see the value of self-containment and not you know just spinning off and shooting energy out every time you get the urge, but I'm wondering what is the relationship between self-containment and the ability to love somebody. Do you think that it increases that?

GJC: Yeah. I think that if you're not self-contained you can't do anything for anybody or in relationship to anybody until you've got yours together.

PO: Right.

GJC: Now the self-containment issue that I work with in the training helps people really be somewhere inside themselves, instead of living in their environment, living in their situations, or living in their problems.

PO: Uh huh.

GJC: When people work with me in the training what they're able to do is they're able to really get that they are not their problems and they are not their environment but they do in fact live somewhere inside their physical bodies. Most people are only 10%

available, but if you can go from 10% to 20% available, that's 100% increase already, the way it works. So if somebody goes to 40% or 50% available, you know they're doing wonderful. They're completely different people by then. In the way they talk, the way the think. You know there's a horrible poverty mentality that runs through this area here. When people develop this self-containment characteristic that they get from the training, they just recognize it and they're finally able to do something about it.

PO: So really, love is a form of energy and the more energy you have, the more you have to give.

GJC: Yeah, no problem.

PO: Studies have shown that a lot of people, particularly men, are addicted to sex, or addicted to orgasm. Does this training have any value for people in that position?

GJC: Well it depends on if their sex is detrimental to them or not. Most people don't know the difference so it's not a big deal. But if somebody's really aware of how tired they get when they do it, then this is the absolute answer to that particular problem. The problem is, most men don't think it's a "problem." Because you know, they grew up in the 50's or the 40's and they see it on TV and they saw it in the movies and it's just something that's expected. But there are men around that don't view sex the same way as everybody else.

PO: It seems to me, there's an incredible amount of ignorance around the subject in general.

GJC: Yeah, well I don't know what you mean by "the subject."

PO: The subject of human sexuality, of cultivating sexual energy.

GJC: Oh Yeah, yeah, you know, it's almost got to come from another culture before you learn anything about it.

PO: So, I was just over in Europe and I noticed how natural people were with their intimacy and affection and it seems very out of place here.

GJC: Yeah. You go to Chicago, where I come from, and see what happens.

PO: Uh huh. So would you consider that sex is an important opportunity for spiritual development?

GJC: Yes, I would. Absolutely. In fact, if you're doing it the way we're talking about here - yes, if you're talking about it otherwise - no, sex is usually in my book considered something like drinking, drug abuse, or gambling. You know, I mean it can be used really in a bad way for people, as almost a distraction. Whereas if you practice this particular kind of sex, or cultivating internal energy, it develops you as an individual and it sort of sets you up to be self-contained, and self-motivated, and self... and it's very exciting to watch what happens with people. There's a lot of people that I'm been working with in Portland, who really are getting a lot of benefits and some of the benefits are tied into this particular thing.

PO: Uh huh. How do people, let's say that people don't live in a geographical location that's convenient for them to take one of your trainings? What do you suggest for people in general to increase their awareness of these kinds of possibilities, to learn more about it? What would be the first steps for people to take?

GJC: Well they could buy the books.

PO: Uh huh. The Mantak Chia books.

GJC: Or they can contact me and I'm writing a book right now also. It won't be ready for another six months. And it will explain cultivating internal energy, as well as I'm going to tie in the sexual part that will be a special chapter and questions and answers. I think they're in trouble. They've got to find somebody that knows this stuff or come and spend two days with me. This isn't like learning Karate. There's a Karate school on every corner. This is almost hidden. I mean up until my generation this stuff wasn't even talked about. They kept this material for themselves, you know. This was kept secret.

PO: There was another book out called " The Tao of Love and Sex" . Are you familiar with that book?

GJC: Yeah, I am. That's not as technical as Chia's books. Chia's books are a little better, but not much.

PO: Right. In The Tao of Love and Sex, he talks about how in ancient China it was considered much more viral to be self-contained, to never ejaculate. To never ejaculate was the ultimate ideal for a man and conferred immortality upon one. But he talks in that book about...

GJC: See I avoid using terms like that because no one knows what I'm talking about. I spend too much time explaining myself instead of communicating.

PO: Well that book was written by a Chinese man.

GJC: Jolan Chang.

PO: Right. He says in there that's its a good idea for a man who is following this practice to make love very often, if not every day, but to regulate how often he ejaculates. Maybe twice a week is O.K. for somebody's in his 30's.

GJC: Yeah, right.. there's a time.. O.K. they's a seasonal influence and there's also an age influence.

PO: And he says that its a good thing to make love often because both parties pick up...

GJC: There's an exchange of hormones and energy and all kinds of other things.

PO: Right, and there's a spiritual dimension to what's happening.

GJC: Right.

PO: Well, Gary, would you mind telling the audience how they can get in touch with you if they're more interested in this, or any of the trainings that you give because we're running out of time.

GJC: O.K. They can call me at my office in Chicago at (312) 527-1188.

PO: Well that's it for tonight Gary. Thank you very much for being here.

GJC: Thanks for having me on.

PO: It's been a pleasure and it's a fascinating topic. On behalf of KBOO Radio 90.7 FM, this is Paul O'Brien of Pathways, signing off.

This is Community Radio KBOO Portland, broadcasting at 90.7 on your FM dial.
-THE END-

HOW MUCH DO ORGASMS COST YOU?

When a man has an orgasm with a woman, he loses four days of Chi Kung work from before and five days after. To "catch up" after having an orgasm requires a lot of work. Now there are certain ways to have sex with a woman when you lose less, but you must be able to separate your Heaven's Essence from your Earth's Essence. This is a very complicated and specific technique.

Having sex and having orgasms are not considered the same. Don't confuse the two. You can have sex without it ending in an orgasm.

SEX WITHOUT ORGASMS: CHI KUNG WHILE HAVING SEX

Frequency of sexual orgasms during the winter should be restricted to a minimum (None is preferable). In spring, because everything is growing and blooming, you can have them much more frequently, if you are "in practice." During the summer and fall, you should restrict your ejaculations to one per week. I don't expect many students to give up sex altogether, but <u>sex in moderation is strongly suggested</u>. I am not condoning having orgasms, but you should know that one orgasm in winter is worth

100 orgasms in spring, and one drop of sperm is worth 100 drops of blood. I cannot stress this enough. If you are trying to cultivate sexual energy (Jing), can you see the drawbacks of having frequent orgasms?

MASTURBATION IS A TOTAL WASTE

You won't go blind, become insane, or get pimples, but you might feel drained.

There is a distinct difference between having sex and masturbating besides the obvious differences. Hopefully you're not a member of "The Sex Without Partners Club." If you are, resign immediately. Having sex can have its drawbacks in many situations. Masturbating is considered "energy suicide" in relationship to your internal energy cultivation practice. Masturbation is the most important of "Clyman's Four Unbreakable Rules" for this reason. It is death to your Chi Kung practice and must be discontinued and avoided at all cost. Most men think they are doing themselves a favor when they masturbate. They are actually performing the ultimate energy destruction act. Hands Off!

What do you think you are trying to accumulate, cultivate, and circulate when you practice Chi Kung? Your Jing (cultivated sexual energy), that's why masturbating is so destructive. If you think you can continue to masturbate and excel in Chi Kung, <u>you will be wasting your time</u>. Stop now!

HOW MASTURBATION DESTROYS SELF-ESTEEM

Masturbation is a great way to eliminate any resemblances of self-esteem, self-confidence and discipline. If you could be in my shoes and interview as many people as I do, you would see just how humiliating "jerking off" is and what side effects it causes in men's dynamic physical presence, not to mention the huge energy leak it is.

WOMEN AND MASTURBATION

Masturbation for women is also self-destructive because it reduces their attention span and makes them daydream. If tension is what you want to get rid of, go get a massage. If your "life force" is what you want to get rid of, masturbate. Many women already have trouble achieving what they want in life. Masturbating only pours water on your "little spark" that motivates you to strive to get what you deserve, and more. Masturbating tends to lower your "deservingness" which leads to more inaction.

SAVE YOUR SPERM

The topic that always comes up when discussing developing internal energy is what about your "precious thing?" Could there be any validity in the saying "one drop of sperm is worth 100 drops of blood?" I will present old information and let you make up your own mind.

CELIBACY VS. SEMEN RETENTION

A question comes up many times relating to "sex" in marriage or in relationships. The question is "What is better for me?" ("Me" being one of my clients), "giving up sex altogether and being celibate or practicing The Taoist Sexual Technique?" Well, The Taoist Sexual Technique is a good alternative to celibacy. However, celibacy is still a more internal practice where you can get more of your "internal work" done. Because we will soon be in the 1990's, celibacy is not a very common practice for many people. It requires too much discipline and giving up of the world.

Instead of destroying your marriage by taking the sex out, the next best thing is to incorporate The Taoist Sexual Technique into your sex life whenever possible. There will be a need for a lot of negotiation and compromise, but this certainly beats separation, divorce and all the other problems that are associated with this. I repeat, The Taoist Sexual Technique is a good positive alternative to celibacy when celibacy cannot be practiced. It is not practical for people to give up sex. I don't expect anyone to do this, but The Taoist Sexual Technique is a workable alternative. It can save your marriage and relationships as well as lead to Spiritual/Sexual Freedom. Try it, you'll like it!

"BLUE BALLS" NO MORE

A common discussion that is brought up when most men hear about this is, that most men think this is an unhealthy practice or that they will get what's called "blue balls" from practicing The Taoist Sexual Technique without ejaculating. Nothing could be farther from the truth, if the technique is practiced correctly.

ABOUT DUAL CULTIVATION

Little do these men know, there actually is a release, but it's not an external release like an ejaculation, but rather the internal energy is projected into your Micro Cosmic Orbit. If both partners know what they are doing, it is called "dual cultivation." It can be practiced even if only one partner knows how, but it may require some discussion.

When a man practices The Taoist Sexual Technique, it's a little tricky at first, because the tendency is to want to let the pressure off, or ejaculate when he gets excited. If you can direct your mind beyond your immediate situation and urges, you can take that energy and do something different with it. You can obtain a lot of benefits from this practice.

If you can control your mind during sex, you can control it anywhere.

These benefits will show up as improvements in your health, strengthening your constitution, and developing a much more stable emotional state. This kind of love making will actually fulfill your female partner more if you have "the right one" and can explain what you're doing. This is also a good method of birth control when your technique is impeccable and practiced correctly. It is best to also understand her fertility cycle. Do your homework in advance.

INCREASED SEXUAL PERFORMANCE

I have been practicing The Taoist Sexual Technique since I came out of celibacy in 1977. I really works! I discovered this practice out of shear necessity. I felt like I was dying because of losing it after all that practicing, for the first few times. I asked myself, "Do I have to give up sex for the rest of my life to get what I want?" The answer is clearly NO.

The Taoist Sexual Technique, when practiced correctly, can save you many thousands of hours of wasted practice. <u>I do not advise men to attempt to practice The Taoist Sexual Technique until they have a good grasp of Chi Kung in general.</u>

The Taoist Sexual Technique is an extension of your Chi Kung practice and applications. There are a few other books on this subject, but they spend most of their content on posture and fail to teach what the energy and your mind do, while circulating your energy.

The Taoist Sexual Technique can be used for some very specific applications. One of these benefits is to prolong erection in the man, it can be used as a remedy for impotence (lack of erection) or lack of sexual drive. After practicing Chi Kung, sexual performance is usually enhanced, but <u>Chi Kung is the key to your vitality</u>, not just in relation to sex.

TEACHING YOUR WOMAN THE TAOIST SEXUAL TECHNIQUE

Finding "the right partner" that will let you practice The Taoist Sexual Technique is not an easy task. It takes a lot of patience and explanation to help your lover understand a very sensitive subject. Many women think the best way to satisfy a man is to make him ejaculate. This is not true in regard to The Taoist Sexual Technique. It is best to have or find a women that practices Chi Kung, but let's face it, the chances are slim, unless you train her yourself.

I don't even teach The Taoist Sexual Technique to my male clients until their Chi Kung practice has stabilized. As I have mentioned before, you will be using specific techniques such as Condensing Breathing, The Micro Cosmic Orbit, Inside Air, and others while making love.

It is quite common for women not to want to experiment with The Taoist Sexual Technique, but with some it is "workable." Many women are afraid of this practice because they don't want to get pregnant, not a bad fear. If you, the man, have low levels of self-discipline, beginning to practice The Taoist Sexual Technique may be harder than you think (no pun intended). If you don't have the sexual control that is required, I doubt if you will be able to talk your sex partner into anything "new."

BEYOND SELF-HELP: MASTERING PERSONAL POWER™ by Gary J. Clyman

However, there are a few things that might help.

UNDERSTANDING HER MENSTRUAL CYCLE

There are certain times of the month when most women are somewhat predictable (if ever?). I will give a brief explanation of the menstrual cycle. Remember, there are no guarantees with this. These are only to be used as guidelines. Each woman will be different. Do your own homework.

The first seven days after the first day of her period are usually considered SAFE. Still no guarantees.
The second seven days is considered less than safe.
The third seven days is considered DANGEROUS due to ovulation.
The fourth seven days may be safe, but because many women have irregular cycles, this cannot be counted on.

THE USE OF RUBBERS

In order to "prove yourself" to your sex partner and to yourself, the use of condoms may be a much needed helper. Remember, if your woman has been "doing it" all her life a certain way, getting her to change is no small task. For you to learn how to perform The Taoist Sexual Technique will be hard enough (no pun intended). So the use of a condom will add to her confidence in you.

There is one drawback. Wearing a condom tends to "choke you off" and builds up pressure, so you might want to ejaculate. This is not good for your self-discipline reputation. However, there is a kind of condom that is not so tight and won't "choke you off." "Sheep skin" has some added benefits that synthetic brands do not. "Sheep skin" allows for an electromagnetic and hormone exchange, not sperm. "Sheep skin" also does not "squeeze the life out of you." I wonder if this is where that saying got started? "Sheep skin" also has the most natural feeling and is not like taking a shower with a raincoat on. However, there is one drawback with "sheep skin" besides an animal having to give it's life so you could... the one draw back is, "sheep skin" does not give you any protection against AIDS. It is advised that you have healthy sex partners in the first place, so hopefully a rubber for AIDS protection is not that important in your case.

Between using "sheep skin" condoms, and understanding her menstrual cycle, you might have a chance to incorporate The Taoist Sexual Technique into your daily and nightly lives. It might be the hardest thing you ever tried to do, but once you become successful at it, it will be great for both of you. Please note, The Taoist Sexual Technique can be used for birth control, but only when perfected, if ever. No guarantees.

Someone years ago asked me if two men could practice this technique. After I finished puking, I said "no." There is an ingredient of exchanging energies while practicing The Taoist Sexual Technique. I don't know how homosexual men would practice this and I don't care either.

EJACULATION: THE DOOR TO DEPRESSION

Many people, men especially, develop a state of depression related to expending their sexual energy in a way that does not do them any good. Most men look at sex and ejaculation as a release. It is a release, but let us look more closely at ejaculation from a Chi Kung perspective. If the goal of your Chi Kung practice is to develop Jing (internal cultivated sexual energy), you must understand the importance of NOT EJACULATING.

KEEP YOUR SEXUAL ENERGY TO YOURSELF

Excessive sex leads to excessive mood swings, low energy, fatigue, and depression. Most men don't recognize the differences because they are not aware of their sexual energy except when they are engaged in sexual activity. By practicing Chi Kung and regulating the number of orgasms you have depending on your age, the season and the age of your female sex partner, you can stabilize your emotional states greatly and regain your "warrior spirit," which we were all born with, but lost somewhere along the line.

SLEEP LESS & WEIGH LESS

A common benefit many of my male client/students notice when they practice Chi Kung is that they tend to require less sleep. They become more rested with less sleep. This is a very interesting phenonoma. When you learn Chi Kung from me, you learn to utilize your energy in a more efficient fashion, thus allowing you to recuperate quicker and expend less energy on the same daily functions. Another by-product is that most people tend to lose weight, 20-30 pounds in the first 2-3 months without actually changing their diet.

I am not implying that "diet" is not important, but in the very beginning, "diet" is not as important as the actual practice itself. After a student has been practicing Chi Kung for a short period of time and starts to develop more energy and a better attitude, "diet" can be incorporated into your daily routine at a later date. It's not important in the very beginning. If new students try to change too many things at the same time, they may "overload" and not want to do anything. I used to require everything from my Tai Chi students and found this to be too demanding on almost every one of them.

The reasons for becoming celibate and practicing Chi Kung are different than the reasons for becoming celibate without Chi Kung.

Many people become celibate in response to external stimuli or pressure to the outside world. I became celibate for my own personal reasons. I wanted to concentrate on developing my internal energy. That was the most important thing in my world at that time; more important than making money, developing a career, having a girlfriend or family, or even becoming a doctor. Nothing else mattered to me. You will need to find your own personal reasons.

MORE ABOUT SLEEPING

I believe any sleep over 6 hours per night is excessive. In the old days, I only slept 2-4 hours at a time. This broken and limited sleep cycle enabled me to develop internal consistency much quicker because I did not forget where I left off, before taking a break. Remember, when I was training heavily, I used to practice 6-10 hours per day. I don't expect anyone in these modern times to put themselves through this kind of "torturous" training, but if you're up for it, just call me. (Don't worry, I won't be sitting by my phone and waiting.)

Most people that practice Chi Kung that I have taught, after a short period of time, begin to sleep less, usually 4-6 hours on a regular basis. Instead of experiencing fatigue, you actually will have more energy.

WHEN SLEEP SEEMS LIKE A WASTE OF TIME

When a person who practices Chi Kung tries to sleep, many times the feeling is like - you can't sleep or you're not interested in sleeping! What you have here is a physical awareness that has to be directed with your discipline to go to sleep, and when you have as much energy as you can have from your practice, sleep is something you're just not interested in many times. You have to discipline yourself and say, "This is it, time to go to sleep" and turn it off.

POSITIONING YOUR BODY WHILE SLEEPING

Much pain and suffering and the origin of many minor Chiropractic problems are related to what you sleep on and in what position you sleep. If you sleep on your stomach, you're definitely going to have low back problems, whether it be sacral or lumbar. On top of that, you will have what is called by many Chiropractors as "a rib out." When your ribs are not fitting properly with your vertebral joints, what happens is, you feel like you can't breath or your shoulder is "frozen," or there are many other symptoms associated with having "a rib out." When you can't breathe because of "a rib out," it feels as if somebody is standing on your chest. The best way to deal with this problem is in advance – by not sleeping on your stomach and by having the right kind of pillow under your neck.

If you sleep on your side, your spine and your cervical vertebrae should be straight and aligned. Your legs should be bent to fit together with your lower leg more extended than your upper leg. If you sleep on your back, you need a "cervical pillow" that supports your neck properly, so you don't injure yourself while you're asleep. You also need to put a thick pillow under your knees if you sleep on your back. It's worth finding out what kind of pillow to get. Talk to a good Chiropractor. As I said before, many of these Chiropractic problems can be avoided if you take care and are aware of how and what you are sleeping on. Extra firm or hard mattresses are usually advised to give you the lumbar support that most people require for pain free living.

DYNAMIC PHYSICAL PRESENCE AND AWARENESS

The term "higher energy levels" refers to having an awareness of your energy or what I call dynamic physical presence. The application of these "higher energy levels" will show up in your attitude, all your relationships, and your efficiency in performing your ordinary daily tasks. You will also sleep less. Chi Kung helps you be more efficient even when you're sleeping. You get more from your "resting time" because of your efficient energy utilization.

THINK OF ONE THING AT A TIME

It's important for you to understand that when you are practicing The Daily Practice Routine, specifically the first part, you are not "thinking" of anything other than what you are doing "in the moment." That means you are not thinking of what you want, how you want it, your new material, or your old material. This means you are not thinking about anything except what you are doing "right now." You don't even want to be thinking of what you're going to practice next.

The point is, that when you are practicing Chi Kung, you are thinking about the technique you are practicing. That's all. You try to isolate and discipline your mind to do one thing at a time. This is the same principle that you will take into your daily life and activities.

Let's say you've got the innate ability to concentrate for 100 points at one time, but when you start to think about concentrating, you're only capable of concentrating for 5-10%. What a waste!

Your goal in your Chi Kung practice is to develop a greater ability to concentrate. You will soon be able to go up to 20-30% of your ability. Your concentration levels will vary from time to time, depending on what's happening in your life. If you concentrate on one thing at a time, by the time you get through your Chi Kung practice, and into The Heaven and Earth Meditation, Your Daily Affirmations and Your Visualizations, you are also concentrating at a higher percent on those, instead of just doing standard affirmations and visualizations with a 5-10% attention span.

If you can raise your attention span and ability to concentrate while practicing Chi Kung, then by the time you get to the affirmations and visualizations part of the practice, your percentage is higher. So you're doing more in your affirmations and visualizations than if you did them on their own.

If I can teach you how to raise your physical presence and awareness in Chi Kung, then these levels will be higher everywhere else in your life.

This is why many people get results with me so quickly instead of spending a much longer time in therapy or using some other method. Practice my system and you will raise your physical presence and awareness which gives you the ability to do what you want and when you want to do it. This is why so many commodity traders come to work with me. Their results appear in their trading accounts.

If you are always thinking in terms of the future, that reflects a current self-confidence problem. If you have sufficient levels of self-confidence, you know that what you are doing right now is correct and what you will be doing tomorrow will be correct also. By raising your dynamic physical presence and awareness, you can and will overcome your low self-confidence levels. You can't be in the present if you are too much in the future.

IMPORTANCE OR IMPOTENCE: THE CHOICE IS YOURS

Having poor relationships with women, having some mechanical or sexual dysfunction where a man does not think he is "performing" as well as he thinks he should, are common reasons for becoming celibate. These reasons represent an "aversion" to women. Combining Chi Kung with becoming celibate is quite different. It's not as if you are running away from something. If you're celibate and practicing Chi Kung, it's as if you are running toward something. One of my early teachers told me, "It's like giving up the small orgasm for the BIG one."

As I mentioned previously, a large percentage of my internal development had taken place during the two and a half years when I was celibate.

THE BENEFITS OF CELIBACY

One of the benefits of being celibate is that it helps you develop a greater level of self-confidence and internal discipline. When I say "internal discipline," I am referring to the reduction of external distractions that are associated with relationships and having sex. When you go to sleep at night and when you wake up in the morning, it is easier for you to pick up exactly where you left off the night before. This principle will be discussed later.

WHY RE INVENT THE WHEEL

Most people work all day long to get to a certain place, whether it is to feel good, to follow a certain train of thought, or any other extended logical progression. Most people drop the ball in relation to being consistent when they go to sleep. This means much energy is lost in trying to get back what you had at the completion of the previous day or what I call "picking up where you left off." There is very little relation between where they were the day before, and where they begin the next day. When I say "they stopped," I am not referring to practicing Chi Kung, I mean life itself.

SELF-CONTAINMENT: THE KEY TO CONSISTENCY

Being celibate, and combining celibacy with the practice of Chi Kung, develops what I call Self-Containment. My definition of "Self-Containment" is 'to have the ability to be by yourself without any reliance on the outside world or anybody else.' You lose much less energy and develop more consistent energy/thought patterns.

Being celibate with Chi Kung gives you "a handle" that you don't get to experience in normal daily life. The self-containment that is actualized while in this stage of your development will stay with you for the rest of your life. Once you change this way, you don't change back.

BIGGER ORGASMS, WOW!

Sex will never be the same again after giving up the little orgasm for the BIG one. This leads to "immortality and longevity."

Self-Containment while being celibate tends to alter your personality and make you very stable, not at first, but after you get used to the shock of the isolation.

RUNNING AWAY OR RUNNING TOWARD

Many people are celibate without Chi Kung, but they are essentially "running away" from sex, or "running away" from interpersonal relationships and the problems associated with them. They are running away from something, but they are not running toward anything (religious reasons excluded), unless they have a great amount of insight, and most people don't.

Being celibate and running toward something by using Chi Kung is different for each person, but this target primarily represents Self-Containment, which is something that most people don't have or experience.

EXPERIENCE STABILITY THROUGH CELIBACY

When you practice Chi Kung and you are celibate, you will be living in a very stable environment. It's as if you wake up, you are the same way, you work all day long, you are the same way. You go to sleep, you are the same way, and when you wake up the next day, the goal is be where you were the day before, when you went to sleep. This is called "Self-Containment and Internal Discipline."

GIVING UP SEX IS NOT ENOUGH

This result does not come with only being celibate because there are always too many variables. I have spoken with with many people who have tried being celibate without Chi Kung and they do not experience their results in this same way. If you use Chi

Kung as your "grounding," your root, or your anchor, it makes your celibacy more stable and productive. I will use a Buddhist illustration. It is as if you have not slept in 6 months but you're not tired. Your concentration has not been broken for a long time.

INTERNAL DISCIPLINE VS. SELF-DISCIPLINE

Internal Discipline is quite different from self-discipline. Many people have and understand Self-Discipline. However, Internal Discipline is quite different. It is picking up where you left off the day before and without skipping any beats. This is very important in becoming Self-Contained.

PLUGGING THE LEAKS

Celibacy with Chi Kung also leads to "Plugging the Leaks" whether the leaks be spiritual, physical, sexual, or in your personality.

MAKING ROOM FOR MORE

Sometimes it is important for you to have an ejaculation, but not the kind where you "lose your soul," more the kind where you've been cultivating your Jing (cultivated sexual energy). If you've been very successful with The Taoist Sexual Technique and every once in a while, (it's different, depending on your age, your practice ability, and your maturity), you can have an orgasm. You might have a "wet dream" which will allow you to actually do more work and accumulate more energy. Its almost as though you've "condensed in" so much, you can't condense any more, you can't fit any more.

This should not happen on a weekly basis. Please do not misunderstand me. This is a "once in a while" phenomenon that will happen to you almost out of your control. In the old days, "wet dreams" were considered "leaks" by many people, but nowadays, a "leak" is actually good because it makes room for more condensing, more internal energy development and cultivation, but you shouldn't look forward to a leak. It should just be a "natural happening." The difference between having an orgasm while having sex, and having a wet dream, is; say you lose, go down to a -5. When you masturbate you go down to a -100, and when you have a "wet dream" related to making room for your practice, you don't go to 0, but you recuperate much quicker with this kind of orgasm. This is Nature's way of giving you more capacity and space to work.

THE ULTIMATE DISCIPLINE CHALLENGE

If you can control your ejaculations at the time when it's hardest, then you are truly disciplined. You will have discipline everywhere, in every situation, because the hardest place in the world to keep it is while having sex. If you don't ejaculate, you could be and will remain Self-Contained, but if you do ejaculate, you are losing four days before an five days of practice and accumulation after the day you "lose it." That self-destructive feeling about wanting to have an ejaculation is normal in the early stages of developing The Taoist Sexual Technique. If you have read any of the sex books (see suggested book list), it says you can have short periods of sex 10 times a day, but if you ejaculate, you won't be able to. I am not saying that if you ejaculate it is a waste of time to practice Chi Kung, but it will hold you back. You can still get there, but it's more difficult.

The problem with most people is, they do "the right thing," but they don't do "the right thing" long enough, so they don't get all the benefits or the results they hope to. Whether it's related to diet, health, business, discipline, whatever it is, people do the same thing all the time. They stop short of getting what they want.

PORNO HELPS YOUR CHI CIRCULATIONS

I do advise going to X-rated movies if you're celibate, for practicing your Condensing Breathing, Inside Air, and The Micro Cosmic Orbit, while you're watching porno movies. What that does is energize your sexual energy and then you actually have more to circulate. I do not recommend masturbating, without ejaculating for the same reason. These two things are not the same. There is another well known Chi Kung teacher that advises men to practice "masturbating" without ejaculating. I think this is a ridiculous thing to tell people to do. It just doesn't work. By the time your mind and your energy reach your genitals due to manual stimulation, that's too late already. Your energy has dropped too low and is already in your genitals. But if your watching a porno movie, and you're doing Condensing Breathing and all your other techniques, that's different because it really doesn't have anything to do with your genitals at that point.

MORE CONCERNING THE TAOIST SEXUAL TECHNIQUE

I do not intend to stuff my book with philosophy about Taoism and The Taoist Sexual Technique. If you need to find out more about the philosophy, the background, the psychology, there are a few good books written by Jolan Chang, entitled The Tao of Love and Sex and The Tao of The Loving Couple, however, what is missing from these books is the actual technique itself. That you can learn by adapting your Chi Kung practice to love making.

SEXUAL RECUPERATION?

Another way of being able to recuperate after "losing it" is to have sex the next day or the day after and absolutely "not lose it." You must circulate and draw the energy from your partner (woman) and throw it into your Micro Cosmic Orbit and not lose it. You must keep it circulating and quit at a high point of your practice and keep doing Condensing Breathing.

WASH OFF HER JUICES

It is very important after having sex with a woman, for a man to wash off her "loving juices" because your body has developed a sensitivity to that and washing will prevent you from having "wet dreams" after being successful with The Taoist Sexual Technique. You have to wash her scent off, otherwise, it's almost as if you are continuing to have sex. Your body knows what's going on and you might have unexpected, unwanted ejaculation simply because of not washing your lovers feminine juices off you. So, it's very important to remain clean at all times.

LIVING IN TROUBLE AND MISERY DAILY

Most people that I meet and see, whether I accept them as clients or not, are in trouble and misery, and they don't necessarily have to be depressed. Misery and suffering is a human condition according to Buddah. A few are depressed and in trouble, but most, comparing the way they are when they are through working with me, to how they were I met them, will admit they were in trouble, even though when I first meet them, they denied being that way. Their trouble and misery was not so apparent before. Being in trouble is a very common problem, you might say a state of being, that most people learn to live with.

HOW MANY ORGASMS CAN YOU HAVE?

Ejaculating is part of a vicious cycle. Breaking the cycle can be very important to your Chi Kung practice.

How many ejaculations a man in Chi Kung is allowed to have depends on a few factors. The first factor is his age and physical condition. The next is his constitution. Next is the season of the year and weather conditions. These are very important factors that should not be ignored.

HOW TO CHOOSE THE BEST SEX PARTNERS

For men, the optimum choice would be a women that is much younger then him, 10 years at least. If the man is 25 years old, then he has some trouble (jail bait), but we are talking a little older than 25 here. It is best to have a women who has never had children, is considerably younger than you, and has not had a hysterectomy. The only exception to these preferences are if the women has been practicing Chi Kung and has cultivated her own Jing (cultivated sexual energy). There is a hormone exchange that takes place during sex that could be a very important factor to a Chi Kung man if he knew what to do with this added female energy.

For women, it is not as important to have an age gap, since women do not lose energy in the same way men do.

YOU GET WHO YOU ARE: NO MORE, NO LESS

Many people are out there searching desperately for "the right person" to share their lives with, whether it be girlfriend, boyfriend, husband, wife, there's a mad race to find "the right person." The thing that people don't understand is that they aren't going to find "the right person" until they are "the right person" for themselves. Now, I'm not suggesting that you have to adjust your body or your personality, or to be subservient for "the right person," but if you don't have it together, you're going to also keep finding people who also don't have it together. So step #1 in how to find your mate is to make sure that you are stable and you have the important personality skills and spiritual development, so when "the right person" does come by, they know it, you know it, and it works.

I've searched for many years for "the right woman," and in my wild search, I have found many of "the wrong ones." I mean they seemed "right" at the time, but the difference between them and my wife now, is that she is "right," and I didn't have to work hard to put all the pieces together. When you find "the right person," it should be a very "natural" experience. You shouldn't have to "work at it," as many people believe. You shouldn't have to make the pieces fit. If you have to make the pieces fit, you can still do it, but you should also understand that it's probably not "the right thing" to do, but you can do "the wrong thing" in place of doing "no thing."

CHOOSING "THE RIGHT MATE"

What is important in creating "the right relationship?" This question is put to me quite frequently. Loving each other is more important than having hot romance. Hot romance is not important and it's not enough to make it through the long haul. Your mate should be your best friend and you must really like each other. This is completely different than what had been going on. When I first met my wife, we weren't romantically inclined. We just knew we liked each other and liked spending time, and liked doing things, it didn't matter what it was. We really cared about each other. The "love" part of the relationship fell right into place after we already knew each other. Now I'm not a traditional guy but we have a very "traditional" relationship.

OLD MEN WITH YOUNGER WOMEN

Hardly anybody realizes that sex, the act of making love, can be utilized for health benefits. People always think it's funny when they see an old man with a very young wife. Well there are very specific reasons for this. In oriental culture, whether it's Chinese, Filipino, Japanese, what have you, this is not so uncommon. In this country, it's almost considered obscene when old men and young girls are seen together. The reaction that people have to this seems ridiculous. What is available to you when you have sex or make love, is the opportunity to "borrow" energy from your partner and accumulate it in very specific areas of your body. Not the ones you already know about. I'm referring to if you have an injury, you can use the sex act to heal your injury. You can use the Jing you can cultivate while having sex, not after necessarily, but while doing it. You can radiate into these specific areas to reduce pain, improve range of motion and mobility, and put more life in areas that were deficient prior to this practice.

BEYOND SELF-HELP: MASTERING PERSONAL POWER™ by Gary J. Clyman

WOMEN DON'T NEED YOUNG BOYS

Women's cultivated sexual energy is much different and functions differently then men's sexual energy, obviously in a few ways. The difference for a man is that when a man practices Chi Kung and has an orgasm, he actually "loses" his energy. His energy leaves his body in the sperm. The electrical-chemical energy that makes up the sperm actually leaves the body.

WOMEN CAN STILL HAVE ORGASMS

I don't like referring to the movement of women's as "scattering," because in Tantric Yoga, women are not allowed to have orgasms. The same restrictions stand for men also. In "The Taoist Sexual Technique," women are actually encouraged to have orgasms. It's sort of like tapping into the Mother Earth's energy and circulating it. If men know how to tap into or draw off a woman's sexual energy, this can be done without any disturbance or reduction to her energy levels or sources. This is a very exciting part of the practice. Try it, you'll like it.

FOR WOMEN ONLY: ABOUT YOUR PERIOD

If you are having your period, you should not put your mind at Tan Tien. Rather, you should keep your mind at your solar plexus instead (the tip of your xyphoid process) of Point #2. This is because her body is discharging "dead blood" and energy and you won't want to re-absorb any of that. Fresh or good energy that drops down to her vagina will have a tendency to leave her body. You don't want that to happen. Raising your mind to the Xyphoid process will help.

CHI KUNG BEFORE SEX

Remember, before being able to perform "The Taoist Sexual Technique" smoothly, you must become proficient at practicing Chi Kung. This is a different application of the same techniques you have already learned, whether it be The Micro Cosmic Orbit, The Macro Cosmic Orbit, or Inside Air.

CHI KUNG DURING SEX

You are going to be practicing these techniques while you're having sex, embracing or touching each other. You don't really need to make sexual contact to practice "Dual Cultivation." As a matter of fact, depending on your level of practice, sometimes you don't even have to be close to the the other person, You can practice this from a distance. I will expand on this later. This is similar to "distance power sex."

SEX WON'T KILL YOU, BUT?

Many men have asked me, "Is it harmful to my internal practice and how harmful to ejaculate?" The answer to this question tends to differ from person to person. Condensing/squeezing and circulating into The Micro Cosmic Orbit will help prevent an excessive energy loss. The loss can be minimized. It's similar to using the amount of water it takes to prime a pump in relationship to actually "pumping" water. Trying to do The Micro Cosmic Orbit while ejaculating will only produce nominal savings and is not advised. It is best to practice seminal fluid retention as often as possible or as much as your relationship will allow.

CHI KUNG AFTER SEX

Pick a sitting posture and begin condensing. It doesn't matter which sitting position you use. Condense into Tan Tien, as small and as tight as you possibly can. In the same breath, shrink again and again and again up to 6-7 times in one single inhale. Next, relax and let your mind expand out into the Universe. Remember, when doing "Condensing Breathing," only the inhale is important. After shrinking considerably, begin to "Fold Your Jing" so it overlaps itself. Have each part of the same inhale and your "Condensing" shrink, overlap and accelerate. Next, after considerable "Condensing" has been done, begin to incorporate your arms into the program (Macro Cosmic Orbit, Mother Meditation, etc.). Suck into your palms, as if you are sucking in fine silk through your palms. The next step is to link your arms, sucking with your "Mother Meditation," into your Tan Tien while sucking in from one consistent, linked condensing practice. After you have ejaculated, there is more space to "Condense" into.

DUAL CULTIVATION EQUALS BETTER SEX

To practice "Dual Cultivation" between a couple, the man must know what to do. It is not imperative that the woman know how to practice Chi Kung, but it would enhance your lovemaking if you both knew how to do the basic "Chi Circulations." The woman can be coached in a very basic way if the man really knows how to practice The Micro Cosmic Orbit, Condensing Breathing, Inside Air, and a handful of other techniques. For the woman, all she really needs to do is inhale and exhale on command, and follow the instructions of her lover. <u>This practice cannot be done if the only partner that knows the technique is the woman.</u> It will be impossible for him to perform without certain important workable techniques. If you want your man to be able to practice these techniques, give him my book.

"Dual Cultivation" is a very high level energy practice. Not high level as if "spiritual," but high level like it requires a good level of technical proficiency.

Not only can a man get more satisfaction without ejaculation, but the woman can have multiple orgasms more easily while practicing The Taoist Sexual Technique. The practice of Dual Cultivation is exciting, fun, and very fulfilling if done correctly.

THE BEST KEPT SECRET: THE GRAND FINALE

This has been reserved for the end of the sex chapter. Now that you have "mastered" the ability to have sex without ejaculating, and it has become second nature for you, I must tell you there does exist a technique with which you can ejaculate and at the same time not lose a large percentage of your cultivated energy. I call this "Separating Heaven and Earth's Essence."

With this particular kind of ejaculation, you can shoot the very thin watery (Heaven) substance part of your sperm up your spine while you excrete the thick (Earth) substance out. However, you only excrete half to three quarters of your Earth's substance out, not all of it.

This is getting very specific and subtle. Careful practicing is necessary to perfect this part of your technique. In order to perform this, you really have to have control of your cultivated sexual energy (Jing). This is not easy, but you already know this. Separating Heaven and Earth's Essence is possibly the most difficult part of The Taoist Sexual Technique.

To the best of my knowledge, this process has never been explained in any of the books I've seen.

To recuperate from this kind of ejaculation is very easy. You have to continue to practice your Micro-Cosmic Orbit after you have ejaculated Earth's essence only. Again, make sure you do not ejaculate Heaven and Earth together. Heaven's essence goes up the spine, Earth's essence drop's out. This is where the toxins that I mentioned earlier, are in Earth's essence. I will include more about this in my next book.

CHAPTER #9
SPECIALITIY APPLICATIONS
FOR COMMODITY TRADERS

Commodity traders have a different set of requirements in their daily lives than most people. They have got to be able to make important decisions, on their feet without hesitation, many times in a day. Applying the principles from Chi Kung helps traders make more confident and disciplined responses to what the market is doing.

To each different trader, confidence and discipline show up differently. A "discipline" problem shows up as the inability to to get out of losing trades or trades that "go against you" when you know you should. A confidence problem shows up as the inability to stay in a good trade or a trade that is "going your way." That means traders take their profits too soon and leave too much profit behind.

By practicing Chi Kung, it enables commodity traders to have the ability to do what they really know they are supposed to do, thus raising their effectiveness. Most traders have a combination of these two problems.

In other words, "I shorten the gap between what you want to do and when you finally do it."

Another important part of what I do with each of my private trader clients, is we work to find the origin of their self-confidence or self-disciple problem. Then we try to pull that out using the "Hands On, Transfer of Power" technique. When we do "Hands On, Transfer of Power" we can pull out a specific confidence problem. It's actually like deleting the original entry from a computer program so that every time it would have shown up in the computer program, it doesn't. It has actually been removed from many places, simultaneously. When I use the word "self-confidence problem" I don't mean some traders are afraid of their own shadows. I am referring to trading confidence exclusively. Most people that are not traders truly don't have the concept of "self-confidence" as I mean it with traders.

With traders it's not just that Chi Kung effects the way they trade. It also effects their relationships, marriage, and relationships with other traders. This ties in with "Commanding Respect vs. Demanding Respect." Believe it or not, traders need to be part salesman to get along with their fellow traders. Some traders call this "kissing ass" but I would prefer to call it "socializing," a more positive word.

WHY YOUR TRADING WILL IMPROVE

When I accept commodity traders as clients, one of the first things I do is help them by figuring out which of the three major problems affect their trading the most.

BEYOND SELF-HELP: MASTERING PERSONAL POWER™ by Gary J. Clyman

The three major problems with commodity traders are:

1) Low self-confidence
2) Low self-discipline
3) Low self-esteem

All three of these problems exist in all traders to different extents, whether they know it or not. A self-esteem problem shows up in a few different ways. Self-esteem problems primarily show up as a person having the underlying belief that "he does not deserve" something. I have mentioned this in other parts of the book, but it is important enough to repeat here. Many people with self-esteem problems secretly have the hidden fear that they will be discovered or found out not to be what they seem to be. This is very common in all people, not just traders.

There is a difference between "low-self esteem" and "low self-image." "Low self-image" problems fall somewhere between a "self-esteem" problem and a "self-confidence" problem. Many people are under the impression that a self-confidence problem and a self-esteem problem are one in the same. I strongly disagree.

As I have stated in other parts in this book, "with a self-esteem problem, it appears as if you don't deserve something," whereas "with a self-confidence problem it appears as if you don't have the ability, you doubt yourself and this can be related to negative belief systems, which make you feel like you simply can't do something. These are two distinctly different feelings. Look into your own life and see if you can identify what I mean.

TRADER SAYINGS AND AFFIRMATIONS

"It's better to be wrong than wrong and stupid." This is used to help traders cut their losses.

"First comes the *action*, then comes the *proof*." This is used for initiating trades at the correct time.

"2 to 1 is good, but 3 to 1 is better." This is used to help traders stay in a good trade longer.

"Trading income is better than salary." This is used to help new traders forget they are getting paid a salary and will help create urgency so they trader better.

"I'm a Shark, you are a guppie." This is used to help give traders confidence when needed.

Don't misunderstand me. I'm not telling you that I can take a "stupid person" and make him smart. What I can do is I remove self-destructive tendencies that get in your way when you're trading. They can be related to your background (Catholic, Protestant,

Jewish, Middle child, etc.). They can be related to the way you were trained as a trader or the way you weren't trained. They can be related to your money relationship, but I sort of screen these out one at a time and that's how the results come. I don't teach you anything to do with "Market Knowledge" or the way the Market works.

BEYOND SELF-HELP: MASTERING PERSONAL POWER™ by Gary J. Clyman

THE EFFECTS PERSONAL POWER TRAINING™ HAS ON COMMODITY TRADERS!

1. Traders focus energy to make positive behavioral changes.

2. Traders learn to utilize their market knowledge to the best of their ability.

3. Traders learn to identify their own strengths and weaknesses.

4. Traders learn how to monitor and master the workings of their own minds.

5. Traders learn discipline skills which directly lead to higher levels of self-control and self-confidence.

6. **PERSONAL POWER TRAINING™** helps repair self-esteem levels after slight or serious "market beatings."

7. Internal Energy Cultivation Techniques are taught that raise each trader's physical presence and self-awareness.

8. "Trading Discipline" needed for "pulling the trigger" in and out of trades is a special feature in **PERSONAL POWER TRAINING™**.

9. "The eye of the tiger" is restored to my trader clients. This is required to be successful in all life's endeavors.

10. The harmful effects of daily stress, related with trading is reduced by helping each trader perform more effectively, thus helping them become more consistent, productive, and happy.

"With PERSONAL POWER TRAINING™ your trading will never be the same again"

DO YOUR MORNINGS "DRAGGGG ON" FOREVER?

Hypoglycemia in commodity traders shows up as losing your ability to make decisions and concentrate in the late morning. The time this happens will vary with different people depending on what time of day they get up. But if traders get up at 4:30 to 5AM in the morning, they tend to lose their "umph" by about 10:30-11AM. I will expand on this in my next book.

WHEN SNAILS MOVE "TOO FAST"

Most people get up slightly later, say at 7AM. They tend to "lose it" around noon, or possibly a little later. This is a very common problem. This is a problem relating to the adrenal glands and the pancreas and is a condition called Hypoglycemia or "low blood sugar." Again, some old timer doctors are still telling their patients to eat a candy bar when this happens. This is the dumbest thing that can be done for these symptoms. A candy bar will only lead to a higher and faster roller coaster ride.

The test I mentioned elsewhere in this book, The GTT (Glucose Tolerance Test) can be given, but it is not that important. I purposely mention this a few times because it bears repeating. Sugar will end up killing you. It contributes to creating hypoglycemia which is the precursor to diabetes, one of the largest killers of mankind. If sugar came out now, it would not be allowed on the market and would be considered an "addictive and dangerous drug."

In my personal opinion, various nutritional supplements can help alleviate and eliminate this particular problem. You can go to your local nutrition store and get a pancreas and adrenal glandular supplement. Ask for help.

"BAD CHOICES" WHEN TRADING MAY BE SUGAR RELATED

The symptoms that many of my clients report to me, losing their concentration, making stupid mistakes, getting depressed, feeling cold or chills at room temperature. The idea that they have two personalities is common with Hypoglycemics. The primary personality works very well, and the second personality is Dysfunctional in that, when your blood sugar is low, your second personality clicks into gear and takes over. This is when all your "bad choices" and "dumb mistakes" seem to be made.

Depending on the severity and frequency of the symptoms, you can tell in yourself if your blood sugar is low. The second personality comes at the most inopportune times. At important business meetings, before giving a scheduled lecture or presentation, when the market makes a "big move" late in the day, or at any other time. It will feel as if you're missing something or sleeping through the "big" move.

If you go to your local health food store and buy some very simple, but specific nutritional supplements, many of these problems can be alleviated almost immediately if not within the first week of regular use. These problems can and should be expected to disappear. Read other books on nutrition and try to learn more about how your body works.

FOR HEALTH CARE PROFESSIONALS

Chiropractors and other health care professionals have another set of specific applications. The primary applications for Chiropractors are: firstly, improving your technique. You can actually work less hard and get better results. For instance, when Chiropractors apply specific manipulations, what Chi Kung allows them to do is have faster and more accurate responses, not necessarily more forceful, but faster.

The second primary application of Chi Kung for chiropractors is in relationship to "communicating" with your patients.

CHI KUNG WILL MAKE YOU A BETTER DOCTOR

As one Chiropractor has stated, "Chi Kung helps me communicate what Chiropractors call 'inherent, innate intelligence,' from the doctor to the patient." In fact, quoting him further, "Sometimes I just lay my hands on the patient, without any force, and the adjustment takes place all by itself."

CHI KUNG WILL IMPROVE YOUR TECHNIQUE

Chi Kung will improve your "aim" and give you more specific "line of drive" in your adjustments as well as giving you the confidence to perform a technique that you would ordinarily hesitate to do. When a Chiropractor's knowledge is greater than his/her confidence levels, he or she would not give it "all." This is one area where a confidence problem will inhibit your professional performance and effectiveness. Chi Kung gives you more control and sensitivity in do those "hard to get" moves.

This confidence problem shows up in Chiropractors and other health care professionals differently than in traders. It shows up, for instance, in speaking to patients about their conditions. If a Chiropractor has a self-confidence problem, that also means he has a communication problem in relation to explaining the examination, "report of findings," diagnosis, treatment & prognosis, x-ray reports, and other specific intended maneuvers. You owe it to your patients to improve these skills.

"GOOD DOCTOR" OR "GREAT DOCTOR"
MAKING THE RIGHT CHOICE

This communication problem, in effect, will hamper your ability to explain your "intention of treatment" and prognosis. If a Chiropractor or other health care professional has a confidence problem, the patients pick up on it and will not follow his advice as well. Patients know, they seem to have a Sixth sense that tells them something is not exactly right. They will not be able to peg what is wrong, they simply won't do what you tell them. You owe it to all your patients to be the best doctor you can be. They didn't teach you this skill in school, and this one missing ingredient can separate good doctors from great doctors.

IMPROVED COMMUNICATION SKILLS EQUALS MORE REFERRALS

Imagine how this missing ingredient will effect your referral statistics. This and practicing Chi Kung can bring you enough new patients on a monthly basis to make most of your peers green with envy. If you don't think referrals are important, just check last month's books.

These same speaking and communication principles apply to all health care professionals. Referrals are referrals. It doesn't matter if you are a medical doctor, surgeon, osteopath, dentist, podiatrist, optometrist, Chiropractor, etc. A professional and confident self-image is always important.

YOUR PATIENTS WILL NOTICE THE DIFFERENCE

What do you think the results are of improved communication skills in your health care practice? The obvious results are: The patients become more enthusiastic and due to the patients' increased understanding of what their problems are, they can actually improve their conditions quicker. This also extends into referrals. When a patient knows what his/her problem is, that enables him, to talk to friends and family more clearly about it. This conversation among friends and family is very important in relation to getting new patients and referrals.

LOW SELF-IMAGE: A COMMUNICABLE DISEASE

If a Chiropractor has a confidence problem, then the patients don't want to send any new patients or referrals to him. This problem is sort of a "communicable disease" which I call "poor communication, confidence and self-image." This problem is the root of many other problems in a health care practice.

For instance, when I had my own health care practice, using my own healing system, which I no longer practice, I had a lot of personal referrals because my patients or clients used to get results, and understand what I said their problems. Because of that, they were enthusiastic and able to send their friends and family to me. Many times I would get one person from a family and end up treating five or six of their family members.

I even had other Chiropractors and medical doctors sending me their "hard to treat" patients, as a last resort.

Treating patients for me was my "small perfect," where as teaching Chi Kung in **PERSONAL POWER TRAINING**™ is my "large perfect." Again, these same principles apply to all health care professionals regardless of specific profession.

CHAPTER #10
Q & A SECTION

1) TECHNICAL

Q. When I meditate, I always sweat, no matter if it's cold or hot in the room. Why is this? I thought meditation was suppose to relax you?

A. First of all, you don't practice Chi Kung "to relax yourself." You practice Chi Kung to attract, cultivate, circulate, and direct energy. When you draw the energy into your physical system, there is always a "heat accumulation" that takes place. When you practice Chi Kung, you are also stimulating your body's metabolism, not to mention the physical "exercise" aspect of your practice. You should be getting hot. If you aren't getting "hot," you're not doing it correctly.

Q. What relationship do the legs have in circulating your energy while practicing Chi Kung, and how is this difference relating to Tai Chi?

A. Tai Chi has a different focus than Chi Kung. Tai Chi is much more physical. In that I mean, you're using the physical structure of the body, the muscles, the skeletal system, and the cardiovascular system. When you practice Tai Chi, the work is more physically exerting, in Chi Kung the work is not as physically demanding or difficult. As I have stated in the book, Tai Chi is 80% physical and 20% mind training, while Chi Kung is 80% mind training and only 20% physical.

Q. Please explain the involuntary shaking that I experience while practicing Chi Kung.

A. The involuntary shaking that many people experience can be caused by a few things. The most often is that your body is not used to performing the various moves or holding the various postures for any extended length of time and that's hard. The second most common reason for the shaking is similar to the first except that the person experiencing the shaking is in worse physical condition and the body is just "freaking out." Either way, within 3-4 weeks, the shaking will probably stop. The third most common reason for the shaking can be a combination of the first two. This can be related to your energy. This shaking is more rare and is nothing to be afraid of.

These vibrations can be quite violent in appearance, but the mere fact that they have occurred is still a benefit. The person experiencing these violent vibrations should just continue practicing as usual. Shaking due to this reason will take longer to go away. I am not suggesting that you even want them to go away. With "true" energy related vibrations, the best way to deal with these vibrations is to keep practicing so these vibrations can be, "assimilated" into your system. I spent many years working to experience these violent vibrations. Congratulations if you are, indeed, experiencing them. I'm sure you worked hard to get to this level.

Q. Often when I practice Chi Kung, especially the sitting meditations, I become distracted either by sexual/physical sensations or by sexual thoughts. How can I avoid these distractions?

A. These should not be viewed as distractions. The first place where your increased energy or cultivated sexual energy (Jing) will show itself is as an increase in your "sexual" energy. These increases can be experienced as different urges, thoughts, images, or actions. Because Chi Kung works with your Jing first, this is expected. Count your blessings... Many men complain that they experience "low sexual energy." Chi Kung is the perfect remedy for impotence and low levels of sexual energy.

Q. How long should I do each exercise? Is a few minutes for each enough?

A. A few minutes on each is enough in most cases and for most people, unless you are intending to become a professional Tai Chi/Chi Kung practitioner, and most people aren't. A short, single daily practice is more than sufficient as long as you insert additional short practices during the day. Most of my clients practice about 15-20 minutes in the morning and throw in more "here and there" as their day goes on. Nowadays, this seems to be the average way to practice Chi Kung, and it seems to work for most people.

Q. In The Micro Cosmic Orbit, how fast does the energy move?

A. Depending on your level of achievement in your practice, the energy can circulate only one circulation per breath or 1,000 circulations per breath. Each person should determine this for themselves. I personally prefer 1,000 circulations per breath, but you do have to work up to it. Don't be afraid to experiment as long as you stick to what you know.

Q. How does one keep one's feet from going to sleep while practicing our sitting meditation?

A. For beginners, your feet will have a tendency to fall asleep. This is "normal." However, if it gets so bad that it completely distracts you from your Chi Kung practice, sit on a chair or move them around. Remember, the physical body and details are not nearly as important as The Mind Training.

Q. Many books I've read mention exercises to force your sexual energies down and up into your head. Is this possible and if so, how is it done?

A. I don't like the word "force" because it has negative connotations. "Direct with your mind" is a much more appropriate phrase and denotes a more truthful action in relationship to your energy manipulation.

BEYOND SELF-HELP: MASTERING PERSONAL POWER™ by Gary J. Clyman

Q. What do you do when you're meditating and energies that you don't want enter into your body by mistake or some other design?

A. There is not such thing as energies that you don't want, only energy that you are not controlling as well as you would like. If you are experiencing distractions, concentrate more carefully. Don't blame your distractions on other sources. I can practice and have practiced Chi Kung and Tai Chi anywhere, without any distractions. However, it is easier to practice in a stable, controlled, quiet, clean, and warm environment. If you can choose this kind of environment, do so.

Q. When you're doing your visualizations, where do they exist in the body?

A. Different visualizations will live in the chest area, the head area, or Tan Tien area and sometimes even totally outside the body, depending on what you are doing and what they are. Some of your visualizations are not related to your body at all and may exist in your mind only. I can write a book on this question alone. This idea of "Creating your World" will be expanded upon in my next book. You must experience your own.

Q. If you feel that your "Chi" is getting stuck in your head, what do you do?

A. You must suck your attention back into Tan Tien (three inches below your navel and two inches in) and do standard Condensing Breathing. You don't have to worry about completing The Micro Cosmic Orbit. Many times there are "dead spots," (that's what I call them) in The Micro Cosmic Orbit that are areas that are much harder to circulate through. For instance, from the top of C7 at the base of your neck all the way up to and around to the lower lip. This is the most difficult area to circulate through. This area is the most difficult area to move your energy and your mind through. Another area is near the center of your back, near Temporary Step #8 at Point #5. More practice will be the easiest way to "burn through" these hard to circulate areas. Acupuncture can help, but the acupuncturist must be great in Chi Kung. Don't go to someone who does not completely understand your situation. Read what Lou Buscemi wrote about his situation. Contact me if this happens or has happened to you.

Q. Why do I notice a "strange smile" on my face when I practice Chi Kung, especially The Micro Cosmic Orbit and Heaven and Earth Meditation?

A. Various emotional expressions surface while practicing Chi Kung. Different people experience different emotions. If a person is primarily anger-motivated, many times they will experience their primary emotion during the practice. Certain sitting forms also bring out certain specific emotions and they will vary from person to person. The "strange smile" that this question is referring to denotes a certain pleasure that is experienced inside the body. Because these pleasurable sensations are happening internally, our bodies have unusual ways of manifesting them. When I was a student I used to laugh and cry for no apparent reason. This went on for a few years prior to my

"Great Energy Awakening."

Q. Do you perform "Inside Air" at times other than specifically during "Inside Air?"

A. No. The "Inside Air" details are performed exclusively during "Inside Air" practice only. The four sets of details should not bleed into other portions of your "Daily Practice Routine," ever. If it does, this is nothing more than sloppiness. Outside of the Daily Practice Routine, Inside Air can be practiced all day long. Many of my clients, as I've said before, practice briefly in the morning and augment their morning practice with many brief practice sessions. Because of the inconspicuousness of Chi Kung, it gives you the ability and flexibility to practice nearly anywhere, anytime and any place.

Q. Why does my tongue get cramped every time I practice? Kay/Portland

A. The tongue is a muscle and muscles should be used. When you "keep your tongue on the roof of your mouth," it gets tired just like any other muscle in the body. Don't worry, it will get stronger with practice.

Q. Why do my eyes feel "pulled down" in the direction of the energy flow when I'm practicing really good? JAL/Portland.

A. By leading your energy with the mind, your body has tendencies to physically follow the flow of your energy. Closing your eyes is not advised because it leads to day dreaming, sleeping and many other distractions. It is said that "you lead the Chi with your eyes" and in practicing Tai Chi this is true; however, Chi Kung is different. In Tai Chi because the focus is on the musculo-skeletal structure and on movement, the mind goes first, the eye goes second, and the body follows third. In Chi Kung this is slightly different. The mind goes and the Chi follows which has very little to do with the body or the eyes.

Q. What does the phrase "the speed of light" mean?

A. "The speed of light" signifies the incredible velocity of the mind. In that I mean the vibration at which you can circulate your Chi. The "speed of light" as I have mentioned before, is separate from the physical limitations of the body relationship. While circulating your Jing, start by connecting "one circulation per breath." After this has been accomplished, start to circulate two times per breath and so on. As you practice, your first goal should be to pick up where you left off at the last practice. This attitude helps develop the quality of consistency. Consistency" is one of the most important factors needed to be successful at anything. As your speed increases, you will feel gaps in your circulation. Smoothness and fusing the beginning of one circulation to the the end of the last will help connect you. "The speed of light" refers to continuously circulating your Jing as one circulation. The image you can use for doing this is the picture of a fan belt or rubber band with the head and the tail connected, with no gaps.

BEYOND SELF-HELP: MASTERING PERSONAL POWER™ by Gary J. Clyman

Q. When I accelerate to "the speed of light" in my Micro Cosmic Orbit, why does it seem to become a thought process instead of a circulation?

A. "The speed of light" is faster than the body sensations can express. At a slower pace, your nervous system can keep up with your mind. "The speed of light" travels at 1,000 circulations per breath. Attaining this speed should be a goal for advanced practitioners. The illusion of a thought process is related to the mind going so fast that there is a dissociation from the body. This again is related to Chi which is internal energy and Jing which is internal power. This has been explained in other areas of the book already.

Q. What happens to people who use breathing and meditation to achieve altered states of consciousness?

A. Altered states of consciousness come in many versions. Some are positive and act to empower people and some are negative causing distress. First, I'll address the positive. One of the positive aspects of meditation is that it can help people become more physically present and functional in their bodies. The word meditation has many meanings. Using meditation in regards to Chi Kung is quite different than in other systems. Many people's understanding of meditation leans toward diffusing, stress-reducing, relaxing and dispersing of energy; however, in the Chi Kung context, it is the condensing, empowering and raising the practitioner's availability of his or her own personal power that is emphasized. The application of Chi Kung helps many people from all walks of life take more responsibility for their own future and actions. Raising the physical energy availability of the practitioner is equivalent to fitting more "life" into a smaller space. When a practitioner has more life, minuscule tasks are done almost effortlessly while difficult tasks are done more easily.

Another positive application of Chi Kung is its valuable use in relationships. When a practitioner utilizes the internal energy cultivation exercises and becomes more complete, centered and whole, this changes the quality of that person's relationships. Because a practitioner is more self-contained from the practice, this removes many of the wishy-washy traits and characteristics that we all possess, thus making relationships more concrete in general.

The negative sides of using meditation includes the reduction of the decision making capabilities of the novice, but not with Chi Kung. Stress reduction seems to be a positive by-product of meditation; however, by using Chi Kung, stress reduction comes from a different perspective. The Chi Kung perspective of stress reduction relates to the person's ability in decision making and in feeling complete in those decisions, thus reducing stress.

The "groundedness" or lack of it depends on the individual's application of various techniques. The harmful side effects of meditation, not Chi Kung, have lead to mixed opinions on the validity of meditation's benefits. The individual's constitution combined with the particular technique that is practiced will produce side effects, if they are not balanced and are incompatible. If the individual's constitution and technique are compatible, many wonderful benefits can be experienced.

Q. When practicing "Sitting Forms with The Mind Training," should my abdominal area expand and contract?

A. No. "Reverse breathing" should be done throughout your "Chi Kung" practice. "Wrapping" is a term I use to illustrate how you should be holding your abdominal area. It's as if you are wrapped with strong tape. Anyone who has ever had a broken rib can relate to this idea.

Q. What is the vibrating that happens while I am practicing Condensing Breathing sitting? CB/Portland

A. Some of the vibrating is muscular; most of the vibration is your body connecting with your intention. The vibration is in response to the contraction of your internal energy.

Q. Do women do anything different while practicing Chi Kung than men?

A. Yes. The circulations are the same; however, if a woman has her period, instead of keeping her mind at Tan Tien, she should keep her mind at the Xyphoid process (lower tip of the sternum).

Q. Where's the transition point when doing "The Micro Cosmic Orbit?" JMJ Portland

A. The rising of the Jing is considerably easier to direct with the mind than the sinking of the Jing. The transition area can be anywhere from the top of the head to the upper chest. Many beginners experience the common difficulty of losing control in their circulation and regaining control with a gap. The gap has already been explained as a "dead spot."

Q. How tight do you squeeze your urinary and anal sphincter muscles?

A. Many beginners are actually shocked to discover that this is a physical function. Squeezing the sphincter muscles at first should be done with one long solid draw as consistently as possible. As a practitioner becomes more advanced and comfortable with the practice the sphincter muscles can be pumped without fully letting go. <u>This practice should be done on the inhale only, never on the exhale.</u>

Q. Please explain the term "Overlapping Condensing."

A. The term "Overlapping Condensing" is like the opposite of the onion image. The onion concept represents layer after layer being removed. While practicing "Overlapping Condensing," the center is shrunk more and more, all on the same breath. This technique is of great value and can accelerate the recuperation of the energy loss after sex.

Q. What about closing your eyes when practicing? Is that advised?

A. No. Closing the eyes leads to drifting and dispersing and should be avoided during most of your Chi Kung practice. On only one specific technique, and you'll be told which one, is it advised.

Q. What are "Shooters" and how do they effect your Micro Cosmic Orbit.

A. The image of "a boiler" accumulating steam and periodically releasing an excess of steam is the image utilized to understand shooters. "Shooters" are a sudden surge of energy released into the central nervous system during practice. "Shooters" can go in either direction, up or down, or in both directions at the same time. In my own personal practice many years ago, "Shooters" preceded a major opening and the completion of my own Micro Cosmic Orbit or my "Great Energy Awakening." "Shooters" should not be feared; there's no cause for alarm.

Q. When generating heat, why is it easier in the beginning stages than at higher levels?

A. For beginners, the sensation of heat is more noticeable because their energy is much more scattered. As your practice develops your body heat is contained in the torso. The primary function of the body heat is to guarantee the organs protection, warmth, and sufficient energy to perform their physiological duties. In an advanced practitioner, because their energy is already gathered and accumulated, the sensation of heat is much more familiar. If a practitioner becomes sick, the cold is felt more and restoration is appreciated more fully.

Q. When circulating, how do you coordinate your breath with your orbit?

A. The breath, in The Micro Cosmic Orbit, at beginning stages, should be in unison with the Chi circulation. By this I mean, inhale, and the Chi rises, exhale and the Chi declines. After you've developed more skill, you can then circulate more than one circulation per breath. The end result of this practice with the circulation acceleration leads to circulating at "the speed of light" or 1,000 circulations per breath. With this, I mean, at a certain point in your progress, your Chi circulations in The Micro Cosmic Orbit only do not rely on your inhales or exhales. In order to circulate 1,000 circulations per breath, the mind training at more advanced levels becomes independent of the breath.

Q. Please explain the concept "extending the mind?"

A. Extending the mind utilizes one of my four basic principles called "Projecting." Extending the mind is practiced in many of the techniques. The application of "extending the mind" implies the mind is larger than the body. In this I mean you are capable of doing circulations beyond the "physical boundaries" of the physical body. This will happen naturally. You do not need instruction in how to do this if you practice.

Q. Please explain "Heaven and Earth Meditation," "The Hour Glass Meditation," "Double Funnel Meditation," or "Twin Tornadoes Meditation" in depth?...

A. "Heaven and Earth Meditation" is used in conjunction with condensing on the inhale and projecting on the exhale. "Heaven and Earth Meditation" is the base technique for applying your affirmations, visualizations and impregnating the universe segments of the daily practice routine. ""Heaven and Earth" meditation has other names which signify the function of the practice itself. These other names are: "Double Funnel," "Twin Tornados," and "The Hour Glass Meditation."

Q. What is known as "A Nine Channeled Pearl?"

A. The term "A Nine Channeled Pearl" describes an increase in "density and intention" in moving the Chi with the mind. The image is symbolic of trying to breathe through very small openings in a physical object, like pores of a porous stone. This has basically two applications. The first is trying to thread a string through the various convulsions or channels with a thread. By this I mean, sensitivity is required to penetrate the delicate unseen openings of a fragile pearl. The second is as if you are trying to suck a golf ball through a garden hose. This action would require intense air pressure to cause movement. Pressure from the mind can increase the intensity and fullness of the circulation. This is similar to blowing a whistle or a wind instrument that is plugged up. This is an excellent image to use for increasing the velocity and fullness of your internal circulation.

Q. What are the various sitting posture alternatives?

A. Sitting cross-legged is my first choice since most people can do this without excessive physical stress but for those who cannot tolerate this simple posture, sitting on a chair in The Lock Off Position is an acceptable alternative, considering most of my readers have no Tai Chi or martial art background. For those who are physically fit and/or have previous experience with "long term" sitting, you can sit with your insteps flat on the ground, on your heels, you can sit with the soles of your feet facing out to your sides, which is the most difficult posture. I do not advise half or full lotus postures because they are physically too hard for most people and may lead to unnecessary energy blockages. Remember: the physical postures and details are of secondary importance, in my system. The Mind Training always takes priority.

Q. How tight should you squeeze your urinary and anal sphincter muscles?

A. When contracting the urinary and anal sphincter muscles, many people have the conception that they only "think" of putting their attention on these muscles. This is wrong; this is not enough. When I say squeeze the urinary and anal sphincter muscles, that's exactly what I mean. To contract the urinary sphincter, for men and women both, is like retracting your urethra upon completion of urination. With this I mean, you actually "suck up" so you don't "wet" your pants. To contract your anal sphincter muscle, I use the humorous metaphor of having eaten Mexican food for lunch and riding on a crowded elevator back to work and not wanting to embarrass yourself and everybody else that is with you. Actually physically squeeze your urinary and anal sphincter muscles, don't just think about it.

Q. When I finish practicing, I feel like my energy is leaking out. How do I stop it? EK/Portland, OR

A. If you feel it leaking out, it is. The energy leaks out because your mind is not directing it to stay in. If you end your Daily Practice Routine with "Layered Condensing," the energy will not leak out at all. If you end any other way, you're not following my prescribed method.

Q. What about closing your eyes when practicing? Is that advised?

A. Closing your eyes is advised against during most of your technique. Remember as stated in the beginning of lesson #1: keep your eyes half open and half closed. The reason for this is if you close your eyes all the way, you become unaware of your external environment or daydream. If you open your eyes all the way or glare, you become unaware of your internal environment. The phrase: half opened and half closed implies keeping attention on both your internal and external environments.

Q. Is there any "perfect time" to practice Chi Kung?

A. Whenever and wherever you can.

Q. Please give a time breakdown of "The Daily Practice Routine."

A. Condensing Breathing - 3 minutes, Basic Path Training - 6 minutes, Inside Air - 1 minute, Sitting Forms with The Mind Training - 10 minutes, Palms on Knees - 2 minutes, The Micro Cosmic Orbit - 5 minutes, Heaven and Earth Meditation - 3 minutes, Daily affirmations - 3 minutes, Impregnating the Universe - 5 minutes, Bone Marrow Exercises - 2 minutes, **TOTAL TIME = 40 MINUTES**.

Q. When practicing "Inside Air," do you practice it a few times, then take normal breaths, or do you practice it once, then take a normal breath?

A. No. You practice it over and over again, using the four sets of details, without taking breaks in between.

Q. When do you release the sphincter muscles when you are doing "Inside Air?"

A. It is important to understand that all the squeezing is always performed on the inhales only. As for this answer, as soon as you begin your "short exhale," that is when you loosen the urinary and anal sphincter muscles. The sphincter muscles are an important part of making your Chi Kung practice physically based.

Q. How thick is the thread in "The Stickman?"

A. When practicing Condensing Breathing, you start with a solid thread and as you practice, it is as if you are building thickness on the outside of the tread, so the tread is transformed into a string. The string turns into a cord, the cord turns into a rope. The rope turns into a cable and the end result will be that the thread will eventually become as thick as your body. So it's consistent with your constitution.

Q. Why did you put "Temporary Step #8 at Point #5" in, when teaching The Micro Cosmic Orbit?

A. Because this area is considered a "Dead Spot" and it's much easier to make the complete circulation to the Point #8 if you put an interim point in between.

Q. When doing Condensing Breathing into "The Stickman," on the exhale, where does the mind go? How far, at what speed, etc.

A. While practicing Condensing Breathing the inhale is of primary importance; the saying "without first condensing there can be no explosion" means you spend most of your waking life expelling, utilizing and in most cases, wasting energy. All our lives we never have a method for attracting, collecting and truly directing energy. The exhale in "Condensing Breathing" is not important. The answer concerning where the energy goes, should be self explanatory. Unless you are in a Tai Chi context, you utilize the energy accumulated from "Condensing Breathing" in your life. If you have a Tai Chi perspective, you utilize this collected energy in your martial art, healing, and physical presence.

Q. What is the phrase "like scotch tape" referring to? JMJ/Portland

A. The phrase "like scotch tape" refers to "detaching and releasing your intention." By this I mean, you conceptualize a portion of your personal energy and release it, intact, into the universe. If you want your physical environment to change, this is a very important part of creating that change.

Q. When practicing Upward and Downward or Inward and Outward Meditation, I feel the energy flowing to Tan Tien, is that the right way? I also feel the energy flowing up my legs, to Tan Tien, is that accurate? JMJ/Portland

A. After a student learns Basic Path Training in The Daily Practice Routine, extra details can be "layered" in on top. Some of these additional details are "on the inhale, as you suck energy in the palms and forearms, you also suck energy in the inside surfaces of the thighs." This added detail I do not teach in the first method of Basic Path Training and should not be practiced until you become more acquainted and proficient in Chi Kung.

Q. How many different ways are there to circulate my energy in Tai Chi stance? I feel a sensation in my chest area, is that my heart?

A. There are as many Chi circulations as the mind can conceive but teaching this way leads nowhere. The strength of my system lies in the fact that I have formatted the essentials and you should stick to the outline. The Chi Circulation and Tai Chi Stance Meditation is practiced going from one palm around through the arms, across the back, through the other arm ending in the opposite palm. In the daily practice routine, The Chi Circulation in Tai Chi Stance Meditation can be to circulate continuously around and around and around in the same direction, thereby, crossing the gap between the fingertips. Again, this advanced circulation should be adopted in the Daily Practice Routine after you have become somewhat proficient.

Q. Concerning Inside Air, is the mind stretching from Tan Tien to the infinite, or is it conceived like a rubber band? JMJ/Portland

A. The image of a "rubber band" stretching up and down from the center, the center being Tan Tien, is used to illustrate extending the mind while remaining in Tan Tien. This is like "chewing gum and walking" in that you are doing two distinct things separately with the mind at the same time.

Q Do you notice any differences among the four directions, when drawing in energy?

A. North or East tends to lead more to accumulating energy. Facing North because of the magnetic pole and facing East because that's where the sun comes up. Facing South or West I notice has a somewhat draining effect. The same principle applies when sleeping. The top of your head should face North or East when resting.

Q. Should you do Chi Kung in bed before falling asleep?

A. Practicing Chi Kung before going to sleep may cause you to not sleep well; that's why I advise early morning practice to be the best. However, this question is different. If you want to practice Chi Kung in bed before falling asleep and it doesn't cause you to lose sleep, you can have a lot of fun. You can do The Micro Cosmic Orbit while falling asleep and actually get more out of your sleep. It's as if you've been meditating all night. However, this does not count as practice time.

Q. In Bow Fists, what are the different qualities, between fully extended arm motions, and more condensed motions?

A. As I have explained previously, the phrase "the larger the movement, the smaller the circulation" and "the smaller the movement, the larger the circulation" applies to this question. When practicing Bow Fists or any of the other Sitting Forms with The Mind Training, after you have become familiar with the physical movements, they can be gently "shrunk." In this I mean, since the physical details are not as important and the circulations, the size of the physical movements should be reduced. This reduction enhances the velocity of your Chi circulations.

Q. When doing Bow Fists, and exhaling the energy out the heal of the hand; is this the only place the energy leaves?

A. Yes. In keeping with the Kiss principle, for all practical purposes, the outside surface of the right fist is the only exit the energy uses.

Q. In Tai Chi Ball Mediation, what is going on with the arms?

A. The simple expansion and contraction of The Tai Chi Ball while sitting is all that's necessary since the Chi circulation is of primary importance.

Q. In Sideways Fan Through Back, I find I do a jerky motion. What is this from?

A. As the energy travels in the body, many times it is not of uniform speed. There's a tendency for energy to accumulate at the articulations or joints. When this energy passes through the joints, this acceleration is sometimes seen as jerky movements. This does not signify "Chi problems." Jerky movements in the beginning stages of your Chi Kung practice are not uncommon and are not a big deal.

Q. What is meant by the word "Internal?"

A. "Internal" in the martial arts context means the energy of the punch kick, or any other technique is present inside the body, before the technique is applied. "External," in contrast, means "what you see is what you get." By this I mean with an external punch, kick or whatever, the vibration is the actual technique itself. "Internal" is similar to an explosion waiting to happen. Whereas "external" is the projectile.

Now "internal" in the Chi Kung context refers to the energy inside the body that is not reliant on external forms, postures, or movements. Condensing Breathing is the first and most important step in developing internal energy.

Q. What is the effect of accelerating the speed in any of the movements? I find there seems to be an acceleration of speed from the first movement to the last, in one sequence. It seems to get faster as I practice? Is it a build up from excitement, energy, or what? I think I notice that when I start to speed up, my mind rises up from Tan Tien.

A. This increase in speed in most cases, is due to your improved practice. When performing the first moves of a particular set many times we have to "clear the cobwebs." By this I mean if you haven't practiced shortly before, your energy must be reburned through your channels. In the beginning stages the feeling of "being rusty" is common. That's why you get more results when you practice more frequently. In some cases, this increase in speed might be related to being excited or to your natural tendency to want to get to the next technique. When you notice this, simply slow down.

Q. What are "shooters" and how do they effect your Micro Cosmic Orbit?

A. I have never heard any other reference to what I've named "shooters." All I have is my own personal experience. In 1976, prior to my Great Energy Awakening, I had the feeling of electricity shooting up and down my spine, in opposite directions at the same time. These sensations were quite alarming but not scary. The excitement involved with receiving these strange sensations propelled me to ask my teachers for advice. No one seemed to understand what I was talking about. The frequency of these "shooters" increased and they began waking me up from a sound sleep. This period of my practice was very exciting. A few months later while practicing Chi Kung something extremely unusual happened to me. I had retraced and experienced my conception and my life changed forever.

Q. Explain more about your Great Energy Awakening?

A. Many times my Tai Chi Master told us that one day something would happen and we would clearly be different. He was quite vague in his explanation of this future event. Most people were afraid; however, I was very excited. This excitement or energy for life propelled me to accelerate my own personal practice. At this time I was practicing an average of six to ten hours a day. And suddenly without warning, I was different. This happened after approximately four years of full time practice. Very shortly after that, I quit working altogether just to practice without being distracted by working. I spent many years becoming detached and avoiding responsibility. It all paid off. During this period I lived in my car for three months and practiced nearly all my waking hours. Two years later I opened my first Tai Chi school.

Q. When doing "Double Palms, Down and Out" your instructions are suck in the knees and in the palms, on the inhale, and blow out only through the palms, Why?

A. This form and many others fall into the category of Macro Cosmic Circulation, not to be mistaken with The Micro Cosmic Orbit. Macro Cosmic Circulations which are explained elsewhere in the book, are Chi circulations that connect the four extremities and the torso. Regardless of which particular form is being practiced, this may be the underlying principle in many forms. <u>To suck into the knees and palms at the same time is a very common practice.</u> This sucking action, not to be confused with Condensing Breathing can also be practiced in standing postures such as: Basic Path Training.

Q. In the Circulations, when exhaling, where does the energy come from? Does it in fact, go from Tan Tien out your arm?

A. The energy fills us. When practicing Condensing Breathing we can actually absorb energy from our environment. When we expel energy out of our bodies, the energy stays connected to us in our energy reservoir called Tan Tien. This refers back to the "rubber band" principle.

Q. What is the relationship between Tan Tien and The Micro Cosmic Orbit?

A. Tan Tien should be thought of as a boiler that creates pressure and steam. When this steam accumulates to a substantial force, it can be released and harnessed into The Micro Cosmic Orbit. This practice is done very frequently whether you know that you're doing it or not. I purposely have structured my system to be "fool proof," if you will only stick to the format.

Q. The cycle appears to be, Palms On Knees Meditation, sucking in the knees, drawing from the arms to Tan Tien, then, from Tan Tien exploding into the arms, and out back into the knees, and the reservoir of Tan Tien, is that the correct image?

A. Yes. One of my oldest Tai Chi students, was instructed by me to practice Palms on Knees Meditation before I taught him anything else. He practiced this particular meditation for five years before I gave him any other technique. The reason for this was, in the old days, I believed people had to go through the whole system to get it. This belief system, according to the way I was taught, was correct. Since then, however, and with the creation of the Personal Power Training™ I have proven my old belief system "wrong." Not that it was not right, but just that I have created an option.

Q. What is the difference between "a circulation practice" and "an acceleration practice? Micro Cosmic Orbit vs. Inside Air, Which comes first?

A. "A circulation practice" is a very generic term referring to the mind training. An acceleration practice refers specifically to "speeding up" the frequency of your micro cosmic orbit circulation. This acceleration practice I teach to my clients and students after they have performed the Daily Practice Routine with proficiency.

Q. Where's the transition point when doing The Micro Cosmic Orbit?

A. The transition point in The Micro Cosmic Orbit is the spot where your circulation changes direction. Different people change direction in different places, depending on their ability. These areas are anywhere from the crown point, top of the head, to the chin. As a beginner, the location of the direction change is not important. This area is related to what I call "dead spots."

Q. In The Daily Practice Routine, what's the difference between "Impregnating the Universe" & "Heaven and Earth Meditation?"

A. Heaven and Earth Meditation is a practice involving sucking from two primary and opposite directions, up and down. Heaven and Earth meditation consists of creating a vacuum and blowing it out. Heaven and Earth Meditation is the "base technique" used when practicing your affirmations and visualizations. The extension of Heaven and Earth Meditation which I've named "Impregnating the Universe" is practiced on the exhale, by blowing out the top funnel only. This is very important in relationship to changing your world, creating results, and seeing what you want before it exists. This is practiced near the end of The Daily Practice Routine.

Q. Please explain the term "Layered Condensing?"

A. "Layered Condensing" is the name of a technique that I've created for sucking in more and more. Everybody understands the concept of peeling onion skins. This is the opposite. This means when you practice layered condensing, you continually increase your "density." An example of this is pouring a gallon of water into a quart bottle, and then pouring another gallon of water into the same quart bottle, etc. In concept, this makes a lot of sense to me. Since we are talking about energy and not water, you have an unlimited capacity to store and conserve it. Remember, your ability to explode is directly reliant on your ability to first condense. Internal power must be cultivated before it is used, not when needed.

2) SEX

Q. Does Chi Kung allow a man to have sex with a woman, especially since its purpose is to circulate and store sexual energy?

A. The Taoist Sexual Technique is a direct application of Chi Kung while having sex. Ejaculation control is the primary focus. Since the purpose of Chi Kung is to cultivate energy, ejaculating may prove disastrous to your Chi Kung practice. For best results, "seminal fluid retention" is advised. However, since this is near the 21st Century, these practices have become nearly extinct. Nowadays, The Taoist Sexual Technique can be used for the treatment of impotency and to prolong sexual intercourse. It can actually be used to lengthen the amount of time you make love before ejaculating.

I do not expect many people to become celibate; however, the practice of The Taoist Sexual Technique as explained elsewhere in the book, is an excellent alternative.

Q. What is the difference between masturbating your energies away and ejaculating them with the help of a sexual partner?

A. To some people "masturbating" is considered having sex; however to me, they are clearly different. When you masturbate, yes you, you get nothing back in return; O.K., at least it's "safe sex." However, it is unproductive. The problem with masturbating is there is no energy exchange, no hormone exchange, and no emotional exchange unless you're masturbating with another person (spare me!). When you, a man or woman, have an orgasm while masturbating, you get nothing back in return. This is a waste and is not advised if you're trying to cultivate internal energy.

Q. How do you know that all exchange of energy and hormones is positive or healthy?

A. Energy, in my opinion, is neither positive nor negative. However, through having heterosexual sex, ordinarily there are hormones exchanged with or without ejaculation. This is because there are other secretions excreted besides just sperm. It is important for men to absorb these "female juices" and for women to absorb these "male juices," sperm not included. While using condoms, absorbing female juices through a man's penis is inhibited unless he's using sheepskin. However, sheepskin condoms, though a good birth control device, do not provide protection against AIDS. This lack of protection is due to the permeability. However, this permeability acts as a screen to keep sperm from leaving. That's because sperm are large enough to not pass through a sheepskin membrane, but viruses are smaller and can get through without obstruction. Concerning the hormone exchange, I believe the hormones readily pass through the sheepskin membrane, thus allowing for absorption. Whether AIDS can be passed through hormone exchange, I'm not sure if anybody knows the truth on this. So know your lovers.

Q. What's the advantage of absorbing someone's hormones? EW/Chicago

A. As I've mentioned elsewhere in the book, a man needs some Yin energy and a woman needs some Yang energy. If a woman gets a wimp, this Yang energy might exist in small quantities. If a woman has larger biceps than you, tattoos on her arms and a mustache, I think her Yin energy might be relatively limited. I personally like very feminine women.

Q. What about homosexual energy exchange?

A. I'm a "straight" kind of guy. The thought of exchanging body fluids with another man is revolting. I have had a few gay men as clients, very few, and some of them have asked me questions on this topic. Since I have no homosexual tendencies, my opinion regarding homosexual energy exchange is irrelevant to say the least.

Q. What if the person doesn't have any energy?

A. All people have different levels of energy. Energy always flows to the lower level between two people. In this I mean, if you have a great deal of energy and you have sex with your lover who has less energy, you will have a tendency to feel somewhat depleted; however, you can prevent this depletion from happening to a large extent if you practice Chi Kung and apply it to The Taoist Sexual Technique. However, prevention of energy depletion is why my advice to my male clients is to find a lover at least 10 years younger.

Q. Over a long period of time (for me, three months), Chi Kung seems to make me more sexually active. While I don't mind this, how can I convert this sexual energy into something more productive, rather than wasting it every Friday night? AW/Chicago

A. Don't go anywhere on Friday nights and practice Chi Kung instead, by yourself or learn The Taoist Sexual Technique. It really works.

Q. How does a man recuperate after ejaculation?

A. "The 10 Steps to Sexual Recuperation" are the following: 1) Layered Condensing, 2) Standing Condensing, 3) Mother Meditation, 4) Sitting-Stillness Condensing, 5) Micro Cosmic Orbit, 6) Sitting Forms with The Mind Training, 7) Standing Condensing, 8) Bone Marrow Exercises, 9) Floor Stretching, and 10) Standing Condensing. This order I have personally found to work quite effectively.

Q. Please explain the influence the moon has on sex drive and why "menstrual sex" is different?

A. Our bodies are mostly water. The moon affects tides and human fluids. Hormones flow much more freely and they tend to be more reactive. Having sex with a woman during her period can have negative side effects for the man. "Menstrual sex" has a higher vaginal temperature and men have tendencies to ejaculate more freely, losing their seed, their WILL and their Jing (cultivated sexual energy).

Q. How do I control my ejaculation?

A. While having sex, the number one important thing for a man is to **not ejaculate and lose his seed or spirit**. Applying the Chi Kung techniques taught in PERSONAL POWER TRAINING™ are directly related to man's ability to do this most difficult task. Condensing Breathing and The Micro Cosmic Orbit are the 2 main techniques used while having sex. One important alteration in the downward cycle of The Micro Cosmic Orbit is to bypass the genitals and go directly to the tip of the tail bone. If a man does not do this correctly, he is in big trouble. Women do not have to worry about losing this because nature works the opposite way. The Micro Cosmic Orbit can be used by both men and women with excellent results while having sex.

Q. How does one practice "Dual Cultivation?"

A. "Dual Cultivation" can be practiced between 2 Chi Kung practitioners. Sexual contact is not necessary but it makes it easier. "Dual Cultivation" is 2 people doing The Micro Cosmic Orbit together at the same time. The energies mix, and each person helps complete the other partner's internal circulation. This can be performed in many positions and postures.

Q. Why does the mind become scattered concerning sex?

A. While performing sex, the Jing is agitated and scattered. The manifestation of the scattering shows itself as confusion, forgetfulness, and low energy. The cure for this condition is to practice Condensing Breathing, or "Layered Condensing" to be more specifically. Direct accumulation of Jing is the only other way to counter this distraction other than not ejaculating.

Q. How much progress is lost when a man ejaculates?

A. After a man ejaculates, he loses 4 days before and 5 days after worth of his practice. Ejaculation is the most destructive and disruptive action to your Chi Kung practice. Women don't really lose their Jing like men do, they just re-distribute it or move it around.

Q. Regarding an "energy loss," what is the difference between masturbation and having normal sex?

A. The effects of masturbation totally deplete your cultivated sexual energy reserves. Normal sex, that is sex with a partner, does not totally destroy your energy reserves. On a scale of I to 10, masturbation reduces your energy reserves to 0 while sex can reduce it anywhere from 8 to 2 depending on how much you lose. When I say how much you lose, I'm not referring to how much sperm you lose rather at the moment of ejaculation. What you do with your mind is more important. This is a subtle practice. Ejaculation is possible without losing high percentages of your cultivated sexual energy but you must be very good at Chi Kung.

Q. Can women be energized by sex? EW/Chicago

A. Yes. A women's relationship with energy is much different than that of men. When women have orgasms, usually they do not lose excessive amounts of energy. These female orgasms many times circulate the energy throughout their body. By nature, women can have multiple orgasms and become energized. Some women even can borrow or steal energy from their male sex partners. Men however, depending on their age, usually cannot have 10 orgasms in a row. That's because energy leaves the body upon ejaculations and does not simply re-circulate. Anatomically speaking, women gather energy during sex and men disperse it. However, if a man practices The Taoist Sexual Technique, he can apply the "gathering" principle during sex.

Q. Sometimes when I practice "Ovarian Circulations" the energy gets stuck at my sacrum. Is there anything I can do to move it? EK/Portland

A. The problem is that you're not making a "loop" at the bottom of your circulation to bypass your genitals as you practice The Micro Cosmic Orbit

Q. At what point and how do you stop the ejaculate response?

A. First of all, when having sex and practicing The Taoist Sexual Technique, you have to stay ahead of the game. If you wait until the last possible second to try to prevent your orgasm, you're a gonner. By this I mean, "ejaculation control" must be practiced before your sperm and prostate fluid are travelling up your tubes. If you wait for the last possible second, it's usually impossible to control your ejaculation. My advice is to practice Condensing Breathing, Inside Air, and The Micro Cosmic Orbit, then try to apply them while having sex.

Q. What harmful side effects can come from "ejaculation control" and how do you prevent this?
A. If practiced properly, The Taoist Sexual Technique has relatively few to no side effects. However, when beginners practice, many times they wait too long to decide to not ejaculate; in this instance, The Taoist Sexual Technique is not a reliable form of birth control. As for the stress of the moment, controlling your ejaculation must be determined prior to the critical point. There is no turning back.

Q. Please explain the various "hand to genital circulations" and how do you use them?
A. This will go in my next book.

Q. What's the proper way to circulate your Jing while having sex?

A. First of all, never let your mind get stuck in your genitals. Even when practicing The Micro Cosmic Orbit or Inside Air while having sex, at no time should you lower your mind. This means, you practice your Chi Kung exercises while having sex as if you're not having sex. If you can do this, you truly can control your mind.

Q. At what point and at what regularity do you do the technique?

A. The Taoist Sexual Technique can be practiced many times a day or twice a month. The frequency is up to the practitioners. I have no specific recommendations except "do what you can handle."

Q. In your opinion, what is most difficult time to control your mind?

A. If you can concentrate and control your thoughts and mind during sex, you can do it any and all the time.

Q. Does a man actually have an orgasm when circulating while having sex or does only "part" come out? If it doesn't come out, where does it go?

A. If it's done right, "part" doesn't come out. If "part" does come out, for all practical purposes "all" comes out. The point is: you don't want to ejaculate. When you don't ejaculate, you take your cultivated sexual energy and inject it into your Micro Cosmic Orbit. If you ejaculate, you can't inject your Jing into your Micro Cosmic Orbit. This is a goal in The Taoist Sexual Technique.

Q. When does the sperm start to form. Explain the thick (Earth's essence) and the thin (Heaven's essence) sperm and their relationship to each other.

A. Separating Heaven and Earth's essence is a very high level and difficult practice. This is actually ejaculating but retaining a certain part of your discharge. When you ejaculate while practicing The Taoist Sexual Technique, you might notice sometimes your sperm is very thin like water or very thick like Jello. In my opinion, the thick discharge is Earth and the thin watery discharge is Heaven's essence. I have noticed slight to severe energy losses depending on which has been excreted.

3) PSYCHOLOGICAL

Q. Explain the word "Embodiment."

A. The term "Embodiment" refers to aligning your purpose in the present. By this I mean you become who and what you want to become.

Q. Explain in detail visualizations and affirmations after Heaven and Earth Meditation.

A While practicing the Daily Practice Routine, affirmations and visualizations are added to your Heaven and Earth Meditation. Remember, I have structured the Daily Practice Routine so each fragment or technique leads to the next step. It is important to understand that you continue to practice Heaven and Earth Meditation as you add your affirmations and visualizations to it. This combining or stacking makes affirmations and visualizations much more potent.

Q. Why, after finishing my practice, do I feel like I want to take a nap?

A. If your energy exceeds your body's ability to absorb, you will have a tendency to "check out," by thinking you want to take a nap. Your WILL can override this tendency if applied correctly.

Q. Sometimes I find myself backing away when my practice reaches new heights. How can I use this fear to push myself ahead?

A. Breaking new ground scares many people. As humans, many of us have fears of the unknown. In training your WILL, this fear of the unknown must be realized, accepted, and <u>ignored</u>. The development of this attitude leads to greater levels of excellence in everything you do.

Q. When do I start floating while practicing? CB/Portland

A. The term "floating" is used in "TM." Using Chi Kung, you will never float; however, what can happen is you can connect your internal circulations in such a way that your physical body can bounce or vibrate intensely. In high level Chi Kung practice, these vibrations become high velocity in nature.

Q. How do I redirect the aggression after The Sitting Forms with The Mind Training? RS/Chicago

A. Hopefully when you finish your sitting forms you will have become stable, prior to leaving. It is important while practicing not to get up while under the influence of Chi Kung.

Q. Explain "the Monkey Concept."

A. "The Monkey Concept" exemplifies being physically present. When you go to the zoo and you look at a monkey hanging around, he's not worrying, he's simply being. When practicing Tai Chi or Chi Kung, you should concentrate only on what you are doing; not on what you just finished and certainly not on what you're about to do.

Q. How do we utilize Condensing Breathing in our business lives and why aren't we instructed on what to do on the exhale.

A. The exhale is not important! Use your Condensing Breathing while you are trading commodities or healing someone. It will raise your level of awareness and physical presence and can be practiced anywhere.

Q. How do you heal with Chi Kung?

A. This cannot be answered briefly. This will be a major topic in my next book.

4) HEALTH

Q. What about organ displacement and gravity? Explain the importance of the position the pelvis is held in while practicing.

A. Gravity constantly pushes down on us. The skeletal system, more specifically the pelvis, is the foundation for proper postural alignment. If the pelvis is tucked under, the abdominal organs fall into their appropriate position, thus improving their function. If the pelvis is not in the correct location, this will cause all kinds of problems including back aches, poor posture, low energy, stiff or tight hamstring muscles, not to mention making you look like you have a "pooch."

Q. What effect does Chi Kung have on posture?

A. This is related to the previous question, but slightly different. Since "reaching for the ceiling with the top of your head, elongating your spine, and tucking your pelvis under" are standard characteristics, many people experience improved posture, reduced back pain, greater circulation and more effective digestion. The combination of these benefits result in a more efficient body system, weight loss, more energy and youthful vitality. Chi Kung and Chiropractic treatments are the perfect compliment to each other.

Q. What are the effects of alcohol in relation to hypoglycemia, severe mood swings and low energy levels?

A. Briefly, many alcoholics suffer from hypoglycemia (low blood sugar). This is because of the close similarities between sugar and alcohol. When the blood sugar is suddenly elevated, the pancreas is triggered to dispense insulin into the bloodstream. This trigger response mechanism in drinkers is the same as for sugar abusers. As stated in the hypoglycemia article in this book, this is the beginning and a contributing factor of adult onset diabetes. More will be discussed in my second book which will also include specific nutritional supplementation to remedy many common human ailments.

Q. What is meant by the term "Internal Kung Fu?"

A. "Internal Kung Fu" means different things to different people. In a Tai Chi perspective, "Internal Kung Fu" refers to the energy being stored and ready to be released in the body in a martial art situation. In a Chi Kung perspective, "Internal Kung Fu" refers to the art of circulating energy inside the body. The difference is the Tai Chi expression has structural applications and the Chi Kung expression is more on the level of personality, thus usually lacking the fighting implications.

5) EMOTIONAL

Q. Please explain the relationships between fear, anger, depression, sorrow, joy, rage, anguish, bitterness, stubbornness, guilt, abandonment, etc.?

A. Fear is related to the kidneys. Anger is related to the liver. Sorrow is related to the lungs. Joy is related to the heart. Depression is related to the liver thus being the opposite emotion of anger. Rage is related to liver/gall bladder which is different but related to anger. Bitterness and stubbornness are both related to stomach/pancreas. Anguish is related to lungs. Guilt is located above the ovaries on women and near the testicles on men. Abandonment is found and removed from the thymus area on the sternum. These emotions are the primary focus of Hands On, Transfer of Power™.

Q. Explain the emotional and physical relationship in Five Element Theory.

A. The answer to this specific question requires much more in depth presentation and discussion. This topic will be covered in detail in my second book.

6) GENERAL

Q. If I want to practice Chi Kung and Tai Chi, which should I practice first?

A. Depending on your level of proficiency in either art, this is a complicated question and must be dealt with on an individual basis.

Q. How important is it to do the exercises in the order learned?

A. I've worked hard so you don't have to. The Daily Practice Routine has been designed to get the maximum results with the minimum effort. You can spend as much time as you like. Most people practice between 20 to 40 minutes a day, and some even less.

Q. If I don't do the complete Daily Practice Routine, but only a section, will I get the same benefits?

A. You might, but there's no guarantee; however, many people have received enormous benefits using my prescribed routine. If you want to be creative, that's O.K., but only after you've successfully learned the Daily Practice Routine.

Q. If I do Condensing Breathing and then skip The Sitting Forms and jump to The Micro Cosmic Orbit and Heaven and Earth Meditation, will I still get the same effect?

A. Possibly, but this is pulling out major pieces of the Chi Kung skeleton. Try it-- you tell me.

Q. Should I try to practice Tai Chi and do The Mind Circulations at the same time?

A. No. It's impossible to concentrate on both. If I can't do it, how are you going to be able to? However, the closest thing to combining Tai Chi and Chi Kung or the physical movement in combination with The Mind Circulation is a set of meditations from Temple style Tai Chi called "Tai Chi Connective Meditations." These are like the mix or the combination of the two practices, but this is not Tai Chi and it's not Chi Kung.

Q. If you only have five minutes to practice, what should you do? EW/Chicago

A. Being the efficiency expert that you are, five minutes for you could be the equivalent of two hours for somebody else. However, five minutes for a "normal" person is not quite enough. I prescribe 40 minutes but most people do half of what I say.

Q. How do we as students tell our friends the difference between Chi Kung and Tai Chi?

A. When you explain to your friends, tell them, Tai Chi is primarily the physical aspect of "The Tai Chi/Chi Kung Relationship," sort of second cousins. Tai Chi works with the physical body by altering the musculo-skeletal system and creating a relationship with the body and the ground through the practice of "forms" and other physical practices. Chi Kung, however, creates a relationship with your energy, your mind, your spirit, and your WILL. Your body is involved but to a much lessor degree than with Tai Chi.

Q. What is the difference between "Practicing" and "Running Through" Chi Kung?

A. "Practicing" means spending sufficient time working at your technique, while "Running Through" means you stop short or quit when you feel just O.K. "Practicing" is a much more productive and superior way rather than always feeling rushed. Rushing is a common mistake. Take your time!

Q. What do people gain from this practice?

A. Read this book.

Q. How long does it take to implement these techniques?

A. As soon as you learn them, they're implemented.

Q. How do the results show up in peoples lives?

A. I wrote a whole book on this one too.

BEYOND SELF-HELP: MASTERING PERSONAL POWER™ by Gary J. Clyman

OTHER SUGGESTED BOOKS

Information such as philosophy, health, history, and many of the psychological aspects have been purposely left out of my book. Some of these books cover them satisfactorily. This suggested book list is to be used as an adjunct to my book.

Taoist Yoga by Charles Luk
The Secrets of Chinese Meditation by Charles Luk
Tao Te Ching by Lao Tsu, the Feng/English Edition
Chuang Tsu, the Feng/English Edition
Awaken Healing Energy Through The Tao by Mantak Chia
Cultivating Male Sexual Energy by Mantak Chia
Cultivating Female Sexual Energy by Mantak Chia,
The Tao of Love and Sex by Jolan Chang
The Tao of the Loving Couple by Jolan Chang
Any and all books by Jou, Tsung Hwa on Tai Chi and Chi Kung
The Web That Has No Weaver by Ted J. Kaptchuk
Unlimited Power by Anthony Robbins
Dynamic Laws of Prosperity by Catherine Ponder
The Millionaire of Nazareth by Catherine Ponder
Open Your Mind to Prosperity by Catherine Ponder
Cutting Through Spiritual Materialism by Chogyam Trungpa
Earl Mindell's Vitamin Bible by Earl Mindell, Ph.D.
Mega-Nutrition by Richard A. Kunin, M.D.
The Missing Diagnosis by Orian Truss, M.D.
The Yeast Connection by Billy Krook, M.D.
Orthomolecular Nutrition by Abram Hoffer, M.D.
Chronic Fatigue Syndrome by Jesse Stoff, M.D.

REGIONAL PERSONAL POWER TRAINING™ ASSOCIATES

Portland, OR
Salem, OR
Salt Lake City, UT
Boston, MA
Austin, TX
Flint, MI
New York City, NY
San Diego, CA
San Francisco, CA
Los Angeles, CA
San Jose, CA
Aspen, CO
Ontario, Canada
Leibnitz, Austria, Europe

Gary J. Clyman
Tai Chi Master & Martial Artist

Made in the USA
Charleston, SC
28 October 2011